STUDIES IN COGNITIVE DEVELOPMENT

STUDIES IN COGNITIVE DEVELOPMENT

Essays in Honor of Jean Piaget

DAVID ELKIND

JOHN H. FLAVELL

NEW YORK

OXFORD UNIVERSITY PRESS

LONDON   TORONTO

1969

Contributors

BEILIN, HARRY, Professor of Psychology, Institute for Child Development, City University of New York.

BRUNER, JEROME S., Professor of Psychology, Harvard University.

CHARLESWORTH, WILLIAM R., Associate Professor of Psychology, Institute of Child Development, University of Minnesota.

ELKIND, DAVID, Professor of Psychology, University of Rochester.

FLAVELL, JOHN H., Professor of Psychology, Institute of Child Development, University of Minnesota.

GOODNOW, JACQUELINE J., Associate Professor of Psychology, The George Washington University.

HUNT, JOSEPH McV., Professor of Psychology, University of Illinois.

INHELDER, BÄRBEL, Professor of Developmental Psychology, Institute of Educational Science, University of Geneva.

LAURENDEAU, MONIQUE, Professor of Psychology, University of Montreal.

PINARD, ADRIEN, Professor of Psychology, University of Montreal.

POLLACK, ROBERT H., Ph.D., Institute for Juvenile Research, Department of Mental Health, Chicago.

SIGEL, IRVING E., Chairman of Research, Merrill Palmer Institute of Human Development and Family Life, Detroit.

SINCLAIR-DE-ZWART, HERMINA, Director of Research, Institute of Educational Science, University of Geneva.

WALLACH, LISE, Research Associate in Philosophy, University of North Carolina.

WHITE, BURTON L., Research Associate in Education, Laboratory of Human Development, Harvard University.

WOHLWILL, JOACHIM F., Associate Professor of Psychology, Clark University.

Contents

Research Perspectives

Applied Perspectives

Introduction

How does one honor a great man? In the scientific community, it has long been recognized that perhaps the highest honor students can bestow upon their teacher is to continue the work he has begun. This is the sentiment out of which the tradition of the Festschrift arose. It is a means whereby the students can join together and communicate to their teacher what they have learned and how they are getting on with the work. Indeed, what better way could there be to demonstrate to a man, whose life has been devoted to his research, that his endeavors have not been in vain—that they continue to live and beget life? It was in this spirit that the present Festschrift was conceived and written.

As a Festschrift, however, the present volume is perhaps unique in the sense that only two of the contributors, Inhelder and Sinclair, were Piaget's students in the literal interpretation of having taken a degree under his direction. Some of the contributors may, in fact, have never met Piaget in person. It is a special tribute to Piaget that so many psychologists who do not speak his language and who have never attended his classes or

seminars, nonetheless consider him their teacher. This is due, not
only to the breadth and originality of his research and theory,
but also to his long and courageous persistence with problems
and concepts totally uncongenial to the prevailing *Zeitgeist*.
Piaget's vindication lies in the fact that, despite having begun his
research more than forty years ago, his work is today regarded
not only as contemporary but even as avant-garde.

We have said that the Festschrift is meant as a sort of progress
report on enterprises initiated by the teacher. In the case of
Piaget, there is such a wealth of starting points, so much to build
upon and expand, that it is hard to know where to begin. Some
of our contributors have addressed themselves principally to the
analysis and explication of Piaget's conceptualizations, some to
the research problems and possibilities raised by the Genevan
investigations, and some to the practical applications of Piaget's
work. We have therefore grouped the papers in this volume according to their primary concern, whether with conceptual, research, or practical issues and shall introduce them in that order.
Each of the contributors to this book is likely to have at one time
or another concerned himself with each of these approaches to
Piaget's opus, so their present contributions should be regarded
as reflecting only upon their present preoccupations and not
upon the full range of their concerns.

Theoretical perspectives

Piaget's concepts were born in biology and were nurtured by
logic. When one first reads Piaget, such concepts as *assimilation,
accommodation, schemata, stages,* and *operations* are likely to
seem utterly foreign. American psychologists, at any rate, have
not been accustomed to thinking of behavior in these terms, and
the tendency is to suppose that Piaget is using these concepts as
analogy. Nothing could be further from his intention. For Piaget,
when an infant puts everything he grasps into his mouth this *is*
assimilation and the scheme actually abides in the action itself.

The continuing attempt to assimilate Piagetian concepts
within American psychology is reflected in the papers of the first

section. Hunt makes this progressive assimilation explicit by suggesting how Piaget's conceptualizations compare and contrast with other leading conceptualizations and how they have fed into the current critiques of our traditional views regarding motivation, learning and intelligence. Although Hunt is appreciative of the Piagetian concepts and recognizes that they have played an important role in the revitalization of psychological theorizing, he nonetheless argues that they are a starting point only and that the bulk of the work needed to explicate and refine them remains to be done.

In a sense, the succeeding papers in the section on conceptual issues attempt such explications and refinements of the Piagetian concepts. The most general of these attempts is that of Flavell and Wohlwill, who attack a number of fundamental and abiding issues in developmental psychology. These authors examine some of the Piagetian concepts from the standpoint of competence and performance models derived from modern psycholinguistics. The focus is on some of the difficulties and biases built into our traditional developmental concepts. Although it is in part a position paper, pointing to and searching for a clarification of the notions of structure, process, and stage, it also presents a concrete model for attacking some of the issues in question.

A somewhat more limited focus is taken by Pinard and Laurendeau. These writers deal in considerable detail with the concept of stages. Developmental psychologists are perennially troubled by this concept. Like an old, comfortable pair of shoes, the concept of stages is hard to throw away even though one is aware that fashions have changed. Pinard and Laurendeau provide an explicit and detailed defense of the stage construct as it is used by Piaget. It is a good defense and one that is based on organismic considerations that are usually ignored when, as is frequently the case, we are dealing with isolated experiments. At the heart of the stage concept is the idea of organization, and it is upon the demonstration of changes in mental organization that the battle of stages must be fought.

Just as Piaget's work has reemphasized the perennial problem of stages so too has his method of assessing concepts challenged conventional views of concept formation. The psychological theory of concept formation, based on the ideas of abstraction and generalization, is perhaps one of the least satisfactory constructions in psychology. It has been under repeated attack not only by psychologists such as Lewin (1931), Osgood (1953), and more recently Kendler (1964), but also by philosophers such as Cassirer (1923). Elkind argues that Piaget's conservation problems presuppose a theory of concept formation that differs from the abstraction-generalization model in three significant respects, but that the Piagetian version of the concept complements rather than supplants the classical one. The parallel between these two conceptions of the concept and the Lewinian distinction between Aristotelian and Galilean modes of conception is utilized to heighten the contrast between the two approaches.

While Elkind takes up the conception of a concept implicit in the conservation problems, Wallach deals with the phenomenon of conservation itself. The extent to which the Piagetian conservation problems have captured psychologists' fancy can only be appreciated by looking at the very large number of studies that have been and are being done in this area. These problems are, moreover, being used as exercises in many developmental laboratory courses around the country. They have, in fact, become a sort of Piagetian trademark with which his name is immediately associated. In her lucid analysis, Wallach takes us step by step through the logical and empirical anomalies raised by these conservation problems and arrives at an original and unexpected solution to the problem of the role of experience in attaining conservation.

Research perspectives

If one were to survey the areas of greatest research activity in contemporary child psychology, it is obvious that cognition, infancy, language, and perception would all poll close to the top. In each of these areas Piaget's influence is clearly evident. This is all the more extraordinary when one remembers that Piaget's own work has been more epistemological then psychological in its intended focus. In effect Piaget has attempted to answer, or to provide still another answer, to such traditional problems of epistemology as the nature of the number concept, the role of perception in knowledge, and the relations between language and thought. It is probably because, at least in part, Piaget approached these problems from such a different frame of reference that his work is so original.

For the psychological researcher, Piaget's investigations pose a great many difficulties. Quite aside from his disregard of the accepted canons of conducting and reporting psychological research, he has concerned himself with questions of content as well as with questions of process. In traditional experimental studies of process, content is usually sacrificed as a confounding variable. This accounts for the frequent use of nonsense syllables and geometric forms in psychological investigations of such cognitive processes as memory and concept attainment. Piaget has demonstrated, most dramatically perhaps in his studies of conservation, that in the study of process one does not have to sacrifice relevant content. Experimentally trained psychologists are, however, still not comfortable with content and often center upon the process aspect of the Piagetian investigations. While the process aspects are important, the content aspects are equally significant, and it is to be hoped that these aspects of Piaget's investigations will be given more attention in future research studies.

Some of the papers in the research section move in the direction of clarifying some of the processes that Piaget revealed, while others take content into account as well. In presenting these studies we shall consider first the investigations concerning infancy and follow with studies of language, memory, perception, and conservation.

INFANCY

Piaget's work on infancy was sort of an intermezzo between his earlier investigations of the spontaneous thought of the child and his later investigations of operational intelligence. Although Piaget's work on infancy has something in common with the

early baby biographies, such as those of Teideman (1787) and
Shinn (1900), it differs in important respects. First, Piaget did
not limit himself to simply observing behavior as it occurred; he
also conducted successive little experiments. More important,
and one senses this in all of Piaget's work, he had very definite
ideas of what he was looking for and the intuitive genius for
arranging those situations that would best reveal the kinds of
behavior he sought. Like Freud, Piaget found in the earliest
sensorimotor coordinations of infants protypical analogues of
adult thought and behavior.

The observations Piaget made of his own three children have
now been replicated and extended by many different workers.
Some of these investigations have attempted to elaborate on
some of the conditions and factors that affect sensorimotor development. Others have taken Piaget's work as a starting point for
making new observations of phenomena related to those that he
had noted. To be sure, the onrush of research in infancy so
prominent in contemporary psychology is only in part derived
from Piaget's seminal studies. Most investigators in this area,
however, acknowledge their indebtedness to him in one way or
another.

Although it is presented only briefly here, Bruner's work on
infancy is intriguing in several respects. For one thing, he ties his
observations of infant behavior to more general issues, such as
the relation of human infancy to societal and cultural progress.
Some of his observations and findings are, moreover, quite unexpected and exciting in their own right. They should lead to even
greater activity in this already busy area of research.

White's studies of infant behavior are more directly related to
Piaget's work than are Bruner's, and he and his colleagues have
been concerned with some of the experiential determinants of
the coordinations noted by Piaget. Institutions for children provide a natural laboratory for studying the effects of environmental stimulation and of caretakers on the development of sensorimotor intelligence. In addition to reporting his research,
White makes a plea for more naturalistic study, arguing that
there are behavioral riches that are all too often lost in more
rigorously controlled types of investigation.

This stress on the need for more varied methodology is carried further in the Charlesworth's paper on the concept of surprise. This paper deals with both a theoretical and a methodological issue. On the theoretical issue, it attempts to relate the phenomenon of surprise reaction to recent motivational concepts such as novelty and the orienting reflex and to demonstrate the role of surprise as a determinant of cognitive growth. On the methodological issue, Charlesworth makes a very strong case, buttressed with his own research, for using surprise behavior as an index of particular cognitive structures. The use of surprise as a measure of cognitive structure proves to be a very useful addition to the developmental psychologist's armamentarium.

LANGUAGE

Psychologists have ranged between two extreme positions in their views on the relation between language and thought. At one end of the continuum are those who would reduce thought to language or representational functioning. In this camp one might place such men as Ryle (1949), Whorf (1956), and perhaps Luria (1959). On the other side are those who would make language a product of thought. Psychoanalysis would seem to be in this camp to the extent that it regards language as being under the control of primary and secondary thought processes. A "new look" with respect to this issue has emerged with modern psycholinguistics, mightily stimulated by the work of Chomsky (1957). Language, from this new point of view, is a relatively independent system with its own generative rules. The growth of language as a system can be studied in itself; its relation to thought constitutes a separate problem.

The Piagetian position with respect to the language-thought issue is reviewed by Sinclair. In many respects this position, explicit or implied, is quite in agreement with that of modern psycholinguistic theory. As Sinclair points out, however, there are also some important points of divergence. In addition, she also reviews some of her own ingenious research regarding the child's spontaneous use of quantitative terms in relation to his success on various conservation problems. This research should go far toward answering the "verbal misunderstanding" objections to research findings on conservation. It provides also a useful research paradigm for exploring relations between languge and cognitive growth.

MEMORY

One of the salient criteria of a good theory is fruitfulness. On this criterion, Piaget's theoretical constructions have acquitted themselves very well indeed. In recent years, the major thrust of the Genevan group has been toward using the basic findings on the development of operational thinking as a framework for exploring many different psychological processes. A case in point is the work of mental imagery and operational thinking that has recently been published (Piaget & Inhelder, 1966). One of the most recent processes to be explored within this framework is that of memory, and a book is soon to issue on this topic. In her paper, Inhelder provides us with a preview of this forthcoming book. As in the case of imagery, the Piagetian theory has engendered a number of novel experiments with, as the reader will see, truly remarkable results.

PERCEPTION

Although Piaget is best known for his work on intelligence, he has had also a long standing interest in perception. Considering his epistemological interests, this is quite understandable. The empiricist position has always been that knowledge derives from perception, whereas for Piaget knowledge derives from activity. It was necessary, therefore, as a counterpoint to his research on the development of intelligence, to demonstrate that perception could not be regarded as *the* source of knowledge although it most assuredly plays an important role in knowledge acquisition. For Piaget, perception is a separate system that develops according to its own rules and has its own regulations and principles of organization. While these regulations resemble the operations of intelligence, they are only *partially isomorphic* with them.

Piaget's "minor" (as one of us put it, Flavell, 1963) in perception gave rise to a long series of studies on perceptual development published in the Genevan house organ, *Archives de Psychologie*. Not surprisingly, there finally emerged a book (Piaget, 1961) that summarizes all this work and puts forth Piaget's general theory of perceptual development and his position on the relations between perception and intellectual functioning. Robert Pollack is one of the few investigators who have been following up some of Piaget's work in this area. In his careful and methodologically sophisticated research, Pollack not only has added considerably to our factual knowledge about perceptual development but also has offered some intriguing hypotheses to account for his research findings.

CONSERVATION

We have already noted that Piaget's conservation problems have attracted more attention in this country than any of his other research. The fascination of these problems is easy to understand. The procedures are so simple to understand and administer that anyone can use them, including parents in the home or teachers in the classroom. Too, they can usually be counted on to evoke the expected response. Rare indeed is a four-year-old so perverse as to manifest conservation on these tasks! Finally, the results are so surprising and unexpected to uninitiated that adults immediately raise objections and questions. These objections and questions often eventuate in additional research investigations.

The research reported by Beilin illustrates nicely two basic strategies that American researchers have adopted regarding Piaget's investigations in general and his conservation problems in particular. One of these strategies is to vary systematically some of the standard procedures and materials. In Beilin's case he has devised an electronic board that simulates the situation Piaget used to study area conservation. The value of such an analogue is demonstrated by the interesting results Beilin reports. The second strategy employed by other research workers, and recently by the Genevans themselves, is to devise training procedures that get nonconserving children to arrive at conservation. Beilin's training procedures and his discussion of quasiconservation make a very real contribution to the burgeoning literature on conservation.

Conservation and other Piagetian tasks have been administered to children in virtually every corner of the globe. Such cross-cultural replication studies are rare in research on cognitive development and are of considerable importance for understanding the role of tutelage and cultural milieu in the development of intelligence. Goodnow's paper is a model of how to exploit the potential of this sort of research.

Practical applications

It is probably fair to say that Piaget views himself as a biologically oriented genetic epistemologist first, a psychologist second, and an educator not at all. The ontogenetic origins of number, time, space, and causality and other concepts have been his major concerns, not the most efficacious ways such concepts could or should be taught in the schools. To be sure, Piaget has occasionally addressed himself to educational issues (e.g. Piaget, 1964), but always in the most general terms and without ever being very specific as to just what teachers and children should be doing in any concrete case. It is perhaps not really fair to demand of Piaget that he give us such direction. There is, after all, only so much that one man can do—even Piaget—and it is hardly for the rest of us to tell him how and where to direct his energies. Moreover, Piaget occasionally argues that our knowledge of mental development is still not sufficiently thorough to serve as a basis for a scientific pedagogy, and he may be right.

Nonetheless, many educators and psychologists have been intrigued by the possible relevance of Piaget's work for curriculum revision and for teaching practice. The Sigel paper attempts to show the ways in which Piaget's findings and theories can be used by the teacher and by those who are preparing curricula. Sigel also recounts some of his own research with teachers that indicates the cognitive blinders (in the form of fixed notions about how concepts are to be defined) that often stand between teacher and child. Sigel feels that these blinders are not irremovable and offers suggestions as to how they can be overcome.

This, in overview, is the perspective of the present volume. It presents a sampling, but only a sampling, of the many directions that students of Piaget are taking in carrying out the work he has begun. We think that it is a reasonably representative sampling, however, and that it exemplifies the impact of Piaget upon current research and thinking in developmental psychology. We hope it also demonstrates our indebtedness to Piaget and how we have, each in his own way, assimilated his teachings. It is for you, *Patron*, to judge how well we have succeeded.   D. E.

J. H. F.

References

Cassirer, E. *Substance and function and Einstein's theory of relativity.* Chicago: Open Court, 1923.

Chomsky, N. *Syntactic structures.* The Hague: Mouton & Co., 1957.

Flavell, J. H. *The developmental psychology of Jean Piaget.* Princeton, N.J.: Van Nostrand, 1963.

Kendler, H. H. The concept of a concept. In A. W. Melton (Ed.), *Categories of human learning.* New York: Academic Press, 1964. Pp. 212–236.

Lewin, K. The conflict between Aristotelian and Galileian modes of thought in contemporary psychology. *J. gen. Psychol.,* 1931, 5, 141–177.

Luria, A. R. The directive function of speech: its development in early childhood. *Word,* 1959, 15: 341–352.

Osgood, C. E. *Method and theory in experimental psychology.* New York: Oxford Univer. Press, 1953.

Piaget, J. *Les mécanismes perceptifs.* Paris: Presses Univer. France, 1961.

Piaget, J. Development and learning. In R. E. Ripple & V. N. Rockcastle (Eds.), *Piaget rediscovered.* New York: Cornell University, 1964. Pp. 7–20.

Piaget, J. & Inhelder, Bärbel. *L'image mentale chez l'enfant. Étude sur le développement des représentations imagées.* Paris: Presses Univer. France, 1966.

Ryle, G. *The concept of mind.* New York: Barnes & Noble, 1949.

Shinn, Millicent, W. *Biography of a baby.* Boston: Houghton Mifflin, 1900.

Tiedemann, D. *Beobachtungen uber die Entwicklung der Seelenfahrigkeiten bei Kindern.* Altenburg: Bonde, 1787.

Whorf, B. L. Science and linguistics. In J. Carroll (Ed.), *Language, thought, and reality.* Cambridge, Mass.: The Technology Press and Wiley, 1956. Pp. 207–219.

THEORETICAL PERSPECTIVES

The Impact and Limitations of the Giant of Developmental Psychology

J. MCV. HUNT

It is my guess that when the history of developmental psychology in the twentieth century is ultimately written, the name of Jean Piaget will stand out above all others. His name will stand out because he has reported highly revealing observations of early child development as an ongoing process of interaction between the infant and his circumstances. Moreover, he has drawn important theoretical hypotheses from these observations—hypotheses that impinge not only upon other conceptualizations of behavioral development but also upon conceptualizations of intelligence and of motivation. Piaget's observations and theories, however, provide definitive answers to few questions. Rather, they serve to open doors and to make issues for investigation.

I wish to indicate first the twists Piaget's observations and conceptions provide for several of the still dominant theoretical conceptions that have been bequeathed to us from various lead-

The preparation of this paper has been supported by a grant (MH K6-1857) from the United States Public Health Service.

3

ing investigators of the past. Second, although I believe Piaget will influence the wave of the future, I wish also to point out some of the limitations in what he calls the invariants of process, namely, his constructs of accommodation and assimilation, and also in his conception of stages. Finally, I wish to express an appreciation of his contributions.

The three periods of Piaget's life-work

Piaget's life-work falls into three periods. The first period includes studies of the child's language and thought (1923), judgement and reasoning (1924), conception of the world (1926), conception of physical causality (1927), and moral judgements (1932). In these early studies, Piaget's empirical data came almost completely from the language behavior of pairs of children observed in preschool situations at the Rousseau Institute in Geneva. These early works, and, especially, his notions of the prevalence of egocentric thought in children under age seven, were severely criticized. Piaget has since admitted that, "My method of studying logic in the child was much too verbal at first, dealing particularly with the relation between thought and language" (1953, p. 32).

The second period began with his observations of the origins of intelligence and reality constructions in his own three infant children. In these works, Piaget (1936, 1937) revised his method of observation to focus on the child's actions in the course of repeated encounters with objects, persons, and situations. In these observations of his own infant children Piaget, in effect, carried out Hilgard's (1948, p. 353) suggestion that it would be highly desirable for someone to follow a child around to discover the circumstances under which he learns, what performances provide for recall, for problem-solving, and the like. It should be noted, however, that Piaget began these observations more than twenty years before Hilgard made this suggestion, and published them a dozen years before his suggestion. These observational studies have been almost as pregnant with suggestions for theory as Hilgard hoped they might be. As I understand the sweep of

Piaget's life-work, it was in these longitudinal observations (Piaget 1936, 1937) of his own children during the sensorimotor phase of their progressive development, and to some degree while they were forming symbolic processes and acquiring the beginnings of language (Piaget, 1945), that Piaget found the basis for, or perhaps the justification for, his view of development as an ongoing process of continuous sensorimotor interaction between the infant and his environmental circumstances. Such interaction is given explicit theoretical recognition by Piaget in his process invariants, namely, accommodation and assimilation. Moreover, this interaction is seen to result in an epigenetic series of changes in the structure of the child's behavior and in his constructions of reality. Much of Piaget's most general theoretical work (Piaget, 1947) derives largely from this second period of his life's work.

The third period of Piaget's work begins with the studies that he and his collaborators made of the development of the concrete operations from preconceptual thought. These concrete operations are interpreted to underlie conservation (of quantity, length, and number), the formation of classes, and serializing asymmetrical relations (Piaget, 1941, 1942a, 1942b; Piaget & Inhelder, 1940, 1947, 1948; Piaget, Inhelder, & Szeminska, 1948; Piaget & Szeminska, 1939, 1941). The studies in this group extend the epigenesis in the structure of thought from the symbolic preconceptual stage, through the stages of intuitive processes and concrete operations, which appear at age seven or eight, to the stage of formal operations (Inhelder & Piaget, 1955) that appear with adolescence. The studies of this third group include also the constructions beyond the sensorimotor stage, of such categories of reality as movement (Piaget, 1946), chance (Piaget, 1950), probability (Piaget, 1955b; Piaget, Albertini, & Rossi, 1944), space (Piaget & Inhelder, 1948; Piaget, Inhelder, & Szeminska, 1948), and time (Piaget, 1955a). The studies in this third period include also those of Piaget and Lambercier (1943a, 1943b, 1944, 1946, 1953) on changes in perception, and especially in the perception of illusions with age, and Piaget's (1952, 1953) elaborations of the transformations of thought in terms of logical operations. In this third period, Piaget and his collabora-

tors fill out much of the empirical promise of the general theory
of intelligence that Piaget (1947) formulated earlier.

Some implications of Piaget's observations and theoretical conceptions

Piaget's observations and his theorizing provide a basis for a
critical reevaluation and assessment of various of the theoretical
beliefs that many of us hold because we were taught them by
Piaget's predecessors or by some of his contemporaries. Important among these is the contrast between the views of behavioral
development formulated by Gesell and by Piaget.

PIAGET VERSUS GESELL

As I read the writings of contemporary students of developmental psychology, I glean that the depth of the dissonance
between the outlooks and conceptions of Piaget and Gesell has
hardly yet been fully appreciated. It is true that their methods
and results show certain similarities. Both have employed the
cross-sectional method of confronting children of various ages
with situations and materials and then observing how these children behave. Both describe behaviors typical of children at successive ages. Both recognize an epigenetic system of change in
the structure of behavior as essentially predetermined. Piaget,
however, views them as products of the sensorimotor interaction
between the infant or child and his environmental circumstances. Moreover, in his observations of his own three children,
Piaget employed a longitudinal method. He observed them repeatedly in similar situations and confronted them repeatedly
with given objects and materials.

To be sure, Gesell and his collaborators occasionally discussed
organism-environment interaction. Thus, Gesell (1928) wrote,
"The constitution and conditions of the organism are intimately
interdependent. The organismic pattern of one moment, responsive to both internal and external environment, influences the
pattern of succeeding moments. In a measure previous environ-

mental effects are perpetuated by incorporation with constitution." This statement, in itself, is an excellent expression of interactionism. Elsewhere, Gesell et al. (1940) noted, ". . . this serve(s) to show how supremely important it is for society to achieve through education and family life an optimal culture to insure a maximum of growth to infants and children. Culture provides the milieu . . . the conditions of growth. It provides a vast complex of symbols, cues, and foci of interest, which are assimilated into the very texture of the growing personality. Culture operates most profoundly and projectively in the first five years of life." In one of his still later publications, Gesell wrote, "Infancy is the period in which the individual realizes his racial inheritance . . . but infancy itself is a product of evolution. It was evolved not only to perpetuate a groundwork of racial inheritance, but also to add thereto a contingent margin of specific modifiability" (1954, p. 335).

In terms of the general impact of Gesell's contributions, however, these statements are little more than lip service. His work was basically normative in nature. He described the patterns of behavior typical, or statistically modal, for each age. In the *First Five Years of Life*, Gesell described mental growth as, "A progressive morphogenesis of patterns of behavior . . ." (1940, p. 7). Moreover, in a majority of his statements about the causal basis for mental growth, he said, in one form or another, the following, "The basic configurations, correlations, and successions of behavior patterns are *determined by the innate process of growth called maturation*" (Gesell, 1945, italics are mine). In the introduction to his film, *Life Begins*, he emphasized the importance of "intrinsic growth." Elsewhere he defined intrinsic growth as, "the unfolding of behavior with anatomical maturation."

In his theorizing, Gesell articulated several principles. All are essentially descriptive in character, and all but one reflect his emphasis on genetic predeterminism. In introducing his principles, Gesell wrote, "The growth of tissues, of organs, and of behavior is obedient to identical laws of development morphology" (1954, p. 337). Gesell's (1954) principles numbered five: (1) developmental direction, (2) reciprocal interweaving, (3) functional asymmetry, (4) individuating maturation, (5) self-regulatory fluctuation. In the first three and the fifth Gesell explicitly put the causal basis for behavioral development on anatomical maturation. The developmental processes go on in time, to be sure, but Gesell's conception of them gave no indication that he considered them to be plastic, or subject to appreciable modification by the circumstances encountered. Only the fourth of these principles, that of "individuating maturation," makes an explicit place for environmental influence. In opening his discussion of this principle, he made these statements, "This principle may help us to recognize the mechanism by means of which the behavioral organism achieves its species characteristics and yet at the same time, makes specific adaptations within its environmental field. From the moment of fertilization, intrinsic and extrinsic factors cooperate in a unitary manner, but the original impulse of growth and the matrix of morphogenesis is endogenous rather than exogenous. The so-called environment, whether internal or external, does not generate the progressions of development. Environmental factors support, inflect, and specify; but they do not engender the basic forms and sequences of ontogenesis" (Gesell, 1954, p. 354). In the subsequent sections of this theoretical paper on growth and development, Gesell discusses "self-regulatory fluctuation," "the individuality of growth careers," and "the stability of mental growth careers." In each of these sections, as their headings imply, Gesell contended, and supported his contention with evidence of a sort, that the individual's behavioral development is essentially predetermined. Moreover, in his consideration of predeterminism, Gesell made no distinction between the rate of development and the order in which the patterns of behavior appear.

In his theory of the causal basis for the epigenetic changes in behavior and thought, Piaget (1936, 1937, 1943, 1947) continually emphasizes accommodation, assimilation, and the lack of equilibrium between aspects of the infant's behavioral repertoire and the circumstances encountered. These are his terms for the adaptive changes that organisms make in their encounters with environmental circumstances. Accommodation may be defined as that modification in a sensorimotor organization (or schema—to use Piaget's term), or in a conceptual operation or construction, that comes about in the course of encounters with new circumstances where the existing organization does not quite fit. Assimilation is the term given to the internalization of the accommodative change. One knows that assimilation has occurred when the infant or child employs the newly modified sensorimotor or conceptual organization in a novel situation. One might say that one recognizes assimilation when an accommodative change in behavior or thought (as reflected in language) generalizes to a new situation.

The concept of equilibrium is more difficult to explain. Equilibrium is Piaget's (1947, pp. 6–8) term for the stability of a behavioral organization. In the case of sensorimotor organizations, including all perceptions and motor habits, the equilibrium is limited to certain circumstances. Each such sensorimotor organization involves cognitive and affective regulation (which I would term its motivational aspect). On the inside of the organism, this regulation is based on interest, effort, and such. On the outside, it is based on the value of the objects concerned in this search and in the solutions sought. When the infant or child encounters circumstances beyond the limits of his sensorimotor systems the equilibrium is upset. This lack of equilibrium of sensorimotor and preconceptual systems leads continually to accommodative modifications in them until certain of them achieve either the limits set by the genotype or achieve structures that can generalize indefinitely to the circumstances encountered. If the circumstance is not too far beyond the limits of his sensorimotor systems, these systems become modified in the attempt to accommodate the new circumstances.

In the locomotor domain, the infant gyrates on his stomach and squirms toward objects desired; then he creeps or scoots toward them; then he gets up onto his feet and cruises and toddles, until he can finally walk and run. The child's strides may increase in length with his skeletal growth, and he may obtain minor increases in force, duration, and rate of strides with special training, if he aspires to be an athlete. Otherwise, these locomotor skills remain essentially stable as they are employed as means in an endless variety of goal-directed activities. They achieve their genotypic limits. Only as men supplement their locomotor abilities mechanically with bicycles, automobiles, airplanes, and rockets can men alter these abilities appreciably.

In the intellectual domain, ready-made systems of information-processing become extended with use. Each becomes coordinated through accommodations with other such systems, until sensori-motor action systems become internalized as imaginal symbolic systems that are combined with vocal imitation in language. These preconceptual named-images are transformed through accommodative modifications, demanded perhaps largely by efforts at communication, into what Piaget calls intuitive regulations. These regulations are then further transformed into the concrete intellectual operations that permit classifying, serializing of asymmetrical comparisons, and counting. These concrete intellectual operations acquire an equilibrium because classifying, serializing, and counting can be generalized to new circumstances indefinitely. Yet, since they constitute thought processes directed entirely by encounters with circumstances, they are inadequate to provide a basis for an examination of those operations. The lack of equilibrium induced by examining these operations in linguistic propositions leads to the formation of those formal operations of thought that Piaget (1947) and his collaborators (Inhelder & Piaget, 1955) find appearing during adolescence. At this stage, thought directs perception in investigation, and the imaginal standards of what life and society might be supply the standards that motivate the adolescent toward reforming the world that exists. Piaget (1947, p. 27) contends that "logic is the mirror of thought." The classificatory logic of Aristotle reflected the thought of the Aristotelian era. The formal logic of Boole (1854) represents the thought that man, in his scientific efforts, has developed largely since the Renaissance. Piaget has contended further that man may yet invent new modes of thought in the process of coping with the new instruments of his own invention.

In sum, then, Gesell and Piaget propose radically different interpretations of behavioral development. Yet, their interpretations do not represent the opposite poles on a polarity of emphasis on heredity and environment. While Gesell has presented a picture of behavioral development as something based essentially on anatomical maturation that is predetermined by heredity, Piaget has presented a picture of behavioral development as a process of changes in the structure of behavior and of thought that come with the infant's or child's interacting with his circumstances. Piaget's position is neither hereditarian nor environmentalistic; it is both. It is interactionist.

PIAGET VERSUS S-R BEHAVIOR THEORY

Piaget's view of development is not the polar opposite of Gesell's. The opposite of Gesell's predeterminism is extreme environmentalism. Environmentalism has its conceptual roots in John Locke's (1690) famous *Essay Concerning Human Understanding*. In the first book of this essay, Locke took his epistemological stand against innate ideas and against the notion that anything need be true simply because it has the weight of traditional authority. The first sentence in the second paragraph of Book II may be paraphrased as follows: "Let us then suppose the mind to be, as we say, white paper void of all characters without any ideas; how comes it to be furnished?" The answer given by Locke to this question came in the words: "From EXPERIENCE."

Taken from the domain of mind in general and applied to individual organisms, and especially infant human beings, this assumption of the organism as a tabula rasa implies that the organism is something statically passive and that the course of knowledge resides in receptor input from environmental circumstances. While no serious theory of behavioral development has ever accepted fully these assumptions about the nature of living organisms, and especially of human beings, several of the central conceptions of stimulus-response (S-R) behavior theory have approached such extreme environmentalism.

S-R behavior theory appears to derive its origin from revolts against three relatively unrelated views that were dominant in the latter half of the nineteenth century. Two of these views were part and parcel of post-Darwinian thought. First, Darwin was especially interested in the continuity of evolution between the infrahuman species of animals and man. He was interested in showing this continuity of evolution both in anatomy (Darwin, 1859) and in behavior. Darwin's (1872) behavioral efforts are to be found in his studies of the expression of emotions in man and animals. The theory of psychological faculties prevailed in the nineteenth century. Emotion was one faculty, intelligence another. Darwin was interested equally in seeing a continuity of evolution demonstrated for the faculty of intelligence as for that of emotion. Romanes (1883a, 1883b) attempted to do for intelligence what Darwin had already done for the expressions of the emotional faculty. Moreover, Darwin's younger cousin, Francis Galton (1869, 1883, 1886), extended the notion of predeterminism in individuals into that of fixed faculties and abilities. These he proposed to measure with his anthropometric tests, and he hoped to develop human excellence in these tested traits through eugenics.

Second, both the biologists and psychologists of the post-Darwinian period tended to conceive not only of the sources of action but also of the patternings of action in terms of instincts predetermined by the heredity of the species or of the individual. Probably the most recent statement of instinct theory applied to human behavior is to be found in William McDougall's (1908) *Social Psychology*.

Third, the human psychology of the late nineteenth century was largely concerned with consciousness and it took as its method introspection. This is true of the psychology of America (witness James, Hall, & Ladd), of England (witness the mental chemistry of John Stuart Mill, the physiological psychology of Bain, and the evolutionary associationism of Herbert Spencer), of France (witness the psychopathologies of Charcot and Janet), and of Germany (witness the work of Fechner and Wundt).

S-R behavior theory arose as a rejection of all three of these positions. Its conceptual roots may be found in the mechanistic philosophy of the eighteenth century, in the theory of tropistic behavior by Jacques Loeb (1890, 1912), in the critical extirpation of the intelligence faculty, imputed by Romanes (1883; a, b), from the causation of animal behavior by C. Lloyd Morgan (1894), and in the experimental studies of problem-solving in animals carried out by E. L. Thorndike (1898, 1911) in the basement of William James's home. S-R theory got a tremendous boost in popularity, moreover, in the polemics over the instinct theory. From the day of Thorndike onward, most of the S-R theorists were students of animal learning. Their studies of animal learning provided evidence against the intinct theory. In the polemics, Dunlap (1919) uttered the battle-cry, and John B. Watson (1924) and many others took up the cudgels shortly after World War I. Finally, behaviorism came into being as a reaction against the psychology of consciousness. Boring (1929) dates the beginning of the behavioristic movement from Watson's (1913) first polemic entitled *Psychology as the Behaviorist Views It.* Shortly thereafter he published *Behavior, an Introduction to Comparative Psychology* (Watson, 1914). The behavioristic movement adopted the objective methods of classical conditioning (Pavlov, 1927) and of trial-and-error learning (Thorndike, 1898, 1911).

In coming to an approximation of the Lockian tabula rasa, however, the revolt against the instinct theory is most important. In consequence of the evidence coming from the laboratories of animal psychology and the arguments made in the polemics over instinct theory, the S-R behavior theories of such leading Americans as Thorndike (1911, 1935), Watson (1914, 1924), Weiss (1925), Hull (1943, 1952), and Skinner (1938, 1953) developed what became the dominant view in American psychology. While substantial differences existed among the theories of these men (Hilgard, 1956), they embraced in common not only something approaching the tabula rasa of original nature but also several other conceptions for which Piaget's observations and theorizing yield a relevant dissonance.

Original nature as an abundant repertoire of minute reflexes. The approximation of the tabula rasa in S-R behavior theory derives from the assumption that the original nature of mammalian organisms including man consists in an abundant repertoire of minute reflexes. Instinct theory had held that even highly complex patterns of behavior could have their organizations predetermined from the innate constitution of the species or the individual, and this made the problem of the criteria of innate behavior important (Marquis, 1930). When the instinct theory was largely rejected (and it was never completely rejected by such behaviorists as Hunter (1920) and Thorndike (1935)), the alternative conception of original nature came to consist of a large number of minute, elementary, reflexes for which the knee-jerk was an approximate model. It was this conception that Dewey (1896) inveighed against in his famous paper on the reflex. Inasmuch as it was also conceived that any given reflex could be evoked through conditioning by any stimulus or combination of stimuli, and also that these minute reflexive actions could be combined without appreciable restraint into any sort of organization, this view constituted a near equivalent to the tabula rasa of John Locke. In this context John B. Watson (1928) claimed that, with the control of the circumstances to be encountered by any healthy infant from birth to seven years, he could make of that infant anything desired. This has been the nature of environmentalism at its most extreme. It is a view that also emphasizes action in the process of learning and that minimizes the role of perception and of central processes. It is a view that has largely failed to take into account the developmental aspect of behavior, for those embracing S-R behavior theory have, in their investigations, employed as subjects chiefly nearly adult rats, often characterized as naïve because they have not participated in a preceding experiment, nearly adult dogs, nearly adult monkeys, and at the human level, chiefly college sophomores who were available because they were students in the first course in psychology.

Piaget's (1936, 1937) observations are highly dissonant with such a form of extreme environmentalism. In place of a repertoire of numerous minuscule reflexes, Piaget finds in the human neonate a very limited number of quite highly organized behavioral systems. These include: (a) sucking, (b) looking, (c) listening, (d) vocalizing, (e) grasping, and (f) the various motor activities of the trunk and limbs. Piaget emphasizes that each of these is a ready-made sensorimotor organization at the human infant's birth. Unlike the investigators of the embryology of behavior (Carmichael, 1954; Kuo, 1921, 1922, 1932a, 1932b,

1932c, 1932d, 1932e), Piaget has not concerned himself with how these ready-made organizations came into being before birth. It is interesting, however, that in his *Design for a Brain,* Ashby (1952) suggests precisely such component ready-made organizations. In his argument, Ashby suggests that if one were to design a complex electronic automaton to do what all mammals do, one would almost necessarily have to begin with a limited number of subsystems that the encounters with circumstances would then reorganize. Such a conception is, at once, a long way from the notion of instincts and a long way from the S-R behavior theorists' notion of an innate repertoire consisting of a set of numerous simple reflexes. It is perhaps more important for the empirical validity of the notion, however, to note that the sensorimotor schemata that Piaget reports from his observations of his own three infants show a rather substantial degree of correspondence with the systems that neuro-anatomists have uncovered in their anatomical explorations of the brain as related to function (Papez, 1929). The neurologists find not only the visual system for looking and the auditory system for listening but also an olfactory system, a complex system for contact reception, and a vestibular system. While neurologists have never spoken of a grasping system or a vocalizing system, the motor portion of the brain has considerable differentiation, and there is a definite speech area. This problem of defining units in behavior is both old and difficult, but the correspondence here between Piaget's sensorimotor organizations and those systems traditional in neurology is sufficient to be impressive.

The existence of a few component organizations rather than a repertoire of numerous minuscule reflexes implies a theoretical conception of the nature of behavioral organization at birth intermediate between the predeterministic view on the one hand and the extreme environmentalism on the other. Piaget's (1936) observations tend to confirm such an intermediate view. These observations attest to an ample place for the effect of encounters with circumstances, but the infant organism is seen to be far from a blank page on which experience can write without constraint. Orderliness in the course of development derives not only from genetic preprogramming, but also from the nature of the manner in which these ready-made sensorimotor systems are capable of being coordinated and differentiated in the course of the infant's interaction with his environmental circumstances.

The ontogenesis of "operants" Piaget's observations and his theorizing provide evidence and conceptions dissonant with the conception prevalent among S-R behavior theorists that organisms, including human beings, tend to be passive and inactive until driven into action by impelling stimulation. Among S-R behaviorists, Skinner (1938, 1953) is an exception to the rule that they are drive theorists, especially in the case of what he calls "operant" activities. These are activities for which the instigating events in the environment cannot be specified, and they are to be contrasted with "respondents" for which the instigating event can be specified.

In his aversion to theory, Skinner (1950) accepts the existence of "operants" and "respondents" as given. He is unconcerned with enlarging the nomological net to include either their ontogenetic origins or their physiological bases. Moreover, he avoids so completely conceptions based on the experimental subject's report that he eliminates consideration of such conceptions as expectations and intentions. The result is an almost endless list of empirical relationships with almost no principles (Ferster & Skinner, 1957).

Piaget's (1936) observations provide evidence of ontogenetic origins of actions that Skinner probably would call "operants," and also of an epigenetic shift from "respondent" status to "operant" status. Immediately following birth, during the first sensorimotor stage, Piaget finds the human neonate with various ready-made systems—already named above—that are essentially responsive in character. At first, for instance, the sucking movements can be elicited only by contact of the lips with some external object, even under what Skinner calls the "setting condition" of hunger from going several hours without food. In his observations of his son Laurent, Piaget noted that,

After the first feedings, one observes . . . sucking-like movements in which it is difficult not to see a sort of auto-excitation . . . [and] one is compelled to state that, in such a case, there is a tendency toward

repetition, or, in objective terms, cumulative repetition . . . this need
for repetition is only one aspect of a more general process which we
can qualify as assimilation. The tendency of the reflex being to repro-
duce itself, it incorporates into itself every object capable of fulfilling
the function of excitant . . . [this] assimilation belonging to the
adaptive process appears in three forms: cumulative repetition, generalization of the activity with incorporation of new objects to it, and
finally, motor recognition.* But, in the last analysis, these three forms
are but one: the reflex must be conceived as an organized totality
whose nature is to preserve itself in functioning and consequently to
function sooner or later for its own sake (repetition) while incorporating into itself objects propitious to its functioning (generalizing assimilation) and discerning situations necessary to certain modes of its
activity (motor recognition) . . . the progressive adaptation of reflexive schemata [such as sucking], therefore, presupposes their organization (1936, pp. 343–8).

Thus, even in the case of such a reflexive motor schema as
sucking, successive encounters with the nipple and the breast
and with other objects that touch the lips are observed to lead
from what, in Skinner's (1953) language, would be the status of
a "respondent" to the status of an "operant."

This progressive adaptation continues through the second
sensorimotor stage during which reflexive looking, to use the
language of Piaget, incorporates things heard so that the things
heard become something to look at as the infant acquires what is
commonly termed "auditory localization." This process exemplifies coordination between looking and listening. In this process
of the second stage of sensorimotor development, it should be
noted that Piaget's observations imply a redefinition of "stimulus." Instead of mere energy delivered at receptors, the effective
instigators of reflexive looking and reflexive listening appear to
be changes in the ongoing characteristics of the light or of the
sound impinging on the neonate's eyes or ears. The reflexive

---

* Piaget illustrates each of these with concrete observations of the behavior of his
children. Elsewhere, I have selected observations to illustrate the points Piaget
makes. Here, there is no space to present them, and the reader is invited to examine Piaget's (1936, Chapter 1) own observations or my selection (Hunt, 1961,
p. 117 ff).

looking and the reflexive listening appear to be special cases of what the Russian investigators, since Pavlov, have called the "orienting reflex" (Berlyne, 1960; Razran, 1961). This being the case, assimilating things heard into the looking schema appears to be a special case of stimulus to stimulus conditioning for which the motivation consists in changes in the ongoing characteristics of the input.

Piaget observed that as his children exercised a schema such as looking, and as the exercise brought them in perceptual contact with objects seen or heard in the external environment, they exhibited "new behavior relating to the objects which have disappeared" (1936, p. 155). Piaget's observations seem to indicate that these new efforts brought on by the escape of objects from perceptual contact occur only after the child has had repeated perceptual contact with those objects. The infant's efforts appear to be directed toward retaining or regaining the perceptual contact with these recognitively familiar objects, persons, and places. Even in a very young infant, recognitive familiarity appears to be the chief basis for what Piaget has termed "spectacles of interest." Everyone who has jounced an infant on his knee is familiar with this phenomenon, even though the example cited typically occurs some months after infants manifest their first efforts to retain or regain perceptual contact with objects becoming recognitively familiar. When the adult jouncer stops his jouncing, the infant typically begins a jouncing of his own. It is extremely difficult to escape the interpretation that the infant, when he starts a jouncing of his own, intends to renew his own perceptual contact with the jouncing event. It is hard to escape the interpretation that the infant anticipates the goal of his action, for when the adult jouncer resumes his jouncing, the infant quickly stops his own efforts, manifests a benign expression, and appears to enjoy what he anticipated all along. In his long third chapter on the "secondary circular reactions" that constitute sensorimotor stage three, Piaget (1936) cites many examples of such behavior. At this point, the human infant clearly ceases to be a reactive responder and becomes an initiator of a great many different kinds of activities in which certain of his sensorimotor schemata are goals clearly anticipated, while others serve as means to the anticipated goals or ends.

One may, following Skinner (1938, 1953), call these self-instigated activities "operants," if one wishes, but such mere naming of a category of nonrespondents fails to consider their developmental origin. Such naming fails to consider that these activities emerge as a product of the infant's early encounters with his circumstances in the course of his development. Skinner's (1950) aversion to theorizing and to consideration of the developmental process leaves him with a pair of categories of activities, "respondents" and "operants," that are of little interest because they are tied neither to hypotheses of their origin nor to hypotheses of the physiological processes which mediate them. From the fact that, as Hebb (1949) has pointed out, central processes run off more rapidly than do events, one gains a hypothetical physiological basis for self-instigation growing out of encounters with circumstances. Combining Piaget's observations of the ontogenetic origins of self-instigated activities with such a hypothesis of their physiological basis yields, in turn, a foundation for "expectations" and "intentions" that is quite consonant with a mechanistic view of living beings.

The S-R conception of learning Piaget's observations and theorizing are highly relevant to the S-R conception of learning. They imply a variety of kinds of learning to which attention is seldom given, and a variety differing greatly from that to which Gagné (1965, Ch. 2) comes from reviewing the investigative work on learning and problem solving. In fact, Piaget's conceptions of accommodation and assimilation and his concept of the lack of equilibrium constitute a domain essentially equivalent to the concept of learning broadly defined. I shall return to this topic in my critique of these constructs below.

Piaget's observations and theorizing call into question also the traditional conception of what in an organism's encounters with circumstances induces modifications in behavior. In our traditional formulations, modification of behavior has been attributed to events that follow behavioral acts. Thus, in the theorizing of Thorndike (1911, 1935a) it is a matter of whether the action or behavior leads to annoyance or to satisfaction. Hull's (1943) position was somewhat similar. Actions that failed to reduce the drive that evoked them were gradually extinguished,

others took their place at the top of the hierarchy. Only those
actions that led to a reduction in drive survived. If I understand
Skinner's (1958) formulation, it also depends upon reinforcement, where reinforcement is any event following the action of
the organism that results in an increase in the readiness of the
action or in a modification of the action to occur. As Skinner put
it, "We observe the frequency of a selected response (operant
level) then make an event contingent upon it and observe any
change in frequency. If there is a change, we classify the event
as reinforcing to the organism under the existing circumstances"
(1953, p. 73). Such modification appears to be chiefly one of
motivation. Yet in the case of shaping behavior, about which we
now hear so much in the work of Skinner and his collaborators,
the modification is a genuine alteration in the structure of the
activity. This shaping is cognitive in nature in the sense that it
must involve a change in the organization in the central processes that mediate the change in behavior. Although Piaget
professes concern only with matters cognitive and epistemological, we have here in the S-R theory of reinforcement something
closely related to Piaget's notion of "lack of equilibrium" and its
role in behavioral and conceptual development.

According to Skinner (1958) and to behavior theorists generally, the modifications in behavior that constitute the shaping
occur because of the rewarding events that follow their occurrence. Piaget's observations, on the other hand, suggest strongly
that the modifications in behavior come at the point in time that
the learner encounters circumstances that will not permit him to
proceed as he anticipated. These are circumstances that upset
the child's equilibrium and force him into accommodative modifications. Relevant observations include those concerned with
modifications of sophisticated sucking, of sophisticated grasping, and of manual groping to solve various problems (Piaget,
1963, Ch. 1, 3, & 5), modifications in the intuitive regulations
leading to the concrete conceptual operations (Piaget, 1943;
Piaget & Inhelder, 1940; Piaget & Szeminska, 1939), and the
modifications in thought that derive from encounters with problems for which concrete operations are inadequate and result in
the development of formal conceptual operations (Inhelder &

Piaget, 1955). Piaget views the child in all of these various situations as highly active. He holds that the child has an end in view, and it seems that the child does have an end in view because he ceases striving once he achieves that end. Moreover, one would expect ends-in-view from the fact that in familiar situations central processes run off faster than events. Thus, from a physiological standpoint, the child can be expected to anticipate what is coming and to have intentional ends in view. The modifications in the structure of behavior or thought, then, can be viewed as an active, creative, coping operation. The modification becomes part of the child's standard repertoire only when it has achieved the child's anticipated goals repeatedly in a number of situations for which it was adequate. In the language of Piaget, then, reinforcement would consist in achieving the child's anticipated goals, would permit at least some degree of equilibrium, and would aid the assimilation of the creative modification in the behavioral structure that came about with the encounter with circumstances novel but not beyond the child's accommodative limits. It is interesting to note that Piaget's view is highly consonant with the view of social psychologists that changes in attitude and belief come directly from encounters with new and dissonant information (Festinger, 1957; Hovland, Mandell, et al. 1957). It is also interesting, in passing, to note that the studies of change in attitude and belief from encounters with dissonant information generally have not been considered to belong within the traditional domain of learning.

PIAGET VERSUS GESTALT PSYCHOLOGY

Piaget (1947, p. 60) clearly accepts the essential, organized "wholeness" of sensorimotor, perceptual, and conceptual structures or schemata. His acceptance of their Gestaltish nature is a major reason for his preference for the notion of accommodative groping in new circumstances over the notion of trial-and-error. According to the theory of trial-and-error, the subject is seen to emit by chance a series of discrete responses. Each one is a trial. Each one is also an error until by chance one occurs that achieves success. The one that repeatedly succeeds survives because it is somehow reinforced. Piaget admits the descriptive accuracy of such an account for instances in which "the problem transcends the subject's intellectual level or knowledge" (1936, pp. 397–398). Under such circumstances, however, success brings little intellectual growth. When the subject grasps a problem, or sees it as akin to others he has already solved, the role of chance is greatly reduced. Instead, the subject brings to bear his ready-made perceptual organization of the situation and his prepared coping strategy. When the fit between this organization and the actual situation is such as to be relevant but inadequate, the subject typically modifies in creative fashion his organized perception and coping strategy to get a solution that consists of an elaboration of the previous organization and brings with it new understanding.

According to the central idea of Gestalt theory, the sensorimotor, perceptual, or conceptual organizations never consist of an association of elements that exist in isolation before they come together. They exist rather in configurations or complex structures that are organized wholes from the outset. They obey such Gestalt laws as simplicity, regularity, proximity, symmetry, and *Prägnanz*. According to Gestalt theory, these laws of organization are simply the principles of the equilibrium that governs the neuro-excitation released by perceptual contact with external objects combined in a field that embraces the organism and its immediate environment simultaneously. Köhler (1929) viewed this field as comparable to an electromagnetic field of forces and considered it to be governed by analogous principles, such for instance, as that of least action.

The notion that the psychological field is comparable to an electromagnetic field implied that the laws of organization must be universal and therefore common to all stages of both evolutionary and ontogenetic development. Gestalt psychologists (Köhler, 1929; Wertheimer, 1920), even those concerned explicitly with developmental psychology (see Koffka, 1924; Werner, 1948), have devoted themselves to accumulating an impressive series of illustrations of perceptual and conceptual structures that are the same in various mammals along the evolutionary scale, and the same in young children as in adults. Moreover,

Gestalt psychologists (Duncker, 1935; Wertheimer, 1920) have attempted to explain intelligent activity as a sudden restructuring of perception that comes with an "aha" moment of insight. Gestalt students of intelligence also have attributed a minimal importance to past experience. From their point of view, both the basic perceptual organizations and these restructurings are essentially preformed in the sense that they arise inherently out of the nature of neural processes evoked by organism's perceptual encounter with its circumstances. In this sense, Gestalt psychologists belong to the tradition of the nativists, and their theory remains as a psychological vestige of preformationism.

Piaget (1947, p. 60 ff) has taken explicit issue with the hypothesis of universal "physical Gestalten." He points out that the dilemma of either organized wholes or the atomism of isolated sensations or reflexes is quite unnecessary. Instead of these two terms, he finds three. In his own words as translated, Piaget states:

A perception may be a synthesis of elements, or else it may constitute a single whole, or it may be a system of relations (each relation being itself a whole, but the complete whole becoming unanalyzable and not relying at all on atomism). This being the case, there is no reason why complex structures should not be regarded as the product of a progressive construction which arises, not from "syntheses" [of atomistic elements], but from adaptive differentiations and combined assimilations, nor is there any reason why this construction should not be related to an intelligence capable of genuine activity as opposed to an interplay of pre-established structures (1947, pp. 63–64).

To support his third alternative view, Piaget reviews work showing a progressive development of size constancy during the first year of life, other work showing that the "systematic error of the standard" in paired-comparisons of heights at a distance is underestimated by children of five to seven years of age but is overestimated by adults, and that the incidence of size constancy increases in children up to nearly ten years of age.

These findings suggest that the phenomena of size constancy, like that of object permanence described below (p. 35), depend upon the solidity of representative central processes that derive their existence from repeated sensorimotor encounters with distances, sizes, and objects.

In his observations of the early psychological development of his own three children, Piaget (1936) noted sensorimotor adaptations not unlike those observed by Köhler (1924) on the use of implements by chimpanzees. Köhler noted that a chimpanzee failed to use a stick in his efforts to obtain a banana beyond reach except when that stick was available to be perceived at the same time that the animal was looking at the out-of-reach banana. Paralleling this observation of Köhler's, Piaget noted repeatedly that, at ages ranging from three to five months, his children would grasp seen objects only when the hand and the object were simultaneously in view (1936, Ch. 2). From such observations, Piaget argues that eye-hand coordination comes about only as the schemata of hand motion and grasping become incorporated in looking to constitute a new Gestalt organization. He argues further that,

Wherever we may speak of conditioned reflexes being stabilized as the result of experience, we always perceive that a schema of the whole organizes the parts of the associations. If the nursling seeks the breast when he is in a position to nurse, follows moving objects with his eyes, tends to look at the people whose voice he hears, grasps objects he perceives, etc., it is because the schemata of sucking, vision, and prehension have assimilated increasingly numerous realities, through this very fact of endowing them with meaning. Accommodation and assimilation combined, peculiar to each schema, insure its usefulness and coordinate it to the others, and it is the global act of complementary assimilation and accommodation which explains why the relationships of the parts which presuppose the schema are confirmed by experience (Piaget, 1963, p. 128).

In similar fashion, Piaget explains the successive coordinations which, when combined with differentiation, provide the basis for the hierarchical nature of intelligence and intellectual functions. Following the six stages of the sensorimotor development, the sensorimotor systems of the infant become internalized as imitative imagery combines with the imitated vocal signs of early language. These are gradually modified in the accommodations demanded by communication into intuitive regulations that, in turn, are coalesced or grouped into the concrete operations of intelligence of which Piaget and his collaborators find evidence in the children of Geneva at about seven to eight years of age (Inhelder & Piaget, 1955). At this stage, the child becomes able to manipulate hierarchies of classes, to serialize asymmetrical relations and appreciate transpositions, and to employ additive compensations that enable him to conserve quantity, length, and number. At each stage, after the first sensorimotor one, the child's anticipation of the end or goal of his action or thought serves to unify the system. Even though concrete thought continues to be directed by encounters with circumstances, the "groupings" of regulatory expectations serve to organize conceptually the classes, asymmetrical relations, and compensatory additive combinations.

Such coordination is then repeated when the concrete additive operations become recoordinated and reorganized into formal, multiplicative operations (Inhelder & Piaget, 1955). At this final stage, the thought of adolescents confronted with various kinds of problems begins to reflect various of Boole's (1854) logical structures. These logical structures include the proportionality which underlies the "education of correlates" that Spearman (1923) considered to be one of the distinguishing characteristics of intelligent action or thought, "the 16 binary operations of two-valued propositional logic," and the "INRC group." Piaget (1953) views each of these systems of formal operations as a Gestaltish whole.

Thus, while Piaget can readily accept the Gestalt principles of organization, the main burden of his life-work, in uncovering a progressive epigenesis of actional, imaginal, and intellectual structures and of epistemological constructions, is maximally dissonant with the notion that "the laws of organization" are constant in the course of human development. Rather, the systems of behavior and of thought are seen to develop into more complex hierarchical organizations in the course of the child's sensorimotor and informational interaction with his environmental circumstances.

PIAGET VERSUS PSYCHOANALYSIS AND DRIVE THEORY

Piaget (1952) began his scientific career as a zoologist, but his first psychological concerns were psychoanalytic. His first publications concerned the anatomical variations in mollusks developing under various ecological conditions. These publications began appearing when he was but fifteen years old. He earned his doctorate in zoology with a thesis on mollusks. Only then did he turn to psychology in Zurich. There he worked part-time in Bleuler's psychiatric clinic, and he attributes his initial concern with psychoanalysis to the personal factor of his mother's poor mental health (Piaget, 1952). In Bleuler's clinic, he learned the interview method. He used this method in his early studies, first, at the Sorbonne where he was concerned with the reasons children failed on Burt's tests and, later, in the first group of studies at the Rousseau Institute in Geneva (Piaget, 1923, 1924, 1926, 1927, 1932).

Despite this background in psychoanalysis, Piaget's later work, beginning with his observations of the behavior of his own infant children in their repeated encounters with everyday things, has been concerned almost entirely with the development of intelligence and with children's construction of the Kantian categories of reality. A concern with affectivity appears only incidentally in the role of a lack of equilibrium in accommodative modifications of intellectual and epistemological structures. It is undoubtedly in the difference between Piaget's concerns and the concerns of psychoanalytic observers, as well as in the differences between the two vantage points of observation, that one finds the origin of such a radical difference in concern and findings with respect to affectivity and motivation. While Freud and the other psychoanalysts were concerned with understanding the origins of neurotic and psychotic behavior, Piaget concerned himself with the development of intelligent procedures for coping with environmental circumstances and with the construction of the various Kantian categories of reality. Where Freud and the other analysts started with neurotically distressed, adult patients and attempted to reconstruct the basis for their distress from their reported memories or from their free associations, Piaget observed the behavior and talk of infants and young children, typically well-fed and well-cared for, when they were confronted repeatedly with various environmental situations. The resulting difference in findings—the tremendous importance of the affective aspect of life in psychoanalysis and the tremendous place of the cognitive aspect of life by Piaget—comes inevitably.

Freud's revolt against the rationalism of the conscious in the psychology of his day was made inevitable by the vantage point from which he observed life and attempted to reconstruct lives. The theory of drives (*Treiben*) as the springs of behavior, Freud found almost ready-made in the thought of the German version of the Romantic Movement. Freud's drive theory can be found in part in Schopenhauer's notion that man finds his essence in will or desire, in part in Feuerbach's related notion of the wish coupled with his notion that happiness is founded upon the universal impulse of sexual love, in part in Bückner's physiologizing of will and wish as drive which von Hartmann also espoused. Freud's theory of the unconscious can also be found almost ready-made; it had been explicit in the psychological theory of Herbart, and it became popular with the wide-spread reading of von Hartmann's (1869) *The Philosophy of the Unconscious*. Freud combined these ideas of drives and of the unconscious with his observations made through his interviews with his patients and through their free associations to create his theory of psychosexual development (Freud, 1905). What was originally the Freudian wish became explicitly tied to physiological stimulation in his paper, "Instincts and Their Vicissitudes" (Freud, 1915).

The concept of drive got support in America from the physiological investigations of Walter B. Cannon (1915) concerned with the bodily changes in pain, hunger, fear, and rage. It got further support from the psychological investigations of Curt Richter (1922, 1927), from the theorizing of Woodworth (1918), and finally, it got incorporated into the dominant motivational theories of psychology by such expositors as Dashiell (1925), Dollard & Miller (1950), Guthrie (1938), Hull (1943), Mowrer (1950), and Thorndike (1935); (see also Hunt, 1963a).

According to this drive theory, organisms are instigated to act only by strong and painful external stimuli, or by such internal needs as hunger, thirst, sex, or by innocuous stimuli that have been associated with (conditioned to emotional responses evoked by) either painful external or internal stimuli. When these conditions cease to operate, the drive ceases and the behavior is supposed to stop. Freud (1915) made explicit that the "aim" of all behavior is to remove the stimuli that produce excitation and to minimize the excitation in the nervous system. Moreover, according to Freud's (1905) theory of psychosexual development, the individual's character, neurotic or healthy, is largely a function of the fate of these instinctual drives and the emotional conditions related to them. Certainly, in those patients who come for psychotherapy, distressing emotions do loom large in the impressions that the psychotherapist gets from his patients' talk.

In the children observed by Piaget, however, the emotions loomed far less large. Although Piaget (1936) has been avowedly unconcerned with emotion and motivation, his observations are an interesting source for hypotheses concerning the development of motivation (Hunt, 1963b). Piaget's own children were typically without pain, without hunger, without thirst, and presumably without sexually strong excitement at the points at which he made the observations reported. Nevertheless, his children were highly active and highly interested from a motivational standpoint, and were not without affectivity—delight when they achieved their intentional ends and distress when they failed. Presumably they were active by virtue of motivation based on their sensorimotor interaction with their environmental circumstances, interaction based largely on input chiefly through the eyes and the ears but also from tactual contact with things and kinesthetic feedback from the muscles. If the other abundant evidence for motivation inherent in information processing and action (Hunt, 1963a) did not exist, Piaget's observations would strongly suggest that something in the infant's informational commerce with his environment through the eyes and ears contains a basis for motivation. Moreover, as I have said elsewhere (Hunt, 1963b, 1965a), Piaget's observations give us at least a first approximation of the nature of the epigenesis of this motivation intrinsic to the infant's informational interaction with his circumstances.

Piaget's observations suggest an epigenesis in which there are four phases. At birth, the human infant is essentially responsive from the motivational standpoint. During this phase, the effective instigator appears, as noted above, to be less a matter of energy delivered at the receptor than one of change in some characteristics of the light and sound delivered to the eyes and ears and, perhaps, change in the characteristics of contact with the receptors in the skin. The second stage begins with the appearance of intentional activities calculated to retain or regain perceptual contact with objects, persons, and places made desirable through recognitive familiarity. As the infant shifts from efforts to gain mere perceptual contact with desired objects to efforts to grasp them, his intentional efforts gradually change to primitive plans in which one of his schemata serves as the goal while others serve as instrumental means. In the observations of Piaget (1936), few of the ends for which his infant children strove were even remotely concerned with relief from pain, with getting objects with which to gratify homeostatic needs, or with sex. Precisely what makes objects desirable during this second motivational phase remains problematical, but from considering the fact that Piaget's children appeared first to desire objects made recognitively familiar with repeated perceptual encounters in conjunction with the phenomenon of imprinting in birds and various mammals, as described by Lorenz (1937), I have been led to the hypothesis that recognitive familiarity is perhaps central. In the third stage, the infant becomes interested in what is new and novel within a complex of familiar circumstances (Hunt, 1963b, 1965b). Finally, as the child achieves language, he comes to the stage of informational interaction in which we all find ourselves. At this final fourth stage, there are two kinds of informational interaction, one through linguistic communication, the other through the perception of reality. The discrepancy between the constructions of reality deriving from these two sources of information provides a never-ending process of motivation and interest as Festinger (1957), Kelly (1955), and Rogers (1951) have recognized in their theoretical writings.

In each of these stages, one can find a motivational basis for many of those infant activities that have long been considered predetermined in their appearance because they do have an autogenic basis (Hunt, 1965b, p. 231 ff). Although I have tended to emphasize information-processing, many correspondences exist between my concept of intrinsic motivation, which the observations of Piaget (1936) helped to justify, and Robert White's (1959) conception of "competence motivation," which emphasizes the action side of sensorimotor organizations. I suspect that the perceptual and the active aspects of the sensorimotor organizations of the infant or child are but two sides of the same coin whose substance is their intentionality. Piaget's observations clearly imply that during a major share of his time, the human infant developing in a middle-class home is little concerned with his instinctual needs. He is looking and listening, manipulating and locomoting, and he is continually increasing the complexity of his self-directed activities. I suspect that it is the fate of these, his own intentions, that control his psychological development rather than the fate of his instinctual needs—except where such needs intrude to become the basis for intentions (Hunt, 1965b).

Although Piaget has concerned himself centrally with intelligence and epistemological constructions, he has not denied the affective side of life. Rather, he regards the affective and the intellectual as inseparable because "all interaction with the environment involves both a structuring and evaluation . . . we cannot reason, even in pure mathematics, without experiencing certain feelings, and conversely, no affect can exist without a minimum of understanding or of discrimination" (Piaget, 1947, p. 6). These propositions imply a basis for motivation inherent in information processing and action. As such, they constitute a view of motivation highly dissonant with that in psychoanalytic theory and also with the drive conception so widely accepted by S-R behavior theorists.

Piaget's work as a beginning

Despite the tremendous amount of observational evidence that Piaget and his collaborators have produced, despite the variety of theoretical conceptions for which the implications of their observations provide an intriguing and relevant dissonance, the work of Piaget is, I believe, but a beginning. His work leaves little fully established except probably that psychological development is much less an automatic unfolding with anatomical maturation than it is a joint product of that maturation of the infant continuously interacting with his circumstances and with even maturation in part a function of the interaction. Although the notion that every sensorimotor advance is organized in Gestalt fashion is a cornerstone of his conceptualizing, this is essentially an interpretive assertion. As the evidence stands now, an S-R behavior theorist can utilize another body of observations and make an alternative interpretation with nearly equal justification. As of now, moreover, it is no easy matter to confront these alternative interpretations with evidence that unequivocally weakens one and strengthens the other except as one widens the nomological net to include evidence from observations of behavior, from neurophysiology, and from the method of report, as I have tried to do above. Piaget's theoretical constructs also leave considerable to be wished for. This holds true for his concepts of accommodation and assimilation, his concept of the role of lack of equilibrium in development, and his concept of stages in the epigenesis of intellectual development. Nevertheless, because of their implications for other views, Piaget's observations and interpretations open doors. They are highly significant in the same sense that the initial observation of Sir Alexander Fleming was significant when, in 1928, he left in open air some culture plates of *Staphyloccus aureus* and returned to find that a speck of mold had settled on the plate and that the bacteria had failed to grow in the neighborhood of the mold. When he quickly drew the implication that something in the mold had killed the bacteria, he had taken the lid off a Pandora-like box whence, instead of ills, came the blessings of antibiotics. I suspect that Piaget's observations and interpretations leave those of us concerned with early child development and early childhood education about where the bacteriologists were with respect to antibiotics when Alexander Fleming made his observation and drew this pregnant implication. It took a tremendous amount of research and development to bring about the social consequences we know as the result of antibiotics. In view of the tremendously greater complexity of human behavioral development as compared with bacterial development, it will take a tremendously greater amount of research and development before we can realize either the developmental or the educational potentialities of Piaget's work. I suspect that Piaget's observations and theorizing, through the work they lead to, are turning some fundamental corners also in systematic psychology.

ACCOMMODATION, ASSIMILATION, AND LACK OF EQUILIBRIUM

Accommodation and assimilation, taken together with the notion of lack of equilibrium, constitute Piaget's theory of ontogenetic, developmental adaptation. These concepts are exceedingly general. In fact, they are as general as the concept of learning. Perhaps it is more accurate to say that these theoretical constructs of Piaget are even more general than the notion of learning. If one defines learning to include only those phenomena of behavioral change typically described in textbook chapters on learning, then, Piaget's accommodation, assimilation, and lack of equilibrium incapsulate a considerably broader domain than has traditionally been incapsulated by learning. Elsewhere (Hunt, 1966) I have described a dozen adaptive phenomena deriving from informational interaction with environmental circumstances that are seldom included within our chapters on learning. The chapters on learning in our standard textbooks are based almost completely on the investigative traditions that stem from the four pioneering experimental programs of (1) Ebbinghous (1885) on memory and rote learning, (2) of Bryan and Harter (1897) on skill learning, (3) of Pavlov (1927) on classical conditioning, and (4) of Thorndike (1898) on trial-and-error learning that has been extended by others, especially Hull (1943, 1952) and Skinner (1938, 1953). Almost never included in these chapters on learning, not even in such categorizations of learning processes and their conditions as Gagné (1965) has constructed with educational ends in view, are the following phenomena which Piaget (1936) has noted in his observations of the psychological development of his own three children and in his studies of children of various ages.

(1) The phenomenon of input habituation: repeated encounters with a given pattern of change in input as the consequence of extinguishing the arousal and attention that initially accompany such changes of input. This consequence of repeated encounters with change of input is illustrated nicely in a study by Sharpless and Jasper (1956) wherein the electroencephalographic signs of arousal to the onset of a loud tone disappear with repeated presentations. Habituation appears to have great significance for the role of what the Russians call the "orienting response" (Razran, 1961; Simon, 1957).

(2) Schema development with use: sensorimotor systems regularly involved in an infant's interaction with his environmental circumstances develop much more rapidly than they would if not used. One of Piaget's favorite aphorisms states that "use is the aliment of the schema." Moreover, Piaget (1936, p. 115) noted that the behavioral landmark he described as "looking and grasping" and interpreted as a "double schema of assimilation" or a coordination between reflexive looking and reflexive grasping first appeared in his son, Laurent, at three months of age, and in his daughter, Jacqueline, at six months of age. Piaget writes: "However, nothing justifies us in considering Jacqueline retarded . . . the explanation is very simple: Jacqueline, born January 9th and spending her days outdoors on a balcony, was much less active in the beginning than Laurent, born in May. Furthermore and by virtue of this very fact, I made many fewer experiments on her during the first months, whereas I was constantly busy with Laurent" (1936, p. 115). In my own laboratory, David Greenberg and Ina Uzgiris (unpublished) have shown that placing a stabile pattern within view over the cribs of home-reared infants, beginning when they are five weeks of age, results in the

appearance of the blink response at an average of seven weeks of age, whereas this blink response fails to appear in home-reared infants with no pattern within constant view until an average of over ten weeks of age. As White and Held (1966) suggest, an opportunity to look at objects may hasten the development of visual accommodation upon which the blink response is based. They, moreover, have shown that the development of visual attention is a function of circumstances and that the development of the final form of eye-hand coordination in mature reaching can be reduced in orphanage-reared infants from a median of 145 days to a median of 87 days (White & Held, 1966) by providing with enrichments in the circumstances which evoke looking and hand motion.

(3) Neural maturation and the development of brain structure and brain chemistry appear to be influenced appreciably by environmental encounters. Such a possibility, implied in Piaget's aphorism that "Use is the aliment of the schema" derived from his observation that even reflexive systems decay without use (1936, p. 30, and 42 ff). Evidence that the absence of an opportunity to use the eyes to see light and patterns results in failure of the anatomical apparatus of the visual system to develop appears in the various studies of the histological and histochemical effects of dark-rearing in rabbits (Brattgård, 1952), in chimpanzees (Rash, Swift, Riesen & Chow, 1961), in kittens (Weiskrantz, 1958), and even in the lowly rat (Liberman, 1962). The retinal ganglia of dark-reared animals from these several species have been found to be deficient in ganglion cells, in Mueller fibers, and also in RNA production. Conversely, evidence of increased growth of central brain structures of rats developing in circumstances deliberately made extra complex have been repeatedly reported (Altman & Das, 1964; Bennet, Diamond, Krech, & Rosenzweig, 1964).

(4) Image formation: repeated encounters with objects, persons, and places with increasing degrees of permanence. Piaget's (1936, 1937) several descriptions of the construction of the object and of object permanence are of central importance, yet they appear to have been completely missed by other observers of child development.

During the first several weeks after birth, infants grow more and more proficient in following objects with their eyes, but when the object followed disappears from view, the infant's gaze wanders immediately from the point of disappearance. Once out of sight, the object is also out of mind. At this stage, infants cannot play peek-a-boo. Later, after more looking, when the object followed disappears, the infant's gaze lingers at the point of disappearance. At this stage, they typically reach for and pick up partially covered objects that they desire. Yet, if the object is completely covered, they immediately lose interest in it. Later, after a variety of other encounters with objects, an object that disappears under a single screen evokes efforts to remove the screen. At this stage, infants do play peek-a-boo. With further visual encounters that occur with time, such efforts become more and more persistent so that an infant can remove not only one screen but two and three or more. Then slightly later, he can follow objects that disappear successively under each of several screens. There finally comes a time when the desired object is hidden in a container, the container disappears under a screen and comes back empty, and when the infant fails to find the desired object in the returned container, he turns immediately to the place where the container disappeared (see sound-motion picture by Uzgiris & Hunt, 1967; Uzgiris & Hunt, 1969). When such behavior has appeared, an infant can typically be observed also to imitate models that are no longer present and to solve problems mentally without the process of motor groping.

(5) Reversibility of imagery: with still more sensorimotor encounters with objects, persons, and places, children come to manifest behavior implying a reversibility of their representative central processes. Thus, when a desired object is placed out of sight within a box, and that box is then hidden successively behind a series of covers, the child begins his hunt for the object with the last cover under which the box containing the desired object disappeared. When he fails to find it there, he proceeds to the next-to-last cover, then to the next-to-next-to-last, etc. Here it is as if the child could play his representative processes backward as well as forward. The hypothesis that these changes of behavior imply central processes that can represent objects, per-

sons, and places is strengthened considerably by the recent findings, mentioned above, that sensorimotor interaction with objects influences the development of brain structures and brain chemistry. It is in this domain of the increasing dominance of central processes over perceptual inputs that Piaget, in his collaborations with Lambercier, has made genuine experimental contributions as experimental contributions are defined by American investigators (Piaget & Lambercier, 1943a, 1943b, 1944, 1946, 1953; and Piaget, Lambercier, Boesch, & Albertini, 1942). With psychophysical experiments, these investigators have shown definite changes in the nature of perceptual illusions with age. The fact that object constancy increases with age, and the fact that the "error of the standard" is somewhat underestimated by children age five to seven years but is overestimated by adults, taken together, imply an increasing role of central processes in perception. The increase in the role of these processes in the development of intelligence is even more marked than it is in perception (Hunt, 1961, p. 288 ff). Perhaps it should also be noted here that this process of image formation corresponds rather closely to Hebb's (1949) conception of the formation of "cell assemblies" in early or "primary" learning, but both Piaget's observations and the ingenious experiments of Held (e.g. White & Held, 1966) and his collaborators indicate that action also plays a major role, perhaps to show that the visual anticipation of the infant or animal as to location or shape is wrong and to call for an accommodative change.

(6) Sequential organizations: encountering a sequence of changes in the character or the pattern of receptor inputs has as its consequence sequential organizations of central processes. Piaget (1936) saw the basis for the coordination between such ready-made systems as looking and listening, looking and grasping, listening and vocalization, as a basis for his notion that accommodation comes about in one way through the combining of ready-made sensorimotor systems. From another standpoint, one can see these sequential organizations deriving from the simple fact that sensory processes run off faster than do events. These phenomena led Hebb (1949) to invent the concept of "phase sequences." In the language of common sense, these

sequential organizations manifest themselves as expectations. In a sense, they come about through a process very much like Pavlovian, classical conditioning. There, however, the sequential organizations examined have been typically between stimulus inputs and motor outputs. In the coordinations that Piaget has observed, the sequential organizations are typically stimulus-stimulus relationships, and from the work of Maltzman & Raskin (1965), the motivational basis for these sequential organizations appears to reside in the attention and arousal of the "orienting response." Once a given kind of change of input has been encountered sufficiently often to become habituated and to extinguish thereby the attention and arousal constituting the orienting response, that kind of change in input cannot become a conditional stimulus in any new sequential organization. This is a point of great educational significance, but elaborating it lies beyond the scope of this paper.

(7) The hypothetical epigenesis of intrinsic motivation: as I have indicated above in the section on "Piaget versus Psychoanalysis and Drive Theory," even if there were not a large body of other evidence for a system of motivation inherent in information processing and action (Hunt, 1963a), Piaget's observations are sufficiently explicit in their implications of such a system that one would have to start looking for the evidence. Moreover, as also indicated above, his observations appear clearly to imply a developmental epigenesis of such motivation underlying the adaptive accommodations on which Piaget has placed his primary attention. While accommodation and assimilation may be invariants, the lack of equilibrium that forces accommodative modifications in a child's organizations of action and thought in the course of development undergoes change in its basic nature. During the first phase, the human infant is basically responsive to changes of input, and the attention and arousal evoked by these changes in input appear to motivate the development of the sequential organizations that serve to coordinate the ready-made systems for receiving information. With repeated encounters of a given pattern of change in input from given objects, persons, and places comes recognitive familiarity that, as it is developing, appears to make those objects, persons, and places

attractive. Elsewhere (Hunt, 1963b, 1965b) I have suggested that the "imprinting" of the ethologists, which Lorenz (1937) has seen as the chief basis for attraction in the development of emotional attachments in birds and various mammals, may well be a special case of this attractiveness that comes with the development of recognitive familiarity. From Piaget's (1936) observations, I gleaned it was commonly and repeatedly encountered objects that induced his children to make efforts to hold the objects within perceptual range (Hunt, 1963b). In an exploratory experimental test of this hypothesis, my colleague, Dr. Uzgiris, and I found that infants two months of age did look longer at a pattern that had been hanging over the crib for a month than they looked at an unfamiliar pattern of relatively similar character (Hunt & Uzgiris, 1968), but the evidence from some studies has been less impressive. Although I still believe that a genuine motivational phenomenon resides here, I am less certain that I am properly describing the conditions for it.

Repeated perceptual encounters with objects, persons, and places already recognitively familiar, lead directly to an interest in the novel and in changed situations. In part, this change probably results from the process of input habituation, and the boredom that results with repeated encounters. In part, however, it may also result from becoming recognitively familiar with a wide variety of objects, persons, and places so that the infant gradually develops a kind of "learning set" or rule which can be stated as "things should be recognizable." At this point, unrecognizable objects, persons, and places provide the infant with a kind of task—a kind of generalized goal for his perceptual activity. This goal may well motivate what Woodworth (1947) characterized as the "trial-and-check process of perceiving." He saw the goal of this process as clear perceptual meaning and the identification or recognition of what is being examined. Such a learning set may well be an important factor in an older infant's persistent looking at unfamiliar objects.

(8) Intentionality and competence: Attempting successfully to maintain or regain perceptual contact with objects, persons, or places that have become recognitively attractive appears, from Piaget's (1936) observations, to have the consequence of

producing intentions, or, intrinsically motivated plans (Hunt, 1963b, 1965b). In their earliest form, intentions appear merely to be actions responsive to the loss of perceptual contact with an object repeatedly encountered. But, as I have indicated above, it would appear that the human infant discovers something akin to "operant" activities through his effort to hold on to or regain perceptual contact with what has become recognitively attractive. Gradually, however, this too appears to result in a kind of rule that might be verbalized as: "If I do things, I can make interesting things happen." In such a generalized functional form, this anticipatory intentionality appears to shift gradually, from mere attempts to retain or regain perceptual contact to active attempts to gain tactual contact and to manipulate desired objects. As the infant makes this change, he comes into a kind of relationship with his environmental circumstances that enables him to increase continually the level of the complexity in his actions and in the materials he can examine. This is at least one interpretation of the basis for what Robert White (1959) has termed "competence motivation." Insofar as infants do develop a kind of rule that "If I do things, I can make interesting things happen and I can find interesting things to do," it is very likely that the persistence of such motivation may be strongly influenced by the nature of the "schedules of reinforcement" (Ferster & Skinner, 1957) with which the environmental circumstances of children have permitted them to achieve their various intentions. In fact, from this standpoint, reinforcement in such action could well be defined as the achievement of intentional goals. One would guess that persistent or courageous competence-motivation probably derives from experiences of success intermixed with an increasing proportion of failures and from successes won only at the expense of prolonged effort. Although Piaget's notions of equilibrium and lack of equilibrium have certain vague implications of the sort indicated, I readily confess that I am extending this line of thought well beyond his conceptions and have, perhaps, rendered his conceptions unrecognizable.

Inasmuch as all of these eight phenomena, or processes, come within the domain of Piaget's so-called invariants of process, accommodation and assimilation, or the domain of equilibrium and its lack, they, like the term "learning," can refer to little more than the general domain of the influence of encounters with circumstances on the development of the organism and its behavior. On the other hand, the observations that Piaget has made within this domain are pregnant with implications. In my own personal case it was the effort involved in becoming reasonably conversant with Piaget's concrete observations as well as with his theorizing that prepared me to be receptive to the implications of the investigative evidence to which I have alluded in synopsizing the nature of these eight (Hunt, 1961), and other phenomena (Hunt, 1966). On none of these phenomena, which I believe do belong within the general domain of learning, or the domains of learning and motivation, do we have anything like the evidence that exists for the four standard kinds of learning. Neither have we begun to exploit their implications for education. By education, here, I mean the fostering of the development of competence, and of those kinds of motivations and standards of conduct appropriate for full participation in the highly technological culture which now, and for the unseeable future, constitutes the ecological niche of human beings in our society. It is, thus, that I contend that Piaget's observations and theorizing constitute but a beginning, but a highly important beginning.

THE CONCEPT OF STAGES IN BEHAVIORAL DEVELOPMENT

The concept of stages in psychological development appears to me to constitute at best but a first approximation of the order that may exist in the development of those organizations of behavior and the central processes that comprise intelligence, motivation, the constructions of reality, and the standards of conduct. Piaget's observations of an epigenesis in psychological development, interpreted as stages, have the merit of suggesting very strongly that there is a very definite order in the successive patterns of behavior and thought. Such a notion meets with a great deal of resistance in those who have imbibed their psychological conceptions from S-R behavior theorists. The S-R behavior theory that original nature consists of an abundant variety of reflexes hardly permits of such natural ordering, although, as Gagné (1965) has suggested, it can be made to permit of a hierarchical ordering of varieties of learning based on differing conditions of acquisition. The view of S-R theorists has always been at odds with that of Gesell. Although Gesell and such investigators as Mary Shirley (1933) reported a definite order in the development of such functions as locomotion, prehension, etc., they both considered this order to be predetermined by the genes in both rate and succession of patterns. The notion of the constant IQ was founded on the principle of predetermined development. When the S-R behavior theorists rejected this predeterminism, they tended also to reject the very notion of any natural order in development, be it predetermined or otherwise.

One can readily find several sources for definite order in the successive patterns of psychological development, however, and these lend support, at a most general level, to the notion of order that is implicit in Piaget's conception of stages. One of these sources is the traditional one of hereditary preprogramming. In every vertebrate species known, for instance, development begins with the head-end, and proceeds tailward. Coghill's (1929) cephalocaudal principle is universal, at least among vertebrates. This preprogramming may well extend to other aspects of development. There may also be critical periods in maturation when certain kinds of encounters with circumstances are maximally productive in effecting the acquisition of certain organizations of behavior and thought. On the other hand, it is too easy to assume such a state of affairs merely because a number of behavioral discontinuities tend to occur at given ages. They may occur at these given ages merely because the culture brings children into encounters with various sets of circumstances simultaneously at a given rate. Moreover, even when there is a preprogrammed order in the development of certain functions, the rate of develoment, as we are beginning to see from various studies of animal subjects and of human infants in the work of White and Held (1966), can be modified substantially. But definite limits must exist in the degree to which the rate of development can be modified. Moreover, it is likely that genetically based individual differences may exist in the degree to which the rates of development for various functions can be modified by the circumstances encountered. Genetic preprogramming, however, is only one source of order in the development of behavior and thought.

A second source of order emerges out of successive processes of coordinating organized systems into new and more comprehensively organized systems. Such a view underlies the conception of intelligence as a hierarchical organization of abilities for which Piaget's observations and theorizing are but one source (Ferguson, 1954; Gagné, 1965; Gagné & Paradise, 1961; Hunt, 1961, p. 109 ff). This notion of a hierarchy of organized sensorimotor systems is perhaps most clearly exemplified in Piaget's (1936) observations of psychological development during the first two years. Thus, during Piaget's second sensorimotor stage, looking and listening become coordinated as things heard become something to look at, and as the infant acquires auditory localization. Thus also do such coordinations occur as things looked at become something to grasp, and as patterns of sound heard become something to vocalize. During the third and fourth stages, these first habitual coordinations become coordinated at a new hierarchical level in various means-end relationships through which representative central processes gradually develop. This notion of hierarchical organization is continued, moreover, in Piaget's (1943) conception of the origin of symbolic processes and language. The child coordinates his images with imitations of standard vocal patterns. At first these images are idiosyncratic congeries arising out of exciting events of which imitated vocal patterns are a part (Hunt, 1961, pp. 185 ff). Such organizations give rise to pseudowords with sufficient semantic specificity to permit limited communication. As the number of pseudowords increases, the child appears to acquire a "learning set" (Harlow, 1949) that "things have names." This stage is typically marked by endless questions of "what's that?" Still later, largely through efforts at communication, these semantic referents become more and more standard. In turn, the child develops various "intuitive regulations" that enable him to anticipate a good many events. These, however, leave many of his expectations dissonant with his observation. As

I understand Piaget (1943, 1947), this dissonance between expectations and perceptions gives rise to the disequilibrium that forces accommodative modifications. This continues until these regulations are coordinated, or—to use Piaget's (1947) term—grouped, into the additive, concrete operations of thought that permit the reversible "nestings of classes, relations, and numbers." These concrete operations persist but get regrouped into the multiplicative, formal operations of the adult that begin to appear in adolescence. The empirical foundations for this conceptual schema are less pretty than the schema itself, especially beyond the sensorimotor phase. Piaget's observations of his own children became sketchy after they were about two years of age. Moreover, in his studies of children beyond four years of age he reverted to the cross-sectional method of confronting groups of children of successive ages with his various problem situations. Nevertheless, the general conception of coordinating-systems, where it is empirically valid, implies that it is impossible to obtain a coordination between two subordinate coordinations until both those subordinate systems are already formed in the child's repertoire. This view, I should note again, is in essential congruence with that of Gagné (1965), which is based on kinds of learning differentiated by their conditions of acquisition. This implication, moreover, provides a very definite basis for ordinality in psychological development that is quite independent of any genetic preprogramming.

A third basis for a definite order in behavioral development is to be found as central processes with increasing duration of persistence grow up out of the young organism's perceptual encounters with objects, persons, and places. The order in such behavioral development has already been described above. A very clean ordinal scale of behavioral landmarks can be found in this development of object permanence (Uzgiris & Hunt, 1968). Now these behavioral landmarks are not preprogrammed. That they are clearly a product of the infant's visuo-motor interaction with his circumstances is implied by their failure to develop in dark-reared chimpanzees (Riesen, 1958). Just how much variation in the age at which each major landmark makes its appearance in human infants can be produced by variations in the circumstances an infant encounters perceptually remains to be investigated, but the retardation in orphanage-reared infants and in cage-reared animals appears to derive in large part from lack of opportunity to encounter variety in patterns of perceptual input. No matter how rapidly or how slowly this order of behavioral landmarks takes place, its nature and its order, growing out of the perceptual interaction of the infant with his circumtances, remain essentially fixed.

Here, then, are three quite distinct bases for order in psychological development. Only one of these derives from genetic preprogramming. Uzgiris and Hunt (1969) have also uncovered others in developing their ordinal scales of infant psychological development. Still others may exist whose nature we have not yet gleaned. Nevertheless, the point that order growing out of encounters with circumstances can be fixed in nature without being genetically preprogrammed is, I believe, established.

On the other hand, a great deal of the order that Piaget has reported in the development of his illustrative accounts of the development of his own three children followed longitudinally and in his groups of children studied cross-sectionally may well be an artifact of the culture in which they were developing. It may well have been an artifact of the combination of circumstances that these children were encountering repeatedly at a relatively fixed and common rate. Although the order might be common to the children in other families reared in the same general culture, it could be a matter neither of preprogramming nor of anything inevitable in an infant's interaction with his circumstances. In Piaget's observations of his own children, for instance, I get the impression that they manifest ear-vocal coordinations before they manifest eye-hand coordinations. I make this statement without great confidence, for it is no easy matter to make such a comparison merely from an examination of Piaget's observations. I can say with considerable confidence that ear-vocal coordinations do appear, as evidenced by pseudoimitations of familiar vocal patterns, well before eye-hand coordinations, evidenced in visually directed reaching, in the home-reared infants who served as subjects for Uzgiris and Hunt (1969). Contrariwise, in the infants of the Tewksbury Hospital, where White and Held (1966) have conducted their splendid experiments, eye-hand coordination, as manifested in visually directed reaching following their enrichment programs, came well ahead of any evidences of any ear-vocal coordination. In other words, the age at which any given sensorimotor coordination of this sort appears may be early or late (in the case of mature reaching, for example, at a median age of 87 days for those Tewksbury infants who encountered the enrichment, and a mean age of 145 days for those who were subjects in the original normative study without such enrichment). Which of two such coordinations appears first is clearly a matter of the nature of the circumstances most frequently encountered, the order for such sensorimotor coordinations is highly plastic. While their appearance may take an ordinal form among children developing under any given set of circumstances, there is no ordinality fixed in the nature of things. Yet, on the other hand, any coordination of two such coordinations must presume the existence of both coordinations before the new level in the hierarchy can be achieved.

Such a logical analysis implies that a great deal of investigation will be required before we can ascertain precisely which behavioral and conceptual landmarks in psychological development come in an inevitably fixed order and which do not.*

* I recognize, of course, that one may come at the matter of order in psychological development from an opposite standpoint. My position in this discussion has been dictated by the issues posed by the development of inevitable ordinal scales with which to assess development. Another standpoint is that of Gagné (1965) and Gagné and Paradise (1961), which Bereiter and Engelmann (1966) have found fruitful in their planning of curricula with which to help culturally disadvantaged children get the abilities required for success in first grades that employ what has become a fairly standard curriculum. This other standpoint takes off from what is to be required of the child, on the one hand, and from what is missing from his repertoire, on the other hand. From my observations of the children who constituted their first group, I believe Bereiter and Englemann (1966) had considerable success. They failed, however, with 4 of the 15 disadvantaged children in their original group. Whether this failure was inevitable on hereditary grounds is a matter of conjecture. Whether such an approach will or will not succeed is, I believe, also a matter of the degree to which the curriculum devised, from an analysis of social goals, to achieve these goals provides what I have termed elsewhere an appropriate *match* (Hunt, 1961, pp. 267–288; 1966, pp. 118 ff) between the development of the child and the circumstances which he encounters in the curriculum. I believe this *match* must be such as will hold the attention of the child and yet call forth modifications in the cognitive systems he brings to the

Ausubel (1963, pp. 112–122) has pointed out how basically
irrelevant investigations with cross-sectional samples of children
at various ages can be to this issue. It will be important in such
investigations to employ longitudinal methods in which the same
subjects are examined repeatedly over a period of time sufficient
to determine the relationships among a set of landmarks in
behavior considered to be orderly in their appearance. It will
also be necessary to provide the subjects in such longitudinal
studies with encounters with circumstances especially designed
to alter the order presumed to be fixed.

Piaget's stages, as he has described them, are based on no such
combination of longitudinal studies in which the circumstances
encountered have been deliberately arranged to modify the
order in which the behavioral landmarks appear. Only those
stages of the sensorimotor phase from birth to approximately two
years of age (Piaget, 1936, 1937) and those during the development of symbolic thought from about two to four years of age
(Piaget, 1943) are based on longitudinal observations—of Piaget's own children. The stages of the intuitive phase from
about four to seven or eight years of age, when concrete operational thought appears (Piaget & Inhelder, 1948; Piaget &
Szeminska, 1941), and those leading from concrete operational
thought to the development of formal operations in adolescence
(Inhelder & Piaget, 1955) are all based on cross-sectional
studies, in which groups of children of various ages are confronted with the various kinds of problem situations, and on
cross-sectional studies alone.

As he has described them, Piaget's stages consist in phases of
transition that terminate in landmarks of behavioral discontinu-

curriculum. It should also be noted that the work of Skinner's followers indicates
that interests themselves can be cultivated—at least in the sense that inputs which
are not originally reinforcing can be made to be reinforcing by becoming sequentially organized with inputs or events which are reinforcing (Addison & Homme,
1966; Kelleher & Gollub, 1962; Homme, et al., 1963). This work indicates that, in
the programming of instruction toward socially prescribed ends, it may be essential to program the development of appropriate interests first. It is my guess,
however, that such approaches are indicated only when cultural disadvantages or
social pathology have resulted in what is essentially the need for a special kind of
therapy to permit cognitive development and socialization to continue with intrinsic motivation.

ity whence new phases of transition begin. I shall limit my illustrations to the major phases and to the behavioral landmarks that designate the terminus of each and the beginning of the next. Thus, the sensorimotor phase terminates in various kinds of behavior implying the presence of stable imagery. These kinds of behavior include imitation of models no longer present, solving problems while looking at them and without motor groping, and following desired objects that are out of sight in a box through a series of hidings in which only the box is visible. Since these three kinds of behavior appeared at about the same time in his children, Piaget presumed that they came at once with the development of stable imagery. Perhaps they do, but to my knowledge, no one has attempted to arrange encounters with circumstances to encourage one of these imagery-implying kinds of behavior while eliminating opportunities to acquire the other kinds. In Piaget's (1947, Ch. 5) description, these kinds of behavior implying imagery mark the terminus of the sensori-motor phase and the beginnings of the preconceptual phase.

The preconceptual phase is concerned successively with the development of symbolic thought and language and with the development of progressively extended and more accurate intuitive regulations. This phase terminates in the development of what is described as a Gestalt-like system of concrete reasoning operations at about the age of seven or eight years. The onset of concrete reasoning is marked by the conservation of quantity, length, and number, by the ability to manipulate reversible nestings of hierarchies of classes and of relations, and by the inference pattern of transitivity for length, quantity, degree of darkness, etc. Although Piaget and his collaborators have devised a variety of tests to diagnose the presence of this system of concrete reasoning operations, they have typically given only one at a time to each series of age groupings, and from such evidence they have drawn the inference that the reasoning system comes into being all at once as a grouping of intuitive regulations. Thus, Piaget has written:

To divide developmental continuity into stages recognizable by some set of external criteria is not the most profitable of occupations; the crucial turning-point for the beginning of operations shows itself in a kind of equilibration, which is rapid and sometimes sudden, which affects the complex of ideas forming a single system and which needs explaining on its own account. In this there is something comparable to the abrupt complex restructuring described in Gestalt theory, except that, when it occurs, there arises the very opposite of a crystallization embracing all relations in a single static network; operations, on the contrary, are found formed by a kind of thawing out of intuitive structures, by a sudden mobility which animates and coordinates the configurations that were hitherto more or less rigid despite their progressive articulation (1947, p. 139).

These concrete operations of thought are, however, limited to concrete materials; they do not extend to verbal tests of similar structure. In the case of conservation, moreover, the children who conserve quantity at age seven or eight fail to conserve with the same materials when the questions concern weight— typically till age nine to ten in the findings of Piaget and Inhelder (1947). And those who conserve weight at nine or ten fail to conserve, again with the same materials, when the questions concern volume—typically till age eleven to twelve (Piaget & Inhelder, 1947). During this same period, changes take place in the child's conceptions of space (Piaget & Inhelder, 1948) and of geometry (Piaget, Inhelder & Szeminska, 1948). The developments of this phase of concrete operations terminate in what Piaget (1947, p. 148) calls the "second-degree grouping of operations" in formal thought. These are marked behaviorally by the ability to conserve volume and to decode properly propositions involving classes and utilizing the terms *some*, *all*, and *none* as related to a given nesting of classes, by thought reflecting the hypothetico-deductive method (wherein thought directs observation), by the proportionality schema, by the 16 binary operations of two-valued propositional logic, and by the INRC group in attempting to solve various problems (Inhelder & Piaget, 1955). Cross-sectional descriptive studies by other investigators generally confirm the findings of Piaget and his collaborators (Wallach, 1963).

Various other investigators have uncovered what appear to be discontinuities in various performances and various neurophysiological events at the ages at which Piaget finds the onsets both of concrete operations and of formal operations. S. H. White (1965, 1966) has reviewed a variety of such changes associated with about age six—an age more typical than seven to eight for the appearance of the behavioral landmarks of concrete operations in American children. Smith and Greene (1963) have found a discontinuity in ability to organize inverted, reversed, and inverted-and-reversed feedback in order to write, draw, or dot at age ten to twelve in children when they are guided only by a view of their movement through television. Other discontinuities have also been reported at this age at which Piaget and his collaborators have found the onset of formal operations. Harway (1963) has reported a marked decrease in errors involved in judgments of distance at this age. Katz and Deutsch (1963) have reported evidence of auditory-visual shifting in the reaction-times of non-readers, and Ratner, Gawronski, and Rice (1964) have reported the appearance of an adult-like adjustment to delayed speech-feedback, both in the range of ages from ten to twelve. In general, these investigators have tended to attribute the discontinuities in these various functions to maturation. Smith and Greene (1963), particularly, mention "a critical period in the maturation of performance," even though the typical definition of a "critical period" is one during which encounters with a given kind of circumstance are especially effective in the acquisition of a given pattern of behavior, and even though the authors evince no special concern with the role of encounters with any kind of circumstances.

Attributing such discontinuities in behavior too readily to maturation is our traditional blind alley because it has long served to stop investigation of the role of experience in their occurrence. Despite the enlargement in the domain of learning implied by Piaget's observations and interpretations in terms of disequilibrium, accommodation, and assimilation, he has been satisfied with his descriptions and interpretations. He has been singularly unconcerned with determining the conditions of a disequilibrium and of testing experimentally the implications of his interpretations, even though his interpretations clearly require validating and even though the implications of his interpretative constructs have great significance for education.

In considering the issues of the role of circumstances encountered in (1) determining whether the order in the behavioral landmarks is necessary and (2) in determining the age at which these
landmarks occur, it is important to distinguish between the
immediate effects of the short-term encounters typical of traditional learning experiments and the effects of long-term, repeated
encounters with problematic circumstances of a given kind. To
my knowledge, the first issue has not really been investigated.
All too seldom, moreover, have the effects of the short-term
encounters with the circumstances of typical learning experiments been appreciably effective in hastening the onset of either
concrete operations or formal operations (Gruen, 1965; Smedslund, 1961a, 1961b, 1961c, 1961d, 1962, 1963a, 1963c). When
short-term experiences have been appreciably effective, they
tend to have been devoted to teaching verbal rules (Beilin, 1965;
Gruen, 1965; Ojemann & Pritchett, 1963), to the teaching of
addition and subtraction as a reversible intellectual operation in
which each can nullify the other (Smedslund, 1916d, 1961e,
1963c), or to have been effective in producing transfer only with
children who already show some evidence of concrete operations
(Beilin & Franklin, 1962). Verbal rules have also shown a close
relationship to the resistance of conservation responses to extinction; high resistance goes with ability to give good verbal explanations (Smedslund, 1961e). Various of the studies that have
attempted to modify the acquisition of the behavioral landmarks
of concrete operations have shown a misunderstanding of
Piaget's concepts or of what operations are relevant to them (see
Smedslund, 1963b, for a critique).

On the other hand, evidence indicating that long-term experience influences the ages at which the various behavioral landmarks appear is clear—and not only for infancy. Conservation of
quantity is typically delayed in deaf children (Furth, 1964; Nass,
1964). When combined with the findings concerning the importance of verbal rules for both the acquisition of and resistance of
conservation responses to extinction, this finding indicates considerable importance for language in conservation. Deafness that
cuts a child off from the auditory category of informational input
can apparently also influence greatly the order, the ages, and the

stability of various behavioral marks of the concrete operations appearance. I have myself examined a deaf girl age fifteen who had not learned the standard manual signs of the deaf. Although this girl spontaneously inquired through written questions (without syntax) about my family tree, and showed excellent understanding of the branching relationships back through several generations while evidencing in her facial expression appreciative wonder that I knew so many of their names, she did not conserve quantity as assessed by the two-ball technique. In fact, she considered a quantity labeled "mine" [the examiner's] as larger than even a much larger quantity labeled "yours" [meaning hers]. Despite her confusion over conservation, this girl also understood road maps and their relationships to road signs. She would argue with her parents in her idiosyncratic system of gestural communication about which of several routes from Estes Park, Colorado, to New York City might be preferable. This, I believe, called for a visually based symbolic sophistication about space well beyond that typical of children age seven and eight, when conservation of quantity has typically developed. Those concepts that she could develop from information through the visual channel, she appeared to have despite near-sightedness, but those calling for language and the concepts embedded in language, she lacked. It is interesting that at age seventeen, and after some six months of sophisticated special education that emphasized language and brought her to the point of communication through writing with sentences and appropriate syntax, she did conserve quantity with certainty.

Other evidence attesting the importance of long-term experience in children's development of the behavioral marks of concrete operations derives from their retardation in the culturally deprived (Wachs, Uzgiris, & Hunt, 1967). The extent of this delay has been dramatized in a cross-cultural study of the performances of Australian aborigines on a series of the diagnostic tests of concrete operations by de Lemos (1966). The ages at which these tests were passed by these subjects varied from a minimum of eight years to a maximum of nineteen, and the variable most obviously associated inversely with the age of passing was either amount of mission schooling or amount of

contact with people of European culture (the latter was sometimes
confounded with racial mixture).

Such bits of evidence, still limited to be sure, suggest strongly
that one is justified in questioning the attribution of the behavioral landmarks of the various stages to maturation. They suggest
strongly also that to attempt to alter the age at which these
landmarks appear or the order in which they appear by means of
short-term encounters with the circumstances characteristic of
traditional learning experiments is the wrong focus. We need to
develop an experimental methodology that provides individuals
with relatively long-term encounters with circumstances hypo-
thetically calculated to have various specified effects. It is precisely such long-term encounters with circumstances that have
been so effective in demonstrating the plasticity in the development of various functions during infancy (Greenberg, Uzgiris, &
Hunt, 1968; White & Held, 1966). Perhaps the method of choice,
where damage to that motivation inherent in information processing and action has not occurred, will be a preparation of the environment with materials with which infants and children can
play at will. This prepared environment can well be programmed
to enable each child to build constructively on his own cumulat-
ing experience.

Indirect evidence for the importance of long-term experience
in the development of the behavioral landmarks of various stages
comes from yet another source. This indirect evidence also calls
into some question Piaget's conception of discontinuous stages
—at least as I understand it and have described it above. One
form of this indirect evidence consists in a failure of various
investigators to find consistency in the performances of individual children across a range of the diagnostics tests of concrete
operations. Even Piaget's collaborator Szeminska (1965) has
reported difficulties in attempts to assess transitions in the development of thought when either different materials or children
differing in formal training are concerned. In a study of adolescents, Case and Collinson (1962) found in most of their subjects
evidence of their having reached the stage of formal operations,
but regression to an earlier stage occurred frequently when the
subjects lacked either specific information or the requisite vocab-

ulary. In studies of younger children, Dodwell (1962) found that scores on a test of number concepts correlated only .20 with scores on a test of understanding the logic of classes. In perhaps the most sophisticated and careful of such studies, Smedslund found that "the generality of overt observable inference patterns over goal objects and percepts is quite limited" (1964, p. 27), and this is especially true over a range of ages from five to eight years when children are presumably developing these concrete operations that Smedslund terms *inference patterns.* In an attempt to determine order among various stages in the development of classificatory concepts, Kofsky (1966) found an order of difficult items that corresponded to that predicted by Piaget, but those who passed the more difficult items did not necessarily pass all the earlier ones.

Another form of this indirect evidence consists in a failure of various investigators to find consistency in the performances of individual children in a given diagnostic test across a range of materials. Dodwell (1963) found that 80 percent of his nearly 200 children had to be classified as "mixed" with respect to the stages of spatial-concept formation they exhibited in six problems all concerned with the composition of lines. Johnson (1962) confirmed Piaget's description of sequential order in children's moral judgments associated with age, but the levels of maturity of individual children exhibited little generality across the situations judged. When Uzgiris (1964) examined 140 children, 20 each from kindergarten through sixth grade, with a standard test for conservation of quantity, weight, and volume with four different materials, she found no instance in which an individual who conserved volume failed to conserve both weight and quantity and no instance where an individual who conserved weight failed to conserve quantity *with any given material,* but this rule held quite imperfectly across materials. There were many instances of variance by a single step in the ordinality of volume, weight, and quantity for differing materials, and some instances where the conservation performances varied by two steps across materials.

From these two kinds of evidence, it is clear that the discontinuities in behavior that Piaget uses to mark the transitions

between his successive stages are less Gestalt-like, are less *structures d'ensemble,* than the cross-sectional evidence from groups
of various ages on given diagnostic tests has led Piaget to believe. Despite these evidences of lack of generality for these
behavioral landmarks across diagnostic tests and across materials
or situations, especially during the phase of acquisition leading
to the mark of discontinuity, I continue to find myself impressed
with the reality of these landmarks. I also find myself impressed
with the resemblance of the notion of acquisition in one situation
after another to that of Harlow's (1949) conception of "learning
sets." I suspect that Piaget is correct in asserting that the concrete operations become Gestalt-like operational structures in
which one can find reflected the logical operations he has attributed to them. But I suspect also that Piaget is wrong in asserting
that these emerge quickly and all at once. Rather, they appear to
emerge tentatively from coping with a given kind of problem in
one situation, then again with that kind of problem in another
situation, in another, and in another, and so on, then from
coping with related kinds of problems in a variety of situations
until the rules for the solution become generalized. How important it is for this generalization that the solution be imbedded in
linguistic explanations is not fully established, but the existing
evidence, especially from Smedslund (1961e), indicates that
resistance to extinction is very much a matter of the rules for the
solution becoming verbalizable. While anatomical maturation
may have a role in the emergence of these behavioral landmarks,
it does not guarantee their emergence, or they would emerge in
the deaf as well as in the hearing and in the culturally disadvantaged as well as in the culturally advantaged (unless one insists
in the face of the accumulating evidence that cultural retardation and poverty derive from heritable abilities). Rather, it
appears that these landmarks emerge through long-term and
repeated encounters with certain kinds of problem circumstances. These problem circumstances presumably produce a
cognitive dissonance that forces accommodative modifications in
the operational structures of intelligence and in the constructions
of reality. While Piaget's observations and theoretical interpretations tell us all too little about these circumstances, they do

strongly suggest that these circumstances must be information-
ally relevant to that which the child has already stored, be
somewhat novel but not too strange, and sufficiently complex to
call for some elaboration of the child's operations yet not call for
elaborations beyond his accommodative limits. In other words,
Piaget's observations suggest what I have elsewhere called the
"problem of the match" (Hunt, 1961, pp. 267–288; 1965b, pp.
226–231). From the fact that we still lack instruments appropriate for the diagnosis of children's informational and operational
levels, I have elsewhere urged that the best cues for an appropriate match of circumstances and child are the evidences of
spontaneous interest and surprise (Hunt, 1966, pp. 131–132).

Doors opened by a giant

Piaget's stature as the giant of developmental psychology, then,
resides less in what he has completed, much as it is, than in the
many beginnings his many observations and his theoretical interpretations provide. These observations and theoretical interpretations not only figure heavily in the resurgence of and the new
look of developmental psychology but also impinge, as I have
tried to indicate above, on almost every aspect of systematic
psychology. They have helped to extend the domain of learning,
and they open doors to the investigation of the effects of circumstances in new ways. They summate with other evidence to delineate the nature of an intrinsic system of motivation inherent in
information processing and action, and, although he did not
interpret them himself, Piaget's observations suggest the outlines
of the developmental epigenesis of this intrinsic system of motivation. The stages that Piaget has described in intellectual development have already stimulated an abundance of informative
investigations. While the evidence from these investigations appears to call for some changes in Piaget's interpretive account,
his account also has the merit of opening the door to a new
approach to assessing psychological development and to testing
intelligence. Finally, despite the fact that Piaget has been unconcerned with the nature of the circumstances that induce learn-

ing, his notions of disequilibrium and accommodation suggest a new view of what in the organism's encounters with circumstances brings about the accommodative modifications in the structures of behavior and thought that constitute learning. Moreover, his observations suggest, interest and surprise are the behavioral cues required for the investigation of the relationship between children's intellectual development and environmental circumstances that is the prerequisite to a theory of instruction. Anyone who has opened so many doors to the future is the giant of his age, not only in developmental psychology but also in general psychology.

References

Addison, R. M., & Homme, L. E. The reinforcement event menu. *Nat. Soc. Program. Instruc. J.*, 1966, **5** (1), 8–9.

Altman, J., & Das, G. D. Autoradiographic examination of the effects of enriched environment on the rate of glial multiplication in the adult rat brain. *Nature*, 1964, **204**, 1161–1165.

Ashby, W. R. *Design for a brain.* New York: Wiley, 1952.

Ausubel, D. P. *The psychology of meaningful verbal learning.* New York: Grune & Stratton, 1963.

Beilin, H. Learning and operational convergence in logical thought development. *J. exp. Child Psychol.*, 1965, **2**, 317–339.

Beilin, H., & Franklin, I. C. Logical operations in area and length measurement: age and training effects. *Child Develpm.*, 1962, **33**, 607–618.

Bennett, E. L., Diamond, M. C., Krech, D., & Rosenzweig, M. R. Chemical and anatomical plasticity of brain. *Science*, 1964, **146**, 610–619.

Bereiter, C., & Engelmann, S. *Teaching disadvantaged children in the preschool.* Englewood Cliffs, N.J.: Prentice-Hall, 1966.

Berlyne, D. E. *Conflict, arousal, and curiosity.* New York: McGraw-Hill, 1960.

Boole, G. *An investigation of the laws of thought.* New York: Dover, 1953. (Originally published in 1854.)

Boring, E. G. *A history of experimental psychology.* New York: Century, 1929.

Brattgård, S. O. The importance of adequate stimulation for the chemical composition of retinal ganglion cells during early postnatal development. *Acta Radiologica*, 1952, Stockholm, Suppl. **96**, 1–80.

Bryan, W. L., & Harter, N. Studies in the physiology and psychology of the telegraphic language. *Psychol. Rev.*, 1897, **4**, 27–53.

Cannon, W. B. *Bodily changes in pain, hunger, fear, and rage.* (2nd ed.) New York: Appleton-Century, 1929. (Originally published in 1915.)

Carmichael, L. The onset and early development of behavior. In L. Carmichael (Ed.), *Manual of child psychology.* New York: Wiley, 1954. Ch. 2.

Case, D., & Collinson, J. M. The development of formal thinking in verbal comprehension. *British J. educ. Psychol.*, 1962, **32**, 103–111.

Coghill, G. E. *Anatomy and the problem of behavior.* Cambridge: Cambridge Univer. Press; New York: Macmillan, 1929.

Darwin, C. *On the origin of the species.* London: Murray, 1859.

Darwin, C. *The expressions of the emotions in man and animals.* New York: Appleton, 1873. (Originally published in 1872.)

Dashiell, J. F. A quantitative demonstration of animal drive. *J. comp. Psychol.*, 1925, **5**, 205–208.

de Lemos, Marion, M. M. P. The development of the concept of conservation in Australian aboriginal children. Unpublished doctoral dissertation, Canberra, A. C. T.: Australian National Univer., 1966.

Dewey, J. The reflex arc concept in psychology. *Psychol. Rev.*, 1896, **3**, 357–370.

Dodwell, P. C. Relations between the understanding of the logic of classes and of cardinal number in children. *Canad. J. Psychol.*, 1962, **16**, 152–160.

Dodwell, P. C. Children's understanding of spatial concepts. *Canad. J. Psychol.*, 1963, **17**, 141–161.

Dollard, J., & Miller, N. E. *Personality and psychotherapy: an analysis in terms of learning, thinking, and culture.* New York: McGraw-Hill, 1950.

Duncker, K. On Problem-Solving (Transl. by Lynne S. Lees). *Psychol. Monogr.*, 1945, **58**, No. 270, p. 113. (Originally published in 1935.)

Dunlap, K. Are there any instincts? *J. abnorm. soc. Psychol.*, 1919, **14**, 307–311.

Ebbinghaus, H. *Über das Gedächtnis: Untersuchungen zur experimentellen Psychologie.* Leipzig: Duncker und Humblot, 1885. (Transl. as *Memory: a contribution to experimental psychology*, by H. A. Ruger & C. E. Bussenius. New York: Columbia Univer. Teachers College, 1913.)

Ferguson, G. A. On learning and human ability. *Canad. J. Psychol.*, 1954, **8**, 95–112.

Ferster, C. B., & Skinner, B. F. *Schedules of reinforcement.* New York: Appleton-Century-Crofts, 1957.

Festinger, L. *A theory of cognitive dissonance.* Evanston, Ill.: Row, Peterson, 1957.

Freud, S. Three contributions to the theory of sex. In A. A. Brill (Trans. & Ed.), *The basic writings of Sigmund Freud.* New York: Modern Library, 1938. (Originally published in 1905.)

Freud, S. Instincts and their vicissitudes. In *Collected Papers.* Vol. 4. London: Hogarth, 1925. Pp. 60–83. (Originally published in 1915.)

Furth, H. G. Conservation of weight in deaf and hearing children. *Child Develpm.*, 1964, 35, 143–150.

Gagné, R. M. *The conditions of learning.* New York: Holt, Rinehart and Winston, 1965.

Gagné, R. M., & Paradise, N. E. Abilities and learning sets in knowledge acquisition. *Psychol. Monogr.*, 1961, 75, No. 14 (Whole No. 518).

Galton, F. *Hereditary genius: an inquiry into its laws and consequences.* London: Macmillan, 1869.

Galton, F. *Inquiries into human faculty and its development.* London: Macmillan, 1883.

Galton, F. Regression towards mediocrity in heredary stature. *J. Anthrop. Inst.*, 1886, 15, 246–263.

Gesell, A. *Infancy and human growth.* New York: Macmillan, 1928.

Gesell, A. *The embryology of behavior: the beginnings of the human mind.* New York: Harper, 1945.

Gesell, A. The ontogenesis of infant behavior. In L. Carmichael (Ed.), *Manual of child psychology.* New York: Wiley, 1954. Ch. 6.

Gesell, A., et al. *The first five years of life.* New York: Harper, 1940.

Greenberg, D. A., Uzgiris, Ina C., & Hunt, J. McV. The effect of visual stimulation upon the blink response of human infants. *J. genet. Psychol.*, 1968 (in press).

Gruen, G. E. Experiences affecting the development of number conservation in children. *Child Develpm.*, 1965, 36, 964–979.

Guthrie, E. R. *The psychology of human conflict: the clash of motives within the individual.* New York: Harper, 1938.

Harlow, H. F. The formation of learning sets. *Psychol. Rev.*, 1949, 56, 51–65.

Hartmann, K. R. E. von. *The philosophy of the unconscious* (Transl. by W. C. Coupland). New York: Harcourt Brace, 1931. (Originally published in 1869.)

Harway, N. I. Judgments of distance in children and adults. *J. exp. Psychol.*, 1963, 65, 385–390.

Hebb, D. O. *The organization of behavior.* New York: Wiley, 1949.

Hilgard, E. R. *Theories of learning.* New York: Appleton-Century, 1948.

Hilgard, E. R. *Theories of learning.* (2nd ed.) New York: Appleton-Century-Crofts, 1956.

Homme, L. E., deBaca, P. C., Devine, E. J., Steinhorst, R., & Rickert, E. J. Use of the Premack principle in controlling the behavior of nursery school children. *J. exp. Anal. Behav.*, 1963, **6**, 554.

Hovland, C. I., Mandell, W., Campbell, E. H., Brock, T., Luchins, A. S., Cohen, A. R., McGuire, W. J., Janis, I. L., Feierabend, Rosalind L., & Anderson, N. H. *The order of presentation in persuasion.* New Haven: Yale Univer. Press, 1957.

Hull, C. L. *Principles of behavior.* New York: Appleton-Century-Crofts, 1943.

Hull, C. L. *A behavior system.* New Haven: Yale Univer. Press, 1952.

Hunt, J. McV. *Intelligence and experience.* New York: Ronald, 1961.

Hunt, J. McV. Motivation inherent in information processing and action. In O. J. Harvey (Ed.), *Motivation and social interaction: cognitive determinants.* New York: Ronald, 1963. Ch. 3. (a)

Hunt, J. McV. Piaget's observations as a source of hypotheses concerning motivation. *Merrill-Palmer Quart.*, 1963, **9**, 263–275. (b)

Hunt, J. McV. Intrinsic motivation and its role in psychological development. In D. Levine (Ed.), *Neb. Sympos. on Motiv.*, 1965, **13**, 189–282. Lincoln: Univer. of Nebraska Press. (a)

Hunt, J. McV. Traditional personality theory in the light of recent evidence. *Amer. Sci.*, 1965, **53**, 80–96. (b)

Hunt, J. McV. Toward a theory of guided learning in development. In R. H. Ojemann, & Karen Pritchett (Eds.), *Giving emphasis to guided learning.* Cleveland, O.: Educ. Res. Council, 1966. Pp. 98–160.

Hunt, J. McV., & Uzgiris, Ina C. Cathexis from recognitive familiarity: An exploratory study. In P. R. Merrifield (Ed.) *Experiments in multivariate Analysis: Studies in honor of J. P. Sculford.* Kent, Ohio: Kent State Univer. Press (in press).

Hunter, W. S. Modification of instinct from the standpoint of social psychology. *Psychol. Rev.*, 1920, **27**, 247–269.

Inhelder, Bärbel, & Piaget, J. *The growth of logical thinking from childhood to adolescence: an essay on the construction of formal operational structures* (Transl. by Anne Parsons & S. Milgram). New York: Basic Books, 1958. (Originally published in 1955.)

Johnson, R. C. A study of children's moral judgments. *Child Develpm.*, 1962, **33**, 327–354.

Katz, P. A., & Deutsch, M. Relation of auditory-visual shifting to reading achievement. *Percept. mot. Skills*, 1963, **17**, 327–332.

Kelleher, R. T., & Gollub, L. R. A review of positive conditioned reinforcement. *J. exp. Anal. Behav.*, 1962, **5**, 543–597.

Kelly, G. A. *The psychology of personal constructs.* New York: Norton, 1955. 2 vols.

Koffka, K. *The growth of the mind.* (Rev. ed.) Paterson, N. J.: Littlefield, Adams & Co., 1959. (Originally published in 1924.)

Kofsky, E. A scalogram study of classificatory development. *Child Develpm.*, 1966, **37**, 191–204.

Köhler, W. *The mentality of apes* (Transl. by Ella Winter). New York: Vintage Books, 1959. (Originally published in 1924.)

Köhler, W. *Gestalt Psychology.* New York: Mentor Books (MP 363), 1962. (Originally published in 1929.)

Kuo, Z. Y. Give up instincts in psychology. *J. Phil.*, 1921, **18**, 645–664.

Kuo, Z. Y. How are instincts acquired? *Psychol. Rev.*, 1922, **29**, 334–365.

Kuo, Z. Y. Ontogeny of embryonic behavior in aves: I. The chronology and general nature of the behavior in the chick embryo. *J. exp. Zool.*, 1932, **61**, 395–430. (a)

Kuo, Z. Y. Ontogeny of embryonic behavior in aves: II. The mechanical factors in the various stages leading to hatching. *J. exp. Zool.*, 1932, **62**, 453–487. (b)

Kuo, Z. Y. Ontogeny of embryonic behavior in aves: III. The structural and environmental factors in embryonic behavior. *J. comp. Psychol.*, 1932, **13**, 245–271. (c)

Kuo, Z. Y. Ontogeny of embryonic behavior in aves: IV. The influence of embryonic movements upon the behavior after hatching. *J. comp. Psychol.*, 1932, **14**, 109–122. (d)

Kuo, Z. Y. Ontogeny of embryonic behavior in aves: V. The reflex concept in the light of embryonic behavior in birds. *Psychol. Rev.*, 1932, **39**, 499–515. (e)

Liberman, R. Retinal cholinesterase and glycolysis in rats raised in darkness. *Science*, 1962, **135**, 372–373.

Locke, J. An essay concerning the true original extent and end of civil government. In E. A. Burtt (Ed.), *The English philosophers from Bacon to Mill.* New York: Modern Library, 1939. Pp. 403–503. (Originally published in 1690.)

Loeb, J. *Der Heliotropismus der Thiere und Seine Uebereinstimmung mit dem Heliotropismus der Pflanzen.* Wurzberg: Hertz, 1890.

Loeb, J. *The mechanistic conception of life.* Chicago: Univer. of Chicago Press, 1912.

Lorenz, K. The companion in the bird's world. *Auk*, 1937, **54**, 245–273.

McDougall, W. *An introduction to social psychology.* London: Methuen, 1908.

Maltzman, I., & Raskin, D. C. Effects of individual differences in the orienting reflex on conditioning and complex processes. *J. exp. Res. Pers.*, 1965, **1**, 1–16.

Marquis, D. G. The criterion of innate behavior. *Psychol. Rev.*, 1930, **37**, 334–349.

Morgan, C. L. *An introduction to comparative psychology.* (2nd ed.) London: Scott, 1909. (Originally published in 1894.)

Mowrer, O. H. On the psychology of "talking birds"—a contribution to language and personality theory. In O. H. Mowrer (Ed.), *Learning theory and personality dynamics.* New York: Ronald, 1950. Ch. 24.

Nass, M. L. The deaf child's conception of physical causality. *J. abnorm. soc. Psychol.*, 1964, **69**, 669–673.

Ojemann, R. H., & Pritchett, Karen. Piaget and the role of guided experiences in development. *Percept. mot. Skills*, 1963, **17**, 927–940.

Papez, J. W. *Comparative neurology.* New York: Crowell, 1929.

Pavlov, I. P. *Conditioned reflexes* (Transl. by G. V. Anrep). London: Oxford Univer. Press, 1927.

Piaget, J. *The language and thought of the child* (Transl. by Marjorie Worden). New York: Harcourt, Brace, 1926. (Originally published in 1923.)

Piaget, J. *Judgment and reasoning in the child* (Transl. by Marjorie Worden). New York: Harcourt, Brace, 1928. (Originally published in 1924.)

Piaget, J. *The child's conception of the world* (Transl. by Joan and Andrew Tomlinson). New York: Harcourt, Brace, 1929. (Originally published in 1926.)

Piaget, J. *The child's conception of physical causality* (Transl. by Marjorie Worden). New York: Harcourt, Brace, 1930. (Originally published in 1927.)

Piaget, J. *The moral judgment of the child* (Transl. by Marjorie Worden). New York: Harcourt, Brace, 1932.

Piaget, J. *The origins of intelligence in children* (Transl. by Margaret Cook). New York: International Univer. Press, 1952. (Originally published 1936.)

Piaget, J. *The construction of reality in the child* (Transl. by Margaret Cook). New York: Basic Books, 1954. (Originally published in 1937.)

Piaget, J. Le méchanism du développement mental et les lois du "groupement" des opérations. *Arch. Psychol., Genève*, 1941, **28**, 215–285.

Piaget, J. *Classes, relations et nombres. Essai sur les "groupements" de la logistique et la réversibilité de la pensée.* Paris: Vrin, 1942. (a)

Piaget, J. Les trois structures fondamentales de la vie psychique: rythme, régulation, et groupement. *Schweiz. Z. Psychol. Anwend.,* 1942, **1,** 9–21. (b)

Piaget, J. *Play, dreams, and imitation in childhood* (Transl. by C. Gattegno & F. M. Hodgson). New York: Norton, 1951. (Originally published in 1945.)

Piaget, J. *Les notions de mouvement et de vitesse chez l'enfant.* Paris: Presses Univer. France, 1946.

Piaget, J. *The psychology of intelligence* (Transl. by M. Piercy & D. E. Berlyne). Paterson, N. J.: Littlefield, Adams, & Co., 1960. (Originally published in 1947.)

Piaget, J. Une expérience sur la psychologie du hasard chez l'enfant: le tirage au sort des couples. *Acta Psychol.,* 1950, **7,** 323–336.

Piaget, J. Jean Piaget. In E. G. Boring, H. S. Langfeld, H. Werner, & R. M. Yerkes (Eds.), *A history of psychology in autobiography.* Worcester, Mass.: Clark Univer. Press, 1952.

Piaget, J. *Logic and psychology* (Transl. by W. Mays & T. Whitehead). Manchester: Manchester Univer. Press; New York: Basic Books, 1953.

Piaget, J. The development of time concepts in the child. In R. H. Hoch & J. Zubin (Eds.), *Psychopathology of childhood.* New York: Grune & Stratton, 1955. (a)

Piaget, J. Essai d'une nouvelle interpretation probabiliste des effets de centration de la loi de Weber et celle des centrations relatives. *Arch. Psychol., Genève,* 1955, **35,** 1–24. (b)

Piaget, J., Albertini, Barbara von, & Rossi, M. Essai d'interpretation probabiliste de la loi de Weber et celles des centrations relatives. *Arch. Psychol., Genève,* 1944, **30,** 95–138.

Piaget, J., & Inhelder, Bärbel. *Le développement des quantités chez l'enfant. Conservation et atomisme.* Neuchâtel: Delachaux et Niestlé, 1940.

Piaget, J., & Inhelder, Bärbel. Diagnosis of mental operations and theory of intelligence. *Amer. J. ment. Defic.,* 1947, **51** (3), 401–406.

Piaget, J., & Inhelder, Bärbel. *The child's conception of space* (Transl. by F. J. Langdon & J. L. Lunzer). London: Routledge & Kegan Paul, 1956. (Originally published in 1948.)

Piaget, J., Inhelder, Bärbel, & Szeminska, Alina. *The child's conception of geometry* (Transl. by E. A. Lunzer). New York: Basic Books, 1960. (Originally published in 1948.)

Piaget, J., & Lambercier, M. La comparaison visuelle des hauteurs à distances variables dans le plan fronto-parallèle. *Arch. Psychol., Genève,* 1943, **29,** 175–253. (a)

Piaget, J., & Lambercier, M. Le problème de comparaison visuelle en profondeur et l'erreur systématique de l'ètalon. *Arch. Psychol., Genève,* 1943, **29,** 255–308. (b)

Piaget, J., & Lambercier, M. Essai sur un effet d'Einstellung survenant au cours de perceptions visuelles successives (effet Usnadze). *Arch. Psychol., Genève,* 1944, **30,** 140–196.

Piaget, J., & Lambercier, M. Transpositions perceptives et transitivité opératoire dans les comparaisons en profondeur. *Arch. Psychol., Genève,* 1946, **31,** 325–368.

Piaget, J., & Lambercier, M. La comparaison des différences de hauteur dans le plan fronto-parallèle. *Arch. Psychol., Genève,* 1953, **34,** 73–107.

Piaget, J., Lambercier, M., Boesch, E., & Albertini, Barbara von. Introduction à l'étude des perceptions chez l'enfant et analyse d'une illusion relative à la perception visuelle de cercles concentriques (Delboeuf). *Arch. Psychol., Genève, 1942,* **29** (No. 113), 1–107.

Piaget, J. & Szeminska, Alina. Quelques experiences sur la conservation des quantités continues chez l'enfant. *J. Psychol. norm. path.,* 1939, **36,** 36–65.

Piaget, J., & Szeminska, Alina. *The child's conception of number* (Transl. by C. Gattegno & F. M. Hodgson). New York: Humanities Press, 1952. (Originally published in 1941.)

Rash, R., Swift, H., Riesen, A. H., & Chow, K. L. Altered structure and composition of retinal cells in dark-reared mammals. *Exp. Cellular Res.,* 1961, **25,** 348–363.

Ratner, S. C., Gawronski, J. J., & Rice, F. E. The variable of concurrent action in the language of children: effects of delayed speech feedback. *Psychol. Rec.,* 1964, **14,** 47–56.

Razran, G. The observable unconscious and the inferable conscious in current Soviet psychophysiology: interoceptive conditioning, semantic conditioning, and the orienting reflex. *Psychol. Rev.,* 1961, **68,** 81–147.

Richter, C. P. A behavioristic study of the activity of the rat. *Comp. Psychol. Monogr.,* 1922, **1,** No. 2.

Richter, C. P. Animal behavior and internal drives. *Quart. Rev. Biol.,* 1927, **2,** 307–343.

Riesen, A. H. Plasticity of behavior: psychological aspects. In H. F. Harlow & C. N. Woolsey (Eds.), *Biological and biochemical bases of behavior.* Madison: Univer. of Wisconsin Press, 1958. Pp. 425–450.

Rogers, C. R. *Client-centered therapy.* Boston: Houghton Mifflin, 1951.

Romanes, G. J. *Animal intelligence.* New York: Appleton-Century-Crofts, 1883. (a)

Romanes, G. J. *Mental evolution in animals.* New York: Appleton-Century-Crofts, 1883. (b)

Sharpless, S., & Jasper, H. H. Habituation of the arousal reaction. *Brain*, 1956, **79**, 655–680.

Shirley, Mary M. The first two years: a study of 25 babies. Vol II. Intellectual development. *Inst. Child Welf. Monogr. Ser.*, 1933, No. 7, Minneapolis: Univer. of Minnesota Press.

Simon, H. A. *Models of man*. New York: Wiley, 1957.

Skinner, B. F. *The behavior of organisms: an experimental analysis.* New York: Appleton-Century-Crofts, 1938.

Skinner, B. F. Are theories of learning necessary? *Psychol. Rev.*, 1950, **57**, 193–216.

Skinner, B. F. *Science and human behavior.* New York: Macmillan, 1953.

Skinner, B. F. Reinforcement today. *Amer. Psychol.*, 1958, **13**, 94–99.

Smedslund, J. The acquisition of conservation of substance and weight in children. II. External reinforcement of conservation of weight and the operations of additions and subtractions. *Scan. J. Psychol.*, 1961, **2**, 71–84. (a)

Smedslund, J. The acquisition of conservation of substance and weight in children. III. Extinction of conservation of weight acquired "normally" and by means of empirical controls on a balance. *Scan. J. Psychol.*, 1961, **2**, 85–87. (b)

Smedslund, J. The acquisition of conservation of substance and weight in children. IV. Attempt at extinction of the visual components of the weight concept. *Scan. J. Psychol.*, 1961, **2**, 153–155. (c)

Smedslund, J. The acquisition of conservation of substance and weight in children. V. Practice in conflict situations without external reinforcement. *Scan. J. Psychol.*, 1961, **2**, 156–160. (d)

Smedslund, J. The acquisition of conservation of substance and weight in children. VI. Practice on continuous vs. discontinuous material in problem situations without external reinforcement. *Scan. J. Psychol.*, 1961, **2**, 203–210. (e)

Smedslund, J. The acquisition of conservation of substance and weight in children. VII. Conservation of discontinuous quantity and the operations of adding and taking away. *Scan. J. Psychol.*, 1962, **3**, 69–77.

Smedslund, J. The effect of observation on children's representation of the spatial orientation of a water surface. *J. genet. Psychol.*, 1963, **102**, 195–201. (a)

Smedslund, J. Development of concrete transitivity of length in children. *Child Develpm.*, 1963, **35**, 389–405. (b)

Smedslund, J. Patterns of experience and the acquisition of conservation of length. *Scan. J. Psychol.*, 1963, **4**, 257–264. (c)

Smedslund, J. Concrete reasoning: a study of intellectual development. *Monogr., Soc. Res. Child Develpm.*, 1964, **29**, No. 2 (Ser. No. 93), pp. 1–39.

Smith, K. U., & Greene, P. A critical period in maturation of performance with space-displaced vision. *Percept. mot. Skills*, 1963, **17**, 627–639.

Spearman, C. *The nature of intelligence and the principles of cognition.* London: Macmillan, 1923.

Szeminska, Alina. The evolution of thought: some applications of research findings to educational practice. In *European Research in Cognitive Development, Monogr., Soc. Res. Child Develpm.*, 1965, **30**, No. 2 (Ser. No. 100), pp. 47–57.

Thorndike, E. L. Animal intelligence. *Psychol. Rev. Monogr. Suppl.*, 1898, **2**, No. 8, 1–109.

Thorndike, E. L. *Animal intelligence: experimental studies.* New York: Macmillan, 1911.

Thorndike, E. L. *The psychology of wants, interests, and attitudes.* New York: Appleton-Century, 1935.

Uzgiris, Ina C. Situational generality of conservation. *Child Develpm.*, 1964, **35**, 831–841.

Uzgiris, Ina C., & Hunt, J. McV. Object Permanence (sound-motion-picture). Urbana, Ill.: Motion Picture Service, Univer. of Illinois, 1967.

Uzgiris, Ina C., & Hunt, J. McV. *Toward ordinal scales of psychological development in infancy*, 1969. (In preparation.)

Wachs, T., Uzgiris, Ina C., & Hunt, J. McV. Cognitive development in infants of different age levels and from differing environmental backgrounds. Mimeographed paper presented at the Soc. Res. Child Develpm., New York City, March, 1967. Available: Psychological Development Laboratory, Univer. of Illinois.

Wallach, M. A. Research on children's thinking. In *Yearb. nat. Soc. Stud. Educ.*, 1963, **62** (I), 236–276.

Watson, J. B. Psychology as the behaviorist views it. *Psychol. Rev.*, 1913, **20**, 158–177.

Watson, J. B. *Behavior, an introduction to comparative psychology.* New York: Holt, Rinehart, & Winston, 1914.

Watson, J. B. *Behaviorism.* New York: Norton, 1924.

Watson, J. B. *Psychological care of infant and child.* New York: Norton, 1928.

Weiskrantz, L. Sensory deprivation and the cat's optic nervous system. *Nature*, 1958, **181**, 1047–1050.

Weiss, A. P. *A theoretical basis of human behavior.* Columbus, O.: Adams, 1925.

Werner, H. *Comparative psychology of mental development.* New York: Science Editions, 1961. (Originally published in 1948.)

Wertheimer, M. *Productive thinking*. New York: Harper, 1945.

White, B. L., & Held, R. Plasticity of sensorimotor development in the human infant. In Judy F. Rosenblith & W. Alinsmith (Eds.), *The causes of behavior: readings in child development and educational psychology.* (2nd ed.) Boston: Allyn & Bacon, 1966.

White, R. W. Motivation reconsidered: The concept of competence. *Psychol. Rev.,* 1959, **66,** 297–333.

White, S. H. Evidence for a hierarchical arrangement of learning processes. In L. P. Lipsitt, & C. C. Spiker (Eds.), *Advances in child development and behavior,* II. New York: Academic Press, 1965. Pp. 187–220.

White, S. H. The hierarchical organization of intellectual structures. Mimeographed paper presented at Symposium, The Role of Experience in Intellectual Development, Amer. Ass. advance. Sci. Convention, Washington, D. C., December, 1966.

Woodworth, R. S. *Dynamic psychology*. New York: Columbia Univer. Press, 1918.

Woodworth, R. S. Reinforcement of perception. *Amer. J. Psychol.,* 1947, **60,** 119–124.

Formal and Functional Aspects of Cognitive Development

JOHN H. FLAVELL

JOACHIM F. WOHLWILL

The aim of this essay is to present some tentative ideas and opinions regarding the nature of cognitive development. These ideas and opinions are, as the reader will quickly note, distillates from the recent and burgeoning literature on cognition, language, and their ontogenesis. In particular, the seminal work of Jean Piaget and of those who have taken up his ideas has influenced our thinking at every turn as, indeed, they must profoundly influence anyone in our era who thinks about cognitive development.

Any account of development, cognitive or otherwise, must speak to two interdependent aspects of the developmental process: formal and functional. The formal aspect has to do with the "morphology" of the process: the sorts of cognitive entities that make up the successive outputs of development and how these entities are causally, temporally, and otherwise interrelated. The formal-morphological face of development could be regarded as its "merely descriptive" face, although for us this phrase is not in the least pejorative in this context. The other aspect, sometimes distinguishable from the first only by the most strenuous efforts at discrimination and abstraction, has to do with function and mechanism: the activities or processes of the organism, somehow specified in relation to environmental inputs, by which it in fact makes the cognitive progress that has been formally characterized. As a prelude to discussing the formal side, we shall summarize a bit of recent history concerning not cognitive, but language development, with a promise to show its relevance subsequently to our broader topic.

Preliminary considerations

The study of cognitive development, in the light of recent trends in developmental psycholinguistics There has recently been a minor scientific revolution in the field of language development. Prior to the present decade, researchers in this field had models of the output and of the process of language development, both models frequently implicit rather than explicit. The model of the output was, to oversimplify slightly, an adult who had at his disposal: (1) a large vocabulary of words he could pronounce, perceive, and decode correctly, classifiable by an observer into the traditional gross syntactic categories of noun, verb, adjective, etc. (2) an ability, simply stipulated rather than analyzed, to concatenate these words into sentence strings the structure of which was also describable (although not often described) in traditional, grammar-book ways (McCarthy, 1954). The model of the developmental process that yielded such an output was essentially an accretional, quantitative one, tacitly or expressly derived from contemporaneous learning theories. Thus, language development was seen as a gradual but uniform process of getting the appropriate items into the repertoire: of approximating the adult phonology phoneme by phoneme; of acquiring vocabulary word by word; of producing sentences of one-word, then two-word, then three-word length, and so on.

The rest of the historical narrative is far more difficult to describe briefly, and we shall highlight only what we shall later wish to use. The "new wave" in psycholinguistics (Chomsky, 1957, 1965; Katz, 1966; McNeill, 1966) also offers both an output and a process model for language development, but they are radically different from their predecessors. The model of the output is a complex device that includes as part of its equipment a finite set of rules by which it can, in principle (see below), generate all and only the infinite number of grammatical sentences in its native language. This system of rules that characterizes the adult's abstract knowledge of the structure of his language is referred to as his linguistic "competence," and is identical to a formal grammar of that language. This model of linguistic "competence" is not equivalent to a psychological theory of the adult's actual linguistic "performance" in real situations (i.e. as speaker or listener), although it would have to bear an intimate and complex relationship to any models of the latter kind that were devised. For example, the competence model does not represent the psychological operations involved in actually processing and interpreting a sentence heard, although it does represent the grammatical knowledge that must be prerequisite to performing these operations. In particular, various factors on the performance, "psychological-hardware," side may impede or distort the application of the abstract knowledge represented in competence. For instance, memory limitations may lead us to fail to understand or to misunderstand a long complex grammatical sentence, distraction or affective factors may lead to the production of grammatically aberrant sentences, and so on. The competence-performance distinction is akin to the familiar but often-forgotten distinction between learning and performance: to say that someone failed to do A in a given situation need not be equivalent to saying that he was fundamentally incapable of doing A, in that situation or in any other.

The model for the process of acquisition is less well articulated, but runs roughly like this. Language development is analogous to the process of scientific discovery. The infant is endowed by the model with an innate representation of the general characteristics that all human languages have in common (i.e. "linguistic universals" at all levels) and successively tests hypotheses, derived from this innate representation, about the rule structure of the specific language to which he is exposed. Like the scientist, his search for structure is an active process of hypothesis formation, test, and confirmation/disconfirmation; also like the scientist, the particular hypotheses he entertains are selected from the set of possible ones by his preexisting mental structure, in this instance a structure biologically specialized for extracting grammatical rules from linguistic samples. Thus the linguistic input he receives "controls" his linguistic development only in the weak sense that it provides the necessary data for hypothesis testing. Exponents of this rationalistic theory of language development point to worldwide uniformity in the ages at which language development is begun and completed, despite what must be wide variation in the amount, quality, and kind of linguistic input children receive during this period.

This model of the process leads the student of language development to new and different research objectives, objectives scarcely definable within the previous theoretical "paradigm" (Kuhn, 1964). He may be led, for example, to study the order of emergence of the various components of the adult grammar—the successive stages ("pregrammars") in the child's discovery of the specific rules that define linguistic competence in his native language. He may also try to theorize about the role that developmental changes in performance capabilities (e.g. memory span) may play in determining the sequence and timing of these emergents. What he will *not* do, manifestly, is describe grammatical development in terms of such variables—irrelevant for the new output model—as sentence length.

We think that there are lessons to be learned from what has recently happened in the field of language development, lessons which those interested in cognitive development would do well to heed. The first is that one's conception of how development proceeds is constrained by one's model of what this development yields, and that changes in the output model necessarily imply changes in the process model. It stands to reason, in other words, that our image of the formal and functional aspects of any genesis must be shaped by our image of the nature and kind of entities it is thought to yield as successive outcomes—as "precipitates," if you will, of the ontogenetic process. The obvious implication is that we should be as precise and explicit as the state of the science permits about the cognitive makeup of the child at various critical points in his development (and of the adult end product of this development) before constructing a model of this evolution. Needless to say, no one is going to await the Compleat Output Model before making guesses about development. On the other hand, we should at least avoid developmental pretheories that, for want of a careful prior analysis of what the outputs would have to be like *in general,* describe the development of a patently nonhuman cognizer. In effect, the pre-1960 work on language development conveyed just such an impression, and this same problem may still be a significant one in present-day thinking in the area of cognitive development.

The competence-automaton distinction A second lesson centers on Chomsky's distinction between competence and performance. A group at the University of Minnesota Center for Research in Human Learning (Donald J. Foss, Terry G. Halwes, James J. Jenkins, and Robert E. Shaw) is currently working on an approach to theory construction in psychology that, among other things, further elaborates this distinction. These psychologists argue that a psychological theory that accounts for complex behavior will have two principal components: a *competence* model, which is a formal, logical representation of the structure of some domain (e.g. the abstract rules for generating grammatical strings in some language); an *automaton* model (an elaborated version of what Chomsky apparently meant by "performance"), which represents the psychological processes by which the information embodied in competence actually gets accessed and utilized in real situations. The competence model gives an abstract, purely logical representation of what the organism knows or could do in a timeless, ideal environment, whereas the automaton model has the job of describing a real device that could plausibly instance that knowledge or skill, and instance it within the constraints (memory limitations, rapid performance, etc.) under which human beings actually operate. A competence model for mathematical operations, for example, would be some fragment of mathematics. Such a model says nothing, obviously, about the actual mechanisms human beings utilize in performing these operations, nor could it tell us anything about the variables (within the organism or the task) that facilitate or impede this performance. A parsimonious representation of all the psychological variables relevant to executing what is "known" in competence is the ultimate objective of the automaton component of the theory. Note that the competence model is far from being a superfluous entity within the system; without it, the theorist could not define the theoretical objectives of his psychological (i.e. automaton) model—he would not know what the model was to be a model *of*.

This distinction between competence and automaton/performance may turn out to be quite useful in thinking about cognitive-developmental phenomena. Consider the following, by no means hypothetical, situation. Suppose children of different ages are tested extensively for their ability to make transitive inferences, e.g. $X < Y$ together with $Y < Z$ logically implies $X < Z$. Assume further that the following three subjects are identified in the course of the investigation. Child A (age four) never shows anything remotely resembling transitive inference, regardless of how the test situation is structured. Moreover, the investigator is unable to make him understand this pattern of reasoning through brief training or prompting. Child B (age eight) gives indisputable evidence of reasoning in this fashion on some tasks but not on others. Attempts at training on the latter tasks are partially successful, although the child continues to fail to apply, or misapplies, the rule in some of the more complex of these tasks. Child C (age 14) correctly applies the rule, without any training, in virtually every problem given him. An analysis framed in competence-automaton terms "parses" these three cases in an intuitively correct way, assigning similarities and differences in what seem to be the right places. Child A differs from both B and C in that we have no basis for asserting that a transitivity rule has yet become part of his abstract cognitive competence, in the same sense that it could be said that a two-year-old had not yet acquired a particular grammatical transformation. In contrast, the inclusion of a transitivity rule in the competence description is mandatory in the case of C and also, we believe, in the case of B. The difference between B and C is best assigned to a difference in the automaton/performance system, i.e. the machinery by which the subject transforms the task data into suitable coded form, accesses and utilizes the functional equivalent of the transitivity equation, and so on. The approach suggests that, if we knew more about psychological processes and about this subject, we could identify rather precisely the variables that determine whether or not his rule—"his" in the sense of its being in his competence system—can be accessed and used in a given situation. We would want to describe B as really "having" the transitivity rule in some sense, but unable to generalize or transfer it to all tasks for which it is an effective solution procedure. His limitations as regards transfer and generalization, and the lack thereof in the case of child C, are both to be explained with reference to the automaton rather than competence component.* A competence-automaton approach does not ignore or underplay the undeniable capacity difference between B and C, but it wants to assert that it is not the same *kind* of difference as that which distinguishes A and B. It goes without saying that problems of developmental diagnosis do not suddenly vanish with the advent of a competence-automaton analysis. For one thing, there is the recurrent and very thorny problem of just what to write into the competence system—a problem that will surely prove even more troublesome in cogntive development than it has for psycholinguistics. Our only claim is that the distinctions that this analysis wants to capture are real ones, and that it may give us new and fruitful ways of looking at traditional problems in cognitive-developmental theory.

Our position, then, is that an analysis of cognitive development must be guided by some conception of what this development successively precipitates, and also that any such conception would do well to incorporate a competence-automation distinction. The aim of this paper is not to offer a theory of outputs, but instead to present some ideas regarding development itself.

---

* Donaldson (1964) has made an interesting and detailed analysis of the kinds of difficulties children encounter in trying to bring their intellectual skills effectively to bear on the solution of various problems. The "structural," "arbitrary," and "executive" errors she notes could in many instances be interpreted as reflecting shortcomings in the automaton component rather than actual lacunae in the child's competence.

Nonetheless, it would be appropriate to preface the latter with a very brief account of what we think such a theory ought to be like, since our convictions here have helped to shape our developmental views.

We believe that an abstract competence description of what the child knows and can do, at any level of maturity, will be an extremely long and complicated affair. Correspondingly, the automaton model that represents how this knowledge is actually stored, accessed, and utilized by a real human subject will have at least as much complexity of structure and function as the most powerful and flexible computer system presently imaginable. Any competence-automaton representation of developmental outputs less rich than this seems certain to be incomplete at best and wrongheaded at worst.* Simple models just will not do for human cognition, regardless of their seeming advantages in regard to explicability and operational definition. Pursuing the computer analogy, intellectual development is essentially a matter of ontogenetic change in the content and organization of highly intricate "programs," the nature of each program strictly determining what gets inputted from the environment (and from memory storage within the child) and how that input gets dealt with intellectually.

What sorts of contents and characteristics will have to be attributed to these programs? The crude taxonomy given below is inadequate and should not be taken as a serious organizational scheme, but it does convey some of the things we have in mind.

Of paramount importance is a very large and ill-bounded category containing the child's "stored information" about self and world. Included here are the many fundamental concepts and rules the genesis of which Piaget and others have so well described: the early concept of object permanence and the later conservations; the concepts of class, relation, number, measuring unit, proportionality—the list could be extended almost endlessly.

---

* We suspect, in fact, that the cognitive-developmental theorist of the future will need to be well trained in computer simulation lore, in addition to possessing good intuitions about how children think. Our ideal would be a combination of Herbert Simon and Piaget, with perhaps a bit of Chomsky added for writing the competence model!

Also, to be included is information of a somewhat more nebulous and nonspecific kind: for instance, that other minds exist and that this fact implies a multiplicity of cognitive-perceptual perspectives; that there is an appearance-reality distinction—that the world, like language, has both a surface and a deep structure; and that the game of thinking follows certain rules, involving notions of logical implication, noncontradiction, proof, lawfulness, and the like. The information in the child's program can be as specifiable as a concrete concept and as ineffable as a pervasive world-view. An adequate model of what he is and has at a given point in his cognitive growth must somehow take account of both kinds of information.

Also to be specified is the manner in which the child's information is represented and organized. As to representation, Piaget has contrasted sensorimotor and symbolic modes, and Bruner (Bruner, Olver, & Greenfield, 1966) has recently distinguished among enactive, ikonic, and symbolic forms of representing the child's knowledge. Any adequate output model must specify both what the child knows and the manner in which that knowledge is represented. As to organization, Piaget's structural models (his groupings, groups, and lattices) constitute virtually the only available suggestions as to how cognitive elements might be interrelated at each level of development.

Finally, the program must incorporate the child's innate and acquired procedures for extracting, processing, and utilizing information of both the permanently-stored and the presently-inputted variety. The outcome of a cognitive encounter with the environment is never more than partly a function of what the subject knows and of how that knowledge is represented and organized. It also depends upon his ability to deploy and maintain selective attention, to organize perceptual elements into intellectually suitable form, to transport information (and just the *right* information) to and from memory storage in an efficient fashion, and so on. Skills of this type—what might be termed the "handmaidens of the mind"—also show considerable alteration with age and must also figure importantly in models of development's products.

Two traditional questions about the form of development

There appear to be four basic questions or issues regarding the formal as opposed to functional properties of cognitive growth. The four issues are closely interrelated, and positions taken with respect to any one tend to constrain reactions to each of the others. Two of them are briefly discussed in the present section: are developmental changes essentially qualitative or quantitative in nature, and do such changes tend to take place abruptly or gradually? These two questions have been posed many times in the history of the field, and we think that their repeated resurrections (Werner, 1957) attest both to their substantiveness and to their lack of satisfactory resolution. The remaining two—concerning developmental sequences and the problem of stages —are relative newcomers on the scene, and owe much of their present salience to Piaget's theoretical and research accomplishments. Moreover, they appear to be richer and more interesting questions than the traditional ones, and will accordingly be discussed more fully here. Our discussion of the two traditional questions is, in fact, meant to serve primarily as context-setter and preface for a more extended treatment of sequence and stage.

QUALITATIVE CHANGE

The issue here is whether the successive products of the cognitive-developmental process differ from one another qualitatively, i.e. in kind, or only quantitatively, i.e. in degree or amount on one or more dimensions. The kind of position one takes on this issue determines, among other things, whether one is likely to espouse a stage-sequential model of development, such as Piaget's. Since the qualitative-differences position rather than the alternative appears to assert something positive about the nature of development, and seems to offer hope of interesting theory-building in this area, the burden of proof has generally been on those who wish to claim that it is true.

The position has a weaker and a stronger form. The weaker one asserts that there exist *some* changes, of prima facie importance, which are undeniably "qualitative" in any usual meaning of that term. The stronger one asserts that *all* cognitive-developmental changes are best construed as changes in kind rather than degree or amount. There now appears to be overwhelming evidence that the weaker version of the position is true; Piaget's data alone show an abundance of convincing examples. The difference between sensorimotor and symbolic-representational modes of coding experience, for instance, could hardly be characterized as a mere difference in "degree" or "amount" of coding. The difference between inference-based and perception-based reasoning in a conservation task is also a clear instance of a qualitative change. Notice that an assertion of qualitative differences is a claim only about the *formal* relationship between two cognitive processes; as Werner (1957) has pointed out, it does not imply anything about other kinds of relationships that may hold between them. It does not, for example, say whether the transition from the earlier to the later process was gradual or abrupt, complete or incomplete, and the like. The specification of these relationships is, of course, an important task for the developmentalist (see below), but it should not be confused with the question of whether the two intellectual "programs" in question are or are not qualitatively distinct.

The stronger version of the qualitative-differences hypothesis, on the other hand, is surely false. There are innumerable true statements about cognitive growth that have a straightforward quantitative-change character. The question is rather whether any such statements are interesting or "theoretically revealing" to the developmentalist, as qualitative-change assertions almost invariably are. For example, the statement that the number of concepts available to the child grows as he grows is certainly true, but is far less interesting than, say, the statement that the child begins to acquire and use formal operations at a certain age. While we doubt if any quantitative-change findings could ever have quite the allure of qualitative ones, there may be some that are less trivial-looking than that cited above.

For example, suppose a child at a certain point in his development acquires a new strategy for remembering a string of digits,
e.g. he now tries to group them by threes whereas earlier, let us
say, he did no deliberate grouping at all. It is probable that the
number of digits he could recall would continue to augment during the next several years, even supposing he always utilized that
strategy and no other. Thus, while really continuing to do the
"same thing," from a qualitative standpoint, the child gradually
comes to do it better and better. Perhaps the grouping operation
becomes progressively quicker and less effortful; perhaps it becomes more resistant to distraction or other interferences, or
perhaps the number of items (grouped or ungrouped) that he
can hold in short-term memory simply increases somewhat as a
consequence of neurophysiological growth during that period of
years.

This kind of relationship between quantitative and qualitative
aspects of growth may hold rather generally: qualitative-looking
changes in the child's mode of representing reality, in his
problem-solving strategy, and so on; quantitative-looking
changes in the operational efficiency, flexibility, mobility, and
such like, of each of these emergents during all or part of its
developmental life. There are ontogenetic stretches during which
some segment of the child's intellectual program changes only
quantitatively, at the parameter level, and other stretches during
which that segment actually alters its basic character, setting the
stage for renewed quantitative change. Perhaps the relation between the two forms of change goes even deeper than mere
temporal alternation. Maybe the quantitative development that
an emergent undergoes is for one reason or another a necessary
precondition for the advent of its successor. In fact, we read
Piaget as implying this in his assimilation-accommodation-
equilibration model of cognitive development (Flavell, 1963, pp.
49–50, 244–249).

ABRUPTNESS

Two issues have to do with the temporal aspects of cognitive
development. One concerns the temporal order of acquisitions, in

particular whether some or all developmental emergents appear in a fixed and invariant sequence for all children. We shall take up this major issue in the next section. The other concerns the rate at which development proceeds, and particularly whether the rate speeds up (or slows down) at certain points. Thus, there has been a question as to whether cognitive evolution is abrupt, or saltatory, characterized by spurts of intellectual growth, or whether instead it is gradual throughout its span. Alternatively, it has been asked whether this evolution is typically "continuous" or "discontinuous" in nature.* This question about developmental tempo appears to have two rather different forms.

It can be asked whether a given process—comprising only one segment of the child's total cognitive system—will evolve and proliferate rapidly once its evolution has begun. Within our conceptual framework, this version of the question might be paraphrased as follows. Once some cognitive algorithm (an inference rule, say) has finally entered the competence system, how rapidly does it become reliably available to the subject throughout its domain of application, i.e. the set of tasks or problems for which it is adaptive? Or more simply, what is the typical interval of ontogenetic time between the first, tentative and limited but—we shall stipulate—genuine instance of a given cognitive form and its period of generalized availability? The recent Piagetian literature strongly suggests that development is normally gradual rather than abrupt in this sense. The conservation concepts, to take everyone's favorite example of a cognitive form, seem to show a rather extended interval between first-incompetence and always-in-performance. The process of stabilization and generalization of these and perhaps all competence items appears to be a relatively slow and gradual one; we shall

---

* While all of the traditional lexicon for describing development tends to be imprecise, "continuity-discontinuity" is a particularly bad offender. In addition to its connotation of abruptness of change, "discontinuity" seems also to imply: (1) that the change is qualitative rather than quantitative, (2) that the newly developed process extinguishes and replaces its predecessor (the transition lacks the "continuity" that would have obtained if, say, the new process had incorporated the earlier one into itself). Although entrenched in the literature, this antonym pair is best avoided when trying to be clear about the formal properties of cognitive development.

attempt to characterize the typical course of such a process in our discussion of the stage concept. Assuming that this is so, does it attest to a fundamental inertia in the developmental process, or does it only mean that the child's everyday school and home environment is educationally inefficient. Would it be possible, in fact, to reduce the above-mentioned interval by a very considerable amount if only we were apprised of and could institute the proper environmental inputs? This is, of course, a very old question about intellectual development, and a very important one. Obviously one cannot ever prove that a drastic reduction in interval is *impossible*, because the number of yet-to-be-tried input patterns will always be indefinitely large. Our intuition nevertheless tells us that such a reduction is most improbable—that cognitive development, like physical growth, cannot be accelerated beyond certain fairly tight limits, however well-designed and intensive the educational program.* This question, too, will be taken up again, in our concluding section on the functional aspects of development.

Notice that what has just been said does not concern the prior transition from not-in-competence to first-in-competence. How should this transition be conceptualized, and should it be construed as abrupt or gradual in nature? We cannot at present offer any very illuminating suggestions on this matter. One possibility is that the typical competence item (rule, operation) one would be interested in is actually an integrated combination of several subitems. The subitems might individually enter the system quite abruptly, but in staggered order over an extended period of time. From the standpoint of their eventual integration, the competence item could be said to have shown a relatively abrupt emergence; from the standpoint of the separate sub-items, its acquisition could be said to have had an extended course, i.e. to be "gradual" in a certain sense.

* This position reflects no animus against educational-psychological research, let alone against education as a developmental force. First, we are quite prepared to believe that *some* manipulation of the interval is always possible and often desirable. And second, we do not believe that accelerating cognitive development is the only or even the most important educational objective. The object of education, to our mind, is to produce some desired kind of adult, not at first but at last, not the "fustest" but with the "mostest."

There is a second sense in which cognitive development could be characterized as "abrupt," "saltatory," "discontinuous," and the like. There might be certain periods, as contrasted with certain other periods, in which development somehow seems to take a giant step, irrespective of the rapidity of transition from first-in competence to always-in-performance. We might want to say that a relatively large number of new cognitive skills enter competence at about the same time at a certain point in ontogenesis, or that cognitive acquisitions of particular importance emerge then. The impression of a growth spurt here does not derive from the rapidity with which components stabilize and generalize, but rather from the fact that a number of components evolve at the same time, or that what develops is especially conspicuous or noteworthy. The major episodes of transition in Piaget's developmentology come to mind: the movement from sensorimotor intelligence to representational intelligence, from preoperations to concrete operations, and from concrete operations to formal ones. The transition from preoperations to concrete operations has received considerable attention in this respect, and many would agree with White (1965) that something very important happens to the child's cognitive program between five and seven years of age. How accurate is such a picture of cognitive developments—one of peaks and troughs, of alternating periods of greater and lesser change? It is partly a matter of value judgments, of course. If we agree that the acquisitions that typically occur during one ontogenetic period are more numerous, important, far-reaching, or whatever than those of another period, then such a picture is "accurate" by consensus. There is a more interesting consideration here, however. We wonder how much the current picture of uneven development owes to our current knowledge or, if you prefer, our current ignorance. It is largely based on Piaget's theory and research which properly and inevitably, have been highly selective with regard to methods used and phenomena studied. We should not be at all surprised to find some future theorist making an excellent case for the simply momentous cognitive changes that take place, say, during the three- to five-year-old span. Since his discoveries would not likely gainsay the hard core of Piaget's accomplishments, the outcome would be that an apparent unevenness across one segment of childhood is effectively reduced. Developmentalists would then say that some very important things happen between three and five and that some other things, quite different but equally important, happen between five and seven. We have already given as our opinion that development is typically not very saltatory as regards the transition from first-in-competence to always-in-performance for a single component. We would add here that it will also probably appear less and less saltatory in the sense under discussion as the gaps in our factual knowledge about cognitive growth are gradually filled and as new theories emerge to compete with present ones.

Sequential patterning of cognitive structures

The other major question regarding the temporal aspects of cognitive development is: Do some or all cognitive acquisitions enter the child's repertoire in a constant, invariant sequence, or does their order of attainment vary from child to child, within or across cultures. It must be said at the outset that no general and definitive answers can be given to this question at the present time. In the first place, it is most unlikely that the field has yet identified all the cognitive acquisitions, or even all the important ones. In the second place, there are difficult measurement problems in establishing invariant versus variant sequence for those acquisitions that it has identified. Probably the most unambiguous way to state that two acquisitions A and B invariably emerge in that order for all children is to say that A always enters competence before B does. But inferences about competence can be made only on the basis of overt performance, and we have already discussed the problems involved in making such inferences. Any tests used to diagnose the presence of A and B as competence items will necessarily entail a hard-to-assess quantum of automaton "noise." Depending on the relative amounts of such noise in the two tests, one might be led to conclude, erroneously, that B invariably precedes A, or that the order is A-B for some children and B-A for others.

Although, as we have said, substantive answers to the sequence question cannot yet be had, it is possible at least to make a preliminary analysis of the question and to make some plausible guesses about the answers. To begin with, it seems to us that sequential variance or invariance should be regarded as only a symptom or indicator of something far more important, namely, the kind of functional relation that holds among the acquisitions in question. If it turns out that A precedes B in everyone's development, there must be a reason for it, and this reason may be found in the kind of connection obtaining between A and B, or between each of these and other developmental events. Similarly, if the A-B temporal order keeps permuting from individual to individual, this fact could also reflect the nature of the relation linking the two acquisitions. Table 1 shows the principal kinds of functional relations that may hold between any two cognitive acquisitions, and also the temporal relations (variant versus invariant order of emergence) that we think may be associated with each. Let us examine each row of the table in turn.

Table 1   Corresponding Functional and Temporal
Relations for Pairs of Cognitive Acquisitions

Type of Relations	
FUNCTIONAL	TEMPORAL
None or Remote	Variant * or Invariant
Substitution	Invariant (?)
Implicative Mediation	Invariant
Nonimplicative Mediation	Variant or Invariant

* "Variant" includes the possibility of simultaneous acquisition as well as the two possible sequences A-B and B-A.

None or remote   This category refers to the case where A and B are unrelated or very distantly related, e.g. linked only via a long series of intervening acquisitions. It is no surprise that order of emergence may be variable from individual to individual in such instances. All one needs are two acquisitions whose group mean ages of attainment happen to be roughly equal; some individuals will likely attain them in the order A-B, some in the order B-A, and some will attain both at about the same time. The child's initial version of some political concept (e.g. his first coherent image of the President) and the attainment of number conservation might be a case in point: roughly synchronous acquisitions, functionally unrelated or remotely related, and order of emergence variable from child to child.

It is less obvious but equally true that for certain As and Bs in this category the acquisitional sequence may be strictly invariant. Thus, for instance, Piaget's secondary circular reaction surely enters every child's repertoire before the concept of correlation does, but this fact would not lead one to infer much of a functional relation between the two.* In such cases there is, of course, a reason for the sequential invariance, but the developmental psychologist will likely find little profit in uncovering it.

Substitution   The following is the paradigmatic case of Substitution. At some point in development, A emerges as a cognitive item that is utilized in a certain class of situations. At some later time, B enters the repertoire and gradually preempts A's functions, effectively substituting for A in these situations. Furthermore, A and B are formally unrelated; their only similarity lies in the fact that they apply to the same domain. Hence, there is no sense in which one could say that B incorporates A, is an extension or elaboration of A, and so on. A is not typically (and perhaps not ever) banished completely from the repertoire with the advent of B. It remains as a potential substitute for B and

---

* This example illustrates a distinction between what we might call "strong" versus "weak" sequential invariance. A sequence is strongly invariant if it is both universally present and universally fixed in the childhoods of undamaged human beings. For instance, we imagine that all intact human infants achieve primary and tertiary circular reactions, and achieve them in that order only. A sequence is weakly invariant if, when present, it is universally fixed. One may be able to find children who do not attain A, or B, or both; but for all children who do attain both, the order of attainment is the same. For example, individuals in a certain culture may never achieve any kind of naturalistic view of the nature of dreams, or never grasp the concept of correlation, or both, and yet the acquisitional sequence of these two notions may be the same for all individuals—in another culture, perhaps—who do in fact acquire both.

may be actualized under certain conditions, e.g. fatigue, distraction, or other regression-inducing circumstances.

Many of the cognitive-developmental changes that mark the transition from preoperations to concrete operations appear to fit this paradigm. One would hardly say that the four-year-old's perception-dominated approach to conservation and other problems is incorporated into the eight-year-old's inferential approach (as, for example, concrete operations are incorporated into formal ones); rather, one mode of solution is simply displaced by another, quite different mode. Similarly, the young child's moral and causal concepts do not form a part of, or lead to (except temporally) the qualitatively different concepts in these domains that he will subsequently form; again, the relation seems to be simply that of replacement or substitution. In these and other instances of substitution, it is probable that the earlier form coexists with the later one in a state of suppression and may reassert itself from time to time under certain conditions.

Is it the case for all A-B pairs related by Substitution that their order of emergence is invariant across individuals? We suspect that it is at least weakly invariant for all pairs, but as Table 1 implies, we are not sure. The invariance is most certain where B corresponds to the adult cognitive item. For instance, it would be most implausible to find a child who began with inference-based conservation and in later years replaced it with perception-based nonconservation. On the other hand, two immature As and Bs (both eventually replaced, say, by some adult C) could conceivably emerge in the sequence A-B for some individuals and B-A for others.

Implicative mediation A plays a far more constructive role vis-à-vis B in the case of both Implicative and Nonimplicative Mediation than was true for Substitution. The following is the model of an Implicative Mediation relation. First, A develops. Sooner or later thereafter, B develops. The exercise of B always and necessarily implies the exercise of A, because A forms a part or subset of B by definition. It is, of course, quite possible for the child to be capable of A but not yet capable of B; indeed, this is presumably the case for some period of time during his development. However, it is logically impossible for him to be capable of B and incapable of A, because A is literally reenacted whenever B is utilized, together with whatever other conceptual ingredients go to make up B. An A of this kind plays a vital developmental role, not only because it is itself a new and presumably useful addition to the repertoire, but also because it constitutes an insufficient but decidedly necessary condition for the acquisition of B.

This kind of relation between pairs of acquisitions should be of particular interest to the developmental psychologist for two reasons. Instances of this relation are both numerous and important. For example, concrete and formal operations are linked in just this way. Providing one accepts Piaget's characterization of what these operations consist of, it is logically possible for the child to be capable of the former and incapable of the latter, but not conversely. Formal operations are supposed to take the products of concrete operations as their objects, and hence presuppose the capability to exercise these operations. Similarly, preoperations presuppose the attainment of the capacity to symbolize (Piaget's "symbolic function"); the ability to multiply or coordinate two relations presupposes the ability to apprehend the two relations individually; the representation of class hierarchies implies the ability to represent a single class; and so on and on. It is clear that to ignore logico-developmental relations of this sort is to ignore a very substantial portion of our subject matter.

The existence of these relations poses something of a conundrum for the developmental psychologist, however. We are accustomed to thinking of ourselves as students of nature, not of logic, and we seek to discover, rather than reason out, the developmental connections between acquisitions. If somebody predicts that a pair of acquisitions A and B emerge in a fixed and invariant order for all children, our immediate inclination is to want to test the prediction empirically. In the case of acquisitions linked by Implicative Mediation, however, it is hard to see the justification for any kind of empirical test.

This problem of when to test for sequential invariance and when not to has arisen in at least one actual investigation. Dr.

Ellin Kofsky carried out her dissertation study (1966) on the development of classification skills, under the supervision of Flavell. Her particular interest was to establish the developmental order of acquisition of a number of these skills by means of scalogram analysis. For some pairs of skills, the question of order of emergence was very definitely an empirical one; while there might have been a well-reasoned hypothesis that the sequence would be such and such, it was clearly not logically impossible for the hypothesis to be wrong. Other pairs, however, seemed in retrospect (unfortunately not in prospect) to be of just the kind under discussion. For example, she tested the prediction that children would acquire the ability to group two like objects together before they acquired the ability to recognize that such groupings should be exhaustive, i.e. that each and every object possessing the common attribute should be put in the same pile—none should be left apart and unclassified. But it now seems clear that no empirical data could possibly contradict this hypothesis, because being able to think of putting all the red objects on the table together in a pile logically implies that one can think of putting some of them together, while the converse does not hold. Any empirical deviations from this logically necessary sequence have to be attributable to measurement error or other difficulties.

We do not hold, of course, that As and Bs tied together in this peculiar fashion are of no interest to the student of cognitive development. Their existence in the ontogenetic stream is as real as their relation is logical, and hence they must be included in the developmental story. However, testing "hypotheses" about sequential relations in such cases does seem to be an unprofitable exercise where the investigator is sure that the relation is of this type. Fortunately for the empirically minded, not all As that may serve as developmentally productive antecedents to Bs are logically necessary antecedents, as we shall now show.

Nonimplicative mediation   This refers to the situation where the advent of some A may help mediate the subsequent acquisition of some B, but where this mediative role is not assured, as in the previous case, simply from the definitions of A and B. Unlike the case with Substitution, one can see how A really could be a constructive force in the evolution of B; but unlike the case with Implicative Mediation, one can also entertain the possibility of B's developing independently of A. For example, Piaget has suggested that the growing ability to multiply or to coordinate height and width relations plays an important mediative function in the child's acquisition of conservation of liquid quantity. This hypothesis is plausible, in the sense that one could specify the way in which this ability might serve as an important bridge to the conservation concept. At the same time, its validity *could* be doubted and, indeed, it actually has been (Bruner, Olver, & Greenfield, 1966, Ch. 9).

A wide variety of Nonimplicative Mediation patterns is possible, depending upon the nature of the acquisitions in question. The hypothetical pattern most reminiscent of Implicative Mediation is the following: A invariably precedes B in ontogenesis and equally invariably assists in its construction. It might be the case, for example, that while coordination of relations is not logically necessary to the attainment of quantity conservation, all children do in fact acquire them in that order and do in fact make use of the first in attaining the second. Assuming that universal sequences of this kind were to be discovered, how to account for them?

One might try to explain them by appeals to universally shared experiences, commonalities in the environmental inputs to all growing humans. If such experiences could insure the universal acquisition of A, one need only add the assumption that children are constructed in such a way that they will automatically make use of that which is useful, i.e. since A can mediate B, it will eventually be so utilized by children. Thus, a young human mind operating on the "species-typical environment" will inevitably acquire A, so the argument goes, and this same mind will then inevitably use A to get B. This argument carries with it the implication that the A-B sequence is not biologically necessary, and that it might be possible to achieve B by a different route through suitable modifications in the environmental inputs. The alternative possibility is that the A-B sequence is somehow rooted in human cognitive embryology, and that drastic modification of the environment might prevent the acquitision of B, but it could not effect a B that was unmediated by A. Asking why the child invariably achieves A before B would then be akin to asking why his nervous system develops as it does, or why he always acquires milk teeth before adult dentition.

There may be certain pairs of acquisitions, on the other hand, for which the sequence is less fixed and the mediative connection less universal. One conceivable pattern is that in which a certain A is invariably used to help mediate a certain B whenever it is acquired before B, but in point of fact it is not acquired before B in all developmental histories. Alternatively, it may not invariably serve this mediative function even for those children who do acquire A first; that is, only a subset of these children utilize A in this fashion. Both of these patterns imply that the B in question can be mediated by A but can also be mediated otherwise, i.e. there exists some X (or Xs) that can serve as a developmental surrogate for A. There could be yet another pattern that subsumes these two, a pattern in which A and B play reciprocal developmental roles: A will (for some or all children) mediate B if A develops first, and B will (for some or all children) mediate A if B develops first. Something like this reciprocal arrangement might exist even inside a single skin: a child begins to make progress on one of the two acquisitions, this progress helps to mediate a beginning on the other, and so on back and forth, leading eventually to the mastery of both.

These manifold possibilities can also be exemplified in terms of the conservation example. Some children may acquire the ability to coordinate relations prior to acquiring the conservation concept, and some may not. For those who do, this ability may help to mediate the concept in all cases or only in some. Those who do not attain the concept via the coordination of relations can do so in some other fashion, perhaps by making use of their knowledge that no liquid has been added or subtracted during the pouring operation. Of those children who achieve conservation before coordination, some or all may utilize the former in the acquisition of the latter. And finally, some children may achieve them more or less synchronously, each developmental increment in the one (either one) mediating increments in the other.

It is apparent that the definition of Nonimplicative as opposed to Implicative Mediation allows for a wide range of logically possible A-B patterns, and the interesting question is whether any or all of them actually hold true in real ontogenetic histories. Their existence would imply that there can be alternative developmental paths to a given cognitive product, and that children may not all acquire the same things in the same way (Flavell, 1966). Such flexibility in potential means could conceivably be highly adaptive for our species, given all the individual variation in its members and in their life experiences which obtains. A diversity of ontogenetic routes might thus be plausible as well as possible, and empirical probes for the existence of these several patterns might accordingly be a worthwhile research venture.

In this section we have discussed the question of developmental sequence from the standpoint of the various functional relations that may hold between cognitive acquisitions, since, presumably, these relations account for the sequences found. Of the four types of relations described, Substitution, Implicative Mediation, and Nonimplicative Mediation are obviously of greatest interest, and it may be worthwhile to make a brief additional examination of the similarities and differences among these three. It appears that sequences related by Implicative and Nonimplicative Mediation are the real locus of developmental progress, with Substitution pairs constituting a kind of phenotypic reflection of this progress. If B replaces A à la Substitution, how shall this fact be explained? As we have seen, A cannot itself explain or account for the B that eventually substitutes for it. Rather, the explanation must lie in the acquisition of something else (singular or plural) that is capable of playing this constructive role. This something else—call it A′—must then be related to B via Mediation, it seems to us. Thus, while substitutions do mirror the fact of developmental progress, they do not directly mark the essential ingredients of this progress. If an inferential strategy for coping with a conservation problem comes to replace a naïve-perceptual one, we know that cognitive progress has been made, but we do not know what other developmental happenings made the inferential strategy available to the child.

The stage concept and its role in cognitive development

The meaning and significance of the developmental-stage concept   The problem of stages of development has been discussed at length in the literature, but without any real agreement as to the status to be assigned to this concept, or the criteria that might enable us to tell a stage when we see it. The most extended consideration of this question, in a symposium specifically devoted to it (Osterrieth, et al., 1955), brings out above all the great diversity of uses of the term and of opinions as to its value and applicability to different aspects of development.

Most typically, the stage concept is invoked to refer to a mode, pattern, or constellation of behaviors (or dispositions towards behavior) that seems to characterize some definable period in the child's life, be this period specified in terms of chronological age (with the resultant difficulty of taking individual differences in rate of development into account) or in terms of its position in a sequence. The expression, "The stage of infancy," would exemplify the former, while "the crawling stage" would illustrate the latter use.

This immediately brings us to one of the chief questions to be raised with respect to developmental stages, namely the range of behavioral responses that they are intended to encompass. Depending on the answer given to this question, "stage" may vary from a purely descriptive term specifying a particular response or form of behavior appearing at a given time to a convenient though equally descriptive shorthand standing for a wide array of behaviors that appear at approximately the same point in the life span. The two examples just given also serve to illustrate the narrowly specific ("crawling stage") as against the highly nonspecific ("stage of infancy") poles of this dimension of generality.

We suggest that somewhere between these two extremes the stage concept reaches its optimal level of generality, in the sense that it has reference to a diversity of behaviors that are still interrelated, whether by way of certain structural relationships that bind them together or by some common behavioral or functional core. In either case the degree of generality of the behavior referred to invests the stage concept with a status clearly transcending the purely descriptive level and approaching more closely to the level of explanation identified with the hypothetical construct.

This point is well illustrated in the Freudian use of the stage concept. Thus the "oral stage" refers to a constellation of separable responses implicating the zone of the mouth. This concept is most effectively exploited in its application to adult behavior, where it may refer to response tendencies as varied as a penchant for ice cream cones, a habit of chain smoking, or an inclination to engage in vociferous argument.

It is apparent, then, that at such intermediate levels of generality the postulation of a stage can serve to unify a set of otherwise quite disparate and seemingly unrelated behaviors or traits, much as the postulation of a mysterious force called "gravity" brought an underlying unity into a most diverse set of phenomena in physics and astronomy. To the extent, furthermore, that such an array of behaviors appears (or disappears) at the same time during development, the stage concept can help account for this temporal unity. For instance, if we say that little Johnny has started masturbating *because* he has reached the phallic stage, this statement escapes circularity, both because his assignment to that stage can be determined from or verified by other related behaviors (curiosity about the sex organs and the birth process, sex play in nursery school), and because on the basis of his prior passage through the anal stage we would predict him to be in the phallic stage at this time.

This conception of developmental stage is particularly pertinent to the field of cognitive development, notably as formulated by Piaget; in his system this unifying aspect constitutes in fact one of the criteria of the stage concept.

Stage as a structurally defined entity   The explanation of the central place that this aspect of the stage concept occupies in Piaget's system touches on a fundamental property of cognitive development itself, which any viable theory in this area must recognize. Harking back to the competence-automaton distinction invoked in the first part of this paper, it is apparent that any attempt to handle the problems of cognitive development that leaves room for the competence component must be couched in structural terms, that is, involving recourse to constructs such as rules, programs, operations and the like that transcend particular overt responses. For instance, in handling the child's development in the area of classification skills, we require constructs referring to the rules by which the child organizes an array of objects or stimuli into a set of categories, to switching mechanisms by which he shifts from one such rule to another, to nested structures enabling him to deal with subordinate-superordinate class relationships, and so on. These constructs then permit an analysis of the child's development with respect to these various kinds of skills, be they manifested in sorting or matching-from-sample tasks, in the solution of matrix problems, in spontaneous clustering in free recall, or in responses given to Piaget's class-inclusion questions.

The considerable achievement of Piaget is that he has provided us with a system or model of intellectual development that not only affords a basis for conceptualizing children's behaviors in cognitive tasks in such generalized structural terms—as illustrated in his concept of "concrete operations"—but also delineates the process of cognitive development as a series of successive approximations to these structures. Let us look at this matter in more detail.

Piaget's "concrete operations" consist of a set of eight "groupings," representing formal, quasi-logical structures or rules. Not all of these are equally meaningful or relevant to behavior (Flavell, 1963; Wohlwill, 1966a); for purposes of illustration we shall select one of the more useful ones, that concerned with class multiplication. A child who possesses this structure in his repertoire (i.e. whose program includes rules necessary for handling multipleclassification problems) should be able to solve all of the following types of tasks: sorting, oddity-discrimination, matching-from-sample or concept-induction problems entailing multiple cues; class-intersection problems; and matrix problems such as the Raven.

To the extent that tasks as diverse as those just cited are handled in an equivalent fashion by a child, to the extent, that is, that the stages of cognitive development do indeed exhibit this unitary character that Piaget has designated by his term, "structures d'ensemble," we require structural constructs of the concrete-operations type, linking diverse task behaviors, to construct an adequate competence-model of the child's intellectual development. This point seems to be too readily ignored by those who are tempted to chuck Piaget's apparatus of logical and quasilogical structures overboard, on the grounds either of the inconsistencies and contradictions in the system of logic he employs, or of the apparent lack of parsimony of these constructs for the interpretation of the child's overt behavior. To paraphrase Voltaire's dictum concerning the deity: if there were no such structures in the mind of the child, we should have to invent them, to account for the degree of consistency and orderliness that we do find in his cognitive development.

Just how far does this consistency extend? Empirical investigations of intertask consistency in performance have, to be sure, not always revealed the kind of close correspondence between success or failure on structurally equivalent tasks on the part of a given child that Piaget's system appears to demand, and that he has explicitly postulated on many occasions. Both at a theoretical and an empirical level, however, the picture is a good deal more complex than a simple verdict of "case unproven" would indicate.

The problem of the transition period   There are very good reasons, in fact, that empirical tests of the intertask consistency hypothesis implied in Piaget's use of the stage concept are apt to come to grief. Were we to limit ourselves to children who are either well below the stage (e.g. deeply entrenched in the prior stage of preoperational thought) or in whom the stage had already become firmly established (e.g. a group of preadolescents, on the threshold of formal operations), such consistency would be virtually a foregone conclusion: the child would either fail or succeed across the board, though occasional exceptions to the latter might occur as a function of lapse of attention, difficulties at the information-processing level, and so forth. It is only during the period of transition from one stage to the next, therefore, that the consistency question becomes empirically interesting. Thus the strongest version of the intertask consistency postulate would be that the child's responses on a set of interrelated tasks *undergo changes during the course of his development* in a strictly synchronous fashion. Yet, upon closer examination, such a postulate is paradoxically revealed as quite implausible, and it is hardly surprising that data bearing on it should have turned out negatively for the most part.

Let us note, first of all, that Piaget has placed a quite unnecessarily heavy burden of proof upon himself, by stipulating that *all* of the various concrete operations (i.e. all of the several groupings) develop in unison. There appears to be no reason that the *structures d'ensemble* could not be looked at as a family of separate structures, each following its own developmental timetable. While this would clearly delimit the scope of the concepts invoked and would require the specification of stages in more limited terms, referring to particular structures, a considerable degree of unifying power could be retained, as shown above with respect to the multiplication-of-classes case.

But even restricting ourselves to a single grouping, or domain, we can expect to find departure from intertask consistency during the transition period. For it is precisely during this period in which the newly emerging structures are in process of formation that the child's responses may be expected to oscillate from one occasion to the next, to be maximally susceptible to the effects of task-related variables, and accordingly to evince a relative absence of consistency. Piaget has given implicit recognition to this circumstance: he has provided for a stabilization phase, in which newly formed structures are undergoing consolidation, as one of the features of the formation of a stage, and he has proposed his concept of horizontal "décalages" to account for differentials in performance, relating to the particular content of a task or to a variety of situational variables. In the context of his system, these notions represent purely ad hoc constructs. It is possible to look at them, however, as referring to aspects of the automaton side of the model, concerned with the mechanisms for coding and processing information, rather than with the reasoning process as such. As we shall show below, this may enable us to take such differentials into account more systematically and effectively, while staying within the overall framework of Piaget's structural system.

It is apparent from the foregoing analysis that to deal with the facts in this area, and in particular with the interrelationships among structures and performances during the period of transition, a considerable extension and elaboration of Piaget's model will be required. We shall attempt to sketch the outlines of such an extended model presently, in which, incidentally, the notions of transition and consolidation of stages will be invested with new meaning. To set the stage for this effort, it will be useful to consider first a pioneering study on this problem by Nassefat (1963), which brings out in an illuminating fashion the dependence of intertask consistency on the stage-stabilization and -consolidation process. Indeed, in spite of certain severe limitations of a statistical nature, this ambitious investigation stands as a model of the approach to research required to shed light on the manner in which stage-dependent behaviors become established. It will thus repay us to examine it in some detail.

The Nassefat study Nassefat's research concerns the transition from concrete to formal operations in the age period from nine to thirteen years. He selected 150 Ss in this age range, and administered to them a set of 48 items, falling into six domains, dealing with both concrete and formal operations (e.g. probability problems, problems involving the lever principle, conservation of volume, and so on). For each item a number of different response categories were empirically set up into which the responses were classified; the number of such categories varied from a low of 2 (equivalent to Pass-Fail) to as many as 20. Each item was classified as *Concrete* (C) or *Formal* (F), in terms of the operations assumed to be required for adequate performance; roughly one-third of the items were, however, assigned to an *Intermediate* (I) category, based on ambiguities or inconsistencies in the responses actually given by the Ss. The response categories for each item were subsequently combined, and further collapsed to form a four-point ordinal scale, representing different levels of performance in regard to the sorting out of relevant from irrelevant information, combined with failure versus success in the inferences that the child drew from the pertinent information.

The analysis of the data proceeded along a series of fronts. Having first demonstrated the validity of the ordinal response scale as a measure of developmental level attained on a given item (the *taus* for the association between response type and age level were for the most part highly significant), Nassefat turned to an analysis of the scalability of the data in the Guttman sense, based simply on dichotomous, Pass-Fail response measures. Scalability was assessed *separately* for each age level and for each of the three item categories (C, I, and F) in terms of both Green's index of consistency and Loevinger's index of homogeneity. Restricting ourselves to the former, we find consistency generally highest at the age level at which the discriminative power of each item category is maximal, i.e. at age nine for the C items, at age eleven for the I, at age twelve for the F. (Actually, the consistency of items in the F category never exceeds .25, apparently reflecting the fact that even at the oldest age level only a minority of Ss passed them.)

The interesting feature of this scalogram analysis is that it is used, *not* for the usual purpose of establishing a developmental sequence (since the analysis is carried out separately for each age level), but rather to determine the degree of homogeneity, i.e. unitary dimensionality, characterizing a particular item domain. The assumption is that the acquisition of the requisite mental structures is essential to bring out such dimensionality— just as, in measuring attitudes concerning a given topic, responses on a Guttman scale should prove scalable only for respondents who had formed a set of crystallized and articulated attitudes toward that topic. Nassefat regards this progressive homogenization of the item domain as one of the signs of the stabilization of the stage reached by the child; for the C items, this is already present at the youngest age level included in the study (nine years), since the process of acquisition of concrete operations is in general completed by that time; conversely, for the F items, it is clear that the homogenization is still far from complete at age thirteen, i.e. the stage of Formal Operations is still in process of elaboration at the oldest age level included.

Nassefat points to other evidence, partly from interrelations in the responses to items within a category, in support of his concept of the transition period as one during which performance across formally equivalent tasks becomes progressively more consistent. The discrepancy between these correlational analyses and the scalability data belies the interpretation he gives them as representing equivalent measures of the degree of stabilization or homogenization of a stage. Nevertheless, if the data can be taken at face value (and it must be admitted that serious difficulties of a statistical nature arise with respect to Nassefat's treatment of the data, both in the scalability and in the correlational analyses), they seem to fit into an enlarged framework within which the changes occurring during the process of the child's transition from one stage to the next may be encompassed.

A general model for the analysis of the formation of stages of intelligence   Let us distinguish at the outset between two determinants of the child's performance in a cognitive task: A, the rules, structures, or "mental operations" embodied in the task, and B, the actual mechanisms required for processing the input and output. (The correspondence of these two entities to the competence-automaton distinction discussed previously is apparent.)

We may now specify three parameters that jointly determine a child's performance: P_a, the probability that the operation will be functional in a given child; P_b, a coefficient applying to a given task or problem, and determining whether, given a functional operation, the information will be correctly coded and processed; and k, a parameter expressing the weight to be attached to the P_b factor in a given child. P_a and k are thus parameters characterizing a particular child at a given age level, while P_b characterizes a particular item or task. Let us examine these parameters more closely.

P_a reflects the degree to which a given operation has become fully established in a particular child. The assumption here is that, during the period of transition from preoperational to operational thought these structures have a probabilistic character, appearing now in evidence, now absent. This view may seem to run counter to the abruptness or discontinuity position frequently identified with respect to Piaget's concept of stages, but the fact is that his Stage II phenomena abound with instances of children's vacillating between conservation and nonconservation, or between an intuitive and an operational concept of length, for example. This uncertainty and instability, which is convincingly illustrated in many of the protocols to be found throughout Piaget's books, may be expressed in terms of a value of P_a changing from 0 in the preoperational period to 1.0 when the operation has become established.

P_b, according to our model, is an attribute of the task. It represents the likelihood for any given task that the operation, if functional, will in fact be called into play, and its end product be translated into the desired output. The value of this factor may also be expected to vary between 0 and 1, depending on a host of factors related to task-difficulty: the stimulus materials and their familiarity, the manner of presentation of the relevant information and the amount of irrelevant information from which it has to be abstracted, the sheer magnitude of the information load placed on the child in dealing with the problem, the role played by memory and sequential processing of information, and so on. (See Aebli, 1963; Smedslund, 1966, for more detailed treatments of the role of these variables.) Thus, presumably, this factor is responsible for the horizontal *décalages* that we find not only in Piaget's own studies, but also in much Piagetian research generally.

Yet the influence of these task-related variables itself varies with age. For the average five-year-old the likelihood of success in placing a set of 10 stimuli in order of size may be considerably smaller than it would be for only 6 stimuli, for instance, whereas for a ten-year-old there may be little difference. This is the reason for introducing the parameter k, or more particularly its complement, $1-k$, as a power to which P_b is to be raised. The parameter is intended to express the weight that the P_b corresponding to a particular task carries for a given child, depending on that child's ability to abstract the information required to utilize a particular operation, and to code and process information generally. For the sake of simplicity, we shall assume that k varies from 0, at a relatively early phase of the establishment of an operation, to an ideal of 1.0, when the stage has become fully consolidated; accordingly, the influence of P_b, when raised to $(1-k)$, should be expected to decrease progressively over this period.

We may now write the equation

$$P(+) = P_a \times P_b^{1-k}$$

to show the probability of a given child, characterized by particular values P_a and k, solving a task with some particular value of P_b. The course of the formation of a new cognitive structure may accordingly be described in terms of a four-phrase process:

Phase 1: In the initial phase, $P_a = 0$, i.e. the child, lacking a given operation, must fail all of the problems demanding that operation. This corresponds clearly to Piaget's stage of preoperational thought (designated as Stage I in his writings).

Phase 2: In this transitional stage, P_a changes from 0 to 1.0, while k is assumed to remain equal to 0, or close to it. (This would seem to be a reasonable assumption, not only because the role of situational and task-related variables would be expected to be maximal during the period in which the operation is still in process of becoming established, but also because the abstraction of relevant information is necessarily dependent on the establishment of the operation.) Thus $P(+) = P_a \times P_b$. This means that for the most part, during this phase, the child will still fail most tasks based on the operation; for instance, if $P_a = .5$ (e.g. in the middle of this phase), and for a task of medium difficulty for which $P_b = .5$, then $P(+) = .25$. Thus in terms of any criterion of operational-level responses, the child at this phase must still be considered preoperational. He should, moreover, manifest the kinds of oscillations and intermediary forms of reasoning characteristic of this transitional period, which Piaget designates by II-A and II-B.

Phase 3: This is the period of stabilization and consolidation of the operation, which has now become functional, i.e. $P_a = 1.0$. At the start of this period, however, success will still vary with the demands placed on the subject by the particular task, i.e. the value of P_b for that task. During the course of this phase the contribution of this factor progressively decreases, i.e. 1-k decreases from 1.0 towards an ideal state of 0. This would seem to correspond most closely to the stage designated by Piaget as III-A.

Phase 4: This is the terminal phase of univocal success, in which $P_a = 1.0$ and $k = 1.0$, i.e. S is able to bring the operation to bear on the problem successfully, regardless of the situational and task variables involved. In practice one may presume that k always falls somewhat short of 1.0, even at the most advanced levels; but unless P_b is very low (i.e. task difficulty very great, as in a task of ordering a series of tones, for instance), the net result will still be an expectation of success, $P(+)$, close to 1.0.*

Perhaps the most arguable aspect of the above model concerns the distinction proposed between Phases 2 and 3. Why not simply postulate a single transitional stage in which P_a and k are changing concomitantly? It may be that when all the data are in, this will be the most parsimonious view. Yet both conceptual clarity and certain empirical findings compel us to distinguish between the stabilization of the intrinsic components of the stage-related operations (the competence aspect) and the changes in the child's ability to apply these operations to a particular content.†

---

* It is likely that for measures such as latency, the value of 1-k will remain considerably higher. This would be in line with the findings of Suppes, Hyman, and Jerman (1966), in applying a mathematical model based on information-processing considerations to children's performance on a variety of arithmetic problems. In a number of instances there was a strong indication that error data gave rise to functions that were qualitatively different from those for the latency data.

† In this respect, a comparison between our model and that proposed by Aebli (1963), who has similarly concerned himself with the role of task-related variables, may be illuminating. Aebli reduces the level of functioning of the operation demonstrated by a child to a joint multiplicative function of a variety of such variables (number of elements in the task, complexity of the stimulus field, number of cues available, and so on). Thus one obtains, falsely it would seem, a

First, Phases 2 and 3, as we have described them, seem to bear more than an accidental relation to Piaget's Stages II and III-A, thus strengthening the case for treating them as part of an ordered sequence. Second, the evidence adduced by Nassefat that a set of stage-related items goes through a period of low homogeneity before attaining maximal scalability seems to provide one instance of the separability of Phases 2 and 3 (recall our discussion of the meaning to be attached to Nassefat's scalability data, based on the role of task-related variables). A study by Uzgiris (1964) investigating the development of conservation of substance, weight, and volume for three different types of materials, between Grades 1 and 6, also gives evidence of Phase 2 periods during which intercorrelations for performance with the different materials go into relative decline.

Third, a number of instances can be cited that bear out the reality of Phase 3 phenomena, in which the requisite operations appear to have come into existence, but are variably functional, depending on the demands for information-processing that the task places on the subject. These are the many instances of *décalages,* e.g. the acquisition of conservation of number under changes in length of the rows of elements before it is shown for subdivision of a single pile of elements into two or more piles (Winer, 1966); the understanding of transitivity for $A < B$, $B < C$ before it appears for $A < B$, $C > B$ (Glick & Wapner, 1966); the precedence of success in copying a sequence of beads from a "necklace" pattern onto a straight line, over that found for the same task when the model sequence forms a figure eight (Lovell, 1959).

Several major points remain to be resolved, in regard to the definition of P_a, P_b, and k. As concerns P_a, the question arises: how broadly shall we define the domain over which this parameter will be assumed to apply? As pointed out earlier, Piaget treats the stage of "concrete operations" as an integrated, unitary

picture of the level of the child's performance that can be raised or lowered at will according to the nature of the task, no matter what the level of the child's own cognitive development. Most important, there is no room in this model for the structural relationships embodied in Piaget's concept of operations, and no picture of a progression of definable stages emerges from it, as it does from our model.

whole, i.e. a set of *structures d'ensemble*. But we also noted that there was little basis, on either empirical or theoretical grounds, for the assumption made by Piaget that all of the component operations comprising this stage *develop* in unison. The most profitable approach, therefore, would seem to be to let P_a refer to a particular rule or operation, e.g. class-multiplication, and to study each of these separately.

One of the consequences of this restrictive conception of P_a is that it forces us to distinguish between two kinds of horizontal *décalages:* those due to the automaton aspects of the cognitive process, that is, to the differential difficulties of the information-processing requirements of structurally equivalent tasks (e.g. conservation of discontinuous versus continuous quantity), and those relating to the competence aspects, i.e. to a differential rate of formation of the structures themselves—as in the apparent lag of transitivity behind conservation (Smedslund, 1964). It is apparent that only the first of these *décalages* can be handled by our model.

What about the second type? Here we come back to the earlier discussion of sequential relationships. In particular, it seems likely that many of the A → B sequences discussed under the heading of Nonimplicative Mediation represent cases of relationships among structures considered by Piaget to be formally equivalent and thus to emerge synchronously, but which in fact develop in a staggered sequence, due to the mediating role that one plays in the process of the formation of the other. An alternative situation is represented by the two-way relations, A ⇆ B, where A appears to mediate B in some children, while the reverse is true for others. These will not, of course, give rise to *décalages*, but only to randomly distributed deviations from intertask consistency in the study of structures in process of formation. They will obviously remain the most difficult to handle in a systematic account of cognitive development, for to do so one would need to have a basis for predicting which of the alternative courses any given child will follow. Perhaps we shall have to make allowance for a certain degree of indeterminacy in the study of cognitive development, brought about by such instances of vicarious mediation.

The second question to be disposed of concerns the definition of P_b, and its dependence on or independence of subject-related variables. We have tried earlier to give meaning to this parameter, in terms of the "cognitive strain" placed on the subject in dealing with the information-processing aspects of a problem, independently of his level of development, and to indicate denotatively some of the types of variables included under this heading. Yet it would be idle to pretend that we are able, at this time, to offer a fully satisfactory operational definition of this parameter, for to do so would require a complete account of the various task-related variables influencing the child's performance.

Furthermore, the probability of a child's meeting correctly the information-processing demands of a problem is surely a joint function of the problem and of the child who is tackling it. Is this interaction adequately represented by the parameter k? It must be admitted that the psychological meaning of this parameter is not specified in very simple terms; on the one hand it refers to information-coding and -processing ability generally, while on the other it refers to the ability to abstract the information that is relevant to a particular operation, and is thus dependent on the establishment of that operation. For instance, in a conservation-of-number situation, the child with a low value of k may succeed, as long as the elements whose number is to be conserved remain as discrete, discriminable elements under the transformation (e.g. a change in the length of the rows of a set of chips). On the other hand, if the elements lose their identity under the transformation (e.g. placing the chips in a vertical pile), focusing on the relevant information, that is, on the number of elements, may become too difficult to maintain, and conservation will be lost.

A further question is whether it is reasonable to attribute to k the status of a constant, over-all type of tasks. It may well be, for instance, that through training or experience, or conceivably even as a function of purely endogenous factors, some children may be better able to process information for one type of problem, while others will find some other type easier. If so, it would mean that k will have to be defined relative to a particular domain or type of information-processing problem. But in practice it would be difficult in any case to compare or equate the values of P_b for items from very disparate domains, on any except a purely pragmatic basis (e.g. how would one compare the increase in difficulty due to the addition of elements in a seriation task with that represented by a shift from a provoked to an unprovoked number-conservation problem?). It might be noted that this restriction on the generality of P_b and k is approximately on a par with that mentioned earlier for P_a.

Unity of stages reexamined   Finally, let us reexamine now, in the perspective of the model that has been presented above, the meaning of the stage concept itself, and in particular the unity-of-stages question. We have seen this concept recede in importance as a profitable source of empirical investigation on the problem of developmental stages, since this property could be taken for granted in children who had fully acquired it and would rarely be expected to apply during the period of transition.

This property of developmental stages is thus of limited significance as a source of empirically testable hypotheses; nonetheless the concept of *structures d'ensemble* remains of both theoretical and empirical consequence, in the sense that it provides a standard against which the progress of a child along the road to the establishment of the stage can be gauged. This is implicit in our four-phase conception of the transition and stabilization process, which considers consistency in performance across tasks as an ideal end product, and suggests the changing nature of the inter-task relations to be expected over the course of the development of the stage.

Specifically, the picture with respect to the interrelationship among operationally equivalent tasks now shapes up as follows: In Phase 1 there is failure across the board; correlations may thus be expected to be low, for lack of variance. During Phase 2, correlations should be low, due to the oscillations and inconsistencies in response implied by intermediate values of P_a. Towards the end of this phase and the beginning of Phase 3, consistency should become more apparent, with items with equivalent P_b's being passed about equally often, and with items with discrepant P_b's exhibiting a Guttman-type pattern. Finally in

Phase 4 (the terminal phase) there is success across the board, so that inter-item correlations should again drop to near zero.

This formulation, incidentally, points up the need for studies such as Nassefat's and Uzgiris's, in which, rather than being lumped together over an extended age range, these interrelationships are studied separately within fairly narrowly defined age groups. This may be seen more concretely in the Appendix to this paper, which presents a reanalysis of Uzgiris's (1962, 1964) original data, based on the individual Ss' response patterns. This analysis provides convincing evidence of the appropriateness of the four-phase sequence of stage formation that we have presented. However, the most satisfactory approach for the investigation of the process of the formation of a stage remains, of course, the longitudinal one.

The focus on stage as a set of structurally related entities also serves to place into proper perspective attempts to induce this or that individual concept experimentally, or through some short-term experience. Since this problem forms the subject of the concluding section of our paper, suffice it here to point out that, according to Piaget's view, and any similar structurally oriented conception of cognitive development, it is a far cry from the acquisition of a single concept, such as conservation of continuous quantity, to the elaborate network of concepts that mark the attainment of the stage of concrete operations.

Functional implications

In the many discussions and debates that have dealt with one aspect or another of Piaget's work and theoretical system, no topic has given rise to more vociferous argument than the question of the basis for the changes observed to take place in the reasoning processes of the developing child, i.e. the *mechanisms* of cognitive change.

This problem is clearly far too vast to allow us to provide a thorough treatment of it within the confines of this paper. We shall content ourselves with bringing out some of the main implications that we see emerging from our previous discussion of the development of cognitive structures for these functional questions of process and mechanism, and with pointing out some of the major limitations and shortcomings of the approaches that are current in research on these questions.

There are three major points to be brought out. They relate, first, to the competence-automaton distinction itself; second, to the stage concept and its structural characteristics; and third, to the character of the transition and stabilization phases through which cognitive structures in process of development pass.

In regard to the first point, it seems possible to differentiate between approaches that have focused on the automaton side and those that have tried to alter the child's cognitive system at the competence level. Among the first we would include the various attempts that have been made to neutralize irrelevant cues in a conservation task, e.g. Braine and Shank's (1965) approach, aimed at enhancing the child's differentiation between appearance and reality at the linguistic level, and screening techniques such as utilized by Frank (Bruner, Olver, & Greenfield, 1966), designed to shield the child from biasing perceptual cues. Among the second type, directed at the competence aspect itself, we have training in reversibility judgments (Wallach & Sprott, 1964) and addition-and-subtraction training (used by a number of investigators), aimed at inducing conservation; training for class-inclusion by intermediary of practice in class-intersection (Morf, 1959); and possibly approaches involving the learning of rules, such as used by Beilin (1965).

Either of these types of approaches may, of course, prove successful in a given instance, but the distinction we are proposing suggests that there may be important differences in the basis for the learning that results. In the first case we would argue that we are dealing either with one of two kinds of effects. We may have children who have already acquired the operation at the competence level, but fail to apply it in the given situation. The effect of the training, then, would be to facilitate access to the operation, as it were, by "stripping away the cobwebs lying in its path," allowing for more effective abstraction of the relevant information. (In terms of our model, training would increase the value of k, and thus render $P\,(+)$ more nearly equal to P_a, i.e. to unity.) Alternatively we may be dealing with children who are still in a transitional state with respect to the operation; for these, we would argue, the effect of the training is to produce only the semblance of a true operation, lacking the latter's resistance to extinction or generalizability (i.e. the concept may be learned as an empirical rule or fact, without raising P_a materially closer to 1.0). Thus, since the child's operational system will not have been affected, the learning produced should prove readily extinguishable, and show little transfer. Few if any of the observed findings in this area seem to be inconsistent with this interpretation, although the information required to establish its validity is lacking, in most instances.

Let us turn now to the second case, in which the child's operational system is attacked directly. What is the basis for the learning effects that are to be observed here? It is interesting to note that the methods employed in these situations generally entail practice in a concept or operation that is presumably related to the one to be acquired via a relationship of Nonimplicative Mediation, either of the uni- or the bidirectional variety. The repeated success of such approaches argues for the legitimacy of treating the relationship between the training and test concepts as involving true mediation. Yet it is significant that in most instances in which they have been employed little if any learning has taken place with respect to the mediator concepts themselves, raising the question of why they failed to mediate the test concept before training. It seems likely that the experience in these situations, where successful, operated to make functional an operation that probably was close to becoming established already at the start, so that it only required a certain amount of "priming" from the mediator utilized during the training session. It seems fair to state, then, that neither of the two above-mentioned approaches has thus far succeeded in providing any definitive answers to the "hows" and "whys" of cognitive development, or in isolating the necessary and sufficient conditions for cognitive change.

Let us consider the functional implications of the stage concept and its structural properties. It should be apparent that, if we wish to study the mechanisms governing the formation of stage-related concepts, we must recognize that these concepts are acquired as part of an intricate network of interrelated rules of operations, applicable to diverse contents and domains of reasoning and problem-solving behavior.

Note that there is both a vertical and a horizontal aspect to this question; both of these are of consequence for the investigation of the mechanisms of cognitive change. The vertical one refers to the sequence of steps involved in the attainment of a given concept or the formation of a given operation, which will determine the success to be expected from a particular training experience for a given child. Recognition of this vertical component implies a thorough analysis of the interrelationships, implicative and otherwise, that obtain among any constellation of interdependent concepts, along the lines sketched out in the earlier discussion of the sequence problem. It thus presupposes a thorough structural analysis of the concept domain of which the particular concept to be learned forms a part. It is interesting to note that those who have taken this point closest to heart thus far have predominantly represented, not the field of cognitive development, but rather the behaviorist's approach to programming children's learning. Foremost among these, in the degree to which he has rendered explicit the theoretical rationale for his approach, is undoubtedly Gagné, who has presented us with detailed accounts of the steps involved in the learning of certain mathematical rules at the junior high school level (Gagné, 1962) and more recently, in a hypothetical vein, in the acquisition of conservation of continuous quantity (Gagné, 1966).

For psychologists such as Gagné, and more particularly those operating from within a Skinnerian framework, it seems that the problem of the child's "readiness to learn" can in fact be reduced to the question of whether he has mastered all of the steps in the sequence that precede and are prerequisites for the concept to be learned. This assumption appears to ignore the problem of horizontal transfer, i.e. the interrelationships among cognitive structures that are coordinate as to level. Their relevance to the problem of learning derives from the strong possibility that "readiness to learn" is in part a question of what is to be learned, i.e. that the breadth of learning achieved by a given experience will vary as a function of the level attained by the child prior to the onset of the experience (Wohlwill, 1966b). This possibility, and the problem of horizontal transfer more generally, has been largely ignored by those approaching the programming of learning via the essentially linear, Skinnerian model. Again we find Gagné concerning himself more explicitly with this question, notably in his most recent statement (Gagné, 1966), but to a considerable extent his treatment still assumes that learning will take place within a rather narrowly circumscribed domain, and that concepts will not be learned as highly general, but rather as relatively specific entities (e.g. that conservation of liquid will be acquired independently of conservation of number), and, more important, that these concepts remain as separate, unrelated entities, being tied together only in the mind of the psychologist. It is apparent that Gagné's position here is at variance with the emphasis on structurally interrelated concepts forming a stage that we have proposed as an earmark of cognitive development.

It should be noted that our insistence on this horizontal-transfer question in the study of learning effects does not commit us to an a priori assertion concerning the prevalence of broad across-the-board acquisitions in the normal process of cognitive development. It has been pointed out with some justification (Lasry, 1966) that the child who demonstrably has acquired a concept without benefit of practice or special experience may similarly fail, in many instances, to show an understanding of interrelated concepts. Our own analysis of the formation of stages actually points itself to the instability, inconsistency, and lack of generality of concepts during the period of their acquisition.

Nevertheless, horizontal transfer remains of importance as a criterion to evaluate the results of learning. That is, considerable differences in breadth of learning may be anticipated, depending on where the child is at the start. At one extreme it may prove possible to create the appearance of operational structures in children starting at the level of intuitive thought, by means of a suitably programmed sequence of steps, but the end result may be expected to remain of very limited generalizability or transfer value. At the opposite extreme we may be dealing with children in whom the operation has already become established, but who for one reason or another fail at the outset to respond in accordance with it at the performance level; here the training may in effect amount largely to the externalization of the operation, and its effects can be expected to transfer to other situations or structurally related tasks.

Elsewhere one of us (Wohlwill, 1966b) has argued that effects of training in producing vertical progression tend to be inversely proportional to the extent of horizontal transfer:achieved. This inverse relationship represents quite possibly the key to the difference between the effects of training and controlled experience and those of the child's spontaneous, unprogrammed experience. The latter results in vertical progress that is undoubtedly slower and more haphazard, but in compensation it takes place on a much broader scale horizontally. This still does not mean that every structural link between tasks is necessarily realized instantaneously, but only that there is progress on a wide front, with certain concepts spearheading the advance while others are lagging slightly behind, but at the same time without major gaps in the levels of thought demonstrated by the child for different but interrelated concepts.

This brings us to the third point at which our analysis of cognitive development touches on questions of function, and of the role of training or experience in particular. We have proposed that the process of formation of cognitive structures can be looked at as a four-phase process, in which transitional and stabilization phases intervene between the initial preoperational phase and the final full-fledged establishment of the operation. This formulation suggests that very different effects of learning are to be expected, according to the phase in which the child is located at the outset. Children in the preoperational phase should show little evidence of acquisition of concrete-operational concepts—and this is in accordance with the lack of success of most Piagetian learning studies below the age of five. Children in the transitional stage should be variably receptive to influences aimed at speeding up the initial emergence of concrete operations, and for those that do learn, the extent of transfer exhibited should be fairly limited. Children in the stabilization phase would presumably show effects mainly of a consolidation or generalization nature—i.e. the extension of previously established operations to new domains. Finally, those in the final phase cannot give evidence of any learning effects, of course, though they might show greater resistance to artificially induced extinction attempts (Smedslund, 1961), in comparison with those in the transitional phase, at least.

Much of the evidence on the effects of learning currently available is congruent with this analysis, notably the generally limited percentage (typically less than half) of children who show such effects, when samples selected merely on the basis of age are studied, and the relationship between learning and level of performance on pretests, where such information is available. Thus, it is undoubtedly no coincidence that the one study showing close to 100 percent learning effects, that by Wallach and Sprott (1964), utilized children who in terms of their mean age would have been expected to have already attained the concrete-operations level with respect to the concept under investigation, i.e. conservation of number. It does not seem unreasonable, then, to suppose that they had advanced well into Phase 3 at the outset. This case points up the importance of obtaining adequate pretest measures, not only with respect to the concepts to be trained, but also with respect to other related concepts, so as to provide a true picture of the nature of any learning effects observed.

A recently completed pair of masters' theses, carried out as a collaborative venture by Carbonneau (1966) and Fournier (1966) at the University of Montreal, under the direction of Dr. Laurendeau, are of considerable interest in this connection. They bring out succinctly the advantages to be gained by extensive pre- and posttesting, defining the child's status in the formation of concrete-operational thought at the start of training as well as providing a comprehensive picture of the changes resulting from a particular training experience. Their investigation was concerned with the acquisition of conservation of area. The details of the training procedure need not concern us; suffice it to mention that it comprised a series of sessions in which minimal perceptual alterations (which even the nonconserving child could resist) were contrasted to progressively more radical perceptual transformations. Carbonneau's results show a very notable degree of success from this procedure in leading previously nonconserving children to understand area conservation. Fournier's data show evidence, furthermore, of transfer to other tests of area conservation, involving, e.g. continuous vertical surfaces instead of the discrete squares defining the horizontal area used during training. At the same time Fournier provides further pre- and posttest data based on other tasks less closely related to the training task, which enhance very considerably the meaning of the observed training effects. For one thing, a pretest of area conservation involving subdivision of a circular "pie" into smaller sections, showed in the pretest that most of the children had already attained conservation in this situation. This finding—a clear case of horizontal differential—indicates that the children in this study were already some distance along the way to the formation of concrete operations at the start of the experiment. On the other hand, on the pretest the subjects retained for the training lacked not only the criterial concept of area conservation, but also of substance and length conservation (the latter involving the transformation of a straight path into a zig-zag one); transfer to *these* concepts following the training on area conservation was minimal.

Thus far the results cited point only to a gradient of transfer, falling off roughly in inverse proportion to the similarity between the training and transfer concepts. A second posttest, administered three months after the first, showed, however, an interesting tendency for this gradient to flatten: on this posttest, the superiority of the experimental over the control group had substantially decreased on the criterion area-conservation task, as well as on the transfer task of continuous, vertical-area conservation. At the same time there was some indication of a delayed effect of training on the length-conservation task, at least to the extent that a number of children had advanced to Phase 2 on this task.

In sum, the intensive training administered, the broad range of tasks spanned by the pre- and posttests, and the provision for a follow-up test to determine the longer-term effects of the training, all help to bring the true role of this experience into sharper focus. In these respects, the conception and design of the Carbonneau-Fournier investigation might profitably be emulated more generally in research on the role of learning or experience in cognitive development. In essence, the contribution of these investigators is that they have given recognition to a fact that previous workers in this area have been inclined to ignore: that any effects of a particular experience on some aspect of the child's cognitive functioning must be thought of as *superimposed* on his normal development. Thus, a meaningful assessment of these effects should incorporate both the breadth and scope encompassed by this developmental process and the temporal dimension along which it runs its course.

Appendix

Data of direct relevance to the four-phase model outlined in this paper have been presented by Uzgiris (1962) in her dissertation on the attainment of conservation of substance, weight, and volume in children from the first through the sixth grades. Uzgiris's intent was not only to verify the progression from substance to weight to volume, by administering questions relating to these three types of conservation to the same children, but also to examine the situational generality of conservation responses across different concrete materials. Accordingly she selected four materials—plasticine balls, sets of cube-shaped nuts, wire coils, and strands of plastic-covered wire.

For each combination of material and type of conservation there were three items, involving three different transformations of the material prior to asking the conservation question. (Thus, the ball of clay was successively rolled into a "fat" sausage, rolled into a longer, thinner sausage, and subdivided into three pieces; the nuts were arranged in stacks or piles varying in number and conversely in height, and so on.) There were, therefore, a total of 3 x 4 x 3, or 36 responses for each child. Since Uzgiris provides the complete raw data for all of her Ss in an Appendix, it becomes possible to look at the patterns of responses exhibited in the different age groups, and thus to determine whether the succession of phases outlined in our model provides a reasonable fit to these data.*

To this end, each S's pattern of Passes and Fails on the four substance-conservation and four weight-conservation tasks was determined, a pass being awarded for two correct answers out of the three transformations presented for each task. (The volume-conservation data were not utilized, since it was apparent from the low success-rate on volume-conservation even in the oldest age group that it entailed conceptual processes falling outside of the concrete-operations realm tapped by the other two conservations. In any event the volume-conservation responses would have added little useful information to the test of our model.)

The patterns were then divided into five categories, representing respectively Phases 1, 2, ⅔, 3 and 4. The patterns comprising these phases are shown in Table 2.

Phase 2, it will be noted, is defined in terms of an intermediate level of correct responding on substance conservation, regardless of the child's performance on weight conservation. The rationale for doing so is that Phase 2 represents the transitional period in the initial establishment of the operations underlying conservation; this is best indicated in terms of performance on the task for which this concept is first attained, i.e. substance conservation. Furthermore, it is entirely consistent with the transitional character of this phase to find cases of success on the harder task, weight conservation, to some extent independent of performance on substance, although the overall level of performance on weight should, of course, be lower—as it is (cf. below). As for Phase ⅔, it is marked by consistent passing on the easier task, substance conservation, presumably indicating the attainment of conservation at this low level of difficulty. The specification of "0 to 2" passes on weight conservation for this turning point may seem arbitrary, but it is in line with the interpretation of this point as marking the start of the consolidation period for the concept being acquired; thus for the more difficult

* The authors wish to express their gratitude to Ina Uzgiris, for her cooperation in supplying the raw data from her dissertation, and for allowing us to use them for the purposes of this Appendix.

Table 2   Distribution of Response Patterns Characterizing Ss at Different Age Levels *

	Values of P_a and k assumed for each phase		Response Patterns: Number of Passes on Four Tasks of Conservation of:		Number of Ss in Grades:						Number of Oscillations per S
PHASE	P_a	k	SUBSTANCE ($P_b = 1.0$)	WEIGHT ($P_b = .5$)	1	2	3	4	5	6	
1	0	0	0	0	8	4	0	0	0	0	0.75
2	.5	0	1 to 3	0 to 4	6	8	2	3	4	3	1.85
2/3	1.0	0	4	0 to 2	3	3	3	5	2	2	1.50
3	1.0	.5	4	3	3	0	3	1	4	0	1.45
4	1.0	1.0	4	4	0	5	12	11	10	15	0.09
					20	20	20	20	20	20	

* Based on data of Uzgiris (1962)

concept a low, but not necessarily zero-order probability of success on weight conservation would be expected, as indicated by the equation for our model, which at this point specifies $P(+)$ as $= P_b$.

The extent to which this partitioning of Ss into the various phases conforms to the formal specifications of our model can be gauged by considering the assumed values for P_a and k for each phase, and for P_b for the two types of conservation tasks, given in Table 2. The values indicated for P_a in Phase 2 and for k in Phase 3 are to be regarded as modal or average values. The P_b values were obtained by treating all four materials as equivalent (their overall difficulty levels were in fact closely comparable at all age levels), and arbitrarily setting the difficulty-coefficient as $= 1.0$ for the easier of the tasks, substance-conservation. Since for Ss in Phases 2, ⅔ and 3 combined there were exactly twice as many passes on substance as on weight, P_b for the latter was set $= .5$.

These values turn out to be tolerably good estimates as first approximations: they yield predicted means of 2.0 and 1.0 passes in Phase 2 on substance and weight conservation respectively, which are close to the corresponding observed means of 2.3 and 1.2. For Phase ⅔ the fit is less good: the predicted mean for passes on weight conservation is 2.0, whereas the observed one is 1.2. Through iterative procedures it would no doubt be possible to improve upon these approximations, but for our purposes the gain would be negligible.

The main point to be brought out is that, when we assign Ss in the various grades to these phases, based on their response patterns, a very consistent picture emerges (cf. Table 2): Phase 1 is clearly dominant at Grade 1; Phase 2 at Grade 2; and Phase 4 from Grade 3 on, reaching a maximum in Grade 6. Phases ⅔ and 3, while failing to account for a majority of Ss at any age level, do reach a peak at intermediary ages, i.e. in Grades 4 and 5, respectively. Considering the small number of cases in each age group, this distribution is as orderly as could be expected.

Further information relevant to the interpretation of the phases according to our model is provided by the oscillation data. An S was credited with an oscillation if on any task he had

either 1 or 2 correct answers out of the 3 trials (i.e. three transformations) that he was given with each material. The average
number of such oscillations for the Ss assigned for each phase is
shown in the last column of Table 2. (The maximum theoretically possible is 8, i.e. 4 materials $\times$ 2 tasks.) It is apparent that
oscillations are relatively rare in Phases 1 and 4, as would be
predicted where P_a is 0 or 1, and reach a peak in Phase 2, as
expected from the transitional character ascribed to this phase.
This point emerges even more clearly if we consider only those
Ss who are well into this phase, i.e. with 2 or 3 passes on substance conservation: these 19 Ss exhibited an average of 2.2 oscillations per S.

The oscillation rate in Phases $\frac{2}{3}$ and 3, though less than in
Phase 2, remains higher than would seem consistent with an assumption of $P_a = 1.0$. (As might be expected, a large proportion
of these oscillations is contributed by the weight-conservation
items.) This suggests either that these two conservations are
being acquired separately, i.e. that P_a for weight < 1.0 for these
Ss, or that the stabilization period, during which deficiencies in
information-processing remain ($k < 1.0$), will itself be marked by
oscillation of response. Arguing against the separate-acquisition
interpretation is the total absence of any Ss combining 0 or 1
passes on substance conservation with more than 1 pass on
weight, and more significantly, the finding that only two Ss
showed a combination of 4 passes on substance conservation
with 0 on weight.

Altogether, these data provide a certain amount of empirical
support for the adequacy of the model we have outlined, sufficient at least to warrant further research specifically designed to
test it. For such investigation one would require a larger number
of tasks varying in difficulty and a sufficient number of judgments on the same or equivalent forms of these tasks to provide
direct estimates of P_a for any given S.

References

Aebli, H. *Ueber die geistige Entwicklung des Kindes.* Stuttgart: Klett, 1963.
Beilin, H. Learning and operational convergence in logical thought development. *J. exp. Child Psychol.,* 1965, 2, 317–339.

Braine, M. D. S., & Shanks, Betty L. The development of conservation of size. *J. verb. Learn. verb. Behav.*, 1965, 4, 227–242.

Bruner, J. S., Olver, Rose R., & Greenfield, Patricia M. *Studies in cognitive growth.* New York: Wiley, 1966.

Carbonneau, M. Apprentissage de la notion de conservation de surface. Unpublished thesis (lic. philos.), Univer. Montréal, 1966.

Chomsky, N. *Syntactic structures.* The Hague: Mouton, 1957.

Chomsky, N. *Aspects of the theory of syntax.* Cambridge, Mass.: M.I.T. Press, 1965.

Donaldson, Margaret. *A study of children's thinking.* New York: Humanities, 1964.

Flavell, J. H. *The developmental psychology of Jean Piaget.* Princeton, N. J.: Van Nostrand, 1963.

Flavell, J. H. Heinz Werner on the nature of development. In S. Wapner & B. Kaplan (Eds.), *Heinz Werner, 1890–1964: papers in memoriam.* Worcester, Mass.: Clark Univer. Press, 1966. Pp. 25–32.

Fournier, Edith. Généralisation intranotionnelle et internotionelle d'un apprentissage empirique de la notion de conservation de surface. Unpublished thesis (lic. philos.), Univer. Montréal, 1966.

Gagné, R. M. The acquisition of knowledge. *Psychol. Rev.*, 1962, 69, 355–365.

Gagné, R. M. Contributions of learning to human development. Presidential address, Division I, AAAS, presented at AAAS meetings, Washington, D. C., December, 1966.

Glick, J., & Wapner, S. Ontogenetic changes in transitivity. Paper presented at East. Psychol. Ass. meetings, New York City, April, 1966.

Katz, J. J. *The philosophy of language.* New York: Harper & Row, 1966.

Kofsky, Ellin. A scalogram study of classificatory development. *Child Develpm.*, 1966, 37, 191–204.

Kuhn, T. S. *The structure of scientific revolutions.* Chicago: Univer. of Chicago Press (Phoenix), 1964.

Lasry, J. C. Apprentissage empirico-didactique de la notion d'inclusion. Unpublished thesis (lic. philos.), Univer. Montréal, 1966.

Lovell, K. A follow-up study of some aspects of the work of Piaget and Inhelder on the child's conception of space. *Brit. J. educ. Psychol.*, 1959, 29, 104–117.

McCarthy, Dorothea. Language development in children. In L. Carmichael (Ed.), *Manual of child psychology* (2nd ed.). New York: Wiley, 1954. Pp. 492–630.

McNeill, D. Developmental psycholinguistics. In F. Smith & G. A. Miller (Eds.), *The genesis of language: a psycholinguistic approach.* Cambridge, Mass.: M.I.T. Press, 1966. Pp. 15–84.

Morf, A. Apprentissage d'une structure logique concrète (inclusion): effets et limites. In A. Morf, J. Smedslund, Vinh-Bang, & J. F. Wohlwill (*Études d'épistémologie génétique*. Vol. IX). *L'apprentissage des structures logiques*. Paris: Presses Univer. France, 1959. Pp. 15–83.

Nassefat, M. *Étude quantitative sur l'évolution des opérations intellectuelles*. Neuchâtel: Delachaux et Niestlé, 1963.

Osterrieth, P. et al. *Le problème des stades en psychologie de l'enfant*. Paris: Presses Univer. France, 1955.

Smedslund, J. The acquisition of conservation of substance and weight in children. III. Extinction of conservation of weight acquired "normally" and by means of empirical controls on a balance scale. *Scan. J. Psychol.*, 1961, **2**, 85–87.

Smedslund, J. Concrete reasoning: a study of intellectual development. *Monogr., Soc. Res. Child Develpm.*, 1964, **29**, No. 2 (Whole No. 93).

Smedslund, J. Microanalysis of concrete reasoning: III. Theoretical overview. *Scan. J. Psychol.*, 1966, **7**, 164–167.

Suppes, P., Hyman, L., & Jerman, M. Linear structural models for response and latency performance in arithmetic. Unpublished manuscript, 1966.

Uzgiris, Ina. On the situational generality of conservation. Unpublished Ph.D. dissertation, Univer. of Illinois, 1962.

Uzgiris, Ina. Situational generality of conservation. *Child Develpm.*, 1964, **35**, 831–842.

Wallach, Lise, & Sprott, R. L. Inducing number conservation in children. *Child Develpm.*, 1964, **35**, 1057–1071.

Werner, H. The concept of development from a comparative and organismic point of view. In D. B. Harris (Ed.), *The concept of development*. Minneapolis: Univer. of Minnesota Press, 1957. Pp. 125–148.

White, S. H. Evidence for a hierarchical arrangement of learning processes. In L. P. Lipsitt & C. C. Spiker (Eds.), *Advances in child development and behavior*. Vol. 2. New York: Academic Press, 1965. Pp. 187–220.

Winer, G. H. An analysis of the role of set in the child's acquisition of number conservation. Paper presented at East. Psychol. Ass. meetings, New York City, April, 1966.

Wohlwill, J. F. Piaget's theory of the development of intelligence in the concrete-operations period. In M. Garrison (Ed.), Cognitive models and development in mental retardation. *Amer. J. Ment. Def., Monogr. Suppl.*, 1966, **70**(4), 57–78. (a)

Wohlwill, J. F. Readiness, transfer of learning and the development of cognitive structures. Paper presented at meetings of Canad. Psychol. Ass., Montreal, June, 1966. (b)

Wohlwill, J. F., & Katz, M. Factors in young children's responses on class-inclusion problems. Paper presented at meetings of Soc. Res. Child Develpm., New York City, March, 1967.

"Stage" in Piaget's Cognitive-Developmental Theory: Exegesis of a Concept

ADRIEN PINARD

MONIQUE LAURENDEAU

Piaget's system naturally invites one to adopt extreme attitudes of acceptance or rejection. General acceptance will very often result from the particular attraction exerted by certain of Piaget's constructs, such as those of structure, adaptation, equilibrium, and so on, the definitions of which can lend themselves to easy generalizations and allow for numerous implications in more than one area of applied psychology (e.g. educational, clinical). Piaget's difficult system has become enveloped in an aura of prestige irreconcilable with the critical spirit necessary to avoid confusion between hypotheses, opinions, and facts. On the other hand, an attitude of total rejection can draw its inspiration from a spontaneous reflex of scientific purity or exactingness, a reflex set in motion by the putative theoretical and experimental gaps of the system. In the same manner, the noninitiated will instinctively fear the dangers of a system of conceptualization that he judges to be obscure, a system whose "addicts" speak a language more or less esoteric—the "piagenetic" language according to the expression which Piaget (1964b) attributed to

Gréco—and rather inaccessible to those who use the customary scientific vocabulary.

The possibility of such attitudes depends upon several factors. It no doubt arises first from the magnitude of Piaget's work that incites an all or none acceptance and lends itself poorly to eclectic apportionment. It depends equally upon the contrast that opposes, according to some, the breadth of the theoretical system to the scantiness of the experimental data: a breadth that can appeal to those of synthetic nature who are little inclined toward microtomic procedures, but a scantiness that irritates those of analytic bent always on the watch for unparsimonious interpretations.

Another source of conflict arises from profound differences as to the method of explanation that ought to be used in the psychology of behavior. In this respect Piaget (1950b, 1963a) adopts a position that rejects at the same time all forms of reductionism (physiological or phenomenological) and every traditional form of parallelism. To explain the relations that exist between the states of consciousness and the underlying physiological processes, he advocates a sui generis form of isomorphism (without reciprocal action) between two methods of explanation, one based on physical (or physiological) causality, the other on psychological implication.

The level of formalization of Piaget's system is still another factor that gives rise to massive opposition. On one side the advocates of pure methods—be they innovators or mere consumers of theory—severely criticize Piaget's system for its specifically theoretical gaps, that is to say its lack of formal architecture (postulates, theorems, and so on) and of genuinely hypothetical constructs or intermediate variables capable of lending themselves to empirical verification. They will readily consider that Piaget's contribution consists more in posing problems than in providing solutions and that his conclusions belong more to the domain of theoretical fancy than to that of scientific reality. We read, for example, the capricious and negativistic reactions of Birch as well as the severe but much more positive remarks of Zigler in a recent symposium on mental deficiency (Garrison, 1966). The partisans of Piaget's method or the authors less op-

posed to his manner of thinking, on the other hand—moreover
with a variable enthusiasm and a not less variable sagacity (see
the already classic book by Flavell (1963) and, for example, the
excellent article by Wohlwill (1966a) in the above-mentioned
symposium)—will recognize at once the fact that Piaget has not
allowed himself to be imprisoned by the rigid canons of scientific
theorization, that the paucity of explicitly formulated hypotheses
renders the system difficult to verify empirically, and that many
of his interpretations suggest the post hoc. These same, however,
authors at the same time emphasize the danger of sterility that
becomes associated with all forms of hyperformalization and all
rigid interpretations of operational definitions and hypothetico-
deductive cases. It appears, in this respect, that Baldwin (1960)
speaks the language of reason in recalling that the most valuable
scientific contributions were not necessarily born of the most
rigorous theories and in recognizing, after a very lucid analysis
of more and less sophisticated scientific strategies, that we cannot without dogmatism "legislate" that one or the other is useless.

Lastly, a final point that can help us understand these extreme
forms of acceptance or rejection concerns the differences of a
methodological nature that divide the researchers in developmental psychology. To begin with there are the purists—the
"geometrically-minded"—who are firm partisans of the strict experimental method, the only one capable of realizing the establishment of unequivocal causal relations between the variables
involved, and who contend with one another to reiterate that the
chronological age is not as such a significant variable in the theoretical explanation of a developmental phenomena (Bijou &
Baer, 1963, 1966). There are, on the other hand, the so-called
nonpurists—the "subtle-minded," shall we say—among whom
some would readily class the less critical disciples of Piaget, if
not Piaget himself. These often suffer from a certain negative
form of chronic color-blindness (i.e. exclusive attention to the
age variable without systematic analysis of other variables).
They dread the teratological character of rigid laboratory situations and willingly abide by methods of analysis that are correlational rather than more strictly experimental. Everything in-

dicates, however, that both of these two methods of approaching genetic problems are necessary because they are distinct and complementary as Brown (1965), Flavell (1963), Kessen (1960), Laurendeau and Pinard (1966), and Wohlwill (1963a) have all noted.

The discussion of the formal or structural aspects of Piaget's system would be interesting in itself. It seemed preferable, however, to penetrate to the very heart of the system and to analyze closely a particular aspect of its contents. The aspect chosen here is the concept of "stage," a notion abounding in pitfalls and intricacies, but a key one in Piaget's system as a whole. The study of this concept assumes even greater importance from the fact that it raises certain related problems (e.g. concerning *décalages*, learning) the discussion of which often gives rise to all sorts of misunderstandings. A simple and direct method of dealing with the study of this concept is to make a critical analysis of each of the characteristics that Piaget attributes to it. In at least two places (1956, 1960a *), he lists the different attributes which condition, in his opinion, the use of this notion in the study of mental development. For the sake of conciseness, we shall designate by the following names the five criteria proposed by Piaget: *hierarchization, integration, consolidation, structuring* and *equilibration.* These criteria will be discussed in the order mentioned, the order that Piaget himself follows in the first of the articles just cited. (The order adopted in the second article reverses the third and fourth criteria.) It seems, moreover, that the more rigorous the criterion, the more it becomes surrounded with ambiguities and misunderstandings, perhaps because the difficulty of the problems becomes more and more apparent and because empirical verifications decrease in frequency as the criterion increases in rigor. In consequence, the report that follows will deal only briefly with the first two criteria and will dwell at greater length on the latter three.

---

* Piaget refers in this paper to a list that was first established by Inhelder (1956) and that included only three criteria: constant order of succession, integration, and *structures d'ensemble.*

Hierarchization

The first criterion simply states the necessity of a fixed order of succession of the different levels that constitute a developmental sequence. This condition does not thus characterize any particular stage, but the succession as such. It directly poses the problem of the transitivity of stages (the second stage must never precede the first, nor the third the second, and so on). As Piaget has often made clear, the invariance of this order, a requisite for every stage-sequence, says nothing about the chronological ages of accession and does not therefore exclude the possibility that the particularities of the physical, social, or cultural milieu might accelerate or retard the succession, or even prevent a particular stage from appearing (Piaget, 1956). More specifically, in answer to Mead who pointed out the importance of ethnic and cultural factors in the intellectual development, Piaget (1960a) ventured an even more explicit hypothesis, a hypothesis whose level of hypothetico-deductiveness does not perhaps place it in a seventh heaven of formalization, but which nevertheless merits being submitted to experimentation. According to this hypothesis, the extent of the *décalages* or developmental lags between very different cultural milieus will depend upon the nature of the tasks examined: these *décalages* would be maximum for tasks of a nonoperational nature (e.g. precausal beliefs), a bit less for tasks of an operational nature but that call upon symbolic structures (number or language), even less in cases where perceptual configurations are in opposition to operational structurings (e.g. conservations), and least of all where the perceptual configurations and the operational activities mutually support each other (e.g. seriations).* Again, very recently, Piaget (1966) stressed the importance of the comparative studies already initiated in several countries and insisted upon the need for complementary investigations that would specify the relative influence of different developmental factors accord-

* A more general project involving a comparative study of Canadian and African children is currently in preparation and will deal with this particular aspect.

ing to the cultural milieus compared, and that also would determine both the differential rhythms of development and the eventual simplifications (e.g. absence of a formal-operational level)
of the genetic sequence in certain types of cultures.

    This first characteristic attributed by Piaget to the notion of
stage is obvious enough (it is not, moreover, exclusive to that
notion) and does not appear to create any basically theoretical
problems. We could at times ask if a rigid order of succession is
capable of taking into account residual behavior (i.e. that typical of a previous stage) that, as Piaget has frequently noted,
often persists at a given stage, particularly in the evolution of
sensory-motor intelligence, causality, and such like; but we
should see here no more than the manifestation of certain forms
of *horizontal décalages* inherent to a particular level that will be
discussed later (third criterion). Wohlwill (1966a), for one,
questions the interest and the utility of the present criterion, still
the most studied of the five.* He argues that the limited number of stages, almost always reduced to three (lower, intermediate, and higher) in the current verification experiments, decidedly increases the probability of positive results. The criticism
is largely valuable, but it would no doubt be excessive to wish to
explain simply by this artifact the agreement of the numerous
and varied existing observations (Dodwell, 1960, 1961; Dubreuil
& Boisclair, 1960; Elkind, 1961a, 1961b, 1961c, 1961d, 1962,
1964; Goodnow, 1962; Gouin-Décarie, 1962; Laurendeau & Pinard, 1962; Lovell, 1959, 1961; Page, 1959; Pinard & Laurendeau,
in press). It should also be added that a more systematic use of
the subperiods and substages identified by Piaget could serve to
enhance somewhat the dispersions. Let us recall, for example,
that the sensorimotor period subsumes six stages, that the preoperational subperiod alone includes three stages, that the concrete-operational period contains two principal stages, as does
the formal-operational period itself. Furthermore, each of these

---

* It is almost always a question here of simple replications, more or less systematic, of Piaget's experiments. The difficulty in experimentally manipulating this
first characteristic, a difficulty pointed out by Wohlwill (1966a), stems no doubt
from the fact that such a manipulation would assume that we know the mechanism of transition from one stage to another (see criterion 5).

stages can contain several substages, substages that Wohlwill often and justly finds very transient and thus of little use, but that are occasionally clearly identifiable, notably in the realm of space.

Integration

The second characteristic attributed by Piaget to the notion of stage presupposes the preceding one and includes an additional requirement. It asserts that the acquisitions of a given stage S_2 should integrate those of the preceding stage S_1, instead of simple substituting for them or juxtaposing with them. To avoid any misunderstanding, it is essential to stress that this integrating characteristic does not in itself assume the necessity of finding S_1 as such in S_2, as though we were in the presence of a model of additive nature. The possibility of such a misunderstanding may underlie Wohlwill's (1966a) criticism that this characteristic cannot easily apply to the successive stages of one general period, because no one would maintain that operational conservation, for example, "integrates" preoperational nonconservation. Nevertheless, the exact bearing of this characteristic can already be clarified if we think of the integration in a more primitive (or etymological) fashion. We might thus give it a more comprehensive significance by asserting that the "integration" of S_1 by S_2 would constitute a transformation of S_1 into S_2 and would entail the two processes of *restructuring* and *coordination*.

The first of these two processes would be at work especially at the level of between-period genetic relations—the kind of integration relations to which Piaget in general and also Inhelder in particular (1956) confine themselves—and would thus directly entail the phenomenon of *vertical décalage*. We know that, by virtue of these *décalages* (see Piaget, 1941, where they are extensively discussed), the development of a given conceptual content (e.g. causality, space) is accomplished on several successive levels (sensorimotor, concrete-operational, and formal-operational) according to an analogical process in which this content, already structured at a level established by earlier kinds of actions or operations, is restructured at a higher level by a new kind of operation. These *vertical décalages* would also be expressed, again according to Piaget (1941), by a progressive differentiation of the various domains of application of the operations in the process of establishing themselves. Thus it is that before the advent of logico-arithmetic operations, at once distinct from spatial-temporal and practical operations, these three kinds of operations were at the sensorimotor level completely undifferentiated, the initial differentiation being produced between the practical and the reflective or cognitive domain (including logic and sublogic) at the preoperational level. Now these diverse and successive restructurings would not operate in a simple additive or subtractive fashion as if, for example, the logical were added to the sublogical, or as if reflective intelligence suppressed practical intelligence at a given moment; we must rather see in this a phenomenon of liberation (or of emergence) that transforms and enriches the domains a and b, for example, at first indistinguishable within an ab whole.

The process of *coordination*, to which the integrative property can also refer, would be more directly at work at the level of the interstage developmental relations (those within the same major period or subperiod). Examples of such a process abound in Piaget's descriptions. Granted that, in the case of stages of conservation, for example, the initial absence of conservation does not become an integral part of operational conservation, or more generally speaking, granted that the behaviors at level S_1 are not necessarily recognizable as such in the behaviors of level S_2; it is nonetheless true that operational representations do integrate, by coordinating them in a common system of compensatory transformations, progressively more articulated intuitions of the preoperational level and that, even more obviously, the last stage (intuitive) of the preoperational subperiod integrates the less articulated intuitions of the preceding substages. We find, also, this same process of coordination, *mutatis mutandis*, within each of the principal periods of development. It is particularly striking in the series of six stages of the sensorimotor period, leading for example, to object permanence. We also notice it in the usual

problems of conservation, where what Piaget calls Strategy 4
(operational compensation for the modifications involved in the
complementary dimensions A and B) coordinates the oscillations
(between A and B) peculiar to Strategy 3, itself having already
coordinated the isolated behaviors (centration on A and B separately) of the lower-order strategies. The development of perspective (projective space) furnishes several examples of the
same process: the first projective representations, themselves
supported by elementary representations of a topological nature
peculiar to an initial stage, begin by being applied only to some
one of the three projective dimensions (such as the left-right dimension) before constituting a comprehensive system. In short,
in the case of interstage relations, integration finds expression in
the coordination of more and more differentiated schemata (sensorimotor or representative), just as it was expressed, in the case
interperiod relations, by a restructuring of the same conceptual
contents via increasingly complex operations applied to increasingly differentiated fields.

Consolidation

The third essential characteristic proposed by Piaget means that
a period (or a stage) must always involve at once an aspect of
achievement of the recently acquired behavior and an aspect of
preparation for the behavior of the following level. This characteristic is not easy to analyze. Wohlwill (1966a) does not find it
rigorous enough to be useful and feels that it can serve only to
confuse the lines of demarcation separating the different levels.
It is true that the two brief descriptions Piaget makes in this respect are rather ambiguous. In the first (1956) achievement and
preparation explicitly refer to two stages or successive levels of a
same, more general period, the first serving as point of departure
for the accomplishments to be wrought by the second. In the
second description (1960a), on the other hand, the achievement-
preparation relationship would appear to remain intrinsic to a
given stage n whose function would be to complete the stage
$n - 1$ and to prepare for the stage $n + 1$. Thus, assuming that we

wish to retain this criterion along with the others, it would certainly be necessary to vary its meaning as a function of the degree of refinement of the developmental scale (periods, subperiods, stages, and so on) to which we refer, as it had been judged useful to do for the preceding criterion.

In any case, when we place ourselves in the general context of the equilibration model that inspires all of Piaget's theory (the very term "consolidation" spontaneously evokes this model) we may be readier to admit the utility of this consolidation property if it could serve to limit the very complex concept of *horizontal décalage*, very fundamental in Piaget's system. Just as the concept of *vertical décalage* helps to clarify the significance of the preceding characteristic, it is conceivable that the notion of *horizontal décalage* could occupy an equally central position in elucidating the present one by giving it meaning and justification.

As we know, the notion of *horizontal décalage* expresses a chronological difference between the ages of acquisition of operations that bear on different concepts (or contents), but obey identical structural laws. The classic example is that of the difference in age of acquisition of the conservations of substance, weight, and volume. We see at once the importance that this notion could have in the interpretation of problems that arise, for example, in the study of developmental synchronisms among different concepts, or the even more venturesome attempts at confirmation of the stages pertaining to these concepts (attempts that in themselves are legitimate and valuable so long as one avoids the possible confusion between simple convergences and more precisely defined synchronisms that the structural characteristic, to be considered later, seems to demand). But for the notion of *horizontal décalage* to function in this manner and especially for it to be able to clarify the preparation-achievement relationship entailed by the present criterion, this notion should immediately become the object of systematic experimental studies rather than serve as a magic passkey to the post hoc explanation of observed asynchronisms. It would seem equally necessary to return to certain distinctions previously made by Piaget (1941) in his analysis of the different forms of possible relations among the operations (or the actions) of a given set of operations, as a function of whether they bear on one specific concept or on different concepts.

When these operations bear on one particular concept, three types of relations are possible. Piaget speaks first of *identity* to designate the relations among operations bearing on a specific object that is subjected, for example, to various deformations of greater or lesser magnitude in an experiment in conservation. He refers instead to *vicariousness* when the operations bear on several homogeneous objects that are capable of being assembled in a common whole (e.g. different balls of plasticine), because of the possibilities of substitutions or vicariousness of their respective parts. Finally, he talks of *correspondence* when the operations deal with heterogeneous objects if, although not unitable in a simple whole (e.g. conservation of a quantity of plasticine and conservation of a quantity of water), these objects lend themselves to comparisons or correspondences among their respective parts. Now Piaget immediately adds that these three types of relations, at least at the operational level, present no differential difficulty, and that the operations involved should all, as a rule, be constituted at the same time. He admits nevertheless that instances of the *correspondence* relation can sometimes give rise to "slight *décalages*" explainable "by the difference in the perceptual or intuitive conditions" (1941, p. 266).

On the other hand, to designate the relations among similar operations bearing on different concepts (e.g. quantity of material, of weight, and of volume), Piaget will speak rather of *analogy*, meaning that, in spite of their diversity, the concepts involved seem to be structured according to the same operational rules, with the respective groupings being perfectly isomorphic or analagous among themselves. It is by this *analogy* relation that Piaget essentially characterizes the concept of *horizontal décalage*. Contrary to that which intervenes in the preceding three types of relations, the *horizontal décalage* involves a differentiation of concepts, just as the parallel notion of *vertical décalage* refers to a differentiation of domains of application (logical, sublogical, and practical) of the operational groupings. Given that the incidence and the extent of *horizontal décalages* would be conditioned by the variable resistance of "the perceptual or representational obstacles" (1941, p. 270) entailed by different concepts, and that these same factors equally condition the restructurings indigenous to the *vertical décalages*, Piaget concludes that "the *horizontal décalages* express the differences of speed between the *vertical décalages* of distinct concepts" (1941, p. 270). Such a conception is tantamount to asserting, so it seems, the necessity and the complementarity of the integrative and consolidative properties.

The consolidative property becomes easier to understand and to accept once we introduce the distinctions that have just been mentioned. A relative slowing down of development during a particular period would thus be a matter of the progressive liquidation of the perceptual or conceptual obstacles responsible for various asynchronisms or *décalages*. This is why the principal question of knowing the extent to which we can reconcile this consolidative characteristic with the other characteristics attributed to stages by Piaget could not receive a simple and univocal answer.

In the cases of so-called *horizontal décalages* (involving analogous but different concepts), we must consider a relatively extended developmental scale (capable of covering, for example, the two stages of the subperiod of concrete operations). However, these *décalages* between distinct concepts ought not to compromise the economy of stages: (1) in their hierarchal characteristics, so long as the order of succession of the levels peculiar to each of the concepts and the order of appearance of these concepts among themselves remain invariable (which is a distinct problem); (2) in their integrative characteristics, so long as the succession of behaviors peculiar to the different levels of these concepts takes each time the form of a restructuring or a progressive coordination in spite of the differences in their ages of acquisition; (3) in their structural characteristics, so long as the set of groupings relevant to each of these separate concepts is constructed in synchrony (this is also a problem in itself that will require subsequent discussion); (4) and finally, in their equilibration characteristics insofar as the evolution of these concepts could in each case be described in terms of successive levels of equilibrium and where both concepts might become accommodation hypotheses concerning the continuity of development and the transition between stages.

It is perhaps advisable to specify that these *horizontal décalages* do not apply exclusively to certain privileged concepts, such as those of quantity of matter, weight, and volume, where the analogous relations are particularly striking because they are based on a system of successive implications (i.e. weight presupposes matter just as the action of weighing presupposes the action of finding again, and so on) increasingly difficult to differentiate and to objectivize within a common, generic notion of quantity. The analogy establishing the concept of *horizontal décalage* is often less obvious when it deals with notions that are less similar, such as the asynchronisms recently observed by Vinh-Bang and Lunzer (1965), for example, among different types of spatial coordinations and conservations and many others that a comparative analysis of Piaget's work on the development of concepts of causality, space, and time would reveal. We can, however, recognize, in all these asynchronisms, the dual process of progressive dissociation and complementarity that defines the process of *horizontal décalage* wherein several distinct concepts can acquire structure at different ages even though the same operational groupings are involved in each.

The problem becomes complicated, however, if we bring in the distinction among the different kinds of operational groupings (logical, sublogical, etc.), whose differentiation would be, as already noted, a manifestation of *vertical décalage*. At the concrete-operational level, for example, where the domains of logical, sublogical, and practical operations are finally differentiated, one can ask whether these operations are all stabilized at the same time or whether they show certain *décalages*. The theoretical position of Piaget on this question has not changed appreciably. As early as 1941, he spoke expressly (p. 259) of a general synchrony among these three "kinds" of groupings and did not see how it could be otherwise. A general parallelism between the construction of logical and sublogical operations has been repeatedly reaffirmed (Piaget, 1950a; Piaget & Inhelder, 1963a), and it is particularly said to hold within the more limited context of the construction of continuous and discontinuous

wholes (Inhelder & Piaget, 1959). Gréco (1964a) indirectly at-
tacks the same problem in his work on the evolution of spatial
representations. He seems little inclined to feel that logical and
spatial operations are constructed autonomously and independently, or further, to see in the latter operations a simple application of the former to a particular content. Although he
subscribes to an hypothesis of interdependent and synchronous
construction, he emphasizes the possibility of certain particular
asynchronisms.

Assuming that the positions of Piaget and Gréco are confirmed
by more systematic work, such asynchronisms could be considered as *horizontal décalages* (of the *analogy* variety) in view
of structural parallelism of the areas involved. In certain cases
sublogical operations, of a spatial nature for example, might develop earlier than logical operations. This *décalage* could be explained by the privileged character of the spatial images, under
the hypothesis (Piaget, 1961b; Piaget & Inhelder, 1963b, 1966)
that the homogeneity and isomorphism between image and operation are more intimate in the area of space than in the area of
logic. In other cases, logical operations might develop first, as in
the example of conservation of collections (i.e. conservation of
number) versus conservation of length. In this case, Gréco
(1964a) wonders if the developmental priority of the first conservation over the second is the result of a greater resistance on
the part of preoperative kinematic intuitions to the operations of
conservation, or if instead this is a special kind of invariant sequence, to which the usual notion of *horizontal décalage* does
not apply. In short, even in admitting that the differentiation of
the logical and sublogical (and practical) domains attests to the
phenomenon of *vertical décalage* and that these three domains
are constituted synchronously when we consider them in the aggregate, it would remain theoretically possible to imagine certain
horizontal décalages among the particular operations that arise
from one or another of these areas.

If we consider now the asynchronisms that can come about
from object heterogeneity within the same concept domain (relation of *correspondence* among the operations concerned), they
are naturally spread out over much shorter durations (i.e. across

the substages of the same period or subperiod) and run a much lesser risk of compromising any of the conditions required by the notion of stage. Even if the operations pertaining to a common concept should theoretically develop at the same time, it is normal that certain conditions of a perceptual and intuitive nature, relative to a specific content and themselves variable according to the physical and sociocultural experience of the child, would bring about certain temporal deviations entirely reconcilable with the consolidative characteristic under consideration here. As to cases involving *vicariousness* or *identity*, no *décalages* would be expected, once the operational level had been attained. If we really insist on extending the use of the term *décalage* to the point of designating, for example, the delay of the child in admitting the conservation of weight after a more pronounced transformation (or with a second object, similar to the first), with conservation being asserted in the case of slight modification (or with the first object), it must at least be noted that the span of such asynchronisms must be extremely narrow—largely confined to a single intermediary or (lower) stage.

In this general perspective, we see how equivocal can be the global question of knowing to just what degree it is possible, without diluting the concept of stage, to constantly appeal— often post hoc—to factors of a perceptual or representational nature to explain the *décalages* observed. Everything depends, in point of fact, on the scale at which we pose the question, because the likelihood of *décalage* is inversely proportional to the closeness of the relations (*analogy, correspondence, vicariousness* or *identity*) that hold among the presumedly synchronous operations. It is no doubt the cases of *correspondence* that are the most critical. Indeed, if it were true that heterogeneity of objects alone brings about asynchronisms that are both too numerous and too striking, the typical behaviors at the level concerned could entirely lose their identity and the lines of demarcation between levels would be completely blurred. In any event, the primary role that must be accorded to the perceptual and conceptual obstacles in the production of all these *décalage* asynchronisms, as well as the lack of precision still surrounding the designation of these obstacles, clearly indicates the need for more precise experimental analysis. Indeed, only systematic observations and experiments will be able to help us define the true limits of these various *décalages* and their theoretical significance. It may be that the recent work of Piaget and Inhelder (1963b, 1966), and Gréco (1964a, 1964b), on the role of imaginal representations will be the best starting point for attacking these problems.

Structuring

The fourth criterion that the notion of stage proposed by Piaget must satisfy concerns the actual organization of the intellectual behaviors characteristic of a particular level of functioning. According to this criterion, the typical actions or operations of a given level are not simply juxtaposed one with another in an additive fashion, but are organically interconnected by ties of implication and reciprocal dependence that unite and group them into total structures—Piaget's *structures d'ensemble*. This criterion is no doubt one of the most fundamental in Piaget's concept of stage. It is closely linked with the preceding criterion and will henceforth be discussed only in connection with the more general stages (periods or subperiods) constituting genetic levels that are relatively final, such as the termination of the sensorimotor and concrete-operational periods. As with the preceding criteria, if we wish to clear up the ambiguities that can surround the interpretation of certain of Piaget's writings as well as certain of the experiments inspired by his theory, it is necessary to specify the levels of observation we have in mind when speaking of structural characteristics, for the possible diversity of these levels directly influences the rigor of the criterion, and as a result, the range to be given to these so-called *structures d'ensemble*.

We shall want, first, to refer to an *interconcept* level of observation, thereby allotting to the structural characteristic a range large enough to include either specific concepts within a common generic concept (e.g. those of distance, length), or even less directly related concepts (e.g. logical inclusion, spatial conservation). The majority of the interpretations that Piaget gives to the structural characteristics of stages refers to this level of generality. According to Wohlwill (1963b, 1966a), for example, confirmation of this criterion would require that the acquisition of a logical principle or of a particular operation at a given stage implies simultaneous mastery of all the problems or tasks founded on this principle or operation. It is true that Inhelder (1956) assumes such strong generalization when she notes that the structure of concrete operations implies the solution not only of such and such specific problems, but also of all the elementary problems of classification, seriation, and numerical conservation. Piaget and his associates also emphasize on many occasions the structural isomorphism and the genetic synchronism of certain concepts that are quite dissimilar, and even arise from different areas (logical and sublogical): for instance, the hierarchal inclusions of classes and certain spatial constructions of topographical wholes (Inhelder & Piaget, 1959), or the compositions and recompositions of spatial wholes and collections of discontinuous objects (Piaget, Inhelder, & Szeminska, 1948). It is certain, nevertheless, that we could not reduce the structural characteristic under discussion to a simple form of transfer or of generalization between diverse concepts or problems, nor to necessary (but not sufficient) synchronisms that would reflect the operation of this characteristic. The structural characteristic asserts above all a complete functional interdependence and an organic connection among the operations (or actions) that can, in fact, apply to related concepts. It is primarily this that Piaget (1956) and Inhelder (1956) mean when they give as examples of *structures d'ensemble* the group of displacements of the sensorimotor period, the system of functional invariants (conservations) in the first subperiod of concrete-operational thought, or the spatial system of Euclidian and projective references of the second concrete-operational subperiod, and the structure of the INRC group that becomes established at the formal level. Leaving aside the question of experimental verification of these *structures d'ensemble* and of the synchronisms that they imply, it goes without saying that the completed elaboration of such structures would not be expected before the end of each of the corre-

sponding developmental levels. It is indeed necessary to allow
the vertical and horizontal *décalages,* discussed when the two
preceding criteria were treated, to get successively ironed out
according to a process that spreads itself over several levels and
that is expressed each time by a differentiation and coordination
of domains as well as of concepts.

Instead of giving such a range to the structural characteristic,
we can adopt a much stricter interpretation and limit ourselves
to an *intraconcept* level of observation, that is, to the constituent
operations of one specific concept (e.g. that of weight, distance,
class and so on), and dealing with objects that are as homogenous as possible. In thus reducing the influence of the *horizontal décalages,* and the even more innocuous asynchronisms stemming from a heterogeneity of objects within the pale of a single
concept, we find ourselves reducing the range of the *structures
d'ensemble* to the scale of relations among different groupings
(logical or sublogical according to the case and the corresponding quantitative groups) that give structure to the concept considered. On an even more restricted scale are the examples of
structures d'ensemble (grouping and lattice) that Piaget (1956)
gives in the special Symposium on the problem of stages, specifying that the mastery of a structure such as a grouping or a lattice
assures by this very fact the mastery of all the distinct (and at
times very different) operations that constitute it. But it is very
clear that, especially where he deals with the problem expressly,
Piaget goes beyond this intragrouping level and directly places
the structural characteristic of stage at least at the level of relations among the groupings themselves. In his earlier article on
the mechanism of mental development he explicitly affirmed that
"all the forms of groupings appear at the same time without our
being able to seriate (them) into stages" (1941, p. 246), that "at
a given level and for a given concept, the (eight) different possible groupings appear to be constituted at about the same time"
(p. 246), and so on. It is thus that—to recall one of the two
examples cited by Piaget in this connection—the construction of
the concept of weight would simultaneously imply, at about the
age of nine years: the mastery of groupings of simple addition
and of vicariances (conservation of weight); of addition of

asymetrical (seriation of weight) and symetrical (transitivity of equivalences) relations; of biunivocal multiplication of relations or of classes (concept of density by the combination of weight and substance); of counivocal multiplication (conservation of the weight of the particles of flour in the dilated corn); and finally, of the corresponding quantitative groupings, by a fusion of classes and relations. The same synchronism among distinct groupings is noted by Inhelder and Piaget (1959) among the vicariances, classifications, and seriations (simple and multiplicative) pertaining to collections of discontinuous objects, albeit there are variations from one test to another as a function of the specific nature of the material used.* Even more recently, regarding the synchronism found by Smedslund (1959) † between conservation and transitivity of weight, Piaget and Inhelder (1963a) willingly agree with Smedslund that conservation and transitivity would be only two aspects of the same grouping, and see in this synchronism an empirical proof of the structural characteristic essential, according to them, to the very notion of grouping.

More generally, this interdependence of groupings could be said to lie at the very heart of Piaget's system. The logical (or epistemological) analysis of the groupings themselves testifies to this fact: all are strictly isomorphic because all are based on the same combination of fundamental operations (direct composition, inverse composition, associativity, and so on). The psychological analysis of these same groupings reveals the necessary complementarity of the systems of classes, relations, and numbers. The interdependence implied in being able to recognize both similarities and differences among objects, and the simultaneous and integrative involvement of several groupings within a single activity (e.g. class-inclusion and conservation behavior) are certainly easy to understand if one recognizes that classes

---

* It is somewhat paradoxical to note that the authors here expressed some surprise at finding these convergences, given the difference between classification, more favored by language, and seriation, more favored by perception.
† It is true that in a subsequent article, where he reanalyzes his protocols with more rigorous criteria of transitivity, Smedslund (1961a) changes his mind and talks about asynchronism.

and relations deal with the extension and the comprehension of concepts, respectively, and are coordinated among themselves to produce numerical structures. It would seem that this minimum level of structuring is necessary (and perhaps sufficient) to the criterion of stage that is in question here. In short, to affirm the psychological existence of an authentic operational grouping bearing on a given content, this content must at the same time elicit not only the whole set of constituent operations of this grouping, but also the ensemble of parallel and connected groupings. With the exception of the sensorimotor period where the practical equivalent of such a structuring is realized at the final stage, we must no doubt wait for the end of the first concrete-operational subperiod to see constituted the first operational *structures d'ensemble.*

In this perspective what are we to think of the synchronisms and asynchronisms so often called in evidence for or against this structural characteristic? This is not the place to make a critical analysis of the experiments that could bear upon this problem. It will suffice to recall, for example, the low correlations observed by Dodwell (1960, 1961) among different tasks (e.g. one-for-one correspondence, conservation, seriation), all relative to the generic notion of number. The same inconsistency is found again in Lunzer's (1960) subjects, in his experiment on the concepts of volume (its conservation and measurement) and of the continuum, which according to Piaget should be interdependent. We also recall, however, the very strict synchronism observed by Braine (1959) between the recognition of spatial order and the transitivity of length relations.* Attention should, in addition, be called to all the cases of synchronism reported by Piaget and his colleagues (e.g. Inhelder & Piaget, 1959; Piaget & Szeminska, 1941; Piaget, Inhelder, & Szeminska, 1948) among rather distantly-related concepts, and even among different domains (e.g. logical versus sublogical). If one looks at more limited areas, one could cite, if not the (equivocal) results of Smedslund's (1959) study of conservation and transitivity of weight mentioned ear-

---

* As will be noted later, however, an examination of the tests actually used by Braine leaves open the question of whether the two tasks compared are not simply perceptual in nature.

lier, at least the synchronism found by Kofsky (1966) among certain specific tasks (class hierarchies, dual class membership, and such like) within a battery of class-inclusion problems. We must also note, however, the asynchronisms recently observed by Smedslund (1964), this time between conservation and transitivity of both length and quantity, as well as that between conservation and seriation of length subsequently found by Lunzer (1965).

Before this rather inconsistent inventory, must we reject without further consideration the notion of *structures d'ensemble*, or is it better to reserve our judgment until new data can give a more decisive answer? We know how dangerous the interpretation of similar data can be. Partisans of the notion of *structures d'ensemble* will willingly take into account certain developmental synchronisms between concepts that are sometimes very different, without always distinguishing between synchronisms that are theoretically necessary and those that are simply observed to occur. They fail to recognize that the second, instead of confirming ipso facto the existence of the first, can only be the expression of developmental coincidences attributable to factors that are foreign to the very nature of *structures d'ensemble*. It is also no less difficult to resist the temptation of admitting a priori the existence of *structures d'ensemble*, even if one must incessantly invoke the convenient intervention of various *horizontal décalages* to explain the absence of predicted synchronisms. It would not be a failure to recognize the importance and cogency of the *horizontal décalages* to point out the danger of explanations that are in each instance post hoc and made to measure. We are no doubt correct in seeking, for example, to partially explain the developmental primacy of seriation over conservation of length by showing that it is conservation, and not seriation, which entails spatial displacements and requires that the end points of the lengths concerned be put into relation (Lunzer 1965; Piaget 1964b); but again, it is necessary to take notice of the fact that the developmental primacy observed by Lunzer is true only for simple seriation (without elements subsequently interpolated in an already-constructed series), and that Lunzer himself unites in the same developmental group (equivalent ages) conservation of length and this seriation of interpolated elements—recall that Piaget & Szeminska (1941) demonstrated a long time ago that systematic success in such interpolating is necessary to guarantee the operational character of seriation. In the same way, if we still find it legitimate to read into the synchronism first observed by Smedslund (1959) between conservation and transitivity of weight the indication that these two operations are only two aspects of a single grouping, one could scarcely apply the same interpretation to the dyschronisms later observed by Smedslund (1964) between conservation and transitivity of length and of quantity, dyschronisms for which one must try, post hoc, to find a different explanation!

There is scarcely any justification for using frequency of dyschronisms as a pretext for the unequivocal rejection of the hypothesis of *structures d'ensemble*. If we wish to submit this hypothesis to experimentation, it is necessary to conform in the best faith to the structural characteristic assigned by Piaget to the concept of stage and which (1) can have, as we have seen, a more or less precise meaning depending upon the level of observation considered; (2) should characterize a relatively final stage of development, since we should not insist on an interdependence (between concepts or between groupings) at any and all developmental levels; (3) does not require the rejection of the *horizontal décalages* the importance and necessity of which we saw in the preceding paragraph, but about which one must know how to specify the exact nature, stage, and significance. It is true that such criteria render the experimentation difficult to accomplish; but the theoretical importance of the problem of *structures d'ensemble* recommends systematic study. If it is neither wise nor reasonable to reject or to accept a priori the existence of the *structures d'ensemble* postulated by Piaget; it is indeed no wiser and no more reasonable to be content with pointing out the genetic divergences or convergences that may be observed among different tasks constructed for other purposes, compared as an afterthought, and occasionally even administered to different rather than the same subjects.

A systematic analysis of *structures d'ensemble* nevertheless creates serious difficulties. If we look at interconcept generalization, the intervention of *horizontal décalages* linked to differences in content seriously risks blurring the picture. It would already be less ambiguous to limit inquiry to concepts that are logically interrelated, whether they entail the same processes applied each time to new conceptual contents (e.g. a set of conservation tests *), or whether they are part of a common domain, relatively closed and logically coherent (e.g. a set of tasks involving the construction of spatial coordinates). But it is no doubt better, in order to hew more closely to the problem of *structures d'ensemble*, to begin with the intraconcept level of generalization and therefore to ask if, for the same conceptual content (and even material content if possible), the different groupings underlying this concept are achieved in synchrony.† Even when the problem is thus narrowed, the experimental analysis remains full of traps. It is not easy to reconcile the restrictions indigenous to using the same conceptual (and even material, e.g. cubes) content, a source of monotony, with the necessity of maintaining the child's interest. Perhaps, assuming that such extreme homogeneity will prove to be impractical, we should use a sampling of contents (material or even conceptual), the average yield of which could thus characterize the grouping in question. It is no easier to reconcile the qualitative diversity of the groupings to be studied (e.g. simple seriation, biunivocal multiplication of classes) with the necessity of maintaining as constant as possible the purely quantitative level of difficulty of the tests (e.g. avoid comparing a simple seriation of four objects with a multiplicative classification of 16 cases). It may be that, to avoid looking at only a priori synchronisms, we should select tests of varying difficulty, so as to examine the incidence of synchronisms or asynchronisms at each of the different levels. It is equally important that each test be as homogenous as possible so as to probe for a specific and well-defined grouping. One should perhaps avoid, for example, relatively complex tests about which it would be difficult to know whether they imply the operation of only one or of more than one grouping, or even to know un-

---

* The study by Vinh-Bang & Lunzer (1965) on the spatial conservations is a first step in this direction.

† Experiments of this type are currently under way in our laboratory.

ambiguously to which grouping they refer.* The question of age level of the children to be examined also creates a delicate problem: one has to select children who are *old enough* so that the structural characteristic typical of the operational stage would have a chance to appear, and at the same time *young enough* so that all of the groupings will not have already been long since acquired and consolidated—with the earlier multiple *décalages* now imperceptible. In short, we must attempt to find a critical period of development. Only through such a discovery can we begin to resolve the paradox (or break the vicious circle) according to which, by hypothesis, operational level is characterized by *structures d'ensembles* (to be operational it must possess these structures), they themselves being imbued with an operational level of mental functioning (to show these *structures d'ensembles*, it must be operational). We can finally ask if the search for this critical period should be located at the first level of concrete-operational thought or at the second level of this same period; the chances of seeing a synchronous elaboration of all the groupings bearing on a given concept at this second level are no doubt much greater a priori because of the structures already elaborated at the preceding level. It would obviously make sense to experiment at both levels and, as far as is practical, to utilize longitudinal methods to get direct and unambiguous data on the question of developmental concurrences among the groupings.

Assuming ultimately that experimental analysis should disconfirm the hypothesis of *structures d'ensemble,* even at the level of the constituent groupings of a single concept, it will be necessary to find out whether the attendant asynchronism at least shows a regular order of succession, thus permitting us to establish a developmental series or sequence. This is a substitute hypothesis

---

* It should be noted, for example, that a test that obliges the subject to change criteria of classification would constitute, for Wohlwill, a case of multiplication of classes, whereas Flavell sees in it a case of vicariance (see Wohlwill, 1966a). Similarly, Kofsky's elegant study (1966) remains somewhat ambiguous because we cannot be sure if each of the tasks employed taps a clearly delimited grouping. We can ask, for example, if Kofsky's task MM (multiple class membership) really assesses the child's multiplicative grouping of classes, because it requires the successive classification of a given object into two different classes, and may thus reflect only isolated and uncoordinated classificatory activity.

which Wohlwill (1966a), for example, seems disposed to adopt, because of the frequently observed *décalages;* moreover, he believes that such a conception in no way weakens Piaget's system. We must nevertheless recognize that any empirically-established asynchronism among the constituent groupings of a given concept would seriously jeopardize Piaget's conception of stage because it would deny one of its most essential characteristics, and because it would be difficult to reconcile with the very nature of groupings, whose theoretical interdependence on both the psychological and the epistemological level we have seen above. In any case, we should guard against mistaking such asynchronisms for examples of *horizontal décalages,* if given that this form of *décalage* is defined by the successive application of the same groupings to different conceptual contents. In fact, it is rather to a particular form of *vertical décalage* that we should thus attempt to assimilate any asynchronism among groupings.

Equilibration

The last attribute Piaget attributes to the concept of stage emphasizes the necessity of seeing, within an ensemble of stages, a succession of levels of equilibrium at the heart of the evolutionary process. It may appear redundant to consider this equilibratory property as an additional criterion of stage. Strictly speaking, actually, this characteristic does not refer directly to a particular stage (or period); it plays a role, vis-à-vis the entire developmental series, somewhat analogous to that played by the aforementioned consolidative characteristic, vis-à-vis a particular stage. In this sense it lies at the very foundation of the developmental process—no doubt the reason Piaget (1960a) considers it to be the most indispensable of the five criteria—the equilibratory nature of which he emphasizes in insisting that this equilibration is realized in successive degrees.

It would not be useful to discuss here the absence of all apparent forms of plateaus in the usual developmental curves as an initial objection to this notion of degrees of equilibrium. Indeed, no one would think of protesting that it is necessary to distinguish the individual developmental curves, a pursuit we know to be full of hazards and vicissitudes, from the collective curves where individual differences smooth out and become steady to a great extent. In addition, no one should argue that the ages of accession to the various stages of development, whatever criteria of accession are used, have any absolute value whatsoever, being simply averages of different individual ages of acquisition. The equilibratory characteristic does, however, raise two real problems of crucial importance for Piaget's system: the continuity of development and the transition from one level of equilibrium to the next.

CONTINUITY OF DEVELOPMENT

The question of knowing whether or not the concept of level of equilibrium prejudges the continuous versus discontinuous character of development is not so simple as it might appear at first sight. Wohlwill (1966b) considers, for example, that the problem of continuity versus discontinuity is actually a false problem, discontinuity being a necessary consequence of Piaget's system. He is no doubt right if we agree with him that for all developmental psychologists (including Piaget himself), the problem of continuity has nothing to do with continuity as such (a development without levels or without discernible pauses), but consists only of asking if the changes that intervene in the course of development are of a qualitative nature or only quantitative. Piaget (1957b), however, appears extremely conscious of the dangers of oversimplification this problem presents. It is thus that he establishes a clear-cut distinction, for any developmental succession of behaviors, between the polarity of derivation versus substitution and that of continuity versus discontinuity, being careful to specify precisely that derivation can be either continuous or discontinuous.

The first of these polarities concerns the two methods by which the succession of behaviors in a genetic process can take place. There would be a derivation relation between two behaviors if the two possess common characteristics and if the second derives from the first as a consequence of a process of transformation that is divisible into stages. There would instead be a substitution of one behavior for another if the second, instead of deriving from the first by transformation, simply replaced it at a given moment in development under the influence of factors unrelated to the first. This distinction would thus speak to the qualitative dimension of the genetic process. The criterion proposed by Piaget to distinguish derivation and substitution, one which is empirically verifiable to a certain extent, would essentially concern the order of succession of the behaviors: cases of substitution are recognized by the fact that external interventions (i.e. of cultural, social, educative origin) could, if not necessarily alter the basic quality of the successive behaviors, at least change their order of appearance; in contrast, these same interventions, if the sequence is one of derivation, could at best only accelerate or retard the successive emergents. If we recall the requirements entailed by the integrative characteristic of stages, described earlier, it appears evident that Piaget's concept of stage refers primarily to a derivative mode of development. Substitutive evolutions are not in all cases systematically excluded, as is shown, for example, by the analysis of the development of certain forms of causality (Piaget, 1926, 1927; Laurendeau & Pinard, 1962), although it must be admitted that these less frequent cases of behavioral substitutions were always noted within a more general context of derivation. Moreover, as Piaget has observed in several places (e.g. 1957a, 1959a), it seems that if we consider the totality of the stages of a developmental phenomenon (e.g. the succession of "strategies" leading to conservation), the derivative character of the relation among behaviors is much more evident at the level of the early stages than at the level of the final stage. In other words, the elements common to several successive behaviors, derived one from another, are more easily identified during the first phases of a process, whereas the coordination and the integration indigenous to the final stage may mask these partial identities and may give the impression that this stage is independent of the past, while at the same time opening the door to new progress.

The second polarity opposes continuity and discontinuity of development. Although closely linked to the preceding one, this

polarity is nonetheless essentially different from it in that it refers to the fine details of a developmental sequence, independent
of its derivative or substitutive character. It thus touches on the
quantitative aspect of development, at least in the sense that the
variable under consideration must be able to be quantified in
some fashion and thus be expressible in terms of a more or less
differentiated set of intermediary values. The most objective criterion for deciding the continuity or discontinuity of a developmental phenomenon would thus be simply the number of identifiable intermediary steps between the two behaviors concerned.
Piaget hastens to say, however, that the efficiency of this criterion is necessarily restricted by the limits inherent in our research techniques and methods of observation (e.g. the impossibility of repeated examinations at too short intervals of time or
age, the relative ambiguity and insensitivity of both "clinical"
and standardized methods). This is why Piaget is wise in concluding (1957b; 1960a) that the discovery of intermediary values can never be so exhaustive that we will be able to decide
unambiguously whether the continuity or the discontinuity of
the developmental phenomena under consideration must be regarded as absolute or only relative. The decision taken will
naturally be influenced by the nature of each theorist's favored
explanatory model and by the fineness of the scale of measurement to which each chooses to relate his observations. In this
respect, it does seem that Piaget's equilibration model (the concept of successive stages or levels of equilibrium) and his methods of observation (research of a special kind aimed at uncovering behaviors specific to each level) suggest discontinuity rather
than continuity, even if the importance accorded to behavioral
sequences of the derivation type leads him to focus especially on
intermediary behaviors. As he himself recalls, not without a certain malice (1960a), he is variously accused of, on this occasion,
neglecting the continuity suggested by the multiplicity of the
intermediary behaviors, and on that occasion overlooking the
discontinuity apparent in certain new intuitions that suddenly
emerge even amidst very closely related and similar behaviors.
This is undoubtedly the reason he willingly adopts the concept
of equifinality proposed by Bertalanffy (1960a, 1960b) to desig-

nate, within an open system, the phases of relative stability that stud the evolution of the system—themselves interrupted by unstable phases of transition—and that retain their stability until new conditions (internal or external) bring about new progress. We see to what extent this concept, which Bertalanffy illustrates with examples taken from areas as diverse as biology and architecture (the relative stability of species, styles, and such, and the instability of the forms of transition), can easily be adapted to Piaget's concept of stage. It is thus that the integrative and consolidative characteristics of stage, with their associated activities of coordination, differentiation, and generalization, are reminiscent of the equifinality of Bertalanffy's main phases. Similarly, the instability of the transitional forms described by Bertalanffy is analogous to the relative imprecision of the intermediary stages, stages that Piaget (1960a) says always dissolve into a myriad of substages as soon as we attempt to establish their limits.

TRANSITION FROM ONE STAGE TO THE NEXT

The second problem that is directly raised by the equilibration property concerns the thorny question of the factors responsible for the transition between a given level of equilibrium and the following level. It appears that the solution to this problem—no doubt the most fundamental in Piaget's system—is to be sought in an analysis, at once theoretical and experimental, of the very notion of equilibration.

The model of equilibration A thorough discussion is needed of the essential characteristics of this concept, with special emphasis on: the autonomous and integrative function of this equilibration factor in comparison with other developmental factors; the statistical mode of causality peculiar to equilibratory activity; the priority of endogenous factors (constructive assimilation, internal reinforcement, and so on) over the exogenous factors of development; and the possibilities of application of the equilibration model to different areas (perceptual, sensorimotor, and operational) of cognitive activity (see in particular Piaget, 1957a, 1960a, 1960b, 1964a, 1966). It must also be remembered, however, that Piaget, in giving precedence to equilibration factors, obviously does not intend to exclude the complementary necessity of the usual factors (maturation, experience, social and cultural interaction, and such like), but only to indicate their insufficiency. Even though the notion of equilibration is difficult to define and does not easily lend itself to experimental analysis, it would seem unwarranted to reject it a priori as a mere figment of Piaget's imagination or as a purely verbal substitute for more familiar concepts. We must at least recognize that Piaget has several times tried to concretize this equilibration model in terms of his well-known schema of sequential probabilities regulating the evolution of the successive behaviors or strategies of the subject. He has even tried (Piaget, 1957a) to formulate explicitly the economy of this schema in terms of seven fundamental laws whose principal function is to describe, in terms of probability, the privileged character of certain aspects of the objects upon which the subject's actions bear— aspects that are initially apprehended independently, one from the other, then in alternation, and finally in conjunction—as well as the preference accorded by the subjects first to static configurations, then to transformations as such, and so on.

We know that Piaget refuses to explain his equilibration model in terms of current conceptions of learning without submitting these conceptions to basic alterations concerning: (1) the role of external reinforcement, which does not directly figure in the previously cited laws; (2) the role of repetition, the necessity of which is imposed much less by the need for a progressive establishment of a behavior than by the contingencies peculiar to the mechanism of compensation that is in play during the acquisition of this behavior; and (3) the concept of association, for which he wishes to substitute that of assimilation to emphasize the fact that the succession of behaviors one sees reflects the steps of a process of equilibration between the activities of assimilation to earlier schemata and the activities of accommodation to new requirements. This is the reason that he puts so much stress on the internal factors of autoregulation. Piaget is perfectly willing to appeal to the previous experience of the subject to explain certain behaviors postulated by his model: (1)

that the child attends exclusively to certain specific aspects of the objects upon which bears his consideration; (2) that he is initially interested in the result of the transformations undergone by the objects, before becoming aware of the transformations themselves; and (3) that he does not at first note the possible relations among these different aspects or states. But the role of these experiences is then interpreted in terms of assimilation to acquired schemata whose tendency to generalize will sooner or later lead to a confrontation with obstacles of internal or external origin (e.g. the subject's own dissatisfaction, the resistance of objects, perceptual contrasts), and this information will engender a readjustment and differentiation of these existing schemas. In short, if the most primitive behaviors (e.g. isolated consideration of a particular aspect, simple alternation) become progressively less probable than the more evolved behaviors (e.g. conjunction or coordination of complementary or opposed aspects, with particular attention paid to the transformations themselves), it is thanks to these internal or external factors that bring the child to the first decenterings, the multiplication and diversity of which then open the way to anticipatory and retroactive activities leading to more and more perfect forms of equilibrium.

In the specific area of conservations, eminently favorable to the exercise of compensatory mechanisms, this equilibration model finds its most obvious and least controversial applications; but it could be shown also that Piaget (1941, 1957a, 1961a) manages well enough to transpose this same model, *mutatis mutandis*, to other types of cognitive structures (perceptual, sensorimotor, concrete, and even formal operational). It remains, however, as it is pertinently noted by Flavell (1963) and Wohlwill (1966a), that the model is hard to put into concrete form as soon as we go beyond the hypothetical and somewhat artificial situation where a given subject must resolve a particular problem in a limited period of time and as soon as we move to the more general context of the real and spontaneous development of the child over a period of several years. It then becomes very difficult to conceive what the succession of strategies, the growth of sequential probability, the particular role of the internal or external factors mentioned above, might concretely mean in a given developmental phenomenon spread over several years and inserted in a matrix of related phenomena—with all of the *décalages* and interactions that might ensue. This is why it seems better to liberalize the pattern a bit by disregarding those of its elements that are too specific or limited to a particular type of cognitive structure (e.g. necessary conflict between the opposing dimensions of an object, succession or systematic alternation of simple strategies), to return to the fundamental position always advocated by Piaget: that the evolution of behavior within any cognitive sector is characterized by the progressive coordination of actions (overt or interiorized) that are at first isolated one from the other and centered on the results produced each time, rather than on the changes that link these results. This less strict formulation conserves the essentials of the equilibration model, and even of the probabilistic schema, insofar as the successive decenterings just evoked condition and determine the activities of simultaneous compensation of the real or possible transformations, and insofar as this evolution can be divided into stages, themselves interpretable as a sequence of ever more probable behaviors. Thus reduced to its essentials, the equilibration model can first be applied to the succession of stages within each principal period of evolution (i.e. the sensory-motor, concrete operational, and formal operational periods), since it can be shown that each one lends itself to this same fundamental type of analysis.

It is more difficult, however, to apply to the succession of the major periods themselves because the concept of *vertical décalage* rather implies the recommencement—twice repeated—of the same equilibratory process, beginning with an initial state of equilibrium at the end of the sensorimotor level. It is unfortunate, however, that the actual mechanism of these recommencements has not been well specified by Piaget. With reference to the first transition—from sensorimotor to representational thought—he stressed the role of the new demands created by the inadequacy of sensorimotor coordinations (simple empirical reversibility by successive actions) and the limitations of the field of application of these coordinations, i.e. their restric-

tion to immediate time and space (Piaget, 1947).* With reference to the second recommencement—from concrete operational
to formal operational thought—Piaget (1957a; Inhelder &
Piaget, 1955) points to new disequilibria resulting from the
demands of new problems (e.g. the domain of the possible),
which are beyond the field of application of the previous level of
equilibrium. Each of these recommencements results in a new
form of equilibrium that is more comprehensive than its predecessor: thus, the logical and representational reversibility of the
concrete operational level surpasses the simple empirical and experienced reversibility of the sensorimotor level, but it is itself
exceeded by the complete reversibility attained at the formal
level (by fusion of the two partial forms of reversibility—
inversion and reciprocity—up to this point functionally independent, but hereafter united by the requirements of the real
and propositional combinatorial system). Although Piaget insists
on this hierarchization of forms of equilibrium, he is nevertheless
careful to specify that the equilibrium attained at any given
level is itself not abolished at a higher level, but rather retains its
effectiveness within its particular area of application, although
integrated into and surpassed by higher levels of equilibrium.

We recall that Bruner (1959) regards this concept of equilibration as useless, merely a new name used by Piaget to designate properties that he attributes elsewhere to intellectual operations, and as providing not the slightest explanation of how the
child might be thought to pass from a given level of equilibrium
to the following level. However, Piaget has already shown
(1957a) that the concepts of equilibration and reversibility,
complementary though they might be, differ from one another as
a functional mechanism differs from its corresponding structure,
and that unless this internal mechanism of equilibration is added
to the other factors of development, we could explain neither the

* In the same context, see the brief but illuminating recent analysis by Piaget
(1964b) of the dual abstraction necessary for the transition from the sensorimotor
grouping of displacements to the corresponding representational grouping. See
also the very careful analysis that he makes (1961a, 1963b) of the fundamental
difference separating, in spite of very strong isomorphisms, perceptual constancy,
sensorimotor object permanence, and the conceptual conservation of the object.

formation of the operational structures in general, nor certain of
their properties in particular (e.g. the importance of virtual or
possible operations). If it is true that a recourse to equilibration
is not itself sufficient to concretize the mechanism of transition
between two successive levels and that experimental verification
is required in addition, it remains at least possible to conceive, as
Piaget suggests, that the very increase in mobility and in radius
of action of the form of equilibrium peculiar to a given level
raises new problems and provokes a new beginning, on a higher
scale, of the equilibratory mechanism. It is this last aspect which
Papert (1963) wanted to illustrate by his *parabola of balls,** in
insisting on the primacy of internal factors—Papert speaks here
of autonomy, emergence, and so on—in these successive re-
equilibrations, each particular state constituting the best possible
adaptation to the momentary situation. In the same context,
Papert feels that the process of equilibration presupposes what is
essentially a simultaneous evolution of several different operations,† the resulting interactions and contradictions having precisely the effect of rendering possible and of stimulating the
evolution of any particular operation. The problem raised by
Bruner is perhaps, according to Papert, the result of a kind of
confusion between equilibrium and equilibration, the first of
which referring to a relatively final state, and the second implying rather the gradual growth of the system and thus the very
succession of these different states. To help in better formulating
the developmental problem, the same author proposes in the
same article an abstract mathematical model—which he calls the
"genetron" by analogy with the "perception"—representing a
cybernetic system in which the progressive adaptation of behaviors comes about by successive levels of equilibrium. The modifications of the system would here be determined in a sequential

---

* In a simple physical system, of unequally distributed plateaus, the converging
descent of two balls of different temperature towards a lower plateau, so that the
equilibrium of the position thus attained by the balls at a given moment, releases,
by the simple fact of their collision, a second process of equilibration (equilibration of temperature).

† Papert speaks of operations, but the context does not clearly indicate whether or
not he is referring to a single conceptual content.

manner by the kind of "errors" committed, even though the usual cybernetic models are in themselves less suited to represent the development of mental structures in an organism that starts at zero (without previous programming) and must construct them at all points.

The empirical analysis of equilibration   Whatever might be the theoretical or logical plausibility of the equilibration model, nothing can substitute for the empirical sanction of fact. An experimental test could first look to systematic observation of the spontaneous development of the child. Longitudinal methods are no doubt the instruments par excellence for such an observation and are an indispensable complement to cross-sectional methods. As Wohlwill suggests (1966a, 1966c), an intensive analysis of certain well-defined aspects of the behavior of children in their natural surroundings—an analysis that should at least extend over brief ontogenetic periods—is indispensable to those who wish to look closely at the problem of transition between stages and that of developmental concurrences among different conceptual contents, if not among different groupings or operations dealing with the same concept. Such an analytical method also facilitates the tracking down of interactions among contents or operations in process of formation, interactions that Piaget and Papert have said are a necessary part of the equilibration process.

These methods of simple observation must naturally be supplemented by other experimental techniques, namely, systematic interventions capable of stimulating the rhythm of development, that is to facilitate or channel it, if not to accelerate it in the strongest sense of the term. The objective of such interventions, which augment those that normally occur in spontaneous development, is not so much the actual acceleration of the development of a particular concept, as though it were a matter of inducing the subjects to pass rapidly through the normal stages. It rather consists in seeking out and analyzing the factors responsible for any such eventual accelerations, thus furnishing the essential elements of solution to the theoretical and practical problems involved in understanding spontaneous intellectual development and the rational application of this knowledge to educational purposes.

Recourse to these systematic interventions raises directly the fundamental question of the provoked learning or training of logical structures. We know that the very possibility of such training is still sharply discussed, and that the data currently available are not yet really decisive (Laurendeau & Pinard, 1966). When training efforts fail, the temptation can be strong to conclude without further ado that training is impossible, instead of more prudently concluding that the methods employed may have been inefficient and thus asking if these methods had actually touched the essentials of the process to be stimulated; at the same time, one would want to guard against the inherent dangers of a line of reasoning that would amount to assuming, almost a priori, the possibility of such training.* If the experiments are successful, however, the temptation is then strong either to contest post factum the logical character of the structures learned on the grounds that the training of genuinely logical structures is a theoretical impossibility, or to accept the results prima facie, without questioning the authenticity of the observed learning, and to conclude (prematurely) that the techniques employed actually tapped *the* factor responsible for these acquisitions, without taking care to distinguish sufficient from necessary conditions. The misunderstandings that clutter the current literature on the learning-training of logical structures may involve either the methods of training used or the authenticity of the presumed learning itself.

The methods of training   The majority of the training methods used have nothing to do with equilibration itself and are confined to the purely empirical processes of classical learning situations—repeated trials with failures or successes, externally reinforced, simple repetition of empirical feedbacks and such

---

* Where indeed to trace the line of demarcation between the insufficiency of a method and the incapacity of the subject, as Spitz recently asked, for example, in the face of some rather negativistic reactions by Birch and Bijou (Garrison, 1966)?

like. Some will occasionally resort to methods founded on operational exercise, but will then neglect the importance of empirical factors or will resolutely limit themselves, out of fear of inducing pseudolearning, to procedures that are wholly nondirective or perhaps too indirectly linked to equilibration itself (Morf, 1959; Smedslund, 1961b, 1961c; Wohlwill, 1959). Others will ultimately adopt extremely directive, didactic procedures (Kohnstamm, 1963), without always being sufficiently aware of the possibility that such procedures may yield an ungeneralizable pseudolearning. Nevertheless, if we wish to stay within the context of Piaget's system and examine certain of its constructs, we should, before proceeding to a more precise analysis, begin by introducing, all at once via a unified procedure, both factors of an empirical nature (e.g. repetition, reinforcement) and factors of a logical nature (e.g. activities of coordination, of anticipation, of transformation), using all means to avoid the spurious and artificial acquisitions to which an excessively automatic use of empirical factors as well as an overly didactic use of logical factors can lead.

It is true that a method of training founded principally on equilibration is not easy to program; but the major obstacles are already overcome as soon as we have chosen to center the experiment specifically on the concept of grouping and to reduce to a minimum the differences of conceptual content (and even material content) between the training and criterion tasks. In other words, if we choose to limit ourselves to the first level of generalization required by the structural characteristic previously studied, we reduce, by this very fact, unwanted variance due to the different forms of *décalage*. The training can thus bear either upon a particular grouping or on several at once, and in both cases, it can take either a global or an analytic form. If it concerns the learning of a particular grouping, the global technique applies to the whole set of operations involved in that grouping, and its concrete form will depend upon the nature of the task. It could be centered on more or less didactic exercise in the compensation and anticipation of transformations, in the acquisition of a conservation, for example, where the material exhibits clearly complementary dimensions (e.g. height versus width *). The experiments conducted by Carbonneau (1965) and Fournier (1965) well illustrate this method. The technique is especially centered on exercise in coordinating actions in the context of learning to master a classification or seriation task, for example. The essence of this technique is to provoke decentering activity in the subject by the diversity of complementary actions and anticiptations that we ask him to make: thus, in training the child on a task involving the inversion of linear order (Piaget, 1946), wherein the subject must predict the order in which beads inserted in a tube will reemerge from it after one or more rotations of the tube, the experimenter would ask him to predict and verify the result of several rotations in the same or opposite direction, with or without the tube, with fixed or movable elements, with or without a rod that threads the beads, and so on, to prepare the subject to grasp the essential principle of the reciprocal cancellation of two simple rotations. If we instead choose an analytical technique—perhaps combined with, or at least to be compared with the preceding one, the training will then consist in having the subject carry out the elementary operations included in every grouping. Thus, whatever the grouping involved (e.g. classification, seriation), the technique will always amount to giving the subject practice with the same fundamental operations (direct composition, inverse composition, associativity, and so on), although assuming different concrete form according to the particular grouping that is the object of the training (e.g. if it is a question of classification, have the subject perform the various additions and (inverse operation) subtractions of classes, have him note or anticipate the equivalence of two different sets constituted from the same elements, and such like).

Whatever might be the merits of a technique limited to a particular grouping, it would perhaps be even more promising to train the child on more than one grouping at a time (e.g. a clas-

---

* Even when the transformations carried into effect do not emphasize the "competitive" aspect of the dimensions of the material (e.g. the pouring of a quantity of water from a cylindrical vase into an asymetrically shaped vase), the initial and final dimensions remain correlative and lend themselves to compensatory exercises.

sification and a seriation). The situation thus created would then be a little less artificial and theoretically more favorable to the activation of an equilibration process, if we take into considera- tion the structural properties of the concept of stage and the role played in the equilibration process itself by the interactions or even the interferences or conflicts that could then ensue (Papert, 1963).

In short, in spite of their diversity, the techniques advocated here are each directly focused, in one way or another, on the stimulation of the equilibratory mechanism; although sustained by factors of an empirical and even partly didactic nature, the efficiency of these factors remains subordinated to that of the principal, equilibratory one. It would be extremely interesting, however, in trying to analyze the role of social interactions, to adapt the preceding techniques to various group learning situa- tions (e.g. the same experimenter working with several subjects at a time, the subjects being at similar or different initial levels, with free communicative exchanges), as in the experiments of Palmer (1967),[*] and Brison (1965), for example.

The authenticity of acquisitions   There remains to be men- tioned one last question, already sporadically alluded to in the preceding pages, which may constitute a major source of ambi- guities and misunderstandings: it is the question of the authen- ticity of the learning obtained. We know the reservations of the Geneva group concerning the possibility of training logical struc- tures. In connection with several experiments directly inspired by his hypotheses, Piaget (1959c) would no doubt acknowledge the efficacy of certain techniques. However, he would make clear that the learning obtained ("acceleration") is always very lim- ited when it rests on simple empirical feedback instead of being founded on exercises that bear on the operations in question or on related operations. He would insist upon this interdependence among operations, asserting that a given acquisition always de- pends upon earlier acquisitions to which it is functionally linked. In contesting the logical authenticity of certain, apparently suc-

[*] Personal communication. 1967

cessful laboratory acquisitions (Smedslund, 1959), Piaget (1959b, 1964a) is quick to interpret them as purely empirical affairs, bearing more on the physical contents to be structured than on the logical form of the structuring activity itself. In spite of the obvious dangers of such post hoc interpretation, this kind of rejoinder is often very valuable and in particular seems to be justified as regards the Smedslund experiment just cited. The logical character of the successful acquisitions achieved by Kohnstamm (1963) is also questionable because of the extremely directive nature of the training method used, a method that could have led to a subtle form of rote learning (see the criticism of this study by Pascual-Leone & Bovet, 1966). Additional controls of the sort used by Lasry (1965) and by Kohnstamm himself * are clearly needed, although they may not be sufficient. The same question can also be asked when we want to evaluate, even in experiments that do not involve learning, the level of functioning reflected in the subject's solution to putatively logical tasks. Laurendeau & Pinard (1962) have already called attention to examples of such misdiagnoses (Deutsche, 1937; Hazlitt, 1930) in the area of causal thought, and Morf (1957) has made a very pertinent analysis of the differences between types of solution that are purely intuitive and those that are truly formal. Certain authors have occasionally been sensitive to the danger of confusing perceptual and conceptual approaches. Borelli-Vincent (1951, 1956, 1957), for example, recognizes that it is not possible, especially when one cannot rely on the subjects's verbal explanations, to separate the conceptual and perceptual elements in experiments on ordinal seriation and categorical thinking. Furth (1964) also wonders, not without cause, if his experiment on conservation of weight may not simply have assessed kinesthetic sensitivity, and Braine (1962) was likewise concerned as to the extent to which the relation of class inclusion that he taught to very young children with the help of a nonverbal technique could be reduced to mere perceptual discrimination.†

* Personal communication. 1967
† See in this connection the control experiment carried out by Caouette (1961) on the difference between a logical inclusion of classes and a discrimination of a perceptual nature.

Also relevant here is the famous controversy between Fraisse & Vautrey (1952a, 1952b) and Piaget (1957c) on the possible distinctions and confusions between perceptual and conceptual speed. Likewise not to be ignored is the rather byzantine quarrel in which Braine and Smedslund (Braine, 1959, 1964; Smedslund, 1965, 1966) were engaged for a long time, initiated by an experiment conducted by Braine on the transitivity of length. It would no doubt be imprudent, if not impertinent, to reopen that debate. It may have been, however, that the initial criticism made by Smedslund badly diverted this debate by focussing it on a particular form of pseudotransitivity, concerning the number of comparisons the child must make before we can assess the inferential character of his answer. In fact, even in admitting that two comparisons were necessary in Braine's original experiment (e.g. A > B and B > C, B being the common measure under which, however, the child never finds a reward), still nothing seems to oblige the subject to make the logical inference leading to the conclusion A > C; he may only need to observe the two comparisons made before him in turn (simple successive juxtaposition) and to react positively to that one of the two (A > B in the present example) that permits him to apply an already overlearned schema (the task situation itself excluding the possibility of finding the reward under B). In short, out of a wish to purify Piaget's experimental test by stripping it of its verbal and active components, it may be that Braine has thereby taken away its logical and operational character and has transformed it into a simple test of perceptual generalization, without even being able to use the child's verbal explanations to help estimate his level of functioning. Until contrary evidence is offered, the least ambiguous method for studying the aptitude of the child to master logical transitivity still consists in putting him in a situation where he must exert himself actively and examine closely, using all available means (including verbal information), the logic of his comparisons, as in Piaget's classic test for transitivity of the weight relations.

Be that as it may, these various misapprehensions obviously show that we need to turn to more and more rigorous criteria for judging the logicality of what is learned. Piaget (1964a) recalled not long ago the importance of such criteria when he said that we must always ask ourselves, when confronted with an apparently successful case of induced acquisition of logical structures, about the persistence of the acquisition, the extent to which it shows transfer and generalization, and the initial operational level of the subjects trained. Still more recently, Inhelder, Sinclair, Bovet, & Smock (1966) also underlined, a propos the laboratory acquisitions reported by Bruner (1964), the necessity of such criteria to clarify the nature and meaning of the training techniques used, as well as to get a precise estimate of the actual limits of the results obtained. We ought finally to mention the critical analysis made by Kohnstamm (1966) of the multiple criteria that might be used in evaluating the authenticity of an acquisition, either during the course of the training itself (e.g. suddenness of solutions, relative ease of learning), or after the training is completed (e.g. stability over time, transfer to other situations, a sense of logical necessity expressed in the verbal explanations of the subject, resistance to counter-suggestion, comparison with the same behaviors in older subjects). In practice, it does seem that we must use several of those criteria—and still others will surely be added to the list—since each one applies to a different aspect of the same process and has its own particular limits and shortcomings.

This problem of the criteria of logicality, i.e. of the logical-operational status of what is acquired, is much too vast to be systematically discussed here. It is sufficient to note the almost total absence of experimental certitude on this fundamental question. If we wish the study of the induced acquisition of logical structures to throw some light on the equilibratory characteristic of the stage concept, it is indispensable to have at our disposition solid criteria that leave little doubt as to the authenticity of what is apparently acquired. Now it is quite possible, in this respect, that the phenomenon of generalization, that is, the capacity to extend the acquisition of an operational structure to related situations, constitutes the most promising criterion, not only because this criterion lends itself to empirical analyses, but also because it is directly linked to Piaget's conceptions of the nature of operational thought and of developmental stages. It is necessary, however, to specify that the generalization under discussion is not of the interconcept type, involving transfer from some initially acquired conceptual content to one or more different contents not yet mastered at that moment. This type of generalization —similar to the usual forms of transfer—implies by definition the possibility of *horizontal décalages* or of various asynchronisms. The causes of these *décalages* are no doubt interesting and useful to analyze, but their existence obviously precludes the utilization of these forms of generalization as criteria. The generalization here considered is located rather at an intraconcept level, and thus applies to the different groupings or constituent operations of the same conceptual content. We see immediately that such a criterion is in an essential way integrated into the previously analyzed structural characteristic of stages, and that its use is necessarily contingent upon the findings of future experiments on the existence of Piaget's *structures d'ensemble*.

References

Baldwin, A. L. The study of child behavior and development. In P. H. Mussen (Ed.), *Handbook of research methods in child development*. New York: Wiley, 1960. Pp. 3–35.

Bertalanffy, L. von. Comments on Professor Piaget's paper. In J. M. Tanner & Bärbel Inhelder (Eds.), *Discussion on child development*. Volume IV. *The fourth meeting of the World Health Organization Study Group on the psychological development of the child, Geneva, 1956*. London: Tavistock Publications, 1960. Pp. 69–76. (a)

Bertalanffy, L. von. Comments in discussion on general systems theory and the behavioral sciences. In J. M. Tanner & Bärbel Inhelder (Eds.), *Discussions on child development*. Volume IV. *The fourth meeting of the World Health Organization Study Group on the psychological development of the child, Geneva, 1956*. London: Tavistock Publications, 1960. Pp. 155–176. (b)

Bijou, S. W. & Baer, D. M. Some methodological contributions from a functional analysis of child development. In L. P. Lipsitt & C. C. Spiker (Eds.), *Advances in child development and behavior*. Volume I. New York: Academic Press, 1963. Pp. 197–231.

Bijou, S. W. & Baer, D. M. Operant methods in child behavior and development. In W. K. Honig (Ed.), *Operant behavior*. New York: Appleton-Century-Crofts, 1966. Pp. 718–789.

Borelli-Vincent, Michèle. La naissance des opérations logiques chez le sourd-muet. *Enfance*, 1951, 3, 222–228.

Borelli-Vincent, Michèle. Rôle des données perceptives dans l'abstraction: étude d'une épreuve de groupement par ressemblance chez des enfants de 5 à 8 ans. *Enfance*, 1956, 4, 1–21.

Borelli-Vincent, Michèle. Sur le rôle du langage à un niveau élémentaire de pensée abstraite: comparaison d'enfants entendants et sourds-muets à une épreuve de groupement par ressemblance. *Enfance*, 1957, 4, 443–464.

Braine, M. S. The ontogeny of certain logical operations: Piaget's formulation examined by non-verbal methods. *Psychol. Monogr.*, 1959, 73, No. 5 (Whole No. 475).

Braine, M. S. Piaget on reasoning: a methodological critique and alternative proposals. *Monogr., Soc. Res. Child Develpm.*, 1962, 27, No. 2, pp. 41–63.

Braine, M. S. Development of a grasp of transitivity of length: a reply to Smedslund. *Child Develpm.*, 1964, 35, 799–810.

Brison, D. W. Acquisition of conservation of substance in a group situation. Unpublished doctoral dissertation, Univer. of Illinois, 1965.

Brown, R. *Social psychology*. New York: Free Press, 1965.

Bruner, J. S. Inhelder and Piaget's "The growth of logical thinking." I. A psychologist's viewpoint. *Brit. J. Psychol.*, 1959, 50, 363–370.

Bruner, J. S. The course of cognitive development. *Amer. Psychol.*, 1964, 19, 1–16.

Caouette, C. Les opérations de classification chez l'enfant: étude expérimentale au moyen d'une méthode non verbale. Thèse de licence inédite, Univer. Montréal, 1961.

Carbonneau, M. Apprentissage de la notion de conservation des surfaces. Thèse de licence inédite, Univer. Montréal, 1965.

Deutsche, Jean M. *The development of children's concepts of causal relations*. Minneapolis: Univer. of Minnesota Press, 1937.

Dodwell, P. C. Children's understanding of number and related concepts. *Canad. J. Psychol.*, 1960, 14, 191–205.

Dodwell, P. C. Children's understanding of number concepts; characteristics of an individual and of a group test. *Canad. J. Psychol.*, 1961, 15, 29–36.

Dubreuil, G. & Boisclair, Cecile. Le réalisme enfantin à la Martinique et au Canada français: étude génétique et expérimentale. In *Thought from the learned societies of Canada*. Toronto: Gage, 1960. Pp. 83–95.

Elkind, D. The development of quantitative thinking: a systematic replication of Piaget's studies. *J. genet. Psychol.*, 1961, 98, 37–46. (a)

Elkind, D. Children's discovery of the conservation of mass, weight, and volume: Piaget replication study II. *J. genet. Psychol.*, 1961, 98, 219–227. (b)

Elkind, D. The development of the additive composition of classes in the child: Piaget replication study III. *J. genet. Psychol.*, 1961, 99, 51–57. (c)

Elkind, D. Children's conception of right and left: Piaget replication study IV. *J. genet. Psychol.*, 1961, **99**, 269–276. (d)

Elkind, D. Children's conception of brother and sister: Piaget replication study V. *J. genet. Psychol.*, 1962, **100**, 129–136.

Elkind, D. Discrimination, seriation, and numeration of size and dimensional differences in young children: Piaget replication study VI. *J. genet. Psychol.*, 1964, **104**, 275–296.

Flavell, J. H. *The developmental psychology of Jean Piaget.* Princeton, N. J.: Van Nostrand, 1963.

Fournier, Edith. Généralisation intranotionnelle et internotionnelle d'un apprentissage empirique de la notion de conservation des surfaces. Thèse de licence inédite, Univer. Montréal, 1965.

Fraisse, P. & Vautrey, P. La perception de l'espace, de la vitesse et du temps chez l'enfant de cinq ans. I. L'espace et la vitesse. *Enfance,* 1952, **5**, 1–20. (a)

Fraisse, P. & Vautrey, P. La perception de l'espace, de la vitesse et du temps chez l'enfant de cinq ans. II. Le temps. *Enfance,* 1952, **5**, 102–119. (b)

Furth, H. G. Conservation of weight in deaf and hearing children. *Child Develpm.*, 1964, **35**, 143–150.

Garrison, M. (Ed.), Cognitive models and development in mental retardation. *Amer. J. ment. Def., Monogr. Suppl.*, 1966, **70**, 3–149.

Goodnow, Jacqueline J. A test of milieu effects with some of Piaget's tasks. *Psychol. Monogr.*, 1962, **76**, No. 36 (Whole No. 555).

Gouin-Décarie, Thérèse. *Intelligence et affectivité chez le jeune enfant.* Neuchâtel et Paris: Delachaux et Niestlé, 1962.

Gréco, P. "I-VHR," étude génétique d'un système de représentations imagées concernant un groupe de transformations spatiales. In V. Bang, P. Gréco, J. B. Grize, Yvette Hatwell, J. Piaget, G. N. Seagrim, & Eliane Vurpillot, *Études d'épistémologie génétique.* Volume XVIII. *L'épistémologie de l'espace.* Paris: Presses Univer. France, 1964. Pp. 203–255. (a)

Gréco, P. L'organisation progressive des représentations spatiales relatives à une figure complexe (anneau de Moebius). In V. Bang, P. Gréco, J.-B. Grize, Yvette Hatwell, J. Piaget, G. N. Seagrim, & Eliane Vurpillot, *Études d'épistémologie génétique.* Volume XVIII. *L'épistémologie de l'espace.* Paris: Presses Univer. France, 1964. Pp. 257–280. (b)

Hazlitt, Victoria. Children's thinking. *Brit. J. Psychol.*, 1930, **20**, 354–361.

Inhelder, Bärbel. Comments in discussion on the criteria of the stages of mental development. In J. M. Tanner & Bärbel Inhelder (Eds.), *Discussions on child development.* Volume I. *The first meeting of the World Health Organization Study Group on the psychobiological development of the child, Geneva, 1953.* London: Tavistock Publications, 1956. Pp. 75–107.

Inhelder, Bärbel & Piaget, J. *De la logique de l'enfant à la logique de l'adolescent.* Paris: Presses Univer. France, 1955.

Inhelder, Bärbel & Piaget, J. *La genèse des structures logiques élémentaires.* Neuchâtel et Paris: Delachaux et Niestlé, 1959.

Inhelder, Bärbel, Sinclair, Hermine, Bovet, Magali, & Smock, C. D. On cognitive development. *Amer. Psychol.,* 1966 **21,** 160–164.

Kessen, W. Research design in the study of developmental problems. In P. H. Mussen (Ed.), *Handbook of research in child development.* New York: Wiley, 1960. Pp. 36–70.

Kofsky, Ellin. Developmental scalogram analysis of classificatory behavior. *Child Develpm.,* 1966, **37,** 191–205.

Kohnstamm, G. A. An evaluation of part of Piaget's theory. *Acta Psychol.,* 1963, **21,** 313–356.

Kohnstamm, G. A. Experiments on teaching Piagetian thought operations. Paper read at the Conference on Guided Learning, Educ. Res. Council of Greater Cleveland, 1966.

Lasry, J. C. Apprentissage empirico-didactique de la notion d'inclusion. Thèse de licence inédite, Univer. Montréal, 1965.

Laurendeau, Monique & Pinard, A. *La pensée causale.* Paris: Presses Univer. France, 1962.

Laurendeau, Monique & Pinard, A. Réflexions sur l'apprentissage des structures logiques. In F. Bresson & M. de Montmollin (Eds.), *Psychologie et épistémologie génétiques.* Paris: Dunod, 1966. Pp. 191–210.

Lovell, K. A follow-up study of some aspects of the work of Piaget and Inhelder in the child's conception of space. *Brit J. Psychol.,* 1959, **29,** 104–117.

Lovell, K. A follow-up study of Inhelder and Piaget's "The growth of logical thinking." *Brit J. Psychol.,* 1961, **52,** 143–153.

Lunzer, E. Some points of Piagetian theory in the light of experimental criticism. *J. Child Psychol. Psychiat.,* 1960, **1,** 191–202.

Lunzer, E. Les co-ordinations et les conservations dans le domaine de la géométrie. In V. Bang & E. Lunzer, *Études d'épistémologie génétique.* Volume XIX. *Conservations spatiales.* Paris: Presses Univer. France, 1965. Pp. 59–148.

Morf, A. Les relations entre la logique et le langage lors du passage du raisonnement concret au raisonnement formel. In L. Apostel, B. Mandelbrot, & A. Morf, *Études d'épistémologie génétique.* Volume III. *Logique, langage et théorie de l'information.* Paris: Presses Univer. France, 1957. Pp. 173–204.

Morf, A. Apprentissage d'une structure logique concrète (inclusion): effets et limites. In A. Morf, J. Smedslund, V. Bang, & J. F. Wohlwill, *Études d'épistémologie génétique.* Volume IX. *L'apprentissage des structures logiques.* Paris: Presses Univer. France, 1959. Pp. 15–83.

Page, E. I. Haptic perception: a consideration of one of the investigations of Piaget and Inhelder. *Educ. Rev.*, 1959, **11**, 115–124.

Papert, S. Étude comparée de l'intelligence chez l'enfant et chez le robot. In L. Apostel, J.-B. Grize, S. Papert, & J. Piaget, *Études d'épistémologie génétique*. Volume XV. *La filiation des structures*. Paris: Presses Univer. France, 1963. Pp. 131–194.

Pascual-Leone, J. & Bovet, Magali C. Apprentissage de la quantification de l'inclusion et la théorie opératoire. *Acta Psychol.*, 1966, **25**, 334–356.

Piaget, J. *La représentation du monde chez l'enfant*. Paris: Presses Univer. France, 1926.

Piaget, J. *La causalité physique chez l'enfant*. Paris: Alcan, 1927.

Piaget, J. Le mécanisme du développement mental et les lois du groupement des opérations. *Arch. Psychol., Genève*, 1941, **28**, 215–285.

Piaget, J. *Les notions de mouvement et de vitesse chez l'enfant*. Paris: Presses Univer. France, 1946.

Piaget, J. *La psychologie de l'intelligence*. Paris: Colin, 1947.

Piaget, J. *Introduction à l'épistémologie génétique*. Volume II. *La pensée physique*. Paris: Presses Univer. France, 1950. (a)

Piaget, J. *Introduction à l'épistémologie génétique*. Volume III. *La pensée biologique, la pensée psychologique et la pensée sociologique*. Paris: Presses Univer. France, 1950. (b)

Piaget, J. Les stades du développement intellectuel de l'enfant et de l'adolescent. In P. Osterrieth et al. *Le problème des stades en psychologie de l'enfant*. Paris: Presses Univer. France, 1956. Pp. 33–41.

Piaget, J. Logique et équilibre dans les comportements de sujet. In L. Apostel, B. Mandelbrot, & J. Piaget, *Études d'épistémologie génétique*. Volume II. *Logique et équilibre*. Paris: Presses Univer. France, 1957. Pp. 27–117. (a)

Piaget, J. Transposition du problème de l'analytique en termes génétiques. In L. Apostel, W. Mays, A. Morf, & J. Piaget, *Études d'épistémologie génétique*. Volume IV. *Les liaisons analytiques et synthétiques dans les comportements du sujet*. Paris: Presses Univer. France, 1957. Pp. 40–85. (b)

Piaget, J. Les notions de vitesse, d'espace parcouru et de temps chez l'enfant de cinq ans. *Enfance*, 1957, **10**, 9–42. (c)

Piaget, J. Apprentissage et connaissance (première partie). In P. Gréco & J. Piaget, *Études d'épistémologie génétique*. Volume VII. *Apprentissage et connaissance*. Paris: Presses Univer. France, 1959. Pp. 21–67. (a)

Piaget, J. Apprentissage et connaissance (seconde partie). In M. Goustard, P. Gréco, B. Matalon, & J. Piaget, *Études d'épistémologie génétique*. Volume X. *La logique des apprentissages*. Paris: Presses Univer. France, 1959. Pp. 159–188. (b)

Piaget, J. La troisième année d'activité du Centre et le troisième symposium international d'épistémologie génétique. In P. Gréco & J. Piaget, *Études d'épistémologie génétique*. Volume VII. *Apprentissage et connaissance*. Paris: Presses Univer. France, 1959. Pp. 1–20. (c)

Piaget, J. The general problems of the psychobiological development of the child. In J. M. Tanner & Bärbel Inhelder (Eds.), *Discussion on child development*. Volume IV. *The fourth meeting of the World Health Organization Study Group on the psychobiological development of the child, Geneva, 1956*. London: Tavistock Publications, 1960. Pp. 3–27 and *passim*. (a)

Piaget, J. La portée psychologique et épistémologique des essais néohulliens de D. Berlyne. In D. E. Berlyne & J. Piaget, *Études d'épistémologie génétique*. Volume XII. *Théorie du comportement et opérations*. Paris: Presses Univer. France, 1960. Pp. 105–123. (b)

Piaget, J. *Les mécanismes perceptifs*. Paris: Presses Univer. France, 1961. (a)

Piaget, J. Problèmes psychologiques généraux de la pensée logico-mathématique. B. Evidence, intuition et invention. In E. W. Beth & J. Piaget, *Études d'épistémologie génétique*. Volume XIV. *Épistémologie mathématique et psychologie*. Paris: Presses Univer. France, 1961. Pp. 205–241. (b)

Piaget, J. L'explication en psychologie et le parallélisme psycho-physiologique. In P. Fraisse & J. Piaget (Eds.), *Traité de psychologie expérimentale*. Fascicule I. *Histoire et methode*. Paris: Presses Univer. France, 1963. Pp. 121–152. (a)

Piaget, J. Le développement des perceptions en fonctions de l'âge. In P. Fraisse & J. Piaget (Eds.), *Traité de psychologie expérimentale*. Fascicule VI. *La perception*. Paris: Presses Univer. France, 1963. Pp. 1–57. (b)

Piaget, J. Development and learning. In R. E. Ripple & V. N. Rockcastle (Eds.), Piaget rediscovered. Mimeograph report of the Conference on Cognitive Studies and Curriculum Development (Cornell University and University of California), 1964. Pp. 7–21. (a)

Piaget, J. Les travaux de l'année 1960–1961 et le VIe symposium (19–24 juin, 1961) de Centre international d'épistémologie génétique. In V. Bang, P. Gréco, J.-B. Grize, Yvette Hatwell, J. Piaget, G. N. Seagrim, & Eliane Vurpillot, *Études d'épistémologie génétique*. Vol. XVIII. *L'épistémologie de l'espace*. Paris: Presses Univer. France, 1964. Pp. 1–40. (b)

Piaget, J. Nécessité et signification des recherches comparatives en psychologie génétique. *Intern. J. Psychol.*, 1966, 1, 3–15.

Piaget, J. & Inhelder, Bärbel. Les opérations intellectuelles et leur développement. In P. Fraisse & J. Piaget (Eds.), *Traité de psychologie expérimentale*. Fascicule VII. *L'intelligence*. Paris: Presses Univer. France, 1963. Pp. 109–155. (a)

Piaget, J. & Inhelder, Bärbel. Les images mentales. In P. Fraisse & J. Piaget (Eds.), *Traité de psychologie expérimentale*. Fascicule VII. *L'intelligence*. Paris: Presses Univer. France, 1963. Pp. 65–108. (b)

Piaget, J. & Inhelder, Bärbel. L'image mentale chez l'enfant. Paris: Presses Univer. France, 1966.

Piaget, J., Inhelder, Bärbel, & Szeminska, Alina. La géométrie spontanée de l'enfant. Paris: Presses Univer. France, 1948.

Piaget, J. & Szeminska, Alina. La genèse du nombre chez l'enfant. Neuchâtel et Paris: Delachaux et Niestlé, 1941.

Pinard, A. & Laurendeau, Monique. Le caractère topologique des premières représentations spatiales de l'enfant: examen des hypothèses de Piaget. Intern. J. Psychol., 1966, 1, 243–45.

Smedslund, J. Apprentissage des notions de la conservation et de la transitivité du poids. In A. Morf, J. Smedslund, V. Bang, & J. F. Wohlwill, Études d'épistémologie génétique. Volume IX. L'apprentissage des structures logiques. Paris: Presses Univer. France, 1959. Pp. 85–124.

Smedslund, J. The acquisition of conservation of substance and weight in children. II. External reinforcement of conservation of weight and of the operations of addition and substraction. Scand. J. Psychol., 1961, 2, 71–84. (a)

Smedslund, J. The acquisition of conservation of substance and weight in children. V. Practice in conflict situations without external reinforcement. Scand. J. Psychol., 1961, 2, 156–160. (b)

Smedslund, J. The acquisition of conservation of substance and weight in children. VI. Practice on continuous versus discontinuous material in conflict situations without external reinforcement. Scand. J. Psychol., 1961, 2, 203–210. (c)

Smedslund, J. Concrete reasoning: a study of intellectual development. Monogr. Soc. Res. Child Develpm., 1964, 20, No. 93, 1–39.

Smedslund, J. The development of transitivity of length: a comment on Braine's reply. Child Develpm., 1965, 36, 577–580.

Smedslund, J. Performance on measurement and pseudo-measurement tasks by five- to seven-year-old children. Scand. J. Psychol., 1966, 7, 81–92.

Vinh-Bang & Lunzer, E. Études d'épistémologie génétique. Volume XIX. Conservations spatiales. Paris: Presses Univer. France, 1965.

Wohlwill, J. F. Un essai d'apprentissage dans le domaine de la conservation du nombre. In A. Morf, J. Smedslund, V. Bang, & J. F. Wohlwill, Études d'épistémologie génétique. Volume IX. L'apprentissage des structures logiques. Paris: Presses Univer. France, 1959. Pp. 125–135.

Wohlwill, J. F. The development of "overconstancy" in space perception. In L. P. Lipsitt & C. C. Spiker (Eds.), Advances in child development and behavior. New York: Academic Press, 1963. Pp. 265–312. (a)

Wohlwill, J. F. Piaget's system as a source of empirical research. Merrill-Palmer Quart., 1963, 9, 253–262. (b)

Wohlwill, J. F. Piaget's theory of the development of intelligence in the concrete operations period. *Amer. J. ment. Def., Monogr. Suppl.*, 1966, **70**, 57–83. (a)

Wohlwill, J. F. Comments in discussion on the developmental approach of Jean Piaget. *Amer. J. ment. Def., Monogr. Suppl.*, 1966, **70**, 84–105. (b)

Wohlwill, J. F. Readiness, transfer of learning and the development of cognitive structures. Paper read at the Canad. Psychol. Ass., Montreal, 1966. (c)

Conservation and Concept Formation

DAVID ELKIND

Every method of concept assessment presupposes a particular theory of a concept. Whether we ask a subject to define a word, or to sort objects, or to make a perceptual discrimination, some particular conception of a concept is presupposed. The same holds true for Piaget's conservation problems. Whenever we attempt to assess a child's quantitative concepts by having him judge the equivalence of quantitative relations across a transformation in the appearance of one of the components of the relation, a particular theoretical framework is implicit in the procedure. The purpose of the present paper is to describe the approach to the concept that inheres in Piaget's conservation problems.

As might be expected from Piaget's novel method of assessment, his notion of a concept is quite different from that held by the majority of psychologists. It is instructive, therefore, to compare the Piaget conception with the more commonly held version implicit in the discriminative response method of concept evaluation. These two versions, of the concept, the Piagetian and discriminative response versions, will first be compared with respect to the kind of environment variability they assume and then with respect to the nature, function, and content of concepts. A final section of the paper will summarize the discussion in terms of a broader schema of conceptual thought and attempt to draw some general conclusions concerning the psychological conception of the concept.

Environmental variability

Psychologically speaking, concepts are mechanisms by which we attempt to cope with the multiplicity of nature. By means of concepts we are able to deal with new events in terms of past experience and thus effect a psychic economy through the avoidance of additional efforts at adaptation. Environmental variability, however, which is the starting point for all conceptions of the concept, can be regarded as being of two major types. A consideration of both types of variation is necessary if we are to distinguish between the Piagetian and discriminative response versions of the concept. All of the other differences between the two versions of the concept have their origin in this fundamental divergence between types of environmental variability.

The first type of environmental variability, and the one with which we are most familiar, has to do with the variation *between things*. Dogs and cats, houses and cars, people and animals, differ from one another in their spatial discreteness even though they may share some common features or attributes. This is the sort of variation we have in mind when we speak of the concept as a "common response to dissimilar stimuli" (T. S. Kendler, 1961). The most general relations between these diverse elements are those of similarity and difference and these can occur at the level of whole objects, of properties of objects, or at the level of relations between objects or groups of objects. What is central to this form of variation is that the similarities and differences inhere in spatially discrete elements.

In addition to this variability between things, there is also a variability *within things*. A young tree and a child both grow, a block of ice melts, a house gets painted, and a car gets dented. All of these variations, of form, of state, and of appearance occur within a given thing. It is this sort of variation with which the Piaget version of the concept is concerned. Whereas the variations between things confronts us with problems of similarity and difference, the variation within things confronts us with the problem of states and transformations. Piaget's conservation problems are quite clearly designed to ascertain how well the child can cope with the variability within things.

It is probably fair to say that psychology as a whole has tended to ignore the variability within things. Certainly, from a certain point of view, many of these variations are trivial. Yet Piaget has shown that from the standpoint of the child many of these variations are not trivial and pose genuine problems of conception. During infancy, the disappearance of the object is a within-things form of variability to which the child must adapt. Later, the child will have to deal with the various facets of topographical space that appear different from different perspectives. Indeed, at each level of development the child must adapt to new forms of within-things variability. As we shall see in the following sections, a consideration of the problems posed by within-things variability leads to a unique conception of the concept.

The nature of a concept

Within experimental psychology, a concept is usually thought of in terms of psychological *similarity*. Although, as Wallach (1958) has shown, psychological similarity can be defined in at least four ways (as a common stimulus element or elements, as a common response, as a common mediating response, and as a principle or rule) it is always regarded as the essential feature or aspect of the concept. This is not to say that psychological similarity taken as the essence of concepts does not present theoretical difficulties. H. H. Kendler (1964) is only the latest in a long list of writers including Cassirer (1923) to conclude that psychological similarity is always a post hoc determination. This is true because everything that we know is like everything else in some way and psychological similarity does not explain but only describes why some things and not others are grouped together. Meat, cherries, and tomatoes, for example, are all red, sweet, and juicy but are not classed close together. Despite this limitation in its explanatory power, the notion of psychological similarity does provide a useful way of describing the nature of the concept assessed as a discriminative response.

When we turn to Piaget's conservation problems, however, it becomes immediately clear that for Piaget, the essence of a concept does not lie in psychological similarity but rather in psychological *identity* or *conservation.* This view is stated most emphatically in *The Child's Conception of Number:*

> Every notion, whether it be scientific or merely a matter of common sense, presupposes a set of principles of conservation, either implicit or explicit. It is a matter of common knowledge that in the field of empirical sciences the introduction of the principle of inertia (conservation of rectilinear and uniform motion) made possible the development of modern physics, and that the principle of conservation of matter made modern chemistry possible. It is unnecessary to stress the importance in everyday life of the principle of identity; any attempt by thought to build up a system of notions requires a certain permanence in their definitions. In the field of perception, the schema of the permanent object (Piaget, 1954; First published in 1937) presupposes the elaboration of what is no doubt the most primitive of all these principles of conservation. Obviously, conservation, which is a necessary condition of all experience and reasoning, by no means exhausts the representation of reality or the dynamism of the intellectual processes, but that is another matter. Our contention is merely that conservation is a necessary condition for all rational activity and we are not concerned with whether it is sufficient to account for this activity or to explain the nature of reality (1952, p. 3).

The difficulty with this passage and with grasping the principles that Piaget regards as the essence of the concept, lies in the fact that he brings together two seemingly quite different notions, namely, identity and conservation. Each of these ideas needs to be considered in more detail.

The principle of identity is derived from logic and philosophy and has been described by Aristotle as a law of thought:

For not to have one meaning is to have no meaning and if words have no meaning our reasoning with one another and indeed with ourselves, has been annihilated; for it is impossible to think of anything if we do not think of one thing; but if this is possible, one name might be assigned to the thing (Aristotle, 1941 ed. Bk IV, p. 738).

On the logical plane, the principle of identity is often formulated as the tautology $A = A$ and asserts that in any rational argument the definition of a term must remain the same throughout the whole argument.

In contrast to the principle of identity, which is logical in origin, principles of conservation are physical principles that derive from experience and represent the result of physical measurements. Nonetheless, as Bridgman points out in the passage below, physical principles of conservation always idealize experience:

If the statement of arithmetic is to be an exact statement in the mathematical sense the object must be a definite clean-cut thing which preserves its identity in time with no penumbra.* But this sort of thing is never experienced and as far as we know does not correspond to anything in experience. . . . if our objects are tumblers of water, we discover when our observations reach a certain stage of refinement that the amount of water is continually changing by evaporation and condensation and we are bothered by the question of whether the object is still the same after it has waxed and waned. Coming to solids, we eventually discover that even solids evaporate or condense gases on them, and we see that an *object with identity is an abstraction corresponding exactly to nothing in nature* (our italics) (1960, p. 35).

It is clear then that the logical principle of identity is concerned with the definition of an object whereas the principles of conservation deal with an object's measurable sameness across time. What both have in common is their concern with singleness rather than with multiplicity.

From Piaget's standpoint, there is good reason to bring the logical principles of identity and the physical principles of conservation together. This is true because, for Piaget, thought derives both from logic and from reality. The principles of identity and of conservation to which Piaget refers on the psychological

* That is to say, no area of uncertainty (D.E.).

plane are thus analogous to the logical principle of identity and the physical principles of conservation. The psychological principle of identity, for example, is the analogue of the logical principle in the sense that it ensures the permanence of the objects of thought and/or, their definitions. Likewise, the psychological principles of conservation ensure the permanence of real objects across changes in their appearance. The psychological principles of identity and conservation thus parallel the functions of the logical principle of identity and the physical principles of conservation. But they are only parallel. The forms that the psychological principles of identity and conservation take are dependent on mental structures and the rules that govern their activity, and these are only partially isomorphic with the principles of logic and physics.

Once the psychological principles of identity and conservation are posited as being central to every concept, the correctness of the contention is easy to demonstrate. My concept of a dog, for example, presupposes not only that there is a group of creatures that are alike or the same in some way but also that any one of those creatures will retain his "dogness" both in thought and in experience. Without such a presupposition the concept of dog would be useless since the criteria by which I think of, or recognize, dogs would shift from moment to moment. Every concept thus necessitates both a permanence in its definition and in the existence of its exemplars.

The Piagetian version of the essence of a concept does not, therefore, contradict the discriminative response version, it complements that version. Concepts presuppose both principles of similarity and principles of identity and conservation. Psychological similarity has to do with the ties that bind the members of a class to one another whereas conservation and identity have to do with ties that bind together the various states, forms, or appearances of a single exemplar of the class.

The function of a concept

It has already been suggested that the most general function concepts serve is that of adaptation. Concepts can, however, serve the goals of adaptation in multiple ways. From the discriminative response point of view, the major adaptive function of the concept is the classification of new exemplars. By eliminating the need for fresh adaptations each time a new object is encountered, classifficatory responses help to maintain the psychic economy. Conservation and identity also serve an adaptive function but in a somewhat different way. We have already noted that identity preserves the object in thought whereas conservation preserves it in experience, but have not expressed how this is accomplished. In effect, conservation and identity principles enable us to conserve objects in reality by enabling us to distinguish between the *real* and the *apparent* both in thought and in reality. For our purposes only a consideration of this discrimination in experience is required. Before attempting to describe the psychological criteria for this discrimination, a few concrete examples may help to illustrate its behavioral manifestation.

Consider the conservation task concerned with the assessment of the child's conception of substance (Elkind, 1961; Piaget and Inhelder, 1962). The child is shown two balls of clay and is asked if they both contain the "same amount" of clay. After the child agrees that this is the case, one of the balls if rolled out into a "sausage" and the child is asked whether the ball and the sausage contain the same amount of clay. Now when a particular child, who has been presented with this conservation task, says that the ball of clay contains as much clay as the sausage, it is legitimate to say that he has distinguished between appearance and reality; between an appearance of variation and a real identity. This is legitimate because as has been pointed out elsewhere (Elkind, 1967) the ball and the sausage present the child with an illusion such that the sausage "looks like" it has more clay than the ball. A correct judgment on the part of the child thus requires that he overcome this illusion or distinguish between a real and an apparent variation. And, in general, every conservation problem forces the child to distinguish between how things look and how they really are.

Piaget's conservation problems thus point to a new conceptual function, the discrimination between the real and the apparent. Once this function is pointed out, it is obvious that it holds for all concepts. On the plane of concrete concepts, for example, our concept of tree enables us to distinguish between a picture of a tree and a real tree. At a more abstract level, our concept of "democracy" enables us to discriminate between those countries where democracy is real and those where it is only apparent. If we grant, therefore, that the discrimination between the apparent and the real is a function of all concepts, we still need to enquire into the experiential criteria upon which this discrimination is based.

On what grounds, then, do we make this discrimination between the apparent and the real? One possibility might be that the discrimination is geared to those transformations that produce permanent effects as opposed to those which produce reversible effects. According to this criterion, the man who has acquired a suntan has undergone only an apparent transformation since there will be an eventual return to the original skin color. On the other hand, the transformation of sand and other ingredients into glass would be regarded as a real transformation since it is a permanent and nonreversible effect. Many other examples could be cited, but these should suffice to illustrate that one could make a case for the argument that the discrimination between the apparent and the real corresponds to a discrimination between those transformations that have reversible effects as opposed to those transformations that have permanent effects.

Although adequate in some cases, however, this criterion of permanence and reversibility breaks down in many others. Ice, for example, is the result of a reversible transformation but is nonetheless regarded as real and possesses a distinct name. Contrariwise, many permanent transformations, say of an egg from a liquid to a solid state, or of a nut from a shelled to an unshelled state, are regarded as apparent. At least we still call them eggs and nuts. Quite clearly language and culture play a part in these designations, but even so it is nonetheless true that permanence and reversibility of transformations do not provide a reliable guide to the differentiation between what is regarded as real and as apparent.

A more general criterion for this distinction between the apparent and the real would seem to reside in the distinction between within-things and between-things variability. What seems to be crucial in the determination of whether variations are regarded as real or apparent does not lie in the transformations that produced them, so much as whether they are variations within one and the same thing or between different things. Getting a suntan, the hardening of an egg, the shelling of a nut are all within-things variations and hence are regarded as apparent. Variations between things, on the other hand, such as the variations between dogs, or between cars, or between houses are all regarded as real. To be sure there are some exceptions and ice is a case in point since it is a within-things variation that is regarded as real. It seems, nonetheless, that in most cases, the term "real" is attached to variations between things whereas the term "apparent" is attached to within-things variation.

In summary then, the function of concepts implicit in the conservation problems is the discrimination between the apparent and the real. This discrimination, however, does not seem to be made primarily in terms of whether the variations so described are permanent or reversible. On the contrary, the most general criterion on which this discrimination seems to be based is the distinction between within- and between-things variability. Accordingly, it appears that the same type of environmental variation that gives rise to principles of identity and conservation also gives rise to the discrimination between the apparent and the real. This is not really surprising. Once the child discovers, or constructs, the principles that compensate for the various appearances an object or property may take, he has at the same time differentiated between within- and between-things variability, i.e. between real and apparent variation.

The contents of a concept

Every concept has two different kinds of content. There is, first, the realm of objects that the concept points to or denotes and which constitutes its *extensive* content. This is the kind of content with which the discriminative response version of a concept is concerned. From the discriminative response point of view, the content of a concept includes all the exemplars of the concept, say "dog," that the subject can correctly classify. In practice, we seldom test the limits of the extensive content of a subject's concepts directly. Instead, we tend to sample the extensive content by presenting the subject with exemplars that vary rather widely among themselves, say by presenting him with a Great Dane and a Chihuahua.

Concepts, however, have another kind of content that corresponds to the common feature or features connoted by all the exemplars and that constitutes the concept's *intensive* content. This is the kind of content assessed by verbal definition procedures. We arrive at the intensive content of a subject's concept when we ask him to tell us, say, what "vesper" means or the way in which an "apple and a pear are alike or the same." A comparison of the subject's answers with those given by a representative normative group tells us to what extent the subject has acquired the commonly accepted intension of the concept.

It seems reasonable, in view of these two types of content, to expect a certain amount of coordination between them. We would assume, for example, that when a subject gives a definition of a tree, that he would mention the property or properties that actually enable him to classify trees and to differentiate trees from other objects. This does not, however, occur. A child, to illustrate, may be able to classify objects as bicycles with considerable accuracy. Yet when he is asked to say what a bicycle is, he may well reply, "something to ride." While this definition is correct in a certain sense, it could hardly be the actual criterion on which the child bases his classification of such objects as bicycles. There are just too many other things that a child can ride for such a criterion to be decisive. Accordingly, while the child's verbal definition of bicycles tells us something about his idea of a bicycle, it does not tell us the features that in any concrete instance enable him to label a particular object as a bicycle. There is then, little coordination between the extensive content of a concept as revealed by discriminative responses and the intensive content of the same concept as revealed by verbal definition.

If we turn now to Piaget's conservation problems, it is easy to see that they are primarily concerned with the assessment of intensive content. But they are concerned with an intensive content that is much more closely linked to extensive content than is true of the contents revealed by the verbal definition approach. To illustrate why this in fact is the case, it is useful to think of the particular object, property, relation, and so on with which the conservation problems are concerned, as an exemplar of a class of such objects, relations, and such like. In the most general sense, the conservation problems ask the child whether certain transformations affect the exemplar's membership in the class. With respect to the substance conservation task described earlier, the child is in effect asked whether a particular exemplar of the class of relations "same amount" is still a member of that class after one of the components of that relation is changed in appearance.

This is a unique way of defining the intension of a concept. What the conservation problems propose is that the *intensive content of a concept is always relative to the transformations that leave it invariant.*† If, for example, the child says that the sausage has more clay than the ball, and that the two objects have the same amount of clay only when they have the same shape, we know that the intensive content of the child's concept of substance is *form*. On the other hand, if the child says that the ball of clay and the sausage have the same amount of clay, then we know that he has a *units* conception of substance since these are what remain constant across the transformation.

Although Piaget has used the conservation procedure only with quantitative concepts, the method would seem to be quite general. In some pilot work with destructible toy cars, for example, we have found that for young children "carness" was lost with the removal of the wheels and other body parts. For the older children, however, "carness" was retained so long as the motor was present. Similar procedures with apples revealed that for young children, "appleness" was thought of primarily in terms of visual perceptive properties whereas for the older chil-

† For Piaget, form and content are thus always relative to one another.

dren it was thought of in terms of the more esoteric quality of
"flavor." It is clear from these examples that the intensive content revealed by conservation questions is much more closely
related to extensive content than are verbal definitions. "Motor"
and "flavor" are more closely tied to perceptions than are "vehicle" and "fruit."

In summary, then, when conservation problems are conceived
of as concerned with the exemplars of classes, they introduce a
new way of assessing and defining the intensive content of concepts. Traditionally, such content has been explored by means of
verbal definitions that tend to follow the *species* and *differentia*
pattern implicit in our language and that often have little to do
with the actual criteria by which the child identifies objects.
When the intensive content of a concept is conceived in terms of
the transformations that leave the exemplar a member of the
class, we have a direct and novel way of determining which
properties are regarded as critical to the concept. With respect
to conceptual content, then, the conservation problems force us
to expand our understanding of the intensive content of a concept to include those properties that are, in any given case, unaffected by transformations.

Conclusion

To conclude our enquiry into the Piagetian and discriminative
response conceptions of the concept, it might be useful and
interesting to present the results in the context of a more general
and historical schema of conceptual thought. Such a schema has
been provided by Lewin (1931) in his discussion of what he
called the Aristotelian and Galilean modes of concept formation.
Lewin, of course, was concerned with the modes of concept
formation employed in science and not with the modes of conceptualization utilized by the psychological subject. The psychologist is, however, always in a reflexive position with respect to
his description of mental processes since anything he ascribes to
his subjects must be equally true of himself and vice versa. It is
really not inappropriate then to compare the modes of concept

formation found in the history of science with those utilized by the subject in psychology. In general, the ancient version of the concept held by those under the influence of Aristotle differs in three main respects from modern versions of the concept held by those influenced by Galileo.

CONTINUITY VERSUS DISCONTINUITY

One of the differences between the Aristotelian and Galilean modes of thought lies in the relative emphasis upon continuity and discontinuity of conceptual properties. Within the Aristotelian mode, the properties of objects are regarded as discontinuous whereas in the Galilean mode, properties are regarded as continuous. Lewin writes:

Their (logical dichotomies) places are taken by more and more fluid transitions, by gradations which deprived the dichotomies of their antithetical character and represent in logical form a transition stage between the class concept and the serial concept (1931, p. 149).

It is perhaps not too far fetched to say that the discriminative response version of the concept that assumes psychological similarity is the essence of the concept, corresponds to the Aristotelian mode. What, after all, is a discriminative response if not a dichotomizing activity that separates things that are similar from those that are not on an absolute basis. The implication is surely that the properties in question are dichotomous.

In contrast, when the essence of a concept is viewed, as it is by Piaget, as involving principles of identity and conservation we have an example of the Galilean mode of thought. The whole point of such principles lies in their recognition that the properties or dimensions of a given object may vary within themselves. This leads to the quantification of properties, which accompanies the discovery of conservation both in the history of science and in the mental development of the child. In short, the discriminative response version of the concept corresponds to the Aristotelian or ancient version whereas the Piagetian conception corresponds to the modern or Galilean conception of a concept.

HETEROGENEITY VERSUS HOMOGENEITY

A second way in which Aristotelian and Galilean modes of thought differ is how the functions of the concept are conceived. The function of the Aristotelian concept is descriptive and classificatory whereas the Galilean concept is predictive and explanatory.

With the differentiation of phenotype from genotype or more generally, of "descriptive" from "conditional genetic" concepts, and the shifting emphasis to the latter, many old class distinctions lost their significance. The orbits of the planets, the free falling of a stone, the movement of a body on an inclined plane, the oscillation of a pendulum, which if classified according to their phenotype would fall into quite different, indeed into antithetical classes, prove to be various expressions of the same law (Lewin, 1931, p. 149).

The distinction made in the present paper between the function of the concept as a classification of exemplars and as the discrimination between the apparent and the real, corresponds roughly to the Lewian distinction between "descriptive" and "conditional genetic" functions. When a concept is viewed, as it is by the discriminative response approach to concept assessment, as having primarily a classificatory function, it must of necessity remain on the surface of things. On the contrary, if the function of the concept is viewed, as it is by Piaget, as the discrimination between the apparent and the real, then the road is open for traffic in genotypic laws. That is to say, principles of identity and conservation allow one to predict and explain within-things variations.

THE CLASS VERSUS THE PARTICULAR CASE

Still a third difference between the Aristotelian and Galilean modes lies in their approaches to conceptual content. Whereas for Aristotelian thought the particular object takes its significance from the properties of the class, in the Galilean mode the class gains its significance from the consideration of a particular concrete case:

The particular object in all departments of science is determined not only in kind and thereby qualitatively, but it possesses each of its properties in a special intensity or to a definite degree. So long as one rewards as important and conceptually intelligible only such properties of an object as are common to the whole group of objects, the individual differences of degree remain without scientific relevance for in abstractly defined classes these differences more or less disappear. With the increasing aspirations of research toward an understanding of actual events and particular cases, the task of describing the differences in degree that characterized individual cases had necessarily to increase in importance, and finally required actual quantitative determination (Lewin, 1931, pp. 149–150).

Here again we find a clear parallel between the Aristotelian notion of the content of the concept as residing in the class and the discriminative response notion of the content of the class as residing in the set of elements to which the concept applies. In the same way, the Galilean version of the content of the concept as resident in the particular case or exemplar is paralleled by the Piagetian view that the content of the concept can be determined by the variations within a single exemplar.

We can conclude from the foregoing discussion that the discriminative response conception of the concept corresponds to the Aristotelian mode of conceptual thought in the sense that it assumes *discontinuity* of the properties of its objects, *heterogeneity* amongst objects and events and the *irrelevance of particular cases* for comprehending the property of the class. In contrast, the conception of a concept implicit in Piaget's conservation problems presupposes *continuity* of the properties of its objects, *homogeneity* beneath apparently discrepant events and recognition of *the value of the concrete particular case* for understanding the entire class.

Although we have described these two modes of thought in opposing historical terms, they in fact reside together and complement each other from the point of view of the thinking subject. The psychological subject, the behaving individual, no less than the psychologist himself, can think and does think in both the Aristotelian and in the Galilean modes. That is to say, we all think in terms of psychological similarity as well as in terms of psychological identity and conservation. With respect to the psychological subject, the truth of this statement lies in the observation that the subject can make both discriminative responses and identity and conservation judgments. As for ourselves, the scientific observers, we could not conceive of nor grasp the description of these two modes of thought if we were not ourselves capable of engaging in them.

In conclusion then, we have seen that the conception of the concept inherent in Piaget's conservation problems forces us to expand and deepen our discriminative response conception of the nature, function, and content of the concept. This expanded version of the concept will enable us to explore the modes of conceptual thought that characterize not only the ancient world but also the world of modern science. Any comprehensive psychological conception of the concept can aspire to no less than that.

Summary

This paper has attempted to describe the conception of a concept implicit in Piaget's conservation problems and to show the relations of that conception to the version of a concept implicit in the discriminative response approach to concept assessment. Four facets of the conception of a concept were discussed. These were: the nature of environmental variability, the essence of the concept, the function of the concept and the content of the concept. In a final section of the paper the differences between the discriminative response and Piagetian versions of the concept were interpreted within a broader schema of conceptual thought. This summary will present the conclusions of each discussion in capsule form.

It was pointed out, first, that every conception of a concept starts out from some assumptions regarding the nature of environmental variability. The discriminative response conception starts from the notion that environmental variability consists in the variability between things, cats, dogs, horses, etc. The Piagetian conception of the concept, on the other hand, is premised on the variability that goes on within things, the changes in state, form, and appearance that can occur to any given entity. Obviously both types of variability exist and a comprehensive conception of the concept must be premised on both types of variability.

We next took up the question of the essence of the concept. In the discriminative response conception, this essence corresponds to the principle of similarity or to the commonality among things. For the Piagetian conception, however, it is the principles of identity and conservation, that ensure the permanence of things in thought and action, which is regarded as the essence. Once more the two positions complement each other and the full conception of a concept will have to include both the principles of similarity and the principles of identity and conservation. That is to say, every concept has to do both with things in their multiplicity and in their uniqueness.

Following the discussion of the essence of the concept, we considered its function. From the discriminative response point of view, the major function of the concept is the recognition or classification of exemplars. The Piagetian conception, however, assumes that a major function of the concept is the discrimination between the apparent and the real. This discrimination, in turn, can be reduced to the differentiation of between- and within-things types of variability. Here again, a comprehensive conception of a concept must include both functions because in fact every concept does serve both purposes.

Next, we dealt with the content of concepts. It was pointed out that the discriminative response view of content was extensive and concerned with the population of objects to which the concept applies. For Piaget, on the other hand, the content of the concept is primarily intensive and corresponds to the property that is left unchanged across various transformations of the object. In effect, the conservation problems provide a general paradigm for the assessment of intensive content.

Finally, in the concluding section of the paper, the parallels between the modes of concept formation in the psychological subject and in the history of science, were demonstrated. The discriminative response version of the concept was shown to correspond roughly to the Aristotelian mode in the sense that it presupposes the discontinuity of properties, the heterogeneity of events, and the irrelevance of particular cases. The Piagetian version, on the other hand, corresponds to the Galilean mode of thought in the sense that it presupposes the continuity of properties, the homogeneity of events and the significance of the particular case. Within the psychological subject, however, both modes of conceptualization occur side by side, and every psychological concept presupposes both modes of thought.

These, then, are the discriminative response and Piagetian approaches to the concept. Taken singly, either approach provides only a partial understanding of the concept as we know it in the behaving and thinking subject and in the history of scientific enquiry. Taken together, however, these two versions of the concept can provide a comprehensive view of the concept that will account for the modes of conception in both the individual and science. This discussion has, therefore, attempted still another demonstration of what Piaget has perhaps already made self-evident, namely, the significance of developmental considerations for psychological theory in general and for theories of cognition in particular.

References

Aristotle. Metaphysic. In R. McKeon (Ed.) *The basic works of Aristotle.* New York: Random House, 1941.

Bridgman, P. W. *The logic of modern physics.* New York: Macmillan, 1960. (First edition, 1927.)

Cassirer, E. *Substance and function and Einstein's theory of relativity.* Chicago: Open Court, 1923.

Elkind, D. Children's discovery of the conservation of mass, weight and volume. *J. genet. Psychol.,* 1961, **98,** 219–227.

Elkind, D. Piaget's conservation problems. *Child Develpm.,* 1967, **38,** 15–27.

Kendler, H. H. The concept of a concept. In A. W. Melton (Ed.), *Categories of human learning.* New York: Academic Press, 1964. Pp. 212–236.

Kendler, Tracy, S. Concept formation. In P. R. Farnsworth et al. (Eds.), *Ann. Rev. Psychol.,* 1961, vol. 12.

Lewin, K. The conflict between Aristotelian and Galilean modes of thought in contemporary psychology. *J. gen. Psychol.,* 1931, **5,** 141–177.

Piaget, J. *The child's conception of number.* London: Routledge and Kegan Paul, 1952. (Originally published in 1941.)

Piaget, J. *The construction of reality in the child.* New York: Basic Books, 1954. (Originally published in 1937.)

Piaget, J., & Inhelder, Bärbel. *Le développement des quantités physiques chez l'enfant* (2nd ed.). Paris et Neuchâtel: Delachaux et Niestlé, 1962.

Wallach, M. A. On psychological similarity. *Psychol. Rev.,* 1958, **65,** 103–116.

On the Bases of Conservation

LISE WALLACH

How is it that we come to recognize that when water is poured from one container into a different one, the amount of water remains unchanged, or that when objects are placed closer together or farther apart, there are still the same number of objects as there were before? How do we come to recognize that quantities are conserved under such "irrelevant" transformations?

Much as conservation is later taken entirely for granted, Piaget (Piaget & Inhelder, 1941; Piaget, 1952) and others following him (Flavell, 1963; M. A. Wallach, 1963) have shown clearly that until the age of about six or seven children believe that quantities do change under such transformations. What happens at that point? How do these children come, like us, to consider it an absurdity even to ask whether amounts might change with different containers or arrangements?

The question of how conservation is attained is a particularly fascinating one because it is hard to see how experience could possibly provide a basis for conservation, nor yet how conserva-

Discussions with Samuel Fillenbaum, Jay F. Rosenberg, and Terry Goldman Vance have been very helpful in the preparation of this paper.

tion could be developed without a basis in experience. The reason it seems so difficult to see how conservation could be based on experience is that the properties that are conserved typically cannot be observed to remain the same under the transformations in question. Consider the example of liquid poured from one container into another of a quite different shape. One's senses suffice, of course, to enable one to tell that there is now liquid in the second container, and, very roughly, how much liquid, but they do not suffice to enable one to tell that there is the same amount of liquid in the second container as there previously was in the first. A person who does not know that the liquid in the second container was poured there from the first will not be able to tell that the amounts are the same. Or, to take another example, suppose there are two balls of clay, of identical size and shape, and that one of them is transformed into some quite different shape. Again, someone who has not observed or been informed of the transformation will not be able to tell that the amount of clay in the two forms is the same.

The inadequacy of direct observation as the basis for conservation is not due just to the presence of some misleading perceptual cues that need to be overcome, though such cues are clearly often present—in many cases of conservation there simply are not *any* criteria perceptually available that would permit accurate comparisons. The criteria that are normally available become removed by the transformation. When one is to compare the amount of water in two identical glasses, for example, the relation between the heights reached by the water in the two glasses provides a clear perceptual cue for the comparison. But no such cue is available when the water from one of these glasses has been poured into a glass of different proportions from the first so that the water to be compared is in containers of different shapes. At best one may then try to judge height and width differences in relation to each other. This not only becomes fantastically complicated with any but the simplest containers, but also exact compensation by differences in width for differences in height cannot in any case be directly perceived. Again, a person will not be able to judge accurately whether width differences compensate for height differences unless he already knows whether the amounts are the same. All that perception of width in relation to height may do when the differences are in opposite directions is to lead him to recognize either that the difference in one dimension is so large in comparison with the other that the amounts cannot be the same, or that the differences are sufficiently similar that the amounts *might* be the same. Whether the amounts in dissimilar containers *are* the same or not, his senses do not suffice to tell him.*

For some kinds of conservation, there are external criteria in terms of which comparisons can be made after the relevant transformations. The weight of objects, for example, can be compared by weighing them on a scale—which may be done after deforming or rearranging them, and so on, as well as before. Thus one may show by the use of scales that a ball of clay weighs the same after a change in shape as it did previously, or that after deformation it still equals in weight another ball of the same size and shape it was originally. Similarly, the number of a set of objects may be ascertained by counting, and one may show by counting that there are still the same number of things in a row after it has been stretched out as there were before. Recognition of the conservation of weight and number, then, might be based on experiences with weighing and counting, though this is not supported by the available evidence. Experience with counting provided in an experiment by Wohlwill and Lowe (1962) was not effective in leading to number conservation. Indeed, they found that when children had said there were no longer the same number of objects in two rows after one row had been stretched out, they usually perservered in saying this even right after counting the same number of objects in each row! Smedslund (1961b) found that some children did come to assert conservation of weight after experimental training with clay using a scale. However, he found further (1961c) that these children, unlike children who had attained conservation outside

---

* It does not seem to help here to consider the successive perception of the same water first in one container and then in a differently shaped container, instead of the simultaneous perception of two quantities of water in different containers (Elkind, 1967). How exact compensation between differences in height and width should be recognized remains unclear.

of the experiment, readily returned to nonconservation if a bit of clay was surreptitiously taken away when a lump was transformed in shape.

But in any case, whether or not experience with external criteria might provide a basis for some conservations such as weight or number, there are other conservations that cannot possibly be explained in this way, because there are no external criteria for the properties involved. There is nothing analogous to the use of scales or counting that can serve to show that the amount of clay remains the same when a ball is deformed, or that the amount of water is the same after water has been poured from one glass into another. Not does it seem possible to derive these conservations of quantity per se from conservations for which there are external criteria. Conservation of amount of substance appears to be one of the earliest conservations attained, clearly preceding weight and various other measures (Elkind, 1961; Flavell, 1963; Lunzer, 1960; Piaget & Inhelder, 1941; Piaget, Inhelder, & Szeminska, 1960; and Uzgiris, 1964).

What, then, *is* the basis for conservation of quantity per se? How *do* we know that when one of two balls of clay of identical shape and size is deformed, it still has the same amount of clay as the other? How *do* we know that when the water from one of two identical filled glasses is poured into a differently shaped glass, it is still the same amount as in the other glass?

To say that we know the amounts were the same to begin with, and the clay is still the same clay and the water is still the same water (Bruner, Olver, Greenfield, et al., 1966) will not suffice as an answer. How do we know that the clay and the water *are* still the same, in the sense of "sameness" that is critical? How do we know that the clay—and its amount—does not change when the shape is changed, and that the water—and its amount—does not change when it is poured?

It is very hard to see how such knowledge could be established by any sort of experience. One may think of the possibility of returning to the original situation again—reshaping the clay back into a ball, or pouring the water back into the empty member of the pair of identical glasses. The ball would again be the same size as the other, and the water would fill the glass again as it had before—but what is there in our experience to establish that the amounts did not change with the first transformation and change back again when the original situation was restored? Indeed, children often clearly recognize such reversibility and yet fail to recognize conservation (Berlyne, 1965; Bruner, Olver, Greenfield, et al., 1966; Smedslund, 1961a; L. Wallach, Wall & Anderson, 1967). One may also think of measuring the amounts, putting the clay or water into measuring cups, for example, but the question would only repeat itself: how do we know that the amounts of water and clay do not change when water is poured and when clay is squeezed into a measuring cup?

Factors other than sensory experience

How, then, is conservation to be accounted for? A number of factors other than sensory experience have been suggested. Although they seem to be important, although they may facilitate the development of conservation and some of them may even be necessary for it, they do not seem to be capable of solving the problem we have been considering. They provide no viable alternative to sensory experience as the basis for conservation; they are capable of being effective only given that such a basis already exists.

These factors are social learning (Berko & Brown, 1960; Smedslund, 1961a), the ability to think in certain ways (Piaget, 1952, and 1960; Piaget & Inhelder, 1941; Sigel, Roeper, & Hooper), differentiation (Braine & Shanks, 1965a, 1965b; Piaget & Inhelder, 1941; Smedslund, 1961d; Wohlwill, 1962; Wohlwill & Lowe, 1962; Zimiles, 1966), reduction of immediate stimulus dependence (Bruner, 1964; Bruner, Olver, Greenfield, et al., 1966; Feigenbaum & Sulkin, 1964; Piaget, 1952; Wohlwill, 1962), conflict (Bruner, Olver, Greenfield, et al., 1966; Gruen, 1965; Smedslund, 1961e, 1961f, 1963), and inference from the absence of addition and subtraction (Smedslund, 1961b, 1961f, 1962, 1963; Wohlwill & Lowe, 1962).

Let us look at each of these factors in turn, starting with social learning. Might conservation be attained through learning from other people?

Social transmission of information is clearly crucial at least for

the development of particular vocabularies concerning the properties that are conserved. And some experimental procedures set
up so as to try to teach children about conservation (Beilin,
1965; Churchill, 1958; Ito & Hatano, 1963; Sigel, Roeper, &
Hooper) seem to have had a certain amount of success, though
they all involved more than just transmitting the information
that quantity did not change under the transformations in question. However, it is difficult to locate appropriate conditions for
the social learning of conservation in the normal lives of children.

Further, social learning in any case only provides a possible
basis for a belief in conservation by those who have had a chance
to learn it from others. What about those who did not have such a
chance? Why did anyone ever *begin* considering amount as
something that remains the same under transformations of deformation, rearrangement, and so on? That some individuals in
each of the many different cultures involved (Goodnow, 1962;
Price-Williams, 1961) came to think of amount this way and that
their views came to prevail all by mere chance hardly seems
plausible. Some other basis for conservation is still required.

Let us consider the suggestion that conservation comes about
through the development of the ability to think in certain ways.
Specifically, the abilities that have been thought to be significant
are (1) thinking in terms of different yet equivalent units, (2)
thinking in terms of several aspects of a situation at once, and
(3) conceiving of operations as reversible. Each of these would
seem to be necessary for conservation, but again none of them
seems sufficient to account for it in the absence of a basis in sensory experience.

Starting with the notion of different equivalent units, this may
be required even for understanding the very meaning of "the
same quantity" in different configurations. But it does not in
itself tell one *when* different configurations *do* have the same
quantity. Some other basis is still required for that.

The ability to think in terms of several aspects of a situation at
once is also not sufficient to account for conservation. This ability is probably needed to keep a person from thinking that there
must be more liquid in one container than another because it

reaches a higher level there, or that there must be more clay in one piece than another because it is longer, and so forth. But recognizing and dealing with several dimensions at a time is not enough to lead to conservation in the absence of direct perception of compensation. As we have already noted, a person who does not know that there is the same amount of liquid in two dissimilar containers will not be able to tell that the difference in width exactly makes up for the difference in height. This can only be inferred if it is known—on some other basis—that the amounts are the same. Conservation, then, cannot be accounted for by thinking in terms of several dimensions at once.

Two different kinds of things are sometimes intended by speaking of the ability to conceive of operations as reversible. One is the capacity to recognize that in quantity-conserving transformations any change in one dimension, such as height, is "reversed" (or "cancelled") by a change in another, such as width. Such "reversal" is what we have just been speaking of as "compensation." Recognition that compensation necessarily occurs in quantity-conserving transformations would, of course, be sufficient for conservation. But how is this recognition to be explained, in the absence of adequate sensory evidence of compensation? It seems no easier to explain than the recognition of conservation itself; indeed, recognition of the necessity of compensation seems likelier to derive from the belief in conservation than to provide the basis for this belief.

The other kind of thing that is sometimes meant by the ability to conceive of operations as reversible is the capacity to recognize that quantity-conserving transformations themselves can be reversed—that, for example, water poured from one container into another of different shape can be poured back into the original container again, where it will reach the same height as before. But if the sensory experience of such reversibility does not provide an adequate basis for conservation, then the ability to recognize it cannot do so either. We have already pointed out that it would be quite possible for amount to change with one transformation and change back again with another—and that, indeed, preconservation children often maintain that this is what happens.

Next we turn to differentiation. What was meant by this when it was originally proposed to explain conservation is that the property (e.g. amount) which is conserved over an irrelevant transformation (e.g. pouring of liquid) gets differentiated from irrelevant properties (e.g. height of the liquid in the container) that can vary under the transformation. Very recently, Braine & Shanks (1965a, 1965b), finding that children can be led to conservation answers by training them to respond correctly both to questions about appearance and to questions about reality, have proposed that this is the distinction that must be made for conservation to come about.

Certainly the child who recognizes conservation does differentiate both the conserved property from the irrelevant, changing ones, and also real amount, number, weight, and so on, from apparent or phenomenal amount, number, weight, and such. Lack of such differentiation can, it would seem, prevent the recognition of conservation (cf. L. Wallach, Wall & Anderson, 1967), but differentiation cannot in itself account for recognition of conservation. To differentiate the conserved property from the irrelevant, changing one does not provide one with a basis for recognizing the one that is conserved—such a basis is presupposed. Similarly, to differentiate real quantities from phenomenal ones presupposes a basis for judging the real ones. Our problem is just that we do not seem to find such a basis; sensory experience does not seem to provide it. Differentiation, then, does not provide an answer to our problem either.

The situation is very much the same for the suggested factor of reduction of immediate stimulus dependence. It is clear that conservation cannot be attained so long as the child focusses on only the immediate perceptual situation, since nothing in this situation carries the information that the property in question is unchanged. In the typical conservation test situation the perceptual cues are in fact misleading, and conservation has been facilitated by procedures that seem to reduce the use of misleading cues (Bruner, 1964; Bruner, Olver, Greenfield, et al., 1966; Feigenbaum & Sulkin, 1964; Wallach, Wall, & Anderson, 1967), though direct removal of misleading cues is not necessarily effective (Fleischmann, Gilmore, & Ginsburg, 1966). The change from utter dependence on the immediate stimulus situation to increasing reliance on memory and other conceptual processes as a child grows older is without doubt crucial for the possibility of recognizing conservation. On the other hand, this change again can only get rid of some obstacles to conservation; the effectiveness of reduction of immediate stimulus dependence presupposes some other basis for conservation. That the person becomes less dependent on perceptual processes is not enough to explain conservation—what are the processes he does depend on, and how did they develop?

It sometimes seems to be suggested (Bruner, 1964; Bruner, Olver, Greenfield, et al., 1966) that all that one must assume together with reduction of immediate stimulus dependence is some kind of verbal learning. *Direct* verbal learning of conservation has all the problems previously brought up in relation to social learning generally. On the other hand, verbal learning might provide one with the appropriate language for describing the sensory experience involved—e.g. perhaps learning "tall" and "short," and "fat" and "thin" when previously only "big" and "little" was known, would help in recognizing conservation of the amount of liquid poured from one container into another. Children who do not believe in conservation, however, may well know the relevant words—such children may say, for example, "there the water goes up high because the glass is thin; the other is shorter and wider and there is less to drink there" (Inhelder, Bovet, Sinclair & Smock, 1966, p. 163). Further, learning names for dimensions such as height and width could in any case at best do no more than help the child to take these different dimensions into account, and as we have already seen in the discussion of compensation, this is not sufficient to account for conservation.

Next let us consider the proposal that conservation comes about through the factor of conflict. Two kinds of conflict may be suggested: conflict between a tendency to conservation and a tendency against it; and conflict between various contradictory thoughts or beliefs that a person who does not recognize conservation is likely to have. It seems quite likely that the first kind of conflict aids in the stabilization of conservation once begun.

There is some, albeit weak, experimental evidence that supports this (Gruen, 1965; Smedslund, 1961e, 1961f, 1963). This kind of conflict, however, quite explicitly presupposes a prior tendency to conservation and thus is obviously again not in itself sufficient to explain how conservation comes about.

The second kind of conflict might well lead to giving up various kinds of preconservation bases of judgment, but it also cannot in itself provide the appropriate one. A child who, for example, thinks that either height or width suffice as indicators of amount of water in a container will come into conflict when the water is higher in one container and wider in another. But at best this might lead him to realize that he cannot judge on the basis of either dimension except when the other is constant. This still will not enable him to recognize that the amount remains the same when water is poured from one container into another. Some other basis for this, again, must still be assumed.

Finally, we turn to the proposal that recognition of conservation derives from the inference that there cannot be a change in quantity because there has been no addition or subtraction (Smedslund, 1961b, 1961f, 1962, 1963; Wohlwill & Lowe, 1962).

This proposal has the particular virtue of accounting for the apparent necessity of conservation, but again it seems inadequate. Until recently, the available evidence did suggest that understanding addition and subtraction normally precedes conservation (Smedslund, 1961f, 1962; Wohlwill & Lowe, 1962); but this is no longer true (Smedslund, 1964). The results of experimental attempts to induce conservation through experiences with addition and subtraction (Feigenbaum & Sulkin, 1964; Smedslund, 1961b, 1963, 1966; L. Wallach, Wall, & Anderson, 1967) have been somewhat ambiguous but on the whole not very successful.

Further, the factor of inference cannot solve our problem of finding a basis for conservation, because it again presupposes that there already is such a basis. It is only possible to infer the absence of change of quantity under transformations of rearrangement, deformation, and such, from the absence of addition and subtraction when it is already assumed that these transformations do not involve addition or subtraction and that there can be no change in quantity *except* with addition or subtraction. But the preconservation children do not seem to make these assumptions. It is exactly their problem, rather, that they believe that change in quantity can be brought about by deformations and rearrangements as well as by explicit taking away or adding. What leads them to reject this belief? We still have not found any alternative to experience.

None of the factors that have been suggested to account for conservation, then, provides a viable alternative to sensory experience. A number of these factors probably play important roles, but they seem capable of aiding in the explanation of conservation only if sensory experience provides the basis for it. Perhaps we should look again at the possibility of learning about conservation through the senses. After all, conservation would seem to reflect something about the nature of the physical world—it might, perhaps, be a mere invention of man, but it certainly at least appears to be something more on the order of a discovery. Is there really no sensory experience that could provide the basis for it?

Reversibility

What about the experience of reversibility? Might conservation be dependent on the experience of reversibility after all? There seemed to be strong support for this in an experiment in which first-grade children were given training designed to show them the reversibility of rearrangements that they regarded as implying changes in number (L. Wallach & Sprott, 1964). The children realized, prior to the training, that the number of a set of dolls was equal to the number of a set of beds when the beds were lined up with one doll in each of them. However, they thought the numbers were different when subsequently before their eyes the dolls were taken out and placed closer together in a line in front of the beds, so that there was one bed without a doll in front of it. Almost all the children came to recognize that the numbers remained equal after they were repeatedly shown that the dolls could be fitted back into the beds again after they had been taken out and placed closer together or farther apart.

It seemed possible to answer the argument that children may fail to conserve although they recognize reversibility in terms of their not thinking about reversibility at the time of their assertions of nonconservation. The reversibility training procedure led to conservation in children who were immediately able to predict that the dolls would fit back into the beds again as well as in children who were not; it seemed likely that what the training procedure did for the former children was simply to remind them of reversibilty at the appropriate time—to make them take it into account when they were answering questions about conservation.

However, a subsequent experiment (L. Wallach, Wall, & Anderson, 1967) made it clear that children could well assert nonconservation while fully cognizant of reversibility. The subjects were children who said that there was the same amount of liquid in two identical glasses when both glasses were filled to the top, but that there was a different amount when the liquid from one of these glasses was poured, before their eyes, into a wider glass. Repeated observations of the liquid's being poured back and exactly filling the original glass again had relatively little effect on conservation.

This later study, which included a modified repetition of the first one, also led to a proposed reinterpretation of the earlier findings. In an analysis of reasons given by children for conserving in the dolls and beds situation, it was found that the most frequent reason was that there was an extra doll in the line not aligned with a bed—that there was a doll between two beds, or that two dolls were "sharing" a bed, and so on. The dolls and beds reversibility training procedure would seem well suited to making one notice this extra doll if one had not already done so. This procedure, then, may have been effective not because it made the children cognizant of reversibility, but because it made them recognize that a misleading cue—the "extra" bed at the end of the line without a doll in front of it—*was* misleading.

It would certainly seem necessary for conservation that the subject not rely upon misleading cues—and the use of such cues (height) may have been what kept the subjects from conserving in the liquid conservation experiment also. But on the other hand, not relying on misleading cues is not yet sufficient to account for conservation. Again, some other basis is still required. This basis might, indeed, still be the recognition of reversibility. *Both* recognizing reversibility and not relying on misleading cues might be necessary for the attainment of conservation. But there is not now, as there previously seemed to be, any experimental evidence that can be regarded as supporting the role of reversibility.

Further, it never was clear just how the recognition of reversibility might be expected to lead to the attainment of conservation. It was even argued (Berlyne, 1965) that this was impossible, since there exist clear cases where properties are not conserved despite reversibility. The length of a rubber band is not conserved when it is stretched. And the number of a set of objects is not conserved when an object is added—even though addition, too, is reversible, by subtraction. However, conservation never seems to be at issue when properties can be directly perceived, as length or number can in these examples. One speaks of conservation only when there are no appropriate criteria available to the senses. Conservation, in other words, refers to the continuation of something of which there is no adequate sensory evidence at the time.

Given this, it might be possible to understand how there could be a relationship between reversibility and conservation. It might be efficient and economical to assume that a property for which there is no adequate sensory evidence after a reversible transformation continues unchanged, in the sense that this would help one keep track of what the potentialities are (L. Wallach & Sprott, 1964). But to describe this assumption as efficient and economical is still not to explain how it gets to be made. No process has been suggested by which conservation might come about through the recognition of reversibility.

There is, then, neither any understanding of how reversibility should lead to conservation nor any experimental evidence that it does do so. This being the case, is there anywhere else we may look for the basis of conservation?

Berlyne

A different way of attempting to account for conservation through sensory experience has recently been suggested by Berlyne (1965). With a certain modification of mediational stimulus response theory, Berlyne proposes that conservation can be understood in terms of habit family hierarchies.

In the usual mediational stimulus-response view, thinking is regarded as involving a sequence of implicit responses that represent various stimulus situations. The modification that Berlyne introduces is that there are implicit transformational responses that represent the processes that cause stimulus situations to follow one another, as well as implicit responses that represent these stimulus situations themselves. In other words, he is saying that we may (and do when our thinking is directed) think not only of various stimulus situations, but also of how these stimulus situations may be brought about from one another. For example, we may represent to ourselves not only water high in a narrow container and water low in a wide one, but also the process of pouring from one container into another that transforms the first situation into the second.

Like any other responses, responses representing the transformations and responses representing the resulting stimulus situations are thought to become associated through experience and linked in chains. And these chains, like chains of responses generally, will form habit family hierarchies when they are associated with the same initial stimulus situation and end with responses representing the same goal situation.

Now (although this simplifies Berlyne a little) what seems critical for conservation is that some transformations and resulting stimulus situations will make no difference in certain habit family hierarchies, in the sense that the rest of the chains in which they may occur will always be the same whether they are represented or not. This will be the case if, whenever a constituent chain in one of a set of habit family hierarchies includes the representation of the transformation and the stimulus situation that results from it, there is also an otherwise identical constituent chain in this habit family hierarchy that does not include them.

In this view, then, a quantity-conserving transformation is a transformation whose representation makes no difference in habit family hierarchies having to do with quantity. The pouring of liquid, for example—to a person who conserves the amount of liquid—is a transformation whose representation makes no difference in habit family hierarchies concerned with amount of liquid. One recognizes that the amount of liquid is conserved under transformations of pouring when representations of pouring make no difference in the relevant habit family hierarchies.

Although—as will be seen below—in certain ways this proposal may be extremely helpful, the Hullian framework seems unnecessary and, indeed, misleading. It seems very difficult to identify the required habit family hierarchies and to spell out the experiences through which these hierarchies should be developed.

What seems most directly suggested is that there are hierarchies whose goal situations are recognized as the same when quantity is the same and as different when quantity is different; and that these goal situations or the means by which they can be attained are unaffected by transformations, such as pouring, that are irrelevant to quantity. But our capacity to discriminate quantity in situations of direct motivational relevance seems much too weak for this to provide the basis for conservation.

Consider, for example, how one might attempt to apply this suggestion to conservation of the amount of liquid. The goal situation here might involve drinking, and a child might experience that the amount he drinks is unaffected by prior pourings. But our capacity to differentiate amounts of liquid taken in seems very limited. If a child believes that there are different quantities of liquid in two containers that really hold the same amount, it seems highly unlikely that drinking would necessarily lead him to change his mind.

The requisite habit family hierarchies might, perhaps, be developed in other ways than through experiencing that certain goal situations are unaffected by quantity-conserving transformations. One possibility would be that certain verbal responses (e.g. "same," "equal," and such) are learned to stimulus situations resulting from these transformations. This proposal, however, would have all the same difficulties as the interpretations in terms of social learning already discussed above.

Another possibility would be that there is generalization between the simulus situations prior to and following the transformations under which quantity is conserved on the basis of similarity between them. Quantity-conserving transformations, after all, are unlikely to change a situation completely. To explain conservation, however, we need to account not only for generalization between situations before and after quantity-conserving transformations, but also for the difference between this and what happens with transformations that *do* change quantity. Sensory similarity, as we have discussed earlier, does not seem to suffice for this.

It is, then, difficult to spell out just how the habit family hierarchies Berlyne suggests to account for conservation should come about.

The experiential basis of conservation

Let us take another tack. What do we *mean* when we say quantity is conserved under transformations of pouring, deformation, and rearrangement? Clearly, we mean that these transformations leave quantity unchanged—that after them quantity is equal to what it was before.

But what does it mean for quantities to be equal? Sometimes we judge equality or inequality of quantity on the basis of sameness or difference of a property we can perceive. For example, we may judge whether the amounts of two quantities of liquid are equal or unequal on the basis of sameness or difference of the level they reach when they are in containers of identical size and shape. Or we may use sameness or difference of the reading on a scale when they are weighed, or (with less precision) sameness of difference of how they feel when we drink them or of the consistency they have when mixed with equal quantities of some other substance.

But what does it mean for quantities to be equal when we cannot perceive any properties of which sameness indicates equality and difference inequality? What seems critical then is the possibility of arriving at such properties by doing something —anything, so long as the same thing is done to both quantities to be compared. For example, suppose we have before us two quantities of water, in differently shaped containers. If we know that poured into glasses of the same size and shape, the two quantities would reach the same level, we know they are equal. Or suppose we have two lumps of clay in different shapes. We know there is the same amount in each when we know that if they were formed into balls, the balls would be the same size. More generally: when we know that if something—the same thing—were done to each of two quantities to be compared, they would be the same with respect to a perceptible property, sameness of which indicates equality and difference inequality, we judge the two quantities as equal; if we know that they would be different with respect to such a property, we judge them as unequal.

Let us call perceptible properties, sameness of which indicates equality and difference inequality, "indicator properties." Quantities, then, may be compared on the basis of whether indicator properties resulting from the same actions would be the same or different.

It should be clear that quantity need not be conserved by what is done to the quantities being compared. The operation may be one that changes quantity greatly—still, since the same operation will affect both quantities the same way, if performing a certain operation upon each of two quantities results in their having the same value of an indicator property, the quantities must have been equal to begin with. The operation might, for example, be pouring water into a container of a certain shape and size, which is already filled with water to a certain level. This operation will obviously increase the amount of water—but it will increase it equally whenever it is performed. Thus, if the same level is reached when two quantities of water are poured into such containers, the amount of each quantity will have changed but they must already have been equal at the start.

Quantities may also be judged equal on the basis of their

having certain values of different properties. This too seems ultimately to depend on knowledge that when quantities have these values of these properties, indicator properties resulting from the same actions performed on each quantity would be the same. Consider, for example, the fact that we judge as equal quantities of water which fill a pint jar, half-fill a quart jar, and weigh slightly over one pound. We can, of course, get to situations in which water half-fills a quart jar or weighs slightly over one pound from situations in which it fills a pint jar, by operations that conserve quantity. But one need not know about conservation to recognize such quantities as equal. The recognition of equality may be based on knowledge of the fact that if one has three quantities of water, one filling a pint jar, one half-filling a quart jar, and one weighing slightly over one pound, then by doing any one of a number of possible things to each of the three quantities, one will arrive at a situation in which they are the same with respect to an indicator property. For example, if one poured all three quantities into containers of identical shape and size, they would all reach the same level. (And again, it would not matter if what one did changed the amounts, since as long as one did the same thing to each of the three quantities, it would change them all the same way.)

Indeed, the various perceptible properties that are taken to indicate equality by sameness and inequality by difference themselves seem to be linked in terms of the situations at which one can arrive by performing the same operations on different quantities. Why are reaching the same height in any containers of the same size and shape, weighing the same, feeling the same when they are drunk, changing the same amount of some other material to the same consistency, and so on all taken as indicative of there being equal quantities of water, while—for conserving children and adults—sameness of other properties, e.g. height in a container per se, is not? The reason seems to be that all the former properties are linked by the fact that starting with a situation in which any one of them is the same for two quantities, doing the same thing with each quantity can only result in further situations in which they are the same, never in situations in which one is different; and similarly, starting with a situation in which any one of these properties is different for two quantities, doing the same thing with each quantity can only result in further situations in which they are different—and always in the same direction.* For example, if two quantities of water reach the same height in any particular two containers of the same size and shape, they will also reach the same height when poured into any other containers of the same size and shape, they will weigh the same, and so on. And if two quantities of water reach a different height in any particular two containers of the same size and shape, they will also reach a different height in any others, the same one always being higher, and weigh different amounts, the one that was higher weighing more, and so forth. On the other hand, if two quantities of water reach the same height in two containers *not* of the same size and shape, they may or may not reach the same height in containers that are of the same size and shape, weigh the same, and so on.

To sum up, then: in the absence of perceptible properties, sameness of which indicates equality and difference inequality, equality judgments seem to be made on the basis of whether if something were done to each of the quantities to be compared that results in one of these properties, it would result in the same value for both. And these indicator properties themselves, sameness of which is taken to indicate equality and difference inequality, are linked with one another by the fact that if two quantities of the same stuff are the same in any of these properties, doing the same thing to each can lead only to further sameness, never to difference in one of the properties.

Let us now return to the original question. What do we mean

---

* The principle has to be put somewhat differently for perception, since some indicator properties are precise enough to allow differences to be perceived when others are not: starting with a situation in which any one of the indicator properties is perceived as the same, doing the same thing with each quantity can only result in situations in which indicator properties that are equally or less precise are perceived as the same, never in situations in which one is perceived as different; and similarly, starting with a situation in which any one of the indicator properties is perceived as different, doing the same thing with each quantity can only result in situations in which indicator properties that are equally or more precise are perceived as different, never in situations in which one is perceived as the same.

when we say quantity is conserved under transformations of pouring, deformation, and rearrangement? We mean that the quantity of something after any of these transformations is equal to the quantity prior to it. And this, in turn, means either that a perceptible property, sameness of which indicates equality and difference inequality, is the same after the transformation as before; or that if we did something after the transformation that results in such a property, its value would be the same as if we did it before the transformation.*

If this is what conservation means, then the experiential basis for it becomes clear. When a liquid is poured, when a substance is deformed, or when objects are rearranged, no indicator property necessarily remains the same. Neither do the values of any such properties become different—height in a given container, size of a given form, length of a row spaced a certain way, and so on are simply no longer perceptible when the container, form, or spacing is changed. But whenever an action is performed after pouring, deformation, or rearrangement that results in a perceptible property that indicates equality by sameness and inequality by difference, this property will have the same value as it would if the action had been performed before pouring, deformation, or rearrangement. Pouring, deforming, and rearranging do not change the values that indicator properties will have as a result of any actions. The values are always the same, whether the action is performed after these transformations or before.

It is important to realize here again that it is not necessary that the actions performed to bring about the indicator properties themselves should conserve quantity. If this were necessary, we would be presupposing conservation in attempting to explain it. But the action that results in the indicator property may change quantity—it does not matter. Whenever an action is per-

---

* This kind of analysis originally suggested itself as a result of trying to focus on what seemed most essential to Berlyne's proposal. Put in as general terms as possible, Berlyne seemed to be saying: (1) quantity is a dispositional kind of property—for there to be a certain quantity of something means that *if* you do thus-and-so to it (perform certain transformational responses), *then* it will do something-or-other (provide a certain kind of stimulus situation); and (2) the basis for conservation is the realization that this dispositional property is not affected by certain kinds of transformations.

formed after a quantity-conserving transformation, it will always result in the same value of indicator properties as if it had been performed before that transformation, whether the action itself is quantity-conserving or not. The action could, for example, be pouring water into a container already partially filled with water. The result of doing this after or before moving the water about or pouring it into various other empty containers would be the same.

We may, then, tell whether a transformation is quantity-conserving or not if we know whether an action would result in the same value of a property indicating equality by sameness if it was performed after the transformation as before. How do we tell *this?* It will not do simply to perform actions that result in indicator properties both before and after the transformations at issue. *Such* a procedure *would* presuppose that the actions themselves conserve quantity.

What works very well, however, is to start off with two quantities known to be equal—in terms of being the same with respect to an indicator property—then to perform the transformation at issue on one of them, and then to see whether the same value of an indicator property results when the same action is performed on both quantities. For example, we may have two identical containers filled with water to the same height. We may then pour the water from one of these into various other containers, or perform any other transformation for which conservation is at issue, and then pour both quantities into another pair of identical containers and see if they reach the same height, or weigh them and see if they weigh the same, and so on. The actions we performed after the transformation at issue would not themselves need to conserve quantity—we might pour both quantities into identical partially filled containers. If two quantities are equal to start with and a quantity-conserving transformation is performed on one and not the other of them, the same result will still be reached by the same action with each quantity, whether that action is quantity-conserving or not. Thus—if we observe that after a transformation is performed on one and not the other of two quantities that are originally the same with respect to an indicator property, the same action performed on both quantities results in their again being the same with respect to such a property, we have an experiential basis for conservation under that transformation.

Once we have established, in this way, that any transformation is quantity-conserving, then if that transformation itself results in an indicator property, it may of course be used to tell whether other transformations are quantity-conserving in a more direct manner ("measurement"). That is, one then no longer needs to start with two quantities known to be equal—the transformation known to conserve can simply be performed on a quantity both before and after the transformation at issue. If the results are the same, then the intervening transformation also conserves quantity.

For some transformations that themselves result in indicator properties there is also a somewhat simpler procedure for telling whether quantity is conserved. If the transformation can be repeated without intervening operations, such repetition itself will suffice. A transformation that conserves quantity will result in the same value of any indicator property the second time as the first; a transformation that does not conserve quantity will result in a different value. This is simply a special case of the general principle that the same action will result in the same value of indicator properties whether performed after a quantity-conserving transformation or before.

In sum, then, conservation may be explained as follows: We start with the recognition of two quantities as equal when certain perceptible properties they have are the same, and as one's being more than the other when these properties are different. (In fact, to begin with, to say that two quantities are "equal in amount" could just mean that certain of their properties are the same, and to say that one quantity is "more than another" could just mean that these properties differ in a certain direction.) Quantities then also come to be recognized as equal when it is known that they *would* be the same with respect to one of these properties, if it were rendered perceptible by performing the same action on each quantity. This forms the basis for equality and inequality coming to be indicated by sameness and difference of further properties, and also by certain sets of values of differing properties. Further properties come to indicate equality by sameness and inequality by difference (or become part of the meaning of "equality" and "inequality") when it is found that quantities that are the same in these properties always turn out to be the same in properties already recognized as indicators, and quantities that differ in these properties always turn out to differ—in the same direction—in properties already recognized as indicators, when properties already recognized as indicators are rendered perceptible by performing the same action on each quantity. Equality comes to be indicated by certain sets of values of different properties, when it is found that quantities having these values are always the same in properties indicating equality by sameness, when such properties result from performing the same action on each quantity.

When it is recognized that amounts are equal if they are the same with respect to certain perceptible properties, or if they would be the same if one of these properties were rendered perceptible by doing the same thing with each quantity, it is possible to learn that quantity is conserved under a transformation by observing that after this transformation a quantity is still equal to what it was before. Such equality might be shown by a property recognized to indicate equality by sameness remaining perceptible and unchanged after the transformation, but of course this is not usually the case when conservation is at issue. The equality may also be shown by the same value of an indicator property resulting from the same action after the transformation as it would have before, which itself may be shown in several ways: One is by finding that two quantities that start out the same with respect to an indicator property again are the same with respect to such a property as a result of the same action performed on each, when one of them has undergone the transformation and the other has not. Once any transformation is known to conserve quantity, if it itself results in properties of which sameness indicates equality, conservation under another transformation may more directly be shown by finding the same results produced by the transformation known to conserve both before and after the transformation at issue. Or it may be shown that a quantity is equal after a transformation to what it was before by finding that when repeated the transformation itself results in the same value of a property indicating equality by sameness.

These experiences all can serve as the basis for recognition of conservation. In a certain sense—with some qualifications to be discussed momentarily—they seem sufficient to account for such recognition. That is, given that it is criterial for two quantities being equal that they would be the same with respect to a property indicating equality by sameness as a result of the same action's being performed with each, then it would be recognized that a quantity is equal after a transformation to what it was before when it was known that an action would lead to the same value of one of these properties whether the action was performed after or before this transformation. Experiences which showed that an action led to the same value of an indicator property whether performed after a transformation or before would—when this was recognized—then suffice for the recognition that quantity was conserved under that transformation.

For such experiences to be effective, it must, of course, have become criterial for the equality of two quantities that they would be the same with respect to indicator properties as a result of the same actions. For this to become criterial—which is necessary, as we have seen, not only for conservation but for an understanding of quantity much more generally—requires, clearly, the ability to think in certain ways and the absence of complete dependence on immediate stimuli. But once it has become criterial, then—in the absence of any obstacles—the experiences should be enough.

There can, however, be obstacles. A major obstacle that often seems to stand in the way of recognition of conservation by young children is that properties may be taken as indicating equality by sameness and inequality by difference that do not actually do so (cf. the discussions of differentiation and misleading cues, above). A difference in height per se, for example, may be regarded as indicating inequality of amount of liquid, regardless of the width of the container. Similarly, a difference in the length of two rows of objects, regardless of their density, may be taken as indicating a difference in their number, and so forth.

That young children often do use such erroneous properties as indicating equality by sameness or inequality by difference seems clear from the strong belief they frequently show in non-conservation as against mere uncertainty as to whether quantity is conserved or not. The only way it seems possible to explain this belief is on the basis of some perceptible property such as height or length that changes with the transformation being mistakenly taken as evidence for inequality before and after it.

It is not surprising, of course, that young children should take change in such properties as indicating change in amount. These properties *do* indicate equality by sameness and inequality by difference—and are used by older children and adults in making quantitative comparisons—under certain conditions, namely when certain other properties, as width or density, are the same. Young children may well fail to notice that height, length, and so on indicate equality by sameness and inequality by difference only when these conditions are met. Thus, even a child who under most circumstances already takes two quantities as equal when he knows the same value of an indicator property would result from the same action's being performed with each, and who knows that the same value of such a property would result from the same action after a certain transformation as before, may be prevented from recognizing conservation under that transformation, or led into conflict, by perceptible changes in a property as height or length.

But this obstacle of taking properties as indicating inequality by difference that do not actually do so may also be overcome on the basis of experience. As we said earlier in this section, the properties that validly indicate equality by sameness and inequality by difference are linked by the fact that if two quantities of the same substance start out the same in any of these properties, doing the same thing to each can lead only to further sameness, never to difference in one of the properties; and if two quantities of the same substance are different in any of these properties, doing the same thing to each can lead only to further difference, never to sameness. Properties that are not valid indicators are not linked in this way with valid ones, or even with themselves. For example, two quantities of water that reach the same height in containers of different widths will reach different heights when poured into identical containers and weigh different amounts, and two quantities that reach different heights in containers of different widths may reach the same height in identical containers and weigh the same.

Once it becomes criterial for properties indicating equality by sameness and inequality by difference that starting with sameness, the same action can only lead to continued sameness, and starting with difference, the same action can only lead to continued difference, then experience with such facts should lead a child to stop considering properties as indicating equality by sameness and inequality by difference which do not validly do so. Such linkage must, of course, have become criterial, which again requires the ability to think in certain ways and the absence of complete dependence on perceptible stimuli. It might be interesting to test experimentally the effects of showing preconservation children near the age when conservation tends to be attained that even if two quantities originally differ in a property like height, they may become the same in this and other properties they recognize as indicators as a result of the same actions.

Our main point in this section has been that the recognition of transformations as quantity-conserving seems to be based on observing that they have no effect on the values of properties that indicate equality by sameness and inequality by difference brought about by any actions. We have now noted also that a major obstacle to the recognition of conservation, taking inequality to be indicated by differences in properties that are not valid indicators, may be overcome when it is observed that only the valid indicators are linked through action in a certain way. Experience with two kinds of ecological facts, then, seems critical in the development of conservation. Knowledge of these facts alone is not, of course, enough in itself. It must become criterial for two quantities being equal that as a result of the same actions, they would have the same values of properties indicating equality by sameness and inequality by difference. And it must have become criterial for such indicator properties that starting with a situation in which any of them is the same for two quantities of something, doing the same thing with each quantity can only result in further situations in which they are the same, never in situations in which one is different; and starting with a situation in which any of them is different, doing the same thing can only result in further situations in which they are different, never in situations in which one is the same. But once this is the case, conservation should be recognized when the facts are known.

References

Beilin, H. Learning and operational convergence in logical thought development. *J. exp. Child Psychol.*, 1965, 2, 317–339.

Berko, Jean, & Brown, R. Psycholinguistic research methods. In P. H. Mussen (Ed.), *Handbook of research methods in child development*. New York: Wiley, 1960. Pp. 517–557.

Berlyne, D. E. *Structure and direction in thinking*. New York: Wiley, 1965.

Braine, M.D.S., & Shanks, B. L. The conservation of a shape property and a proposal about the origin of the conservations. *Canad. J. Psychol.*, 1965, 19, 197–207. (a)

Braine, M.D.S., & Shanks, B. L. The development of conservation of size. *J. verb. Learn. verb. Behav.*, 1965, 4, 227–242. (b)

Bruner, J. S. The course of cognitive growth. *Amer. Psychol.*, 1964, 19, 1–15.

Bruner, J. S., Olver, Rose R., Greenfield, Patricia M., et al. *Studies in cognitive growth*. New York: Wiley, 1966.

Churchill, Eileen. The number concepts of the young child. *Res. Stud.* Leeds Univer., 1958, 17, 34–39; 18, 28–46.

Elkind, D. Children's discovery of the conservation of mass, weight, and volume: Piaget replication study II. *J. genet. Psychol.*, 1961, 98, 219–227.

Elkind, D. Piaget's conservation problems. *Child Develpm.*, 1967, 38, 15–27.

Feigenbaum, K. D., & Sulkin, H. Piaget's problem of conservation of discontinuous quantities: a teaching experience. *J. genet. Psychol.*, 1964, 105, 91–97.

Flavell, J. H. *The developmental psychology of Jean Piaget*. Princeton, N.J.: Van Nostrand, 1963.

Fleischmann, B., Gilmore, S., & Ginsburg, H. The strength of nonconservation. *J. exp. Child Psychol.*, 1966, 4, 353–368.

Goodnow, Jacqueline J. A test of milieu effects with some of Piaget's tasks. *Psycholog. Monogr.*, 1962, 76, No. 36 (Whole No. 555).

218   THEORETICAL PERSPECTIVES

Gruen, G. E. Experiences affecting the development of number conservation in children. *Child Develpm.*, 1965, **36**, 963–979.

Inhelder, Bärbel, Bovet, Magali, Sinclair, Hermina & Smock, C. D. On cognitive development. *Amer. Psychol.*, 1966, **21**, 160–164.

Ito, Y., & Hatano, G. An experimental education of number conservation. *Jap. Psychol. Res.*, 1963, **5**, 161–170.

Lunzer, E. A. Some points of Piagetian theory in the light of experimental criticism. *J. Child Psychol. Psychiat.*, 1960, **1**, 191–202.

Piaget, J. *The child's conception of number.* New York: Humanities, 1952.

Piaget, J. Equilibration and the development of logical structures. In J. M. Tanner & B. Inhelder (Eds.), *Discussions on child development. Vol. IV. The proceedings of the fourth meeting of the World Health Organization Study Group on the psychobiological development of the child, Geneva, 1956.* New York: International Univer. Press, 1960, 98–105.

Piaget, J., Inhelder, B. *Le développement des quantités chez l'enfant.* Paris: Delachaux and Niestlé, 1941.

Piaget, J., Inhelder, Bärbel, & Szeminska, Alina. *The child's conception of geometry.* London: Routledge and Kegan Paul, 1960.

Price-Williams, D. R. A. A study concerning concepts of conservation of quantities among primitive children. *Acta Psychol.*, 1961, **18**, 297–305.

Sigel, I. E., Roeper, A., & Hooper, F. H. A training procedure for the acquisition of Piaget's conservation of quality: a pilot study and its replication. Unpublished manuscript.

Smedslund, J. The acquisition of conservation of substance and weight in children: I. Introduction. *Scan. J. Psychol.*, 1961, **2**, 11–20. (a)

Smedslund, J. The acquisition of conservation of substance and weight in children: II. External reinforcement of conservation of weight and of the operations of addition and subtraction. *Scan. J. Psychol.*, 1961, **2**, 71–84. (b)

Smedslund, J. The acquisition of conservation of substance and weight in children: III. Extinction of conservation of weight acquired "normally" and by means of empirical controls on a balance. *Scan. J. Psychol.*, 1961, **2**, 85–87. (c)

Smedslund, J. The acquisition of conservation of substance and weight in children: IV. Attempt at extinction of the visual components of the weight concept. *Scan. J. Psychol.*, 1961, **2**, 153–155. (d)

Smedslund, J. The acquisition of conservation of substance and weight in children: V. Practice in conflict situations without external reinforcement. *Scan. J. Psychol.*, 1961, **2**, 156–160. (e)

Smedslund, J. The acquisition of conservation of substance and weight in children: VI. Practice on continuous vs. discontinuous material in problem situations without external reinforcement. *Scan. J. Psychol.*, 1961, **2**, 203–210. (f)

Smedslund, J. The acquisition of conservation of substance and weight in children: VII. Conservation of discontinuous quantity and the operations of adding and taking away. *Scan. J. Psychol.*, 1962, **3**, 69–77.

Smedslund, J. Patterns of experience and the acquisition of conservation of length. *Scan. J. Psychol.*, 1963, **4**, 257–264.

Smedslund, J. Concrete reasoning: a study of intellectual development. *Child Develpm. Monogr.*, 1964, **29**, No. 2 (Serial No. 93), 1–39.

Smedslund, J. Microanalysis of concrete reasoning: I. The difficulty of some combinations of addition and subtraction of one unit. *Scan J. Psychol.*, 1966, **7**, 145–156.

Uzgiris, Ina C. Situational generality of conservation. *Child Develpm.*, 1964, **35**, 831–841.

Wallach, Lise, & Sprott, R. L. Inducing number conservation in children. *Child Develpm.*, 1964, **35**, 1057–1071.

Wallach, Lise, Wall, A. J., & Anderson, Lorna. Number conservation: The roles of reversibility, addition-subtraction and misleading perceptual cues. *Child Develpm.*, 1967, **38**, 425–442.

Wallach, M. A. Research on children's thinking. In H. W. Stevenson (Ed.), Child psychology. Yearb. nat. Soc. Stud. Educ., 1963, pp. 236–272.

Wohlwill, J. F. From perception to inference: a dimension of cognitive development. In W. Kessen & C. Kuhlman (Eds.), Thought in the young child. *Child Develpm. Monogr.*, 1962, **27**, No. 2 (Serial No. 83), pp. 87–107.

Wohlwill, J. F., & Lowe, R. C. Experimental analysis of the development of the conservation of number. *Child Develpm.*, 1962, **33**, 153–167.

Zimiles, H. The development of conservation and differentiation of number. *Child Develpm. Monogr.*, 1966, **31**, No. 6 (Serial No. 108), pp. 1–46.

RESEARCH PERSPECTIVES

Eye, Hand, and Mind

JEROME S. BRUNER

Six years of research on intellectual and perceptual development in children from the third year of life culminated in the publication of a book, *Studies in Cognitive Growth* (1966). In the course of these studies it became apparent that by the time a child has entered his third year, he has developed certain characteristic strategies of processing information. More recently, we have been at work on the first two years of life. Our hope is to explore some of the preliminaries to the growth of mind—to explore that unique set of processes that makes it possible for human beings and no other species to make and use tools and to use language not only for communication but also as an instrument of thought. We are occupied with the growth of those capacities that enable humans to utilize culture as an amplifier of their capacities.

A task of this order would break the spirit unless tamed to manageable and testable proportions. We begin with four traditional, initially intractable questions in the hope of converting them into experimental form. Let me mention them in rough terms to establish our context and then turn to the specific problem with which we shall cope—the integration of eye and hand. All four questions enter into our problem.

The first question concerns the growth of voluntary self-initiated activity, and is as much an issue of neurophysiology as of psychology since it concerns the regulation of anticipatory behavior by corollary discharge or "feed forward" mechanisms.

The second question centers on the growth of skill and on the forms of growth and learning that permit the child to overcome the three major sources of human awkwardness—grossness of movement that violates the fine structure of a task, contradictory systems of action clamoring for a single common path, and imperfect or faltering sequencing of component acts required to carry out a skilled task. We shall have a little to say about each of them.

Our third concern is with the organization of perception and attention, particularly with one critical issue: how the perceptual world of the infant, first governed by the features of stimulation, comes eventually to reflect the requirements of manipulation—how, in short, the play of attention alters in time from being afferently dominated to being efferently relevant.

Finally, and perforce, we are concerned with how the growing infant learns in time to orchestrate several previously separate enterprises synergically, whereas at the outset he is so one-track that he can scarcely both look and suck at once (a special matter that we happen to be studying with some care since it relates to the integration of an appetitive and an orientative system).

Let me say that these matters in aggregate—intention, skill, attention, and integration—do not sum to either language or tool use. We think of them as preliminaries to the use of uniquely human cognitive activity and are searching for clues in their development that presage those higher order functions that link the child with his culture.

The problem we address ourselves to now has to do with the process whereby an infant comes to guide visually the voluntary movement of his hands and, indeed, how he comes to relate the activity of one hand to that of the other under the guidance of vision. It is a process of integration that takes at least two years to complete and the very length and clumsiness of the process may be one important respect in which human beings go beyond their primate ancestry to a uniquely human estate. We have been greatly aided in our studies by the existence of four fine works on the topic, each rather different in objective and approach, but all of great value: the pioneer observations of Piaget on the visually guided reaching of his three children (1952), the painstaking analyses of Halverson (1931) and of McGraw (1941) on infantile prehension, and the controlled observational sampling of White, Castle, and Held (1964) on the development of visually-directed reaching. It is rare in our quickly changing field to have four good travel guides spanning a third of a century!

Before treating directly the integration of the world of the hand and the world of vision, there are two preliminaries to be described. The first has to do with the development of human visual attention during the period when prehension is a very primitive and, in the main, autonomous operation unrelated to vision. Let me characterize that growth briefly as moving from a diffuse distractibility in the weeks immediately following birth to a stage of "stuckness" where attention has an obligatory character, to use Stechler's phrase (1966), to a stage in which it becomes anticipatory and predictive. In the first phase, the infant tends to be pulled hither and yon by objects in the field and particularly by movement in the periphery. Head movements and eye movements at this stage are very coarsely related and compensation between them poor. But as Kessen (1967) has so elegantly shown, the ballistic movement of the eye itself is exquisitely accurate even shortly after birth, given a steady head. Though there is distractibility "from the outside" during the opening weeks of life, the child will show preferences for certain concentric stimulus forms (Koopman & Ames, 1967; Fantz, 1965), for movement, and for human faces (if not their two-dimensional representations, cf. Koopman & Ames, 1967). To observe these preferences, however, the stimulus field needs considerable "stripping down" to prevent the infant's distractibility from taking over.

By six weeks, often earlier, an obligatory or "stuck" pattern has emerged. The infant is now caught by targets that have good figure-ground properties and yield binocular and movement parallax. Eye-head compensation is much improved, and we have seen eight-week-olds trying to pull away from a target (a red ball with black-edged white rings, a black velvet bullseye surmounted by a glossy pearl, all well illuminated against a plain background), turning their heads, only to have their eyes remain fastened on the target, eventually drawing their head back to the midline. When they move off, it is to scan in a rather crudely patterned way until some other target catches them. The attention is directed *outward* to the stimulus world, in search of something on which to fasten.

Gradually, this pattern changes and the infant, to condense the matter, begins to move easily to anticipated objects—pulling away from one target and going to another that is located many visual degrees away without much intermediate drifting. The child, to use Piaget's term (1952), seems to be using a visual schema, placing objects with respect to each other. His attention has now become biphasic in nature—directed outward to the good targets, but guided in change by a primitive internalized schema. Work by Haith (1966) suggests that anticipatory looking begins to be learned at birth, and the work of Lipsitt and his colleagues (1966) suggests early S-S association or habituation. But it does not seem to be until about fifteen or sixteen weeks that the child seems well able to detach from one aspect of the stimulus field and move to another with a plan that is geared to finding what was intended rather than coming to rest on what is merely encountered. It is this aspect of functioning that I should like to call biphasic attention. Indeed, work recently reviewed by Graham and Clifton (1966) suggests that the biphasic autonomic pattern of the orienting response (indicated, for example, by initial acceleration and subsequent deceleration of heart rate in response to a nonsignal stimulus) does not appear until about the sixth month of life, stimulation producing only the first, accelerated response. There is now some reason to believe that it is the second phase of this orienting that is given over to information processing (rather than information receipt). Kahneman's work suggests that during the second phase (he uses pupillary

dilation as his measure, which he has found to be closely correlated with cardiac deceleration), there may actually be a block-
ing of information receipt while previously obtained information
is being processed. I believe this early development of biphasic
attention during the first four or five months of life is crucial, involving as it does not only the regulation of attention *placing* but
also the *withdrawing* and *shifting* of attention. These developments occur before there is much precise coordination between
hand and eye.

The burden of all this is to suggest that there develops first,
before visually guided reaching, an *orientative visual* matrix in
which the seen movement of the hand can be appreciated. This
matrix involves not only vision proper, but the line of sight as
regulated in a compensatory fashion by eye movements and head
movements. It is in the light of such a matrix that early hand
watching should be understood, for the infant is not only recognizing *what* the hand is, but *where* it is visually. Two other
things are also developing during these opening months. One is
the *hand-mouth coordination,* the baby being able to get hand to
mouth in some erratic path by the fifth or sixth day and having
the movement well perfected even before guided prehension is
on the scene. The other is the *vision-mouth anticipation,* again
the baby's learning very early to open his mouth when the appropriate object is visually apprehended. So the mouth, in the
classic sense, early can serve as a *tertium quid* between vision
and the hand and, as we shall see, plays an important role as the
terminus of guided reaching activity.

Now consider some of the steps en route to manipulative prehension. Let me tell you at the outset that our observations on
even the youngest children (six weeks) are made with the child
in a slightly reclining (ca. 30°) but sitting position, in a special,
cushioned chair that has a wide, soft elastic band to support
the abdomen and another around the chest to support the
trunk. This gives great freedom to the head and leaves the
arms very much unencumbered. The observations are from approximately six weeks to about eighteen months, always in a sup-
ported-sitting or, for the older children, in a free-sitting position.

The first analogue of reaching that we observe when an attractive object is presented to the six- to eight-week-old infant and moved back and forth horizontally through thirty degrees of visual arc at about ten inches distance from him is a general "pumping up" or activation response, in which he brings his hands up to the midline but with little bimanual coordination. There are rough "swiping" movements that constitute a diffuse reaching and that ride atop the massive pumping up of activation. If the child's hand (or hands) happens to strike an object while unfisted, there will be a grasping and a retrieval of the object to the mouth.

If the child touches with a single hand, there is somewhat faster bringing forward of the hand in question a second time when the object is immediately presented again. The unattended hand hangs rather limp. Where there is massive activation, achieved by moving the object between the two raised hands, now touching one and now the other, the child, by the sheer anatomy of outward reaching, will close on the object with both hands and immediately bring it to the mouth, insertion into which terminates the act. Repeating this kind of stimulation facilitates its appearance until activation is too high and there is crying. I should like to emphasize that the two hands are not acting to complement each other, but are in synchrony at the midline. One hand will not cross over the midline to help the other get an object to the mouth or even to get a grasp on it.

Our preliminary observations lead us to believe that a successful carrying out of the sequence "Reach—Capture—Retrieve—Mouth" seems to preactivate repetition of the sequence through a corollary discharge or "feed-forward" to the components of the act. Its threshold seems lowered and its components more smoothly articulated. Note that what is grasped is brought directly to the mouth under visual inspection. Let me illustrate the role of the mouth by reference to the protocol of a sixteen-week-old baby. The baby, having closed both hands around an attractive object held in my hand, brought it to his opened mouth. Before he could get the object into his mouth, I inserted the middle finger of my ball-holding hand between his lips, and he immediately began to suck it, holding firmly to the ball all the while. I removed my finger and the ball after several seconds, holding the ball before him again and moving it from extended hand to extended hand until he closed on it again and drew it to his mouth. But before he could get it there, one hand broke away from the ball and was thrust into his mouth, terminating the retrieving act. The anticipatory mouthing aspect of the re- trieval short-circuited the retrieval act, so to speak. The child's mouth had opened typically just as he began to approach the object and served as a kind of "anticipatory binding" to the grasp and retrieval.

Over the succeeding weeks, indeed until the sixth month or so, there is a better and better coordination of the four-part invari- ant sequence: "Reach—Grasp—Retrieve—Mouth," all with vi- sual inspection. The sequence has several interesting features. It is at first mainly successive, with little anticipatory priming of movements. With time, there is more feed forward and priming so that the hand is shaped to grasping as the reach is going for- ward. One has the strong impression that the mouth, before de- scribed as the *tertium quid,* is priming the sequence by opening in advance.

Moreover, the sequence always ends at the mouth—never, be it noted, before the eyes for closer inspection or for bimanual manipulation. That does not come for another month save in a kind of fortuitous conflict between the two hands asymmetrically holding an object in bimanual possession.

Further, the sequence seems to require for its completion a constant visual surveillance. At seven months, for example, we do the following experiment. The child reaches for an object placed on one side of the midline with the ipsilateral hand. As his hand arrives at the object, we drop a light cloth over his hand and the object. He withdraws his hand empty and begins the reach again, but it is interrupted by the visual absence of the object. By nine months, loss of visual contact will not interrupt the act and the infant's hand emerges from under the masking cloth with the object firmly in hand.

During development, the sequential acts of reaching and grasping seem to require cessation of all other enterprises. Like so much of the child's complex behavior, it involves a total commitment. What is interesting, once visually guided reaching achieves some rough competence, is that attention enters a new phase in its deployment. From diffuse distractibility, through stuckness, through anticipation, attention now moves (usually around seven or eight months) to a phase where it is alternately leading and tracking the moving hand toward objects and in its retrieval of objects—again, with the mouth almost invariably the terminus.

I believe that it is at this stage (about eight months) that the final "maturing" of visually guided manipulation begins, and it requires several forms of mastery to get there. The first of these has to do with rendering the sequence "Reach—Grasp—Retrieve—Mouth" less successive and more anticipatory on the one hand and more differentiated on the other—in a word, less "awkward" in the three senses of that word earlier employed. There are, from eight or nine months on, fewer distinctive steps in the sequence and each successive step is primed one or two steps ahead. The steps, moreover, overlap in time and give an increasing sense of smoothness and speed. With respect to differentiation, there is first a gradual dropping out of the first activation or "pumping-up" and the baby, by eight months, can begin a reach without tensing the whole torso. There is also an end to little bimanual tugs-of-war.

Second, there is a freeing of the sequence from mouthing as its terminal phase. When an object is to be brought to the mouth at seven months (or even at fourteen months) the mouth opens wide early in the sequence. But there are occasions at eight or nine months when the infant retrieves so as to explore tactually or visually or kinesthetically (using an object for rhythmic banging, for example). The mouth, having served as *tertium quid*, by helping knit eye and hand systems, now dominates the sequence less.

Third, there is a gradual freeing of the act from the redundancy of input that was originally needed to sustain it. From one year on, the object does not have to be watched so constantly and visual attention, once the hand starts toward its destination, now moves to a next anticipated locus of action. When we compare the time looking at the hand with object of a fourteen-month-old with that of a twenty-seven-month-old baby during visually directed reaching and retrieving, the proportion drops from nearly three-quarter time to less than quarter-time. The difference at twenty-seven months is spent, literally, in "looking ahead." But both ages, fourteen months and twenty-seven, share a certainty in the joint handling of visual and kinesthetic-proprioceptive information from the hand. At seven months, our specially made films show many episodes in which, while the infant is trying to get hold of a moderately heavy drinking cup, he will literally shut his eyes while bringing his hands together on the cup, particularly if a previous, visually guided effort has failed. So we can say that the first effort is to map the kinesthetic-proprioceptive field of the hand on the visual orientation field (with the help of the mouth), and the second task is to utilize the redundancy of the two fields to free the task from constant visual supervision, so that visual anticipation of action may develop.

Fourth, there is a gradual process of learning bimanual, complementary activity. This is indeed a mysterious process. Piaget (1952) urges that it is produced by the clasped hands pulling against each other. I think this is a necessary but not a sufficient condition. It leads to their conjugate or antagonist action, but not to the kind of complementary action where one hand holds something for the other to pick up. Here a word must be said about the mysterious midline barrier. It is a strict one at seven months. If a toy is held before the hand of an infant after he has already grasped something in that hand, the contralateral hand will not reach across the midline to get it. The ipsilateral hand will tense and the infant will bang the new object with a clenched hand holding the original object. Or if an object is hidden beneath a cloth on one side of the midline, the infant will struggle for it with the hand on that side, the contralateral hand lying on its side unattended and unaiding. Perhaps there is what Geschwind (1965) calls a "disconnexion syndrome" with insufficient commissural fibres. But I suggest there is exercise needed even after the fibres are connected. What the nature of this exercise is remains uncertain. It is well to remember a few salient

facts about bimanual operations before taking its development
too much for granted as mere "maturation." Held and Bauer
(1967) have shown that when infant monkeys are reared without view of their hands, they are not able to reach for and grasp
visible objects with the newly seen limb. Moreover, if the experience is given to the animal that is requisite for learning how to
reach and grasp with *one* hand, there is minimum transfer to the
other hand when it is brought out from under the masking ruff.
This had been found previously in studies of adaptation to pris-
matic displacement in adult humans, adaptation of one hand's
not "crossing over" to the other (Efstathiou et al., 1967). Moreover, when *both* hands of the specially reared infant monkeys were
freed and were open to visual guidance, the first one trained was
favored and little or no complementary activity was observed.
Recall that these animals had previously carried out visually un-
guided bimanual activities under the masking ruff, and also that
the experimental monkeys, when tested, were twice as old as
normally reared monkeys who had visually guided bimanual
reaching completely under control.

Fifth, and finally, from about seven months onward there is a
slow but steady dissociation of the gestural components involved
in visually guided reaching from the goal-directed sequence
noted before as beginning with activation and ending with
mouthing. These gestural components might almost be considered the elements to be combined in a syntax of action. Consider
some examples. We present an infant with a grasping-toy, to one
or another side of the midline so as to reduce conflict. As he begins to reach, we cover the toy from view with a drop cloth that
is attached to the table along the edge opposite to the one at
which the infant is seated. The only way that the child can remove the cloth from over the object is either to lift it directly up
and reach under, or to push the cloth away from him. We know
from other experiments that both acts are in the repertory of children of the ages we observe. Now, with a seven- to nine-month-
old, neither of these acts occurs (or very rarely occurs and then
only in precocious children). In infants of this age, to begin
with, the whole act of removing the cloth and getting the toy is
carried out unilaterally (as already noted), and this precludes

success in lifting, though attempts at lifting are quite rare at that. What one *never* observes is pushing away of the covering cloth—whether one uses an opaque or a semitransparent drop cloth. The response in the great majority of instances is an attempt to pull the cloth toward one—in much the same way as one draws the object toward one. Indeed, one is struck by the fact that in the seven-month-old, the act of attempting to remove the screen is hardly distinguishable from the act of reaching for the object. "Pushing away" is a response that is tied to rejection (as any parent can testify who has attempted to feed the child an unfavored food!). It cannot be dissociated from that goal-directed sequence and inserted in a sequence involved in retrieving a desired object. In this sense we may speak of growth's involving a dissociation of gestural components from goal-directed sequences. The fourteen- to sixteen-month-old has begun to master such dissociation.

Yet it is interesting that en route to this achievement there is an awkward stage in which there seems to be conflict between the "retrieve" and "uncover" responses—looking for all the world like a flailing of the arm back and forth in the frontal-lateral line, firmly gripping the drop cloth in hand.

Let me now sum up in a few words. At the outset, there is a growth of biphasic attention that permits the child to register on salient object cues and to anticipate where other objects are so that one can move to them directly. This makes possible not only attention to a specific object but also orderly withdrawal and shift of attention to other objects. This development during the first three or four months involves not only the purely visual field, but also the orientation of the eyes, head, and body toward visual objects. Concurrently, the mouth becomes a kind of common terminus for both visual and manual-kinesthetic anticipation. The child learns to anticipate the visual approach of objects to the mouth, and learns to put his own hands in his mouth. The mouth now becomes a kind of *tertium quid* between vision and manual movement. As the child's initially gross activation response to visual objects becomes sufficiently differentiated to yield a successful open-handed reach-with-contact, he begins visually guided reaching, grasping, and retrieving—the sequence always culminating in mouthing. The act and its components are now dominated by mouthing as an anticipated goal response. Learning during this stage leads to better anticipation, a more integrated act, and finer differentiation.

Full development of visually guided reaching begins with freeing the sequence of reaching-grasping-retrieving from its terminal phase of mouthing. It is freed, also, from the requirement of full visual inspection and control, freed by feed-forward of its slow successiveness, and its component gestures are freed from a fixed sequence. The component acts of reaching, grasping, and retrieving now become subroutines able to fit into a variety of other activities with which they can become integrated. An infant's visually guided prehensile career starts in the service of hand-to-mouth operations and gradually acquires a freedom for use in a variety of contexts that the environment has to offer.

References

Bruner, J. S., Olver, Rose R., & Greenfield, Patricia M. *Studies in Cognitive Growth*. New York: Wiley, 1966.

Efstathiou, A., Bauer, J., Greene, M., & Held, R. Altered reaching following adaptation to optical displacement of the hand. *J. exp. Psychol.*, 1967, **73**, 113–120.

Fantz, R. L. Ontogeny of perception. In A. M. Schrier, H. F. Harlow, & F. Stollnitz (Eds.), *Behavior of nonhuman primates*, Vol. II. New York: Academic Press, 1965. Ch. 10.

Geschwind, N. Disconnexion syndromes in animals and man: Parts I and II. *Brain*, 1965, **88**, 237–294, 585–644.

Graham, Frances K., & Clifton, Rachel Keen. Heart rate change as a component of the orienting response. *Psychol. Bull.*, 1966, **65**, 305–320.

Haith, M. M. The response of the human newborn to visual movement. *J. exp. Psychol.*, 1966, **3**, 235–243.

Halverson, H. M. An experimental study of prehension in infants by means of systematic cinema records. *Genet. Psychol. Monogr.*, 1931, **10**, 107–284.

Held, R., & Bauer, J. A., Jr. Visually guided reaching in infant monkeys after restricted rearing. *Science*, 1967, **155**, 718–720.

Kahneman, D., Tursky, B., Shapiro, D., & Crider, A. Pupillary dilation, heart rate, skin resistance changes during a mental task. *J. exp. Psychol.* (Submitted)

Kessen, W. Sucking and looking: two organized congenital patterns of behavior in the human infant. In H. W. Stevenson, E. H. Hess, & Harriet L. Rheingold (Eds.), *Early behavior: comparative and developmental approaches.* New York: Wiley, 1967.

Koopman, Peggy R., & Ames, Elinor W. Infants' preferences for facial arrangements: a failure to replicate. Presented at Biennial Meeting of the Soc. Res. Child Develpm., New York, 1967.

Lipsitt, L. Learning in the human infant. In H. W. Stevenson, E. H. Hess, & Harriet L. Rheingold (Eds.), *Early behavior: comparative and developmental approaches.* New York: Wiley, 1967.

McGraw, Myrtle B. Neural maturation as exemplified in the reaching-prehensile behavior of the human infant. *J. Psychol.,* 1941, **11,** 127–141.

Piaget, J. *The origins of intelligence in children.* New York: Internat. Univer. Press, 1952.

Stechler, G., & Latz, Elizabeth. Some observations on attention and arousal in the human infant. *J. Amer. Acad. Child Psychiat.,* 1966, **5**(3), 517–525.

White, B. L., Castle, P., & Held, R. Observations on the development of visually-directed reaching. *Child Develpm.,* 1964, **35,** 349–364.

The Initial Coordination of Sensorimotor Schemas in Human Infants—Piaget's Ideas and the Role of Experience

BURTON L. WHITE

During the last ten years, increasing numbers of American psychologists have turned to the study of human infancy. Characteristically, recent research in this country has been carefully designed and executed. Another feature shared by most modern studies is the modesty of their scope. Visual orientation, auditory sensitivity, heart-rate patterns, conditioned reflexes, etc., typify the target phenomena under study. Valuable as these studies are, they seem to leave the student of human development in a state

At various stages, extending over the last six years, this research has received support from Grant M-3657 from the National Institute of Mental Health; Grant 61-234 from the Foundation's Fund for Research in Psychiatry; Grants HD-00761 and HD-K 02054 from the National Institutes of Health, the Optometric Extension Program; Grant NSG-496 from the National Aeronautics and Space Administration; Grant AF-AFOSR354-63 from the Office of Scientific Research, United States Air Force; and the Rockefeller Foundation. The research was conducted at the Tewksbury Hospital, Tewksbury, Massachusetts. I am very grateful for the assistance of Dr. Richard Held, Mr. Peter Castle, and Miss Kitty Riley and for the consideration and aid given by Drs. John Lu, Solomon J. Fleischman, Peter Wolff, and Lois Crowell and head nurses Helen Efstathiou, Frances Craig, and Virginia Donovan.

of deprivation. Some sense of how the entire human infant functions during his first encounters with the world is indispensable
and yet not easily available. It would be fair to say that few
American developmental psychologists have much first-hand
knowledge about infant behavior beyond the scope of their admittedly narrowly defined studies. I think part of the enormous
respect many of us have for Jean Piaget is due to his contribution to our understanding of the nature of the normally functioning human infant.

The Origins of Intelligence in Children (Piaget, 1952), is in
my opinion, far and away the most outstanding body of work we
have on human infancy. It represents the work of a truly remarkable observer, theoretician, and experimenter. It is one of the
few examples of behavioral research on a grand scale. Actually,
the approach Piaget used is more familiar to biologists and
ethologists than to psychologists. Defining intelligence as the
prime human adaptive tool, Piaget traced the etiology of this
vital asset from its first manifestations in the sensorimotor behavior of the newborn to the emergence of ideational forms at the
end of the second year. He did this using a combination of fundamental scientific tools. The combination was a simple one; (1)
selection of the general topic—the ontogenesis of intelligence;
(2) general theorizing—e.g. continuous efforts towards adaptation involving assimilation, accommodation, and schemas; (3) observations—thousands of hours spent identifying the multiplicity
of manifestations of the processes under study; (4) experimentation—e.g. on object permanence, means-ends behavior, and
so on (5) refinement and integration of the theory.

Along the way, Piaget identified behavioral signs of the emergence of several related fundamental processes such as: intentionality, curiosity, symbolic behavior, the transition from trial
and error to insightful behavior, and so on. It is truly amazing
that virtually no one (Charlesworth, 1966, excepted) has pur-
sued subsequently the study of these processes in infants although it has been thirty years since Piaget's observations were
published.

When one describes this work in 1967, one gets a feeling of
remoteness from modern American studies. There is no mention

of independent variables, operational definitions, elaborate experimental design, nonparametric statistics, and so forth, nor their counterparts of the 1930's. Yet, neither is there a feeling of artificiality, arbitrariness, and atomism characteristic of modern studies. Perhaps, the most unique contribution Piaget has made to the study of infancy is to suggest a viable alternative to the conventional approach used in our field.

Bear with me for a moment while I compare the tasks of understanding early human development and manufacturing a suit of clothes. Most modern studies are primarily empirical, restricted in scope, and scientifically respectable. Such studies produce dependable findings. In the preparation of our suit of clothes, these well-shaped findings are comparable to finely cut lapels, or pockets, or buttonholes, or cuffs, or what have you. They are unquestionably excellently made but it is not as if we have all of the pieces that only remain to be put together. Rather, we have perhaps less than 5 percent of the total, and in fact, there are those producing such pieces, lapels perhaps, who would have us believe that the entire suit is simply a very large lapel. I find less to quarrel with with them, however, than with others in our field who claim to have fine suits available when we know they have not taken the time and trouble to procure any fabric let alone lapels or pockets. Their suits are splendidly advertised but seem to lack substance. Piaget, on the other hand, although admittedly having studied only one of several major developmental processes, and only in his own three children, has manufactured a complete suit. It is undoubtedly improperly cut. It would be miraculous if it were a perfect fit. Nonetheless, it has a general shape that probably bears a strong generic relationship to the product we seek. He has very few genuine competitors.

Let me make explicit what I have implied. There seem to be in current use three ways of studying infant development: (1) empirical studies of high dependability and molecular scope; (2) theoretical work, broad in scope but supported by negligible amounts of data (as for example, modern explanatory systems of language acquisition); and (3) bold frontal assaults on the *total* course of the developmental process via intensive first-hand longitudinal observations combined with cumulative experimentation, and an irreligious attitude towards laboratory methods, experimental design, and statistics. It is my contention that Piaget's infancy work is an example of style 3 and constitutes the single most important contribution to our understanding of early human intellectual development. It is the only system based on empirical evidence that addresses the question, "What does the human child know of the world during his first two years of life?" Perhaps, it is time we asked whether the traditional approaches in which we have been investing virtually all of our resources (styles 1 and 2) have been sufficiently productive.

Personally, I find my professional bearings with Piaget's studies. Right or wrong, he offers a powerful framework for guidance in investigating human behavior; a framework that is sufficiently complicated for the obviously complex creature involved, and one that pulls together the bewildering pieces of infant behavior into a believable system. I never cease to be amazed at how often my own observations on several hundred infants confirm Piaget's observations on only three.

Perhaps, the feature of Piaget's theory that attracted me most was its focus on the intimate interaction between infant and enviornment. Here, after all, is where the processes that concern psychologists take place. Even though he did not concern himself with possible optimal arrangements of environmental circumstances or "aliments," he did not open the door for anyone who would care to sponsor schema development, complication, and proliferation. The studies I have been involved with over the last several years (White, et al., 1964; Haynes, et al., 1965; White & Castle, 1964; White & Held, 1966; White, 1967) have been oriented toward the determination of optimal rearing conditions for human infants. I have consciously tried to utilize both styles 2 and 3 in my approach to the problem. As a result, I feel my colleagues and I have gained some dependable knowledge about such fundamental sensorimotor acquisitions as visually-directed reaching, accommodation, and exploration. In addition, we believe we have gained some preliminary but dependable knowledge about the complicated interrelations between early experience and development.

In this report, I should like to present some hitherto unpublished data on one phase of sensorimotor theory. These data concern the integration of schemas or in Piaget's terms the "reciprocal coordinations" of the second stage. During a series of studies on the effects of differential rearing conditions, we routinely included an "object-in-hand" test. According to Piaget, the behavior seen when an object is grasped by an infant of one to five months of age reveals the degree of interrelationship among the grasp, sucking, and looking schemas. The one-month-old infant is capable of grasping a rattle, looking at it, or sucking it. Further, each of these behaviors can be elicited if the rattle is used as directed "aliment," that is, if it is brought to the infant's mouth, he will suck it; if it is pressed in the infant's palm, he will grasp it, and so on. However, at one month of age, according to Piaget, these schemas exist in isolation. This means that, unlike an adult, a one-month-old infant will not look at something he is grasping, nor grasp what he is sucking, and so forth. During the months that follow, these schemas become coordinated. The steps as spelled out by Piaget (1952, pp. 88–122) are as follows:

1–2 MONTHS*—The hand does not grasp an object that is being sucked, even though the hand itself is occasionally brought to the mouth and sucked. Further, the eyes do not regard the object grasped (or the hand). Vision is therefore not so advanced as sucking when compared with control of the hands.

2–3 MONTHS—The eyes follow the motion of the hands but the hands are not under the control of the visual system; they move in and out of the visual field apparently independently. The hand does not try to grasp what the eye sees. Continuing the primacy of sucking as a controlling function, the hand brings grasped objects to the mouth where they are sucked rather than to the visual field for viewing.

3–4 MONTHS—The hand grasps the object that is being sucked and reciprocally the object grasped is brought to the mouth to be sucked. However, if the object is in view before it is grasped, there is a delay before the object is brought to the mouth. In addition, vision seems to influence hand movements, maintaining their presence in the visual field and "augmenting" their activity (Piaget, 1952, p. 102).

* Ages cited are approximations.

4–5 MONTHS—The hand grasps the seen object for the first time. Prehension results when hand and object are simultaneously in view.

5–6 MONTHS—True visually directed reaching emerges. After the object is grasped the infant routinely glances at it before bringing it to the mouth for sucking. Occasionally, viewing is prolonged and the object is not brought to the mouth at all. It should be noted that in sensorimotor theory the intersection of several schemas provides the basis for the emergence of object permanence. An object that is simultaneously looked at, reached for, and felt, as in the prehensory act, is more than a part of a single activity schema. It serves a truly unique function when it participates in three schemas at once, and from this special role true object permanence normally develops (Hunt, 1961).

The data to be presented in this paper address two questions: (1) Does the sequence described by Piaget fit the facts gathered on a larger group of subjects? (2) Do modifications in rearing conditions that accelerate the acquisition of visually directed reaching affect other important steps in the sequence?

Unfortunately, placing an object in the hand of an infant (our method) is an inadequate test of the entire developmental sequence in question. For example, a test situation where an object (perhaps a pacifier) was placed in the infant's mouth would be necessary as well as a situation where the infant could view the object before he grasped it. Nonetheless, we may be able to learn something from this admittedly partial view of the situation when the results are combined with those of tests of prehension in the same subjects.

The test procedure

Once each week, beginning at 36 days, each infant was brought to the testing room. After a five- to ten-minute acclimatization period, the infant was given three opportunities to respond to the presentation of the test object (for details see White, et al., 1965). This procedure took about five minutes. The last phase of the session consisted of the object-in-hand test. The test object was a paper party toy. It was approximately five inches in length and one half inch in diameter along the handle or stem. At one end there was a wooden mouthpiece through which air could be blown to extend a red coiled section. To this coiled section were attached two feathers. When coiled, this section is surrounded by orange and yellow fringes. The overall diameter of this display was about one and a half inches: The object is a common five-and-ten-cent store item and was used because it is easily grasped and retained by young infants and features a complex contour field with highly contrasting orange, red, and yellow lines previously found attractive to most infants (White, et al., 1964).

Subjects were physically normal infants born and reared in an institution. As part of a larger study, some of these infants had been reared in a variety of systematically varied rearing conditions designed to accelerate sensorimotor development. (For details see White & Held, 1966; White, 1967.) The data presented in this paper are from two groups: Forty-three controls including eleven babies who had received extra handling during the first 36 days of life, and sixteen modified enrichment infants. In brief, the experimental group was reared under conditions designed to increase the occurrence of certain forms of motility in sensorily enriched surrounds. Such experiences produced markedly precocious visually directed reaching and heightened visual attentiveness.

Hypotheses

1. Control babies would exhibit behaviors consistent with Piaget's observations on the development of reciprocal coordinations among looking, sucking, and grasping schemas.
2. Increased looking at and palpating of nearby objects (induced via enrichment procedures) would result in acceleration of the coordination process.

Results

1. The normal developmental sequence:
   On the basis of Piaget's discussion of the development of pre-

hension schemas (1952, pp. 88–122) one would expect a developmental pattern somewhat like that described in Table 1.

Table 1   The Normal Developmental Sequence According to Piaget

Test		*Object-in-Hand*	*Prehension*
AGE (months)	N	RESPONSE	RESPONSE
1–2	3	Retains only	—
2–3	"	Brought to mouth for sucking	—
3–4	"	" " " " "	—
4–5	"	" " " " "	Fourth-stage reaching (if hand and object simultaneously in view)
5–6	"	Brief regard then brought to mouth for sucking	
			True reaching
		Prolonged regard	

Responses to the object-in-hand test in our control group are shown in Table 2.

Description of responses:

1. *Retains only*—The infant holds the test object for more than three seconds.
2. *Views*—The infant holds the test object and either glances at it one or more times or regards it steadily for up to two minutes.
3. *Brought to mouth*—The infant holds the object and without viewing, brings it to the mouth one or more times briefly or manages to keep it at the mouth and gum or suck it.
4. *Monitored mutual play*—The object is brought to the midline where it is simultaneously viewed and tactually explored by the other hand.
5. *Views then to mouth*—Responses 2 and 3 combined.
6. *Views—other hand raised*—The infant retains the object and extends and raises both arms while viewing the object.
7. *Views—other hand*—The infant retains the object and views the free hand.
8. *Monitored mutual play—then to mouth*—Responses 4 and 3 combined.

Table 2   The Sequence Exhibited by Control Subjects

Table 2   The Sequence Exhibited by Control Subjects

Test		Object-In-Hand				Prehension	
AGE (Months)	N*	RESPONSE	SUBJECTS EXHIBITING N	RESPONSE † PER CENT	N	RESPONSE	
1.5-2	23	Retains only	22	95.8			
		Brought to mouth	5	21.7			
		Views	3	13.0			
2-2.5	27	Retains only	23	85.2			
		Views other hand	3	11.1			
		Views other hand raised	2	7.4			
2.5-3	25	Retains only	21	84.1			
		Views	18	72.1			
		Brought to mouth	6	24.0			
		Views other hand	5	20.0			
		Monitored mutual play	0	0.0			
3-3.5	27	Views	24	89.0			
		Retains only	16	59.3			
		Monitored mutual play	7	25.9			
		Brought to mouth	6	22.2			
3.5-4	25	Views	20	80.0			
		Monitored mutual play	13	52.0			
		Views then to mouth	7	28.0			
		Retains only	6	24.0			
		Brought to mouth	6	24.0			
		Views other hand raised	6	24.0			
		Monitored mutual play then to mouth	3	12.0			
4-4.5	21	Views	17	81.0	12	Fourth-stage reaching (median—130 days)	
		Monitored mutual play	15	71.5			
		Views other hand raised	7	33.3			
4.5-5	16	Views	12	75.0	14	True reaching (median—147 days)	
		Monitored mutual play	9	56.3			
		Brought to mouth	6	37.5			
		Views then to mouth	6	37.5			
		Monitored mutual play then to mouth	1	6.3			

Total N = 164   Total trials = 560

* Each test consisted of two trials. Average number of tests/subject was 1.71. Average number of responses per trial was 1.21, increasing steadily with age.
† Only the responses occurring in 20 per cent or more of the subjects of either the control or experimental group are recorded.

Although fourth- and fifth-stage reaching occurred about as predicted by Piaget's work, this was not the case for the object-in-hand data. The number of response patterns seen was considerably greater than expected, the influence of the sucking schemas was much less than expected, and that of vision was strikingly greater than expected.

2a. Is the developmental sequence influenced by rearing conditions? Table 3 contains responses to the object-in-hand test shown by the experimental group. Table 4 indicates that the groups differ significantly.

b. Is the rate of coordination of schemas influenced by rearing conditions?

Table 5 shows comparative data for the experimental and control groups. The schemata listed are not necessarily the only ones involved in the behaviors seen.*

It is clear that the coordination of schemas as described in this analysis has been accelerated for the experimental group. With respect to prehension, the median dates of onset for stages four and five were 95 to 89 days respectively compared to 130 and 147 days for the control group. These shifts are highly significant (p < .001—Mann-Whitney U test, Siegel, 1956).

Discussion

The first hypothesis, that the sequences described by Piaget would be repeated in a larger subject group, was only partly con-

---

* Piaget does not give precise guidelines for assigning schemas to behavior. I have tried to be conservative in assigning schemas to the behavior patterns in question. There seem to be at least five schemas involved: (1) the grasp schema—retention of the object; (2) the visual schema—glances or prolonged viewing of the object; (3) the sucking schema—the object is brought to the mouth for attempts at sucking; (4) the tactual schema—the other hand joins with the hand holding the object to either feel it or take it away; and (5) the "other" arm movement schema—the other hand is raised. This last schema reflects the ambiguities in assigning schemas to complicated behavior patterns. Since all behaviors require a schema in Piaget's system, and since hand-raising occurs rather often, I have postulated a schema for it. Actually, hand-raising is a part of another schema, bilateral hand-raising, which is a behavior pattern often seen between 7 and 11 weeks of age in our control group.

Table 3   The Sequence Exhibited by Experimental Subjects

Test			Object-In-Hand			Prehension
AGE (Months)	N *	RESPONSE	SUBJECTS EXHIBITING N	RESPONSE PER CENT	N	RESPONSE
1.5-2	16	Retains only	16	100.0		
		Views	10	62.6		
		Brought to mouth	6	37.5		
2-2.5	16	Retains only	15	93.9		
		Views	10	62.6		
		Views other hand raised	5	31.3		
		Views other hand	4	25.0		
		Brought to mouth	4	25.0		
2.5-3	14	Views	13	93.0	13	True reaching
		Retains only	7	50.0		(median—89 days)
		Views other hand	6	42.8		
		Monitored mutual play	5	35.7		
		Views other hand	4	28.6		
3-3.5	12	Views	10	83.6	8	4th stage reaching
		Retains only	7	58.3		(median—95 days)
		Views other hand	6	50.0		
		Monitored mutual play	4	33.3		
		Views other hand	3	25.0		
3.5-4	12	Views	10	83.6		
		Monitored mutual play	7	58.3		
		Views other hand	4	33.3		
		Monitored mutual play then to mouth	3	25.0		
		Views then to mouth	1	8.3		
		Retains only	1	8.3		
4-4.5	11	Views	9	82.8		
		Monitored mutual play	9	82.8		
		Views other hand	4	36.4		
4.5-5	9	Monitored mutual play	8	88.9		
		Views	7	77.8		
		Views then to mouth	3	33.3		
		Views other hand	3	33.3		
		Monitored mutual play then to mouth	2	22.2		
		Brought to mouth	0	00.0		

Total N = 90   Total trials = 380

* Average number of tests/subject was 1.90. Average number of responses/trial was 1.13, increasing steadily with age.

Table 4   Significance Levels for Differences Between Control and
Experimental Subjects—Object-in-Hand-Test

Response	Percent Subjects Exhibiting Response [*]		t	df	Significance Level (1-tailed tests)
	CONTROLS	EXPERI-MENTALS			
Retains only	24.0	8.3	1.34	35	N.S.
Views	13.0	62.6	3.56	37	<.001
Views with other hand raised	7.4	31.3	1.90	41	N.S.
Brought to mouth	37.5	0.0	3.10	23	<.005
Views—other hand	20.0	42.8	1.47	27	N.S.
Monitored mutual play	35.7	64.3	2.79	27	<.005
Monitored mutual play then to mouth	12.0	25.0	0.93	35	N.S.
Views then to mouth	28.0	8.3	1.64	35	N.S.

[*] In this analysis the following procedure was followed:
  (a) Identify responses that occurred in at least 20 percent of either group
  (b) Determine the number of age periods when each response occurred in at least 20 percent of either group
  (c) Calculate the probability of any single comparison between groups for any two-week interval for an overall significance level of .05 according to the following formula:

$$p = (1 - \alpha_1)^n \text{ where n = number of 2-week periods}$$

where response occurred in at least 20 percent of either group

  (d) Test most extreme group differences against adjusted significance levels

N	1	2	3	4	5	6	7
α_1	.050	.025	.017	.012	.010	.008	.007

Table 5   Distribution of Schemas as a Function of Age for Control and Experimental Groups—Object-in-Hand Test

AGE (months)	Control				Experimental			
	RESPONSE *	SCHEMAS INVOLVED †	PERCENT SHOWING	WEIGHTED SCORE	RESPONSE	SCHEMAS INVOLVED	PERCENT SHOWING	WEIGHTED SCORE
1.5-2	Retains only	1	95.8	95.8	Retains only	1	100.0	100.0
	Brought to mouth	2	21.7	43.4	Views	2	62.6	125.2
					Brought to mouth	2	37.5	75.0
Group score				139.2				300.2
2-2.5	Retains only	1	85.2	85.2	Retains only	1	93.9	93.9
					Views	2	62.6	125.2
					Views other hand raised	3	31.3	93.9
					Views other hand	2	25.0	50.0
					Brought to mouth	2	25.0	50.0
Group score				85.2				413.0
2.5-3	Retains only	1	84.1	84.1	Views	2	93.0	186.0
	Views	2	72.1	144.2	Retains only	1	50.0	50.0
					Views other hand	2	42.8	85.6
					Monitored mutual play	3	35.7	107.1
					Views other hand raised	3	28.6	85.8
Group score				228.3				514.5

Table 5 Distribution of Schemas as a Function of Age for Control and Experimental Groups—Object-in-Hand Test (Continued)

AGE (months)	RESPONSE	Control SCHEMAS INVOLVED	PERCENT SHOWING	WEIGHTED SCORE	RESPONSE	Experimental SCHEMAS INVOLVED	PERCENT SHOWING	WEIGHTED SCORE
3-3.5	Views	2	89.0	178.0	Views	2	83.6	167.3
	Retains only	1	59.3	59.3	Retains only	1	58.3	58.3
	Monitored mutual play	3	25.9	77.7	Views other hand raised	3	50.0	150.0
	Brought to mouth	2	22.2	44.4	Monitored mutual play	3	33.3	99.9
					Views other hand	2	25.0	50.0
Group score				359.4				535.4
3.5-4	Views	2	80.0	160.0	Views	2	83.6	167.2
	Monitored mutual play	3	52.0	156.0	Monitored mutual play	3	58.3	174.9
	Views then to mouth	3	28.0	84.0	Views other hand raised	3	33.3	99.9
	Retains only	1	24.0	24.0	Monitored mutual play	4	25.0	100.0
	Views other hand raised	3	24.0	72.0				
Group score				544.0				542.0
4-4.5	Views	2	81.0	162.0	Views	2	82.8	165.6
	Monitored mutual play	3	71.5	214.5	Monitored mutual play	3	82.8	248.4
	Views other hand raised	3	33.3	100.0	Views other hand raised	3	36.4	109.2
Group score				476.5				523.2

4.5-5	Views	2	75.0	150.0	Monitored mutual play	3	88.9	266.7
	Monitored mutual play	3	56.3	168.9	Views	2	77.8	155.6
	Brought to mouth	2	37.5	75.0	Views then to mouth	3	33.3	99.9
	Views then to mouth	3	37.5	112.5	Views other hand raised	3	33.3	99.9
					Monitored mutual play then to mouth	4	22.2	88.8
	Group score			506.4				710.9

Group differences are significant beyond .02 level [Randomization test (Siegel, 1956)].
* Only responses occurring in at least 20 percent of the subjects are included.
† Schemas were assigned as follows:

RESPONSE	SCHEMAS INVOLVED	TOTAL SCHEMAS
Retains only	Grasp	1
Brought to mouth	Grasp, Sucking	2
Views	Grasp, Vision	2
Views—other hand	Grasp, Vision	2
Views—other hand raised	Grasp, Vision, "Other Arm" Movement	3
Views then to mouth	Grasp, Vision, Sucking	3
Monitored mutual play	Grasp, Vision, Tactual	3
Monitored mutual play then to mouth	Grasp, Vision, Tactual, Sucking	4

firmed. We did not find the sucking schema to be dominant in our groups. Further, the influence of vision was markedly greater than expected. In addition, the complexity of the sequence in terms of number of responses shown was greater than expected. Finally, the influence of postural factors such as the tonic neck reflex and the favored hand was both marked and unexpected. During the third month of life, a child would often view the object placed in his favored hand, and again view that hand when the object was placed in the other hand. Another manifestation of this asymmetry was seen a few weeks later when the infant would merely stare at the object in the favored hand (views object) but would bring the favored hand over to join or tactually explore the object when it was held by the other hand (monitored mutual play). Responses during the second month involved only one hand. During the third and fourth months there was a steady increase in bilateral hand and arm involvement that paralleled the oft-noted reduction in the influence of the tonic neck reflex (Gesell & Amatruda, 1941). This paves the way for the coordination of the visual and tactual schemas of each hand with the other. It is of course possible that the fact that Piaget's children were breast fed, whereas the subjects in this study were not, would account for some or even all of the differences.

The second hypothesis predicting plasticity of development was amply confirmed. The results of both the object-in-hand and the prehension tests indicate important functional relationships between rearing conditions and the developmental processes in question. Further, it is to be noted that the degree of acceleration involved in the experimental group is more than nominal even though the experimental modifications of rearing conditions were little more than first attempts. Of course, at this time no claim can be made for precise understanding of the role of experience; however, some discussion of the design of the experimental rearing conditions is in order at this point.

It is customary to select independent variables primarily on the basis of the theory underlying one's study. In experiments where the subjects are human adults, for example, whether or not the subject is inclined to act as required during the experimental treatment is rarely a problem. If a subject should prove reluctant, he may be replaced. In our studies of infant development as in Piaget's, the situation is different for two reasons. First, we are unable, and in fact, unwilling to demand actions of our subjects that are very different from what they tend to do normally. Second, we depend much more on induction in designing experiments than on existing theories. This latter fact means that we take pains to discover via extensive naturalistic observations what infants actually do in the hope that an analysis of actual experiences when meshed with general theoretical notions will yield experiments of definite relevance to human development. This process has a parallel in studies of the acquisition of language. For many years now, psychologists and educators have marvelled at how quickly all children acquire the complicated rules involved in understanding and producing their native language. It has frequently been noted that little or no active tuition is necessary. But, few, if any, investigators have attempted to learn how this remarkable natural achievement occurs. It seems most likely that we would learn a great deal about the learning processes involved were we to study the details of the experiences involved. Is it not likely that the differential experiences undergone by extreme groups (very fast versus very slow progress in language acquisition) would provide a wealth of information about the processes involved?

During the first six months of life children are not usually able to locomote; in fact, they have limited abilities in most all developmental areas. In addition, their experiential histories are very brief. These factors combined, suggest that an analysis of the opportunities for learning is more feasible for this period than for subsequent ones. Piaget has provided some clues by describing the developing sensorimotor structures. Only lengthy longitudinal observations can complete the picture, however. These, we have done for one population. We have observed several hundred physically normal, hospital-reared infants for three continuous hours each week from birth to six months (White et al., 1964; White & Castle, 1965). The favorite activities of these children when awake and not distressed or drowsy are visual exploration, especially of their own hands, tactual exploration, and combined visual and tactual exploration, again usually of their own hands. From about the fourteenth week on if given the opportunity, they will usually view areas several yards away. When placed in the prone position prior to that time, however, their visual interest and tactual interest seem to be restricted primarily to the 24 inches or so around them. On the basis of unsystematic observations, it would appear that home-reared babies do not differ radically in these respects. The major visual-motor activities of this time of life primarily consist of the internal ocular adjustments of accommodation and position, including convergence and pursuit; rotations of the head; movements of the arm, hand, and fingers within the visual field; head rearing (in the prone position); and from about the fifth month on, turning the torso from side to side and occasionally completely over.

Our modified enrichment group was given extra handling during the first 36 days of life when visual motor activities do not occupy much of the infant's day (White & Held, 1966; White, 1967). During the second month an attempt was made to optimize learning conditions for the acquisition of visual control over the hand that seems to be a major if not *the* major sensori-motor acquisition of the first half year of life. Visually-monitored batting and tactual exploration of nearby objects were induced (White & Held, 1966; White, 1967). During the third month, similar activities plus heightened visual scanning were induced by the presence of new viewable and palpable objects as well as routine prone placement of the subjects (White & Held, 1966; White, 1967).

Obviously, we have dealt with molar experiences rather than isolated independent variables. The scientific task that awaits is the sorting of what is and what is not relevant within the gross experimental treatment. It is here that refined theory is sooner or later necessary; I, however, do not believe that one should proceed hastily towards extended theoretical analyses. Rather, I would advocate modest theoretical distinctions followed by empirical test leading to new theoretical deviations slightly more specific, followed by test, and so on.

Conclusion

Piaget's general position which holds that infant behavior consists at first of sequential activation of isolated schemas and, from the third month on, their reciprocal coordination, is amply supported by this study. On the other hand, two major amplifications are also revealed. First, that the number of schemas involved in prehensory development is, for the subject groups of this study at least, many times what Piaget saw in his own children. In addition, and of obvious importance for developmental psychology, is the demonstration of the functional relevance of experience to the developments in question. Although this study requires replication, and is only an early attempt in a complicated area of investigation, it appears that major effects on the rate of development may be induced with ease using innocuous alterations in rearing conditions. Let me point out, however, that the design of enrichment conditions in this study ("the match" as Hunt would put it) presupposes dependable knowledge about infant capacities and preferences. This information is expensive to obtain coming as it does from hundreds of hours of naturalistic observations and the results of standardized test sessions.

References

Charlesworth, W. R. Persistence of orienting and attending behavior in infants as a function of stimulus-locus uncertainty. *Child Develpm.*, 1966, 37, 473–491.

Gesell, A. & Amatruda, C. *Developmental diagnosis.* New York: Hoeber, 1941.

Haynes, H., White, B. L., & Held, R. Visual accomodation in human infants. *Science*, 1965, 148, 528–530.

Hunt, J. McV. *Intelligence and experience.* New York: Ronald, 1961.

Piaget, J. *The origins of intelligence in children.* (2nd ed.) New York: Internat. Univer. Press, 1952.

Siegel, S. *Nonparametric statistics for the behavioral sciences.* New York: McGraw-Hill, 1956. Pp. 116–127.

White, B. L., & Castle, P. W. Visual exploratory behavior following post-natal handling of human infants. *Percept. mot. Skills,* 1964, **18**, 497–502.

White, B. L., Castle, P. W., & Held, R. M. Observations on the development of visually-directed reaching. *Child Develpm.,* 1964, **35**, 349–364.

White, B. L., & Held, R. Plasticity of sensorimotor development in the human infant. In J. F. Rosenblith & W. Allinsmith (Eds.), *Causes of behavior: readings in child development and educational psychology.* (2nd ed.) Boston, Mass.: Allyn & Bacon, 1966. Pp. 60–71.

White, B. L. An experimental approach to the effects of experience on early human behavior. In J. P. Hill (Ed.), *Minn. Sympos. Child Psychol.* Minneapolis: Univer. of Minn. Press, I, 1967. Pp. 201–226.

The Role of Surprise
in Cognitive Development

WILLIAM R. CHARLESWORTH

Introduction

This essay is a short introduction to two complex and related phenomena: (1) surprise, the word so frequently and casually used when events occur unexpectedly or without warning, and (2) the way in which surprise and expectancies are implicated in the process of cognitive development. It is impossible in the space allotted to treat the topic historically, analytically, and synthetically so as to make it completely amenable to experimental inquiry. This job will be done later. For now a brief introductory treatment of surprise must suffice, and even it needs some qualifications.

This paper was written while the author was supported by Public Health Service Grant MH 10275 and was supported in part by grants to the University of Minnesota, Center for Research in Human Learning, from the National Science Foundation (GS 541), and National Institute of Child Health & Human development (PO-1-HO-01136), and the Graduate School of the University of Minnesota. Gratitude is extended to John Flavell for his valuable criticism and to Joy, secretary with fantastic patience, fortitude, and a secret ability to violate the law of conservation of confusion.

The essay will cover the following: (1) a brief historical analysis of surprise, (2) the relationship of surprise to the orienting reaction, startle, and novelty (3) a description of surprise in terms of a series of events and mechanisms (4) the nature and ontogeny of cognitive structures, expectancies, and their functional relation with surprise, and (5) surprise as a response used to diagnose the presence or absence of cognitive structures, (6) the surprise mechanism in cognitive change, and (7) some final remarks.

Historical analysis

Surprise is such a common phenomenon in the life of higher organisms that many writers have tempted to view it as having significant adaptive value. But clarifying exactly in what way surprise actually functions in the interests of the organism is mostly an unsolved problem despite the fact that thinkers have been wrestling with it at least as far back as Aristotle (Desai, 1939). Most philosophers recognized that surprise was a complex psychological phenomenon with complex consequences for the organism, but never really succeeded in making the nature of these consequences clear enough for the scientist to attack the problem empirically.

It was not until Darwin attempted to develop a precise picture of what surprise entailed behaviorally and physiologically and what possible adaptive function the various surprise reactions served that the way was opened to rigorous scientific analysis. Darwin's argument, appearing in 1872 in *The Expression of the Emotions in Man and Animals,* was simple and straightforward —the main characteristics of surprise included opening the eyes and mouth widely and raising the eyebrows, both easily observable responses that were accompanied by an increase in heart rate and respiration. These responses, Darwin argued, interacted to play a significant role in the organism's ability to perceive and react to novel stimuli as quickly and adaptively as possible. He thus concluded that surprise was an important determinant of the more complex phenomenon of attention. Apart from the fact that attention aided the organism in detecting the presence of predators or food sources, it was also adaptive in another, equally important way. What this way was was discussed by him in another context in *The Descent of Man* where he had a vaguely stated but what appears to be an unprecedented insight. He noted that attention was a "faculty" of extreme importance for "intellectual progress." Progress was defined in terms of different levels of cognitive achievements characterizing different species and different stages in ontogenetic development. He did not speculate further about the possible mechanisms whereby attention brought about such progress, and interestingly enough, he did not deem it necessary to mention in this context the role surprise played in this process. The possibility that surprise, which presupposes expectations (hence cognitive structures), cognitive development, and attention could somehow be functionally linked (Fig. 1) apparently did not occur to him or his

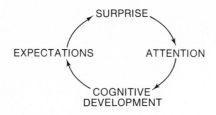

Figure 1

immediate followers, or if it did occur to them, for some reason it was rejected. Whatever the case, the fact that such a connection was not explored until quite recently poses an interesting historical problem. This problem is worth briefly considering since it sheds light on some aspects of surprise that will be discussed later.

Most theoretical writers during and after Darwin's time who were interested in psychology responded to the great excitement created in biology by enthusiastically constructing behavioral taxonomies. The fate of surprise very early in this enterprise was that it was viewed almost exclusively as an emotion—a fact which can be seen in classificatory schemes or textbook chapters starting with Bain (1874) and Ribot (1911) through Wundt (1901), Warren (1920) and Ruckmick (1921) to more recent writers such as Woodworth and Schlosberg (1954). Such writers classified surprise along with such states of the organism as joy and fear, all known to represent internal commotions that, if anything, were generally viewed as disruptive of higher cognitive activities. So far as surprise was concerned, taking such taxonomies seriously meant virtually ignoring the possibility that it had any value (the speculations of earlier philosophers notwithstanding) for cognition or cognitively controlled behavior.

There were some exceptions to such trends, however, and they should be mentioned since their ideas are the proper ancestors of those presented in this essay. James Mark Baldwin (1894) was the most notable exception, and it is interesting that he was perhaps the most heavily influenced by Darwin. While having to face up to the task of defining and classifying emotional states in his own taxonomy, he felt compelled to establish a class of "logical emotions." Such emotions accompanied the "highest reaches of apperception in conception, judgment, and thought" and were invariably associated with various cognitive activities. Surprise was included in this class along with feelings of "routine" (presumably boredom), amazement, anticipation, feelings of contradiction, logical satisfaction, and a number of others. Although Baldwin did not implicate logical emotions as important elements in the development of cognitive structures involved in logical thinking, his insight was one of the important few that ran counter to the trend.

Shortly after Baldwin, and perhaps because of him, Stanley (1895) discussed the intellectual element in surprise, emphasizing both its cognitive and affective aspects, and also making some classical distinctions between surprise and novelty. Later McDougall (1923) went so far as to exclude surprise from the category of true emotions on the argument that surprise had in it important cognitive elements in the form of anticipations and expectations. These writers, as well as a few others, felt certain that surprise had an important cognitive dimension that could not be overlooked. None of them, though, speculated on the possibility that significant developmental changes in cognition may be due to a number of stimulus-producing responses (of which surprise was one) that result when novel or unexpected events occur. This idea took hold much later—sometime during the 1950's.

Apart from the theories and classificatory systems, laboratory emphasis on the importance of surprise or surprise-like phenomena for adaptation was generally lacking during the early post-Darwinian era. There was, however, one major exception. In the early 1900's Pavlov observed and recorded animals' reactions to novel or interruptive stimuli, and on the basis of such observations, he consequently developed the concept of the orienting reflex (OR). He defined the OR as the animal's total behavioral and physiological response to novel stimuli. For Pavlov, as for Darwin, animals capable of the OR had a means of quickly responding to novel stimuli, thereby averting potential danger if the stimuli were dangerous; if they were recognized as nondangerous, the animals were able to inspect them and assimilate them (presumably to eat them or play with them). Pavlov reputedly said nothing about whether animals learned anything about such stimuli, but he did note that ORs of moderate intensity at least clearly facilitated conditioning, if not totally necessary for it to occur. For him the OR was mainly a physiological phenomenon that embraced both the underlying mechanisms and overt behavior forms of curiosity behavior in the broadest sense of the term. He did not identify the OR with the more ambiguous and subjective concept of surprise, and, as it will be shown later, it was fortunate that he did not, since surprise and the OR are not simply different terms for the same phenomenon. Pavlov's antipsychological attitude, as Razran (1961) points out, was very strong and there was little chance that his formulations of the OR would be applied in his laboratory to cognitive or perceptual problems during his time. After his death, the climate in Russia changed and, as will be discussed shortly, recognition of the OR's relevance for understanding cognitive functions became one of the most significant advances in modern Russian psychology.

During the late 1920's and thereafter researchers mainly in England, Germany, and the United States began showing concern for responses to novel or unexpected stimuli.* Examples of such research are studies by Skaggs (1926) who studied changes in pulse and breathing under "conditions of startledness and excited expectancy"; Jacobson (1926) who examined the effects of muscle tonus on sensory and motor responses resulting from an unexpected stimulus; Wilcocks (1928) who conducted experiments on the effect of unexpected heterogeneity on attention; Jersild (1929) who studied the effects of vividness (produced by unexpected changes in stimuli), primacy, and recency on recall; and von Restorff (1933) who discovered that an item that differs from others presented sequentially (hence an unexpected item) is recalled more readily than items more frequently presented in the list. The studies varied widely in content, but in one way or another dealt with the surprise phenomenon.

During the 1930's the first monographs dealing explicitly and exclusively with surprise were published by Patterson (1930) and Desai (1939). While both authors were concerned with experimental rigor, as theoreticians before them, they were not adverse to attacking such problems as whether it was possible to make a distinction between surprise and wonder; whether surprise and astonishment were separated only by a continuum of intensity and not quality; whether surprise mixes with other emotions readily, and whether in order to laugh, we must first be surprised. Today the shortcomings of posing such problems are more evident than they were then. The biggest weakness in attempts to solve such problems appears to be the failure to separate the conditions preceding and/or eliciting surprise responses from the responses themselves, and to distinguish the latter, from their consequences for other behaviors. Furthermore, to complicate matters, confusion between the theoretical and empirical status of the surprise phenomenon was almost never absent—at times surprise was considered as an inferred entity,

---

* An exhaustive coverage of such studies is virtually impossible since titles alone frequently do not contain the term surprise, although the methods used in the study clearly suggest that surprise phenomenon, as defined here, were being produced.

and at other times as a not well-defined set of physiological, facial, and postural responses. But in spite of these confusions, such research was an improvement over most of the earlier philosophical and quasi-scientific studies that relied heavily, if not solely, upon commonsense descriptions, anecdotal evidence, intuitions, introspections, and etymological analyses.

By the end of the thirties the effects of viewing surprise mainly as an emotion and unrelated to other behaviors were still strongly evident. Landis and Hunt (1939), who conducted much work on startle and some on surprise, commented that most of the significant work in the area of the latter had been on "visceral concomitants"—blood pressure, pulse, and respiration. Next to nothing has been done experimentally with surprise in terms of facial expressions and other overt behavioral patterns, and nothing in terms of cognitive structures. The possibility that surprise could be viewed in a broader sense than that implied under the rubric of emotion—a sense that included structural or associative variables as well as motivational or dynamic, nonassociative variables—was not seriously entertained at the time, although, as noted above, certain cognitive functions such as recall were observed to be enhanced by the experience of unexpected stimuli.

In the 1940's virtually no important research with surprise was done. However, a significant event concerning surprise occurred in an unexpected area of psychology. While discussing circular reactions during the sensorimotor period of development, Piaget (1952) observed that surprise may well play an important role in the processes controlling cognitive development. His reason lay in observations he made of his children's behavior during infancy. Laurent, for example, while lying in the cradle is seen flailing his arms more or less randomly. Attached to his wrist is a string that is tied to a number of overhanging rattles. The flailing movements suddenly shake the rattles and they unexpectedly produce interesting novel sounds. Laurent is greatly surprised—this is his first encounter with such a situation—and his first response is to pull the string again and again. Before long he has the rattles well under his control—he has accommodated to and assimilated the surprising situation. Piaget viewed this situation as a classic one involving a particular type of subject-environment interaction (secondary circular reaction) that had important consequences for cognitive growth. The chain of events, which began with surprise, is not too difficult to visualize. Surprise was an important antecedent, if not a direct determinant of, the curiosity behavior that brought the individual into fresh contact with new stimuli. This contact, Piaget reasoned, demanded accommodation on the part of the individual and the accommodation resulted ultimately in permanent changes in existing schemata. Surprise was thus seen as important, but Piaget did not pursue it; his thinking on this matter apparently stopped at this point. In later works he occasionally alluded to surprise, but never discussed it as a relevant variable in cognitive change, although he acknowledged it as "an essential motor in education and in scientific research in general" (Duckworth, 1964).

While there was no immediate response to Piaget's insight, concern for examining the relationship between emotions and cognitive structures and learning began to mount rapidly in the 1950's. Taking up where Pavlov left off, the Russians began demonstrating the importance of the dynamogenic properties of the OR for classical conditioning. Numerous studies appeared in the Russian literature—e.g. a monograph of studies edited by Voronin et al. (1958)—and non-Russian writers, such as Berlyne (1960), Razran (1961), and Lynn (1966), wrote papers summarizing and integrating the rapidly growing corpus of OR literature. In the United States a parallel movement was under way. The role that emotional, affective, and arousal factors played in the restructuring of cognitive dispositions was brought to the attention of other psychologists by such writers as Festinger (1957), Berlyne (1960, 1964) and Hunt (1965). Nonassociative factors other than those generally included under the rubric of motivation were becoming recognized as extremely relevant aspects of the learning process. Such recognition extended beyond the Thorndikian notion that certain affective consequences of a response may be reinforcing. Green (1956), for example, used surprise as an explanatory construct and argued that the von Restorff effect was best accounted for by surprise produced by an unexpected change rather than by Gestalt theory. In short, by the 1950's and 1960's some of the divisive constraints placed upon conceptualizations of emotions and structures by the early taxonomies were collapsing.

Surprise in particular gained entry into the current picture as a result of Berlyne's contributions (1960). Berlyne made the first significant attempt to demonstrate that such stimulus-subject properties as novelty, uncertainty, stimulus complexity, and surprise, which he termed "collative" properties, played a crucial role in the attentional processes concerned in learning, the main focus being on those factors controlling stimulus selection (i.e. curiosity behaviors) that were directly responsible for cognitive change.

No one, however, including Berlyne and those after him, was very specific about how cognitive change took place when once initiated by those collative properties of stimuli. Nonetheless, everyone involved with the problem was (and still is) certain about one thing: when incoming information does not agree with stored information there are a number of ensuing responses, some of which may be classified as "emotional," and these responses are instrumental in initiating processes that ultimately restructure the old information. The concepts of stimulus and schema match and mismatch, as discussed by Hunt (1961), the various feedback models such as the TOTE model of Miller, Pribram and Galanter (1958), and the neurological models of Anokhin (1958) and Sokolov (1960) share this basic idea.

To summarize, surprise as an object of study has had a long, but attenuated preexperimental history, beginning with the Greeks and continuing into the twentieth century. In the 1920's and 1930's it became an object of serious, but sporadic experimental inquiry that has lasted until the present, although aspects of it were studied intensely by the Russians under the concept of the OR. The weak association it has had with cognition has been limited mostly to memory factors, as evidenced by the von Restorff work. Surprise has had no significant association with cognitive development, although hints of such an association were made by Darwin and Piaget, and not until very recently has surprise been viewed as relevant for curiosity behaviors and for the effects such behaviors have upon cognitive change.

In spite of such a relatively impoverished scientific history, the concept of surprise has nevertheless managed to emerge with a number of pertinent generalizations and insights surrounding it (Patterson, 1930; Desai, 1939). Those relevant for the present essay are the following:

(1) Surprise results when an expectation is not confirmed. (Not all writers agree with this generalization.)

(2) Surprise is sometimes manifested in certain characteristic facial expressions, sometimes by vocalization, frequently by particular changes in gross motor behavior, and always by certain physiological events, such as peripheral vasoconstriction, cerebral vasodilation, changes in respiration, cardiac activity, and skin potential.

(3) Surprise is associated with the cessation of ongoing motor activities and of certain cognitive activities, such as complex symbolic processes.

(4) Surprise is followed by a sudden, frequently involuntary focusing of attention upon the surprise stimulus accompanied by heightened consciousness of the stimulus at the expense of other stimuli.

(5) Surprise diminishes as a result of the attention it arouses, i.e. most of the surprise responses habituate relatively rapidly once the stimulus is attended to. The stimulus is usually not effective in eliciting surprise reactions on subsequent occasions.

(6) Surprise has a mixed effect on the ability to retain in memory stimulus aspects associated with the surprise situation.

More has been said about surprise by earlier writers, but these six points have the most relevance for cognitive development. Everyday conceptions of surprise, which we assume share a common historical basis with the conceptions of early thinkers, do not depart significantly from those points, although common usage of the term is generally imprecise. People say they are surprised by a door's slamming (they may also mean startled); by an expensive gift from a parsimonious friend (they may also mean amazed); and by a dull child who solves a complex math problem (they may also mean astounded). All instances involve certain common psychological processes, but they also differ from one another in obvious, as well as subtle, ways. While clarifying the nature of such differences is not the task of this essay, certain distinctions between surprise and what is generally meant by three concepts often synonomous or associated with surprise—namely startle, novelty, and the OR—are ultimately necessary for future conceptual and experimental analysis.

Surprise versus the OR

In view of the broad meaning attached to the OR and the immense elaboration it has undergone as a concept in the last fifteen or so years, surprise appears at first glance to be a gratuitous concept. To demonstrate that this is not the case requires some careful consideration.

As was already indicated, the OR was developed by Pavlov to account for and describe a number of important behaviors and physiological changes that had in common a functional relationship with certain stimulus conditions. Such conditions could be described in capsule form as involving the onset of a sudden, novel, or unexpected stimulus. What is meant by sudden, novel, or unexpected has been a crucial problem that is still unresolved.

Historically, the OR as a concept has undergone changes since Pavlov first introduced it. Such changes led both toward greater clarification of the physiological mechanisms involved, and paradoxically, toward greater disagreement, if not confusion, as to what exactly the term should cover. Today there is no unanimity as to what OR encompasses and even no agreement as to what the initials stand for. Pavlov usually meant *orienting reflex*. Berlyne (1960, used *orientation reaction* for "the whole complex" of behaviors referred to in the Russian literature and *orienting response* for processes that have an "unmistakable exploratory function." Lynn (1966) in a more recent review of theory and empirical studies of the OR used *orientation reflex*.

Part of this disagreement centers around the number and kind of instrumental responses (activity employing the skeletal musculature) that follow the wide variety of responses elicited at the onset of the novel stimulus. The latter include (1) an increase in sensitivity of the sense organs, (2) a directing of sense receptors toward stimuli by skeletal muscle action, (3) rapid inhibition of ongoing behaviors, (4) a change in EEG, (5) vasoconstriction in the limbs, (6) vasodilation in the head region, (7) a GSR, (8) a change in respiration rate, and (9) a change in heart rate. Some researchers add active curiosity (instrumental behaviors) to this list; others do not. Hence when one talks in general terms about an OR he can mean all of these events or only a few of them.

To make matters more complicated, the kinds of stimuli that can elicit an OR are much more varied than one would first believe. In addition to the onset or offset, or change in a single stimulus, sudden, novel, or surprise stimuli can elicit an OR. A familiar stimulus, such as one's own name, can also do the job, as well as conditioned verbal stimuli, such as the words "Look Out!", moderate to high intensity stimuli in general and to relatively long-term conflictual situations, such as being forced to make fine discriminations. In view of this diversity of eliciting stimuli, it would be virtually impossible to predict the stimulus conditions that elicited a known OR, or if we knew the stimulus conditions, to predict whether or not an OR would follow.

In short, the concept of the OR is magnanimously endowed and while it may have very special and operationally exact meanings for individual researchers, it is too diffuse to use alone or to substitute for other terms such as surprise, or even startle for that matter.

Surprise reactions, on the other hand, may include all or nearly all of the reactions listed above. In this sense the OR is meaningful in helping to describe what is involved in a surprise reaction. Surprise, however, carries with it implications that an OR model may or may not carry depending upon one's interest in central processes. One such implication, which is a major one, is that before the numerous autonomic and gross behavioral OR reactions occur, two identifiable (and hence potentially manipulatable) factors must be involved—an expectancy about the forthcoming event and a stimulus that fails to confirm this expectancy. In other words, surprise usually implies a particular kind of cognitive disposition, a set of stimulus events that have a particular relationship to this disposition and a particular set of responses (some of which are subsumed under the OR) that can be used to index this relationship. This three-element model of surprise (expectancy–nonconfirming event–response plus OR) will be delineated in more detail later. What should be emphasized here is that surprise has an OR component to it, but to reduce surprise to a special case of the OR would neglect those aspects of it that can be useful in approaching certain problems of cognitive development. The OR as it stands now is mainly a response construct that may or may not include the predisposing or antecedent cognitive conditions that are functionally tied to it. Sokolov's neuronal model (see Brazier, 1960) may ultimately account for expectancies, but at present Sokolov rightfully sees no reason or desire to equate the two.

Surprise is differentiated from the OR in two ways—(1) surprise implies that there are expectancies involved and that it is possible both to measure such expectancies and to identify those stimuli that are in accord or not in accord with them and (2) surprise reactions can include all or some of the reactions subsumed under the OR as well as other reactions (e.g. facial expressions) that are not conventionally considered part of the OR. These points will be expanded later when describing surprise as a construct.

Surprise versus startle

Distinctions between surprise and startle are commonly recognized in everyday usage and in the scientific literature. Startle generally implies a reaction to a sudden and/or intense stimulus (frequently auditory) that produces fear, discomfort, or some form of annoyance. In the scientific literature, emphasis has been placed upon the involuntary aspect of the response, the response itself consisting of a rapid, frequently stereotyped pattern of overt behaviors accompanied by pronounced visceral changes, changes in skin conductance and blood pressure (see Strauss, 1929; Landis & Hunt, 1939).

In the Russian literature, according to Lynn (1966), the startle is viewed mostly as a defensive reaction, which is distinctly different from the OR in a number of specific ways. For Sokolov (1960) and Gastaut and Roger (1960), different patterns of vasoconstriction and vasodilation in limbs or head and changes in heart rate and respiration help distinguish startle from the OR. But there is no agreement as to which of the patterns adequately represent one and exclude the other. Tomkins (1962) views both startle and surprise as affective responses possessing more or less the same characteristics, but lying on different points of an intensity continuum, startle being the more intense of the two. The salient characteristic of both, according to Tomkins, is their capacity to interrupt any ongoing activity that may interfere with attentional processes elicited by the startling stimulus.

Whether there are classes of responses that accurately separate stimulus conditions into surprise and startle conditions, as the Russian work suggests, or whether every condition involving unexpected stimulation contains phases of different responses are questions that cannot be answered until there is more clarity about the nature of the stimulus and subject conditions themselves. For purposes of the present analysis, startle can be arbitrarily limited to responses to events that occur too rapidly for expectations to be formed. Such events are *unexpected* and can be classified as interruptive stimuli which vary in intensity. For example, a pistol shot close to the individual's head, as Landis and Hunt (1939) have demonstrated, elicits a pronounced response, due undoubtedly to at least two factors—unexpectedness and intensity. Surprise, on the other hand, as noted earlier, can be viewed as occurring because an event was *misexpected*, i.e. because the actual stimulus outcome contradicted it. This distinction has consensual validation since surprise is usually defined in such a way as to suggest that it has more cognitive, as contrasted with sensory, connotations than startle and other terms accounting for the effects of stimulus onset. Lynn (1966) gives a good example of the distinction between the two when he attempts to distinguish startle from the OR. In this case, however, surprise as it is defined is in this essay a better term to use than OR. The example actually refers to the distinction made by the introspectionists between primary and secondary attention. A nongeologist and a geologist friend are walking in a gorge. "A boulder suddenly falls down in front of them and elicits in both 'primary attention,' the startle-defense reaction. Continuing their walk they come across an unusual rock formation. The nongeologist does not notice it, but the geologist immediately sees and investigates it. This is 'secondary attention,' the orientation reaction, including orientation towards the stimulus for the purpose of further investigation." The stimulus properties of falling rock and the unusual rock are vastly different and so are the responses to them, but what is more interesting is the *difference* in responses on the part of the two men. Both were sensitive to the first rock; only one of them was sensitive to the second. Such a difference obviously refers to the cognitive status of the two men at the time. The nongeologist was not expecting anything in respect to the distribution of rock formations in the area; the geologist, in contrast, was predisposed to believe that a particular class of rocks alone characterized the area and that other rocks were excluded. When an excluded rock was discovered, the geologist was surprised. This example, while helping to make a distinction between startle and surprise, also has bearing on cognitive ontogenesis.

The human's capacity to be startled, as is well-known, is already present in the first few days of life. Surprise, it can be speculated, does not develop until later. Landis & Hunt (1939) point out that young infants are capable solely of a primary startle response and only after the infant reaches a certain age is there an increase in the amount of secondary behavior that we frequently associate with surprise. So far as the OR itself is concerned, Lynn (1966) notes that it too is lacking in early infancy, while the startle (e.g. Moro reflex) is not. The OR emerges later, several weeks after birth. It thus appears that there is an ontogenetic difference in reactions to the onset of novel stimuli. That this difference is related to some extent to the

capacity of the organism to anticipate or prepare for a stimulus
has some support in the literature. Anticipatory responses, as
Spitz (1965) notes, do not appear until after the infant has had
about a week's feeding experience. Only then is the infant capable of producing the "Flaschenerkennungsreaktionen" (bottle
recognition reaction) to the appearance of the bottle, a reaction
that may be interpreted as one of the first expectancies the infant
develops. What happens when such an expectancy is contradicted has not been adequately recorded. In all probability the
reactions to such a contradiction, while not completely interpretable as surprise reactions (if we use facial expressions for
example) resemble startle responses only slightly if at all. There
are some data on older infants where known expectancies were
contradicted. In a study by Charlesworth (1966a) infants who
already had a schema of the object (Stage IV of the object
concept as defined by Piaget) were placed in a trick situation
where a desired object resting on a flat surface "mysteriously"
disappeared from beneath the experimenter's hand. While some
infants showed facial surprise and others behaved in ways difficult to interpret, no reactions to the disappearance of the object
could be equated topographically or in terms of intensity with
the startle reactions the average infant makes when a sudden,
loud noise occurs behind him.

It can be argued then that surprise and startle are two different phenomena because (a) they reflect two different kinds of
stimulus-subject conditions and (b) they involve two different
kinds of responses, although they may share responses in the
sense that every surprise situation may have some components of
startle in it during the first phase of the overall reaction. The
capacity to be startled requires only a "primitive" sensitivity to
sudden intense stimuli; it is a capacity present at birth that persists throughout life. The capacity to be surprised, on the other
hand, requires an ability to recognize a signal and anticipate or
expect the event the signal signifies; it is a capacity that develops
slowly over time and at different rates in different areas of cognitive competence. There is ample anecdotal and observational
evidence indicating that a child can be totally insensitive to the
implications of a particular stimulus situation not being fulfilled

at one age, and then very sensitive a few months later when he shows a pronounced surprise reaction if the sequence is violated. This can certainly not be said of startle.

While such distinctions help delimit the boundaries of the surprise phenomenon, they are still crude and will need to be refined by further analysis of the stimulus conditions and responses involved.

Surprise versus novelty

An exhaustive analysis of the distinctions between surprise and novelty is much too big a problem for this paper, but a start toward such an analysis has some merit, since both concepts, as vexing as they are to deal with scientifically, cannot be ignored when dealing with factors responsible for cognitive change.

As noted earlier, Berlyne (1960) was one of the first to emphasize the importance of novelty and surprise (and similar phenomena) in influencing epistemic curiosity and the resultant effects such curiosity had on the organism's cognitive structures. His ideas are mentioned here because they express the essentials of a well-known paradigm (alluded to earlier) currently used in one way or another by many existing theories dealing with the same phenomena (e.g. the TOTE model of Miller, Galanter, and Pribram (1958) and Piaget's (1967) equilibration model). Intellectual change or growth is the end result of a chain of events beginning with the disruption of cognitive equilibrium by a conflict between incoming information and information already stored in the central nervous system. The conflict produced by the discrepancy between these two sources of information has the capacity to motivate curiosity behavior, and the latter has a high probability of leading to information that can be used by the organism to reduce the conflict. Conflict reduction consequently reinforces the curiosity behavior, thereby insuring continued contact with novel features of the environment. Novelty, for Berlyne, is one aspect of a particular kind of subject-stimulus interaction responsible for disrupting cognitive equilibrium. Unlike stimuli experienced earlier by the individual, a novel stimulus produces conflict. But to make matters complicated, novelty is frequently "accompanied" by other properties of stimuli, such as change, incongruity, and surprise. According to Berlyne, surprise results when there is a disparity between "responses" associated with what is required by the event actually experienced. Surprise thus produces conflict, and in this sense hardly differs from novelty. In a number of pioneering studies, Berlyne (1960; 1961) attempted to separate surprise from novelty operationally. According to Lynn (1966), he did not succeed, but Lynn's counterproposal does not seem convincing either, and leads me to the conviction (after also attempting an operational distinction between surprise and novelty—Charlesworth, 1964) that we are a long way from separating novelty and surprise both conceptually and experimentally. A change in perspective appears necessary, and the following may represent one approach to such a change.

As I see it, surprise and novelty can be differentiated in at least two and perhaps three important ways. The first has to do with the nature of the individual's behavior and internal state before the surprise or novel stimulus impinges upon him; the second has to do with the nature of his immediate reaction to the stimulus; and the third has to do with his later reaction to the stimulus.

The first distinction is the most important for the present thesis. It is the prestimulus condition of the individual that determines heavily whether the forthcoming stimulus is classified as novel, surprise, or familiar. In the case of novelty, the prestimulus state of the individual can be viewed as essentially devoid of any specific expectancy about the forthcoming event. If there is an anticipation of what is going to occur, it is diffuse, imprecise, or just a vague feeling that the event will be new or different than what has already been experienced. If asked what is forthcoming, the subject cannot predict or describe exactly what will happen; if the subject is a preverbal human or a lower animal, his posture or sense receptor orientation will yield little or no information as to the nature of the impending stimulus. Novel events may be ineffective in producing specific expectancies or states of readiness for at least two reasons: (1) they occur without advance warning, i.e. are not preceded by stimuli that are in some way associated with them—in this sense they are unexpected—or (2) if they are preceded by such stimuli, the organism has no previous history of an association between the two stimuli. A child receiving a new toy, an adult seeing an unknown play for the first time, or a rat entering an unfamiliar open field most probably have few or no expectations. In this sense such events are not surprising. The one important property they have in common is that they are new, i.e. they have not been experienced earlier and hence fit under the notion of novelty.

In the case of surprise, on the other hand, the expectancies are much more precise and describable. The individual can expect in two ways: (1) he can know clearly what is to happen, but be unclear about an alternative outcome, or (2) he can know clearly what alternative events could happen but reject all but one of them. In either case, there are precise expectancies and these expectancies presuppose some form of cognitive elaboration—for example, they may range from a simple redintegration of B because B always follows A in the past, to a more complex series of cognitive events, such as we find in a child who expects that the weight of an object will not be affected by simply changing its shape. Such cognitive elaboration presupposes cognitive structures are activated, so to speak, by the presentation of particular stimuli. The stimuli have come to mean, as a result of past experience, that a certain event will ultimately follow.

In addition to prestimulus cognitive elaboration, the individual may actually engage in a number of monitoring behaviors, usually in the form of careful attention to certain stimulus details, to insure or ascertain that the initial stimulus condition is what it appears to be and nothing else. For example, in the conservation of weight problem, the individual would insure that nothing happens to a piece of clay from the time of the first weighing until the second, other than that it was deformed into a ball. The important point is that what makes an event surprising is that the individual misexpects it rather than does not expect it (as in the case of novelty), and that this expectation presupposes previous experience. This previous experience, which for our purposes here can be conceptualized as embedded in and actually constituting a schema or cognitive structure, may control the individual's overt attentional behavior to the extent that we can correctly infer what he is anticipating.

A surprise event can be either novel, in the sense that it is unfamiliar in addition to being unexpected, or not novel, in the sense that the subject has already had experience with it but did not expect it. The concept of "recognitive familiarity," discussed by Hunt (1965), covers examples of the latter—discovering the familiar in the unfamiliar or where it was not expected. So does the classic "aha-Erlebnis," which involves discovering that old principles rearranged in a new way, underlie what was thought to be a completely new phenomenon.

The second distinction between novelty and surprise has to do with differences in the immediate, first-phase reactions to both kinds of stimuli. In the human these reactions occur usually in less than a minute after the onset of the stimulus and involve mostly autonomically-mediated behavior. As already indicated in the section on the OR, there is ample literature on the effects of the onset of stimuli, surprise, novel, or routine and familiar. Since to my knowledge this literature makes no distinctions between novelty and surprise in the sense that the terms are being defined here, there is no data on autonomically mediated responses available that would support a distinction between the two in terms. It is speculated, though, that surprising events (a) would produce more intense OR's than novel stimuli—e.g. greater GSR amplitudes, (b) would produce more pronounced and identifiable expressive behavior—e.g. characteristic changes in facial expression and postural changes, such as a slight backward movement of head and trunk, and (c) could be perceived as slightly more threatening, thereby producing an OR with a greater and more rapid defensive component than novel stimuli. Novel stimuli, if threatening, could also elicit defensive reactions, but such reactions would have longer latencies and may even be topographically different than surprise reactions.

The third distinction between surprise and novelty has to do with the individual's responses that occur after the first-phase response occurs. When the novel stimulus impinges upon the organism, attention is elicited and directed to it and it alone. Such attention can range from a passive taking in of the new stimulus elements (a consummatory act) to an enthusiastic examining of them. In neither case, however, does the individual expend effort in exploring beyond them to determine what made such events possible or brought them about. He may search for additional novel stimuli after having exhausted a particular novel stimulus, but not seek the determinants of the novelty. As a result of this activity, the cognitive restructuring that takes place is limited to the stimuli themselves rather than to the more complex issue of the causal mechanisms underlying them. In this sense novel stimuli comprise a lower form of intellectual stimulation than surprise stimuli.

One final distinction. Like startle and surprise, novelty and surprise do not begin to characterize the individual's experiences at the same time during ontogeny or at the same rate. Almost any stimulus change in the first few days of life is novel and the individual can continue to experience novelty until death, in many cases with hardly any effort on his part in obtaining it. Surprise, as already noted, is only experienced after the infant has built up relevant expectations and can only continue to be experienced if new expectations are continually built up, a task that becomes progressively more demanding as he grows older and gradually exhausts the unexpectedness or uncertainties of his environment.

In conclusion it should be reiterated that there is little to be gained from reducing surprise to the OR, novelty, or startle because of experimental convenience or greater current popularity of any of the latter. The term surprise implies more than any one of them and the implications are worth pursuing, insofar as they relate to cognitive structures and the mechanisms involved in changing them. Before going into the latter, however, surprise must be more explicitly and exhaustively analyzed. This can be done best by a description of surprise in terms of what factors are actually involved and how they interact sequentially over time.

Description of surprise

Surprise can be understood as implying: (1) a known, and hence potentially manipulable set of external stimulus circumstances that bear a particular relationship to (2) certain measurable dispositional properties of the individual loosely referred to as cognitive structures that are viewed as responsible for the production of (3) expectancies that both aid the individual in responding to the stimulus circumstances at the moment and also determine the total physiological changes and overt responses that occur when the expected outcome of the stimulus circumstances is discordant with the stimulus circumstances themselves.* The whole chain of events that entails both structural (cognitive) and dynamic (emotional) systems in the organism properly constitutes the surprise phenomenon and helps distinguish it from such phenomena as startle, the OR, and novelty.

Specifically, surprise can be defined in terms of the following sequence of events: †

PHASE	EVENTS
Initial stimulus (manipulable)	A stimulus, S-1, impinges upon the individual.
	A relatively weak or moderate OR is elicited, accompanied by overt attentional behavior to S-1.
Associative (inferred)	As a result of a schema formed earlier, S-1 is recognized as being associated with a previous experience, S-2. Recognition is defined

* Surprise is presented here as a guess as to what some of the variables are that control the behavior and behavior-produced circumstances in cognitive development. In this sense, surprise is being introduced as a hypothetical construct and ideally should be defined in such a way that the researcher will be able to (1) specify what stimulus conditions are to be manipulated and what responses measured for purposes of testing deductions from the construct, (2) define at a more refined level than currently known relationships between stimulus and response variables that are not yet fully understood, and (3) point to existing physiological mechanisms that underline the surprise mechanism.

† This sequence has in part been anticipated by other writers, notably Woodworth (1954) in his paradigm of sequence learning, a paradigm which as Berlyne (1960) points out, is broad enough to fit classical and instrumental conditioning.

as the process of matching stimulus inputs with already stored information.

Assimilative 1 (inferred)

An expectancy of S-2 is generated by the same schema. This is the schema's first assimilative function—the expectancy is covert and represents the forthcoming situation; it is the first relevant action taken by the individual towards the stimulus.

Assimilative 2 (observable)

The second assimilative act occurs in the form of overt anticipatory or preparatory behaviors to receive, act upon, or bring about S-2. Such behaviors may involve

(a) postural changes that orient the individual's sense receptors toward the anticipated locus of S-2.

(b) maintenance of attention toward the locus of S-2.

(c) actual approach behavior, such as reaching or locomoting toward the anticipated locus.

(d) responses that act upon the environment in such a way as to make perception of S-2 possible—e.g. removal of a barrier between the individual and stimulus locus.

(e) carrying out any number of manipulative operations that will bring about S-2—e.g. arranging sticks in a transitivity task, weighing deformed objects in a conservation task—in other words, any operation to check the validity of the expected outcome.

A relatively weak or moderate OR may be associated with such preparations.

All five classes of behavior demonstrate in varying ways that the individual has had experience with S-1 and S-2, and hence can be used as indicators of S's knowledge of the connection between S-1 and S-2.

Most of the behaviors in this phase are operants, subject to modification through instrumental conditioning.

Surprise stimulus (manipulable)

Instead of S-2, a different stimulus, S-2', impinges upon the individual.

Surprise reaction
(observable)

The individual reacts to S-2′ with a strong OR that is frequently accompanied by an arresting of gross motor behavior immediately followed at times by changes in facial expression and posture.

(a) Attention, in the form of orienting and fixing the sense receptors, is immediately and involuntarily focused upon S-2′.

(b) Higher level cognitive processes are momentarily suspended, hence there is little cognitive processing of S-2′ other than a possible very rapid evaluation of whether it is noxious or not.

(c) The surprise reactions (v. section on Diagnosis) can be used as indicators of S's knowledge of the connection between S-1 and S-2.

(d) Most of the processes in this phase are autonomically mediated, hence less subject to instrumental conditioning than the operants in the first assimilative phases.

Surprise decay
(observable)
Accommodative-
assimilative
(observable)

The various OR components diminish and gross motor behaviors are disinhibited.

Depending upon prior experiences, one of the following classes of overt accommodative or assimilative behaviors can occur:

(a) The individual manifests approach behavior to S-2′ in the form of exploratory behavior—locomotor, attentional, manipulatory, or verbal.

(b) The individual manifests avoidance behavior in the form of orienting towards other stimuli and/or locomoting away from or verbally denying S-2′.

(c) The individual engages in neither approach nor avoidance behavior, but remains indifferent to S-2′ and is ultimately distracted by other stimuli.

Most of these behaviors are operants subject to modification through instrumental conditioning.

Behavioral side effects, such as aimless smiling, expressions of annoyance, change of position, nervous giggling, inconsequential remarks to the observer may accompany the above behaviors. Emotional states associated with these side effects may vary widely. A positive, neutral, or even mildly negative hedonic state may accompany the approach behavior. The same may be said for the avoidance behavior, although such behavior is most probably accompanied by a moderate to strong negative hedonic state. The indifferent behavior is most probably accompanied by a neutral hedonic state.

Outcomes (observable under future test conditions)

At this point the surprise sequence proper terminates and one of a number of outcomes ensues.

(a) The various approach behaviors result in one of the following—(i) the inclusion of S-2' along with S-2, thereby partially modifying the original schema which related S-1 only to S-2; (ii) omitting S-2 and retaining S-2', thereby radically altering the original schema; or (iii) omitting S-2'—dismissing it as an exception or anomaly—and retaining S-2, thereby maintaining the original schema.

A decrease in the efficacy of S-2 to produce an OR on subsequent occasions is associated with the first and third outcomes. If the second outcome occurs, the efficacy of S-2 to produce an OR on a subsequent occasion increases.

The approach behavior itself is most probably reinforced as a result of its consequences (i.e. through acquisition of new knowledge and/or improvement in adaptability).

(b) The outcomes of the avoidance behavior for the schema are slight, if any. All that may result is a slight increase in the probability that an expectancy of S-2' will be

generated on a subsequent occasion and
that S-2′ will lose its efficacy in producing
an OR.
The avoidance behavior itself may be reinforced as a result of its consequences (e.g.
fear-reduction).
(c) The consequences of the indifferent
behavior leave the schema unmodified.
S-2′ probably loses some of its efficacy in
producing an OR on subsequent occasions.
The indifferent behavior itself, however, is
probably reinforced (e.g. possibly because it
momentarily preserves equilibrium). If, however, knowledge that S-2′ and S-1 are associated is necessary for adaptation, indifferent
behavior will ultimately extinguish.

Whether this description completely and accurately accounts
for the major events that take place when an individual is surprised by a misexpected event has still to be demonstrated. As it
stands now, it is complete enough both to allow a closer analysis
of problem solving situations that call into play Piagetian-type
structures and ultimately result in their modification and to
make it possible to improve our current diagnostic techniques.

Cognitive structures, their ontogenesis, and surprise

Surprise as it has just been described is a relevant construct to
apply to Piaget's view of cognitive development for two major
reasons—(1) because of the particular nature of many of the
cognitive structures he deals with, and (2) because of the
manner in which such structures appear to be involved in problem solving situations during ontogenesis.

Most of the cognitive structures elaborated upon by Piaget
share similar beginnings—their first forms develop as a result of
the child's prolonged everyday contact with the physical environment. The outcome of this contact is that such structures
inexorably come to reflect the invariances and lawfulness char-

acterizing physical phenomena.* Toys, furniture, and people preserve themselves even while hidden from view; the substance, weight, and volume of candy, pencils, and water are always conserved despite changes in their form or distribution; arithmetical operations, which Piaget conceives of as derivatives of physical actions upon physical objects, perform their functions with amazing constancy and accuracy; and logical propositions are bound together in wonderfully immutable relationships. And as a further consequence of all this, the child gradually learns what is possible and what is impossible and also the distinction between the two. He develops a sense of necessity that certain events must occur, that others can never occur, and that certain relationships (e.g. transitivity) between objects or representations of them must hold forever. His experiences with lawful phenomena ultimately produce in him a degree of conviction concerning the validity of his knowledge that he cannot enjoy in probabilistic domains of experience that are forever capable of keeping him in uncertainty. The organization and coordination of what he knows into a gradually tightening logical system provides him with a powerful method of reducing a sizable segment of reality to predictable and hence controllable proportions.

There is a further aspect, however, of such growth that is frequently overlooked. Associated with such structural changes is an emotional change in the form of a heightening sensitivity to deviations from the logical system that sets limits to his thought. This sensitivity may never be apparent to others or even to the child himself, until the system fails to account for a misexpected experience. Then the dynamic aspect of the system suddenly becomes apparent. One need only casually perform a magic trick without announcing it as such to detect the latent emotional power of the knowledge concerning the laws of physical reality. The normal surprise reaction is immediate, and frequently dramatic, and when the individual recovers, a series of

---

* Piaget may find this interpretation too empiricistic, but I find it difficult to conceive of the child's constructing environmental invariances. It is easier to imagine that such invariances impress themselves upon the child regardless of tendencies on his part to assimilate them or not.

adjustive responses is set in motion. The intruding event must be either ignored or explained away to preserve the integrity of the existing system; if this fails, the system must undergo modification.

Sensitivity to departures from physical and logical laws and the relation of such to sensitivity intelligence has been acknowledged in psychology, but given little attention. Terman (1916) regarded sensitivity to contradictions as one of the most distinguishing characteristics of a bright and dull person, thus making it a valuable process to tap in an intelligence test. Such sensitivity, though, need not characterize the developing mind at all points in its development, however, as Piaget (1926; 1928) has pointed out, the average child is not sensitive until about eight years old. The value of this aspect of cognitive growth for diagnostic purposes will be discussed in more detail later.

In addition to growing up in a lawful world closed for the most part to anomalies, the child grows up in an open, probabilistic one. If Piaget (1946) is correct, it takes the child about seven years to recognize this and to distinguish between the two. In the probabilistic world, events are not completely predictable, causes not always known, control of objects is subject to the caprice of undeterminable factors. A ball rolls into unpredictable places, glass breaks in unexpected patterns, people appear at unheralded times, friends keep then break their promises, act whimsically without warning, and say and do novel things. The child's cognitive adjustment to this ceaseless variability and apparent lawlessness is eventually assured, but in a way presumably somewhat different from the way he adjusts to the lawful environment.

It is at this point, though, that certain distinctions between novelty and surprise alluded to earlier take on added significance. These dimensions are briefly listed here to point out distinctions between the structures particularly concentrated upon by Piaget and those that reflect the probabilistic aspects of reality. Familiarity is added as a dimension that contrasts with novelty. The sequential description of surprise provided earlier is adhered to here whenever possible.

The relevance of surprise for development of cognitive struc-

Table 1   Dimensions along which surprise, novel, and familiar stimulus situations can be distinguished when dealing with cognitive development as described by Piaget.

	Surprise	*Novel*	*Familiar*
Initial stimulus, S-1 that activates the structure to produce an expectancy	Instance of a known class	Instance of a partially known class	Instance of a known class
	Unambiguous	Ambiguous	Unambiguous
Properties of structures responsible for the associative phase	Determinate	Probabilistic	Probabilistic or determinate
	Logical	Empirical	Empirical or logical
	Deductive	Inductive	Inductive or deductive
	Universal	Local	Local or Universal
Behavior elicited in assimilative phase 2	Clearly definable	Not clearly definable	Clearly definable
	Goal-directed	Not completely goal-directed	Goal-directed
	Rapid	Slow	Rapid
Stimulus outcome	S-2′	S-2″	S-2
	Counter-instance of a known class	Noninstance of a known class	Instance of a known class
	High information value	Moderate information value	No information value
	Was mis-expected	Was un-expected	Was expected
Surprise reaction	Intense OR	Moderate OR	No OR
Surprise reaction decay	Slow	Rapid	——
Accommodation-assimilation phase	Very slow accommodation or rapid assimilation	Moderately slow assimilation and accommodation	Rapid assimilation
Outcome	Drastic or slight modification of original structures	Slight modification of original structures	No modification of original structures other than strengthening them

tures is harder to demonstrate than its relevance for the structures per se. While we can infer structures from organized
behavior, no one has yet *observed* how they develop. Consequently, all existing models of the mechanisms responsible for
development are based almost totally upon speculation. The
conflict models are no exception, but they are worthy of attention. Most of the models have the following essentials: perturbation upsets a cognitive equilibrium, conflict results, endogenous
and learned processes are set in motion to restore the equilibrium, the processes are effective, but as a result the organism's
cognitive status is changed—the extent of change depending
upon the size of the perturbation and other factors. Surprise has
an obvious place in such a model. Exactly how it may fit will be
spelled out in more precise empirical terms in the next section.
How surprise can be said to characterize aspects of the broader
picture of cognitive development requires some speculation.

One can argue that an important goal of the kind of cognitive
development dealt with by Piaget is to reduce environmental
uncertainty. In a sense this implies reducing the probability of
being surprised. When we compare the preoperational or concrete operational child with the mature adolescent, there is little
question that the latter faces less uncertainty in his everyday
contacts with his environment. Up to sixteen years or so the
child operates with structures that have only partial adaptive
value in the sense that they are never quite adequate to cope
with the full range of problems the environment can pose. If
presented with a problem of conservation of substance, the child
at an early age may simply guess at a solution (which is better
than nothing). At a later age he relinquishes guessing in favor of
attending to size (which is better than guessing), and at a still
later age he relinquishes both strategies in favor of insuring, by
different techniques, that nothing is added or taken away during
deformation of the object. Until he reaches the latter, he presumably has a lot of unexpected experiences, most of which
represent failures. In this respect the uncertainty or surprise
and novelty value of his experience is significantly above zero.

After sixteen or some years of failures and contradictions laced
intermittently with successes, the child becomes capable of

anticipating and regulating his environment with greater success and accuracy. That his environment is mainly social at the time—his friends, parents, and teachers demand more logical behavior from him than when he was younger—does not alter the fact that what is demanded of him has roots in his experience in the world of physical objects. The Piagetian adolescent's knowledge, for example, of how to combine and permute allows him to predict or bring about all logical arrangements of objects or events. This means no errors of inclusion and also none of exclusion. Since he can consider all possible outcomes, nothing is unexpected. He may misexpect an outcome because he gave it an erroneous empirical weighting, but unlike the preoperational child he is never, if he so wishes, vulnerable to the unexpected. In other words, the tight logical structure of his thought—the presence of intellectual operations that have properties of a group or of a lattice—places him in the relatively powerful position of accounting for all possible contingencies. In this respect a fairly large segment of his experience has its surprise and novelty value reduced to zero.

There is no space to pursue such speculations further, but they do generate a few questions worth considering briefly. Is it empirically demonstrable that the developing child actually experiences surprise when his cognitive structures unexpectedly fail to meet environmental demands? Is it reasonable to assume that the surprise reaction is experienced only the first time a structure fails to do its job of aiding the individual in correctly anticipating a situation, or many times until it habituates in the course of the structure's evolution? Does the surprise reaction actually become more intense over time as the child improves his capacity to make increasingly more precise expectancies, but less frequent as his expectancies prove to become more and more veridical as a consequence of structural development? Do more dramatic changes in cognitive restructuring take place relatively late in development when the individual makes precise predictions that turn out to be wrong, and less dramatic changes in early development when predictions are few and imprecise? In other words, does novelty, as described in terms of imprecise expectancies, more frequently characterize subject-object interaction during early cognitive ontogenesis, and surprise more frequently characterize the same interaction during late cognitive ontogenesis?

There is nothing in the literature to suggest that any attempts have been made to answer these questions. No one has monitored a child for surprise during a normal transitional period of cognitive restructuring. The task obviously is awesomely difficult, both for technical reasons and because no one is certain exactly when transitional periods take place. To obtain OR measures over an indeterminate period of time without knowing what kind of stimulus conditions we should depend on as markers of cognitive restructuring is for the most part, wasted effort. While it is possible that restructuring takes place during contacts with object—e.g. the child acquires transitivity while playing with sticks of various lengths—it is also possible, albeit less probable, that he spontaneously acquires transitivity while doing nothing but staring passively out of the window. A more profitable endeavor is to monitor surprise reactions during training periods when the probability is presumably increased that a structure will change within a limited period of time.

In brief, it seems intuitively true that surprise does play a significant role in cognitive development, especially if one is convinced that one of the functions of structures or schemas is to generate expectancies to facilitate the forthcoming overt acts of assimilation. Once the expectancy notion obtains a position in our conceptualizations of a cognitive structure, surprise automatically becomes worthy of consideration. To achieve such a goal is not impossible. Expectancies can be measured in a Piagetian task situation, but we have to devise ways of doing it. The first step in this direction falls squarely on the problems of diagnosing structures. This is the substance of the next section.

Diagnosis

There are at least four classes of responses that an experimenter can employ to diagnose a subject's level of cognitive development—(1) verbal responses, (2) motor behavior in the form of overt instrumental responses such as manipulating and ordering objects, (3) involuntary overt motor behavior in the form of expressive responses, such as facial expression and postural changes, and (4) autonomically mediated responses (i.e. emotional responses) such as GSR's, changes in cardiac rate, and respiration. The first two have been conventionally used in testing subjects for level of cognitive competence; the last two classes have been generally ignored by those interested in cognitive and instrumental motor behaviors.

It goes without saying that the widespread use of verbal skill has come about for at least two reasons—they are relatively easy to elicit from subjects, require a minimum of instrumentation and controlled testing conditions and, as everyday behaviors engaged in by the individual, they are considered by most theoreticians to be critically involved in the actual process of forming the structures they are employed to reveal. The disadvantages of working with such behaviors are important to consider. To do this, however, requires discussion of certain theoretical premises concerning the nature of cognitive structures, a point that will be dealt with later.

Expressive responses have been acknowledged by early philosophers and psychologists as having informational value for our understanding of processes and dispositions not evident in overt instrumental behavior (see Kirchhoff, 1965). Such processes and dispositions, however, were generally what we classify today as personality, rather than cognitive constructs. Expressive responses, furthermore, are not usually considered as belonging to the same category of responses used for diagnostic purposes in education and abnormal psychology. For example, the most recent handbook of psychology published in Germany, where extensive work on expressive behavior is carried out, contains a volume on expressive psychology and a separate volume on diagnostic method and principles. In short, there are historical as well as current conceptual reasons that expressive behaviors have been virtually excluded from attempts to diagnose cognitive structures.

Autonomically-mediated responses (such as GSR, cardiac rate, respiration), of course, have long been objects of inquiry, but not until very recently have they been seriously considered relevant for our understanding of changes in performance due to learning and cognitive development (Berlyne, 1960). The sole exception is the line of work begun by Pavlov when he was developing objective methods for studying the analyzing activity of the nervous system. One such method involved using the OR, but as indicated earlier, he felt that it was a relatively unstable response and preferred to use conditioned reflexes instead (Razran, 1961). Later Russian investigators interested in a poly-effector approach to higher nervous system problems considered the OR as an important psychological, as well as a physiological, concept that could reveal significant information on perceptual and low-level cognitive capacities. Bronshtein & Petrova (1952), for example, argued effectively for using inhibition accompanying the OR as an index of the infant's capacity to discriminate various sounds. Most of these studies were on simple cognitive functions in young infants who have poor muscle control and thereby limited means of demonstrating any possible cognitive competencies they may possess. In spite of the Russian work, autonomic behavior has not yet been strongly identified among techniques used in the assessment of cognitive capacities.

As noted above, the theoretical premises concerning the nature of cognitive structures is called into question when one begins to consider a variety of response systems as possible indicators of a cognitive structure. Flavell (1963) was one of the first to bring up the issue while discussing the concerns psychologists have about depending too heavily upon verbal responses when assessing level of cognitive competence. Flavell points out that "the child's linguistic comprehension and usage is not independent of underlying intellectual structure and orientation" and that "there is probably a point beyond which stripping a concept of its verbal-symbolic accoutrements makes of it a different, lower-order concept, or even no concept at all." Such remarks were directed mainly to the issue raised by Braine (1959) and others who employ nonverbal techniques to measure transitivity. The issue is far from being settled at the moment, but it does pose interesting questions that are further complicated when the surprise construct is taken into consideration: (1) what is the justification for defining cognitive structures solely in terms of verbal responses and overt problem solving operations such as ordering and organizing objects? (2) is there warrant for defining them in terms of other response systems as well (expressive and autonomic), and if so, what does this imply—that cognitive structures are actually independent entities that "employ" any response system that happens to be developmentally mature enough or appropriate to the problematic situation? Answers to these questions will dictate the way in which such structures are measured.

Much for the present depends, of course, on how narrowly one wants to define a particular cognitive structure and how many structures one feels necessary to postulate. If the ability to solve a transitivity problem nonverbally by the correct arrangement of objects is not correlated with the ability to verbalize clearly the meaning of transitivity and give examples of it, then there is reason for postulating separate structures. However, nonverbal transitivity appears developmentally earlier than does verbal transitivity and when the latter appears on the scene both exist side by side in the same child. Later acquisitions, however, need not completely destroy or displace earlier ones. It is unparsimonious to postulate two separate structures to account for the behavior at two separate times. It seems more reasonable instead to assume that (a) different response classes help construct the same concept at different times, (b) different response classes can be used to index the same concept at different times, and (c) a single concept undergoes a gradual finishing process through out the whole of ontogeny. In terms of Piaget's system, all concepts are launched in one way or another from a sensorimotor base (pragmatic) and then move toward a verbal symbolic level (epistemic), a process which involves great changes in overt behavior. If there is little physical resemblance between concepts at different age levels, there is a logical one that is expressed in Piaget's concept of vertical décalage.

But suppose we employ noninstrumental behavior systems (expressive and autonomic) instead of those behaviors employed by Piaget? As pointed out elsewhere (Charlesworth, 1968), Piaget's theory rests on the key premise that cognitive structures or operations develop primarily out of acts, i.e. out of the overt instrumental behaviors that the child engages in when coping with the environment. To diagnose such structures the investigator relies on actions or verbal representations of them. What would we discover if we did not use actions to index the child's level of cognitive development, and how would we interpret our findings?

Let us look at the object concept as an example. Development of the concept may begin as a vague awareness that objects placed behind a screen are actually there and have not just ceased to be. At this age the infant perseveres in attending to a corner of the screen, but does not reach toward it to retrieve the object, a response that Piaget (1954) regards as an important indicator of the object concept. The infant does not reach because he cannot—his hand-eye coordination is not mature enough. Now suppose the same infant five minutes later acts visibly surprised when the object, which is hidden under a cup for two seconds, "mysteriously" disappears? Or suppose his surprise reaction is not so overt, but that his OR pattern, whatever it may be, is different from the OR pattern obtained when the object does not disappear. Suppose too that the OR pattern resembles that of a much older child who unquestionably has the concept. How would we interpret this finding? Should we conclude that the infant has the concept of object permanence at an earlier age than we orginally thought, and that we would have never detected it if we had depended upon reaching behaviors? Or should we conclude that what we have detected is a stage of the object concept that we did not know existed and that actually involves cognitive structures that are not primarily sensorimotor (active) in their origin, but sensoriperceptual (receptive)? Answers to these questions should raise some interesting theoretical issues. Piaget (1954) argues that the construction of the object is achieved on the basis of polysensory inputs, the implication being that all available sense systems—visual, proprioceptive, tactual, kinesthetic—and stimulus-producing systems, such as instrumental behaviors (e.g. object manipulation), must be at the disposal of the processes responsible for constructing the object concept. If they are not, his theory seems to imply, the concept will not develop or at least not develop normally. The possibility that the infant may acquire the same structure by "passively" observing objects and learning about their behavior at a distance without acting upon them is not seriously entertained by the theory. As with most diagnostic tests, Piaget's technique relies heavily upon the maturational state of motor systems and is also vulnerable to such performance factors as motivation, attention, and verbal ability, which are subject to control by maturation as well as learning. There is sufficient evidence that motor and verbal systems tend to lag behind perceptual systems in many areas of normal adaptive functioning (Maccoby & Bee, 1965). Hence it is conceivable that when Piaget's techniques are used, the age certain cognitive acquisitions take place has been overestimated, i.e. the tests have produced a lot of false negatives. Testing noninstrumental motor and autonomically-mediated behaviors may produce fewer false negatives, but at present we simply do not know for certain if this is the case. The opposite could be true. The skillful application of Piaget's methods may actually involve more reliance on expressive behaviors than is generally thought, and consequently produce the most reliable index possible of the child's conceptual level. However, we cannot be certain of this either.

Let us expand for a moment on some weaknesses of current test strategies. A major objection to relying solely upon the motor and verbal systems of behavior as faithful indicators of the child's level of cognitive development is that they are highly vulnerable to learning experiences. Since they are used instrumentally in many situations completely unrelated to the concept in question, they are subject to reinforcement contingencies that vary idiosyncratically across individuals or within an individual across different time periods. It is highly probable that a child with poor motor coordination due to parental neglect of some kind may not adequately demonstrate his awareness of object permanency at the mean age for his social class. To test this notion we would need data on the nature of the experiences that go into constructing a particular concept and either help or hinder its development. At present such data are not available.

On the other hand, using expressive and autonomic responses

to diagnose the level of cognitive development has certain obvious advantages if such responses have the properties of unconditioned respondents as Skinner (1938) originally defined them. Since they are under control of eliciting rather than reinforcing stimuli, respondents are less subject to modification over time than are instrumental responses.* One would thus expect that, if used properly, respondents would give more reliable information about cognitive competencies than instrumental behaviors. Being "unconditioned" as well as difficult to condition, respondents can be viewed as less subject to social-class and culture reinforcement contingencies than to instrumental behaviors and less subject to variability across time and tasks, as well as across developmental stages.

Consider, for example, the OR. While the various responses that constitute the OR are subject to uncontrollable variation due to such factors as habituation, these are minor liabilities in light of the other properties of the OR that make it ideal in measuring cognitive structures. The generality of the OR is an example of such a property. The Russians (Sokolov, 1963) have abundant evidence to support the claim that the OR takes the same form regardless of the nature or intensity of the new stimulus and as Razran (1961) points out, regardless of differences in the intrinsic nature of novel stimuli, the OR is "specific only to the novelty and change characteristics of the stimuli that evoke it."

Unfortunately, the properties of the OR are not shared by other surprise response systems that can be inserted or partly inserted into the respondent category. Facial expressions and posture, apart from the fact that they can be both involuntary

---

* There is some recent evidence (Kimmel, 1967), though, that does not support the notion that respondents are immune to shaping through externally controlled reinforcement. But achieving control over blushing or a GSR in a laboratory does not necessarily mean that such responses are significantly modified by reinforcement contingencies during normal ontogeny. The probability of any human's having an everyday experience during ontogeny comparable to most operant lab experiences is close to zero. Using such an ecological validity argument at this point is justified since the issue at the moment is centered on measuring cognitive development in normal infants and children who go about making cognitive progress with minimal consciously controlled intervention from outsiders.

and voluntary, expressive and instrumental, are not easily subject to satisfactory measurement.* Nevertheless, they are sources of information about the subject's internal states and may well be employable for diagnostic purposes at age levels when the subject does not use facial expression and posture to control his environment.

Areas of psychological research outside the realm of cognitive development have employed noninstrumental behaviors to ascertain accurate information about internal states that could easily be lost through intentional distortion or other disruptive performance variables. The work on lie or guilt detectors is an example. Lykken's (1959, 1960) successful use of the GSR in guilty knowledge detection has led him to conclude "that there is a distinctive pattern of physiological response which accompanies lying and which can be distinguished from that which accompanies truth telling." Other researchers such as Hess and Polt (1966) and Hess (1965) have successfully utilized pupil diameter as a sensitive indicator of the subject's mental state at the time. And there is some evidence (as noted earlier, see Charlesworth, 1966) which suggests that expressive responses obtained under Trick Conditions are slightly better predictors of object concept level than verbal (instrumental) responses under the Real Condition.

The way to employ expressive and autonomically-mediated responses diagnostically can easily be imagined now in terms of

---

* Considerable research has already been conducted on the possible use of facial expressions as indicative of internal states such as emotions and attempts have been made to scale such expressions (Schlosberg, 1952). So far the results have not been very exciting, although some more recent attempts by Engen & Levy (1956) and Abelson & Sermat (1962) show promise. It is not difficult to explain the lack of progress in this area if one recognizes that the primary data gathered on facial expressions have historically been in the form of photographs. What could be more unrepresentative of a person's total expressive output of the moment and more misleading than a frozen fraction-of-a-second facial movement? The accumulated wisdom of interpreting facial expressions has developed on the basis of faces in action, not on the basis of still pictures. Motion picture samples of facial expressions are the obvious solution for research purposes. But this approach still has numerous difficult measurement problems to overcome. Hopefully they will not deter the enthusiastic researcher. The first counterproductive step one can take in a research program is to ignore an interesting phenomenon because it is difficult to measure.

all that has been said about surprise. The experimenter's main interest is in whether the subject has a particular expectancy about a forthcoming event, the inference being that if he does, he has a cognitive structure for the event. In the case of the concept of rotation, for example (Charlesworth & Zahn, 1966), the experimenter provides the subject with a row of pegs in a board, covers the board, and rotates it 180 degrees about a central axis. The subject's job is to attend to the rotation carefully and determine where the various pegs are. At the end of the rotation, the experimenter points to a place on the bar—e.g. to the far left side. The subject's job is to wait until the cover is lifted, then quickly reach up to a panel of levers and pull the lever corresponding to the peg on the far left of the row. His reaching to pull the lever is an operant, but the speed with which he starts to respond (latency) and with which he pulls the lever (response speed) is not. Latency and speed are two properties of his response in this task that can be viewed as involuntary, and in this sense as expressive. The experimenter can construct the apparatus such that a 180-degree rotation will produce an inverted order of objects, as it normally would (hence Real Condition), or he can rig the apparatus to produce an order (e.g. the initial one) which is physically impossible under normal rotation conditions (hence Trick Condition). If the subject is convinced that a 180-degree rotation produced an inverted order, then his response time will be significantly different (slower) when he is presented with the Trick apparatus than when presented with the Real. Such a subject would be rated as having the rotation concept. A difference score between a subject's response under the Real Condition and under the Trick Condition can be used as the measure as to whether he is discriminating between the two situations or not. If the subject is convinced that a 180-degree rotation had no effect on the order, then his response would be different when presented with the Real than when presented with the Trick apparatus, but most probably in the opposite direction. If he is not certain what the outcome is going to be, i.e. he has no precise expectancy and hence is guessing, then his response time would be roughly the same for both Real and Trick situations. In the Charlesworth and Zahn study (1966), subjects who were rated on a criterion task as having the rotation concept, showed significantly longer reactions when tricked than when not tricked and tended to be more sensitive to the differences between the two situations than subjects not having the rotation concept. The latter finding was illustrated by a significant biserial correlation ($r_b = .60$) between reaction time and demonstrating understanding of rotation on the criterion task.

The techniques used to measure level of comprehension of rotation are based on principles that can be applied to any assessment situation where Piagetian or other concepts are being tested. The question asked remains the same—is the subject sensitive to apparent violation of the laws governing the events before him? Does he act surprised—make a pronounced OR—when the law is apparently violated and show no surprise when it is not? If he does, it is assumed that his ability to discriminate between the two situations reflects the presence of a cognitive structure that faithfully represents the lawfulness of the situation. If he does not respond differentially, it is assumed that the structure is absent. Independent measures of the structure, for purposes of verification, can be obtained by using instrumental behaviors.

In addition to response differences, response intensity may be a good indicator of the subject's expectations and hence cognitive level. For example, an infant not having the object concept may show no OR when an object placed under a cup suddenly disappears (Trick Condition). When the object does not disappear, the same infant may show at best a moderate OR—perhaps because the object is novel or at least more interesting than the cup or the empty table top. This OR may be of the same intensity as that obtained when the object is first presented to the infant. An infant having the concept, on the other hand, should show a pronounced OR when the object disappears, and at best a moderate OR when it does not. A transitional subject, one who acts as if he has the concept half of the time and as if he does not the other half, should probably show weak or moderate OR's in both conditions or *alternate* between strong and moderate. It would be interesting to test these predictions experimentally.

Another contribution of the expressive and autonomically-mediated response technique is its use in training situations where the experimenter desires a probe test of the subject's progress, or an additional measure to test for generalization.

The idea of using apparent violation of physical or logical laws or some kind of unexpected trick to test a subject's knowledge is not new, although it has been rarely used. Terman (1916) applied the idea in the Stanford-Binet in the form of a test for detecting absurdities; Dixon (1949) used an illusion in an ingenious technique to measure sensitivities to contradictions, and Smedslund (1961) employed a trick as part of an extinction procedure to determine the extent to which subjects in various training situations acquired the concept of weight. Furthermore, Piaget and his colleagues have long employed a variation of the same idea in their technique of countersuggestion. By telling the child without warning that he is wrong, or that someone else came up with an answer different to his, they hoped to test the strength of the child's conviction about the validity of his own solution to a problem. A competent child in such a situation must surely be surprised by the examiner's remark and the examiner, in return, surely influenced enough by his surprise reaction to give some weight to it in his diagnosis.

Whether expressive and autonomically mediated responses prove to be good diagnostic indicators of cognitive growth remains to be seen. While on the whole they are less subjective than the orthodox techniques, they are certainly not as easy to apply. Illusions about the ease with which one can obtain reliable measures of the OR, facial expressions, and the like are quickly dispelled on the first attempt to obtain them. But not to use such measures is to miss both a chance to improve current diagnostic techniques and, worse yet, an opportunity to understand more about the dynamic aspects of cognitive structures and their development. Some suggestions as to what these dynamic aspects may be are presented in the next section on the mechanism of cognitive change.

The surprise mechanism of cognitive change

There are a number of existing descriptions of mechanisms purportedly responsible for cognitive change. As suggested earlier, Berlyne's notion of conflict and Piaget's concept of equilibration are the most relevant for the surprise thesis and there is no question that the latter is indirectly indebted to both of them. The surprise concept is an attempt to list and, hopefully, to specify more exactly than the other two the variety of possible functions conflicting or contradictory stimuli may serve in the developmental advancement of cognitive structures. It is difficult, though, to marshall adequate empirical support for each function. Berlyne's (1964) paper on the emotional aspects of learning and Razran's (1961) on the role the OR plays in conditioning are the best relevant sources, but their range of topics does not completely overlap with what the surprise concept requires. What follows is at best a restricted empirical treatment of the topic and at worst an unrestricted drift into more speculation.

As has been noted earlier the surprise reaction can be viewed from a broad perspective as one of many interfacing events between a point where no progress is being made in the development of cognitive structures (a state of equilibrium) and a point where the individual has the opportunity to take relevant steps toward such progress (a transient state of disequilibrium). It is assumed that, as an event, the surprise reaction has a number of stimulus functions that are capable of either setting conditions for subsequent responses to occur or actually instigating the responses themselves.

One possible cue function is that of aiding the individual to identify as a class those stimuli that have no property in common other than the fact that they are novel or surprising. Once identified as such, the stimuli are then reacted to in an appropriate fashion. The OR, for example, can come to act both as a general signal for the failure of certain schemata to assimilate an unexpected event and as a specific signal for the individual to engage in behaviors that will remedy the situation. Since attentional and curiosity behaviors of one form or another generally constitute the first step in restoring the balance upset by the novel stimuli, they bear a special functional relationship to the OR. However, the connection between the OR and subsequent behaviors as alluded to earlier is by no means firm. Responses other than curiosity may be conditioned to it.*

Nevertheless, the extent to which surprise, attention and curiosity are connected is very important for the study of cognitive development. It is a truism that attention to stimuli is necessary if the stimuli are to become part of and help reshape existing cognitive schemata. And it is becoming almost a truism in Piagetian research with children, that one of the defects of a child's approach to many problems is his weak or nonexisting ability to attend to details, his lack of awareness of certain properties of objects, and his frequent insensitivity to contradictions provided by simultaneously or temporally presented stimulus items. In a conservation task, for example, it is only by paying very close attention, and even at times by being actively curious, that the child can insure himself that the object maintains its major invariant properties under apparent transformations. In short, he must know all the relevant facts that constitute a problematic situation and most of the facts can only be obtained by means of appropriate attentional behaviors. Factors instigating and maintaining attention appear, therefore, to be of primary importance in undertaking cognitive change. There are some data to suggest

---

* It may be that the schemata of attention, active curiosity, or defensive reactions, such as flight, may have different relationships to the OR during different stages of ontogenesis. The association, for example, between attention (focusing sense receptors upon the novel stimulus) and the OR may be built in at birth—i.e. attention starts off with respondent status. But gradually over time a second form of attention develops that submits more to central rather than peripheral or exogenous stimulus control; it becomes an operant under "voluntary" control and hence subject to reinforcement contingencies. Active curiosity behaviors (actual locomotion, manipulation, and verbal inquiry), on the other hand, appear to have their genesis in other non-OR related systems and activities and presumably only gradually become attached through learning to the OR. If this is true, children may actually have to learn to be actively curious after being surprised, and that differences in curiosity behavior in children may be directly due to the way in which curiosity behavior subsequent to surprise is reinforced. The consequences of such differences for cognitive development are obvious.

that high uncertainty (hence in part high surprise) stimulus conditions not only instigate attentional behaviors, but are more effective in maintaining them over relatively long periods of time than are low uncertainty conditions (Charlesworth, 1966b). Such data, though, are based on a relatively restricted stimulus situation. A greater variety of situations should be examined and more thought given to other aspects of the relationship between attention and cognitive change. Fortunately, promising attempts are currently being made in this direction. Jeffrey (1967), for example, makes a plea for focusing effort upon attention as a means of understanding cognitive development and presents a number of arguments that reveal a possible link between schema construction and the OR.

While certain components of the surprise reaction may have an instigatory effect on attentional and curiosity behaviors, other components apparently have an inhibitory effect on other behaviors. As the description of surprise earlier indicated, one result of an unexpected stimulus is to disrupt the behavioral chain by momentarily inhibiting ongoing gross motor behaviors. One apparent effect of this inhibition is to make it easier for attentional or curiosity behavior to occur. Tomkins' (1962) idea of the "clearing" action surprise or startle has on the central nervous system is relevant here.

Besides having more or less specific instigating and inhibiting cue value for the individual, the surprise reaction may also have a general arousal effect that influences stimulus reception and selection as well as the amount of information processing that subsequently follows. A number of fairly recent studies (some of which are reported in Berlyne, 1964) deal with the general arousal effects of unexpected events, the effects being viewed in many ways—as frustrating, generally pleasing, or hedonically neutral. The possibility that unexpected stimuli heighten general drive level in a partial reinforcement situation and thereby contribute to the greater-resistance-to-extinction effect, is suggested by Charlesworth (1966b).

The first phase of the surprise reaction predominantly involves the dynamic effects of the reaction upon attention and other simultaneously occurring behaviors. The reaction's positive effect on higher mediational processes presumably does not become apparent until shortly after this phase. There are numerous such processes; only a few will be treated here.

One of the most introspectively salient but ambiguous effects of an unexpected stimulus on an individual has to do with those cognitive experiences covered by the terms illumination and insight. Both terms refer in part to a relatively sudden increase in consciousness as a result of an intruding event or the sudden solution of a problem.

Early accounts of consciousness maintained that the disruption of smooth-running behavior produced a heightened consciousness frequently resulting in an effort to restructure the existing cognitive structures. Such restructuring ultimately meant taking the disrupting agent into account. Later psychologists, such as Humphrey (1951), who were primarily interested in thought processes, maintained that images that impede the flow of thought tend to be more clear and concrete than those that do not. The Gestaltists' "aha Erlebnis" refers to the same phenomenon, but perhaps on a higher plane—to instances of unexpected clarification of a mystery, or a sudden discovery of a solution to a vexing problem. The array of phenomena referred to here shares in principle a number of the elements in the surprise model—the individual moves along smoothly (assimilating), or attempts to solve a problem and fails (because he is assimilating and not accommodating or vice versa), then a sudden unexpected or misexpected event occurs that arrests behavior and heightens attention or awareness. While those interested in this phenomenon, to my knowledge, have not examined the physiological responses of subjects during moments of such insight, it is conceivable that such responses would fit into the OR framework. Furthermore, if we analyze the antecedent or predisposing conditions for both surprise, as defined here, and insight, they appear to have some elements in common. Surprise has generally been viewed as involving a mismatch between an "internal" expectancy and an external event, but this may be an unnecessarily limiting view. It could well include a mismatch between two internal elements. Piaget makes a distinction between thought being in accord or not in accord with itself. Sensitivity to contradiction can imply being aware of discrepancies between: (1) two external stimuli, (2) an external stimulus and an internal stimulus in the form of a memory trace, or (3) two internal stimuli. All three instances can occur in various degrees of concordance or discordance. It seems reasonable to assume that expressive and autonomically-mediated responses to discordant internal stimuli would share at least some properties in common with the responses to discordance between an external stimulus and an expectancy. If they do, the application of the surprise model to instances of insight is partially vindicated.

Further justification for pushing such similarities can be obtained by demonstrating that in any instance of discordance new information can be accrued. One can accquire new information by piecing together two pieces of old information—as Bochenski (1965) points out "indirect acquisition of knowledge proceeds by inference," i.e. from one symbolic (internal) representation to another. While dropping off to sleep, one may idly put "two and two together," suddenly be surprised at the result, and never be the same thereafter.

Is the surprise reaction experienced at such a moment the same as that when an external event disagrees with an expectancy or when two contradictory pieces of information are conveyed to us at the same time? In pursuing the relevance of such notions for cognitive development, we can ask whether the same mechanism underlying a structure's transition from one developmental stage to another operates in short-term problem-solving instances conventionally calling for insight. Is each significant developmental change in a structure preceded by an attempt at assimilation that fails followed by an increase in consciousness, or awareness of new relationships, and a pronounced OR? Some of these questions will probably be answered before too long if training studies clarify what is actually involved in the acquisition of a Piagetian concept. The possibility that the acquisition of logical concepts may in effect be an all-or-none phenomena (Suppes & Ginsberg, 1963) provides some hope for a productive coalition between discontinuity in learning theory and cognitive development.

In addition to cueing attentional or curiosity behaviors and "illuminating" situations or relationships, the surprise reaction may have other properties that influence the individual's behavior after the first phases of the surprise reaction subside. These properties can be loosely referred to under the rubrics of memory, reinforcement, and habituation.

Desai (1939) discusses the effects of surprise on memory and comes to the conclusion that it is mainly detrimental. In contrast, Jersild (1929), von Restorff (1933), and Green (1956) maintain that unexpected events generally tend to favor recall. Both viewpoints probably are correct in one way and incorrect in others. There are a number of different factors to take into consideration, and one weakness of the surprise notion as it is presented here is that unexpected stimuli can have two opposing effects— they can result in a negative hedonic tone followed by fear and then flight or immediate repression of the surprising circumstances, or they can result in a positive hedonic tone followed by approach behavior or immediate retention of the circumstances. The hedonic tone can also be neutral. Furthermore, to make matters more difficult, it is possible that there is immediate repression or denial of the unexpected stimuli followed much later by almost total recall. For example, if in a debate with a friend, the friend takes one's own "well-thought-out" argument, leads it predictably from one familiar step to another, but then suddenly pushes it to a logical conclusion one never thought of (a conclusion that is in direct contradiction with one's own), the results may be so devastating, incomprehensible, or both that one immediately writes it off as an invalid argument and "forgets" it—forgets it, that is, until a calm, protected day of solitude. Then it all comes back and one's well-thought-out argument is indeed recognized as fallacious. When it is pointed out to children, for example, that their rules governing the behavior of objects are riddled with contradictions, they frequently appear unimpressed. It may well be, however, that such an experience is not lost upon them and that only much later does it "come back" and help them achieve a more veridical picture of reality. Whatever the case, there is little existing knowledge about the effects of an unexpected event on subsequent memory.

When surprise is looked at in terms of reinforcement theory

the ensuing problems are almost as great as when looking at it in terms of memory. There is ample research evidence (Berlyne, 1960; Fowler, 1965; Smock & Holt, 1962; Cantor & Cantor, 1964; Charlesworth, 1964, 1966a) indicating that novelty and surprise are reinforcing in the sense that they instigate and maintain various forms of curiosity behavior. But the same weakness that characterizes a postulated functional connection between surprise reactions and memory, characterizes the relationship between surprise and curiosity behaviors aimed at resolving the problems posed by the unexpected event. Mismatches between stimuli and expectancies may be either reinforcing or not reinforcing. Even if we could identify hedonic states, Hunt's (1965) observation that infants frequently repeat both familiar and unfamiliar stimuli, and Friedlander's (1967) recent finding that children while preferring to listen to a stranger's voice will suddenly begin preferring their mother's disguised voice once they discover it in a "classic old-fashioned 'aha' experience," hardly simplify the issue. More research on this problem is obviously necessary.

The concept of habituation and its relation to the surprise reaction needs little comment—the OR shows a decline in intensity as a function of repeated presentations of the novel stimulus which first elicited it. There are numerous Russian and American studies of habituation where the operations that are employed resemble those required to produce the surprise reaction as described here. There is, however, one aspect of habituation that appears relevant for cognitive development. The process of habituation may in some respects be highly correlated with the formation of cognitive structures. This idea has been developed at the neurophysiological level by Russian writers, such as Sokolov (1960; 1963), who have demonstrated that habituation of the OR, or components of it, takes place as conditioning takes place, and recently at a more molar level by Americans, such as Lewis (1967) and Jeffrey (1967) who are interested in developmental changes in cognitive processes in infants and children. Intuitively, the idea holds great promise. Habituation in the form of response decrement is becoming easy to measure and with the current interest among child psychologists in improving diagnostic techniques it should become increasingly easy to assess the extent to which a structure has evolved within a learning situation. It can be speculated that a structure undergoing transformation during a training situation would probably be associated with the following temporal sequence of measurable events: (1) a period of a large number of erroneous predictions, descriptions, explanations, or other kinds of overt responses accompanied by a fairly stable and characteristic physiological response suggesting that the child is operating fairly smoothly with an inadequate structure, (2) a gradual turning point when errors start to decline and the number of correct responses slowly increases accompanied by overt signs of strain, discomfort, and heightened attention as well as an increase in the intensity and perhaps variability of physiological responses, (3) a sharp turning point in performance when errors decrease suddenly or very rapidly accompanied by a relatively pronounced GSR and other physiological changes indicative of surprise or insight, (4) error-free performance and stable, "normal-for-the-subject" physiological responses—the child is operating smoothly with an adequate structure.

That such a sequence may not be too far from reality is attested to (albeit weakly) by a scattering of studies. Millward (1964), for example, found that in a paired-associate learning task response latency rose to a high level on several trials before the last error (could this be due to the inhibiting effects of a surprise reaction?) and then declined sharply after the last error. Millward felt that such data argued strongly for an "all-or-none interpretation of learning." Kintsch (1965), also working with a paired-associate task, used the GSR as a measure of the strength of the OR and noted that it "increased in magnitude up to the trial of the last error" and then began to habituate; similar results were noted for response latencies. Kintsch described the process in terms of a two-state Markov model. In a second study, the GSR was again correlated with response states, but this time there were three states—the GSR "tended to increase in the initial state, remained at its peak during intermediate trials, and habituated after learning was completed." White and Plum (1964) in a discrimination learning task noted that when the child approaches criterion, there tends to be a significant increase in eye movements, as if he were checking a hypothesis to make sure it is correct. Could he possibly be responding to an unexpected insight into the problem's answer?

Studies such as these serve the important function of illustrating how crucial it is for our understanding of learning to know what the neurophysiological correlates of ongoing learning processes are. Concern with such variables in Piaget training tasks would undoubtedly serve a very useful function in clarifying the nature of those processes involved in the evolution of cognitive structures. Learning and development may in principle not be such different processes as we have for historical reasons been led to believe.

Taking a broader perspective of the processes involved in cognitive change allows some additional commentary on the role of surprise in such change. It can be speculated that under normal environmental conditions, cognitive structures are driven through a predictable ontogenetic sequence of development (if the environment is relatively constant). It is possible that driving and guiding this process is a relatively stable, general mechanism that operates at all age levels in essentially the same way. The operations of this mechanism could be considered as functional invariants (in Piaget's sense of the term) that have been programmed into the organism during phylogenesis and are responsible for the nonrandom changes in behavior that take place during ontogenesis. A number of elements of varying empirical and conceptual status are involved in these operations. For purposes of convenience, these elements can be considered simply as abilities. They include the ability to (1) obtain stimuli by means of attentional and curiosity behaviors; (2) code stimuli into a storageable form and then store it as available information; (3) organize the information into structures such that these structures control and monitor future sensory inputs and motor outputs; (4) retrieve the same information when a stimulus situation calls for it; (5) encode the retrieved information into expectancies appropriate to the stimulus situation; (6) respond with surprise reactions (OR, facial, and postural) when such expectancies are not confirmed and to inhibit such reactions when

they are confirmed; (7) respond to the surprise reactions themselves with appropriate attentional and curiosity behaviors; and
(8) utilize the information obtained by the latter behavior to alter
or transform the original schemas or structures.

There is no space to discuss each of the abilities or the chain
as a whole, however, surprise should be accounted for briefly. In
this framework the surprise reactions themselves, especially the
OR component, can be viewed as multifunctional, hyperstable
properties of the organism that help to insure that the organism
behaves in such a way as to produce new knowledge about
problematic properties of the environment. This does not imply
that such reactions will invariably be elicited by unexpected or
misexpected events. There is some proof, as noted earlier (Kimmel, 1967), that such reactions are conditionable. But it does
imply that under normal environmental conditions surprise reaction and subsequent attentional and curiosity behaviors are very
hard to suppress, and that for this reason they seem to be good
candidates for the mechanisms that insure that most individuals
make the progression from sensorimotor intelligence to formal
thought.

In conclusion, the surprise reaction can be viewed as consisting of a number of complex stimulus-producing responses that
may serve to mediate, cue, arouse, instigate, "illuminate," and
reinforce a variety of other responses that ultimately contribute
to changes in existing cognitive structures. While such magical
properties obviously do not characterize only the surprise reaction—they have been examined in great length in other
contexts—they are worth including in any model of cognitive
development. If they are included they will ultimately require a
close examination of the neuro-physiological mechanisms underlying such development, and this will be healthy.

Final remarks

The gist of this essay is as follows. Surprise is such an ubiquitous
phenomenon in the life of an individual, one cannot help but feel

that it may serve some adaptive purpose. Surprise entails expectancies and these in turn suggest that more permanent structures may underlie them. Hence, it is no great jump to argue that surprise could somehow be implicated in cognitive development, especially since surprise is one of the determinants of attentional process upon which cognitive development depends. If there is some validity to chaining these factors together, we shall be able to detect it both by carefully examining neurophysiological processes involved in instances where we know cognitive change is taking place and by examining the suggestion that surprise reactions may well have mediating, cueing, and response-instigating and reinforcing functions. The neurophysiological processes that would show the greatest promise in such an undertaking comprise most of what we recognize today as the OR. Since surprise as defined here, presupposes expectancies and other cognitive processes of a higher level than are usually associated with either the OR, novelty, or startle, it can serve as a bridging construct between the OR and cognitive development.

It is generally admitted that there has been a lack of a dynamogenic element in most of our existing theories of cognitive development. Bringing the OR into the picture, as the Russians have been doing for years in their studies of conditioning processes, seems to be the most likely way to remedy this lack. Berlyne has made a similar plea many times before, and it is still valid.

The consequences of deciding upon this course of action for our study of Piagetian structures will initially be methodological. Testing and training situations will be carefully constructed to maximize the possibility of creating expectancies and obtaining overt measures of them, of carefully controlling stimulus conditions to insure that stimulus inputs will be in accord or discord with such expectancies, and carefully monitoring the child's subsequent expressive and autonomically-mediated reactions. The results of such efforts may shed light, for example, on whether the same cognitive structure actually progresses through a series of very different phases—from a primitive receptive or perceptual phase, to a motor enactive phase, and finally to a terminal verbal phase that crowns all the rest and affords the individual maximal adaptiveness. Such findings may prove to have interesting implications for Piaget's theory.

References

Abelson, R. P., & Sermat, V. Multidimensional scaling of facial expressions. *J. exp. Psychol.*, 1962, 63, 546–554.

Anokhin, P. K. *The role of the orientation reaction in conditioning, the orientation reaction and orienting-investgating activity.* Moscow: Acad. Pedag. Sciences, 1958.

Bain, A. *The emotions and the will.* (3rd ed.) New York: Appleton, 1874.

Baldwin, J. M. *Handbook of psychology: feeling and will.* New York: Henry Holt, 1894.

Berlyne, D. E. *Conflict, arousal, and curiosity.* New York: McGraw-Hill, 1960.

Berlyne, D. E. Conflict and the orientation reaction. *J. exp. Psychol.*, 1961, 62, 476–483.

Berlyne, D. E. Emotional aspects of learning. *Ann. Rev. Psychol.*, 1964, 15, 115–142.

Bochenski, J. M. *The methods of contemporary thought.* Dordrecht-Holland: D. Reidel Publishing Co., 1965.

Braine, M. S. The ontogeny of certain logical operations: Piaget's formulation examined by nonverbal methods. *Psychol. Monogr.*, 1959, 73, No. 5 (Whole No. 475).

Brazier, Mary A. (Ed.) *The central nervous system and behavior.* New York: J. Macy, 1960.

Bronshtein, A. I., & Petrova, E. P. Issledovanie zvukovogo analizatora novorozhdennyk i detei rannego grudnogo vozrasta. (An investigation of the auditory analyzer in neonates and young infants.) *Zh. vyssh. nerv. Deiatel.*, 1952, 2, 333–343.

Cantor, J. H., & Cantor, G. N. Observing behavior in children as a function of stimulus novelty. *Child. Develpm.*, 1964, 35, 119–128.

Charlesworth, W. R. Instigation and maintenance of curiosity behavior as a function of surprise versus novel and familiar stimuli. *Child Develpm.*, 1964, 35, 1169–1186.

Charlesworth, W. R. Persistence of orienting and attending behavior in infants as a function of stimulus-locus uncertainty. *Child Develpm.*, 1966, 37, 473–491. (a)

Charlesworth, W. R. The development of the object concept: a methodological concept. Paper presented at the meeting of the Amer. Psychol. Ass., New York City, September, 1966. (b)

Charlesworth, W. R. Cognition in infancy: where do we stand in the mid-sixties? *Merrill-Palmer Quart.*, 1968, **14**, #1.

Charlesworth, W. R., & Zahn, Carolyn. Reaction time as a measure of comprehension of the effects produced by rotation on objects. *Child Develpm.*, 1966, **37**, 253–268.

Darwin, C. *The descent of man.* New York: Appleton, 1871.

Darwin, C. *The expression of the emotions in man and animals.* New York: Appleton, 1872.

Desai, M. M. Surprise: a historical and experimental study. *Brit. J. Psychol.*, *Monogr. Suppl.*, 1939, No. 22, pp. 124.

Dixon, J. C. Concept formation and emergence of contradictory relations. *J. exp. Psychol.*, 1949, **39**, 144–149.

Duckworth, Eleanor. Piaget rediscovered. *J. Res. Sci. Teach.*, 1964, **2**, 172–175.

Engen, T., & Levy, N. Constant-sum judgments of facial expressions. *J. exp. Psychol.*, 1956, **51**, 396–398.

Festinger, L. *A theory of cognitive dissonance.* Evanston, Ill.: Roe Peterson, 1957.

Flavell, J. H. *The developmental psychology of Jean Piaget.* Princeton, N.J.: Van Nostrand, 1963.

Fowler, H. *Curiosity and exploratory behavior.* New York: Macmillan Co., 1965.

Friedlander, B. Z. Techniques for attended and unattended studies of human infants' operant play for perceptual reinforcement. Unpublished paper, 1967.

Gastaut, H., & Roger, A. Les mécanismes de l'activité nerveuse supérieure an niveau des grandes structures fonctionelles du cerveau. In H. H. Jasper and G. D. Smirnov (Eds.), Moscow Colloquium on Electroencephalogy of Higher Nervous Activities. *EEG. Clin. Neurophysiol.*, 1960, Suppl. 13.

Green, R. T. Surprise as a factor in the von Restorff effect. *J. exp. Psychol.*, 1956, **52**, 340–344.

Hess, E. Attitude and pupil size. *Sci. Am.*, 1965, **212**, 46–54.

Hess, E., & Polt, J. Pupil diameter and load on memory. *Sci.*, 1966, **154**, 1583–1585.

Humphrey, G. *Thinking: an introduction to its experimental psychology.* New York: Wiley, 1951.

Hunt, J. McV. *Intelligence and experience.* New York: Ronald Press, 1961.

Hunt, J. McV. Intrinsic motivation and its role in psychological development. In D. Levine (Ed.), Nebr. Sympos. on Motiv., Lincoln: Univ. of Nebraska Press, 1965. Pp. 189–282.

Jacobson, E. Response to a sudden unexpected stimulus. *J. exp. Psychol.*, 1926, **9**, 19–25.

Jeffrey, W. E. The orienting reflex and attention in cognitive development. Paper presented at the meeting of the Soc. Res. Child Develpm., New York, April, 1967.

Jersild, A. Primacy, recency, frequency, and vividness. *J. exp. Psychol.,* 1929, **12,** 58–70.

Kimmel, H. D. Instrumental conditioning of autonomically mediated behavior. *Psychol. Bull.,* 1967, **67,** 337–345.

Kintsch, W. Habituation of the GSR component of the orienting reflex during paired-associate learning before and after learning has taken place. *J. mathematical Psychol.,* 1965, **2,** 330–341.

Kirchhoff, R. Ausdruckspsychologie. Vol. 5. H. Thomae (Ed.), *Handbuch der Psychologie.* Göttingen: Verlag für Psychologie, 1965.

Landis, C., & Hunt, W. A. *The startle pattern.* New York: Farrar & Rinehart, 1939.

Lewis, M. Infant attention: response decrement as a measure of cognitive processes, or what's new, baby Jane? Paper presented at the meeting of the Soc. Res. Child Develpm., New York, April, 1967.

Lykken, D. T. The GSR in the detection of guilt. *J. appl. Psychol.,* 1959, **43,** 385–388.

Lykken, D. T. The validity of the guilty knowledge technique: the effects of faking. *J. appl. Psychol.,* 1960, **44,** 258–262.

Lynn, R. *Attention, arousal, and the orientation reaction.* New York: Pergamon Press, 1966.

Maccoby, Eleanor E., & Bee, Helen L. Some speculations concerning the lag between perceiving and performing. *Child Develpm.,* 1965, **36,** 367–377.

McDougall, W. *Outline of psychology.* New York: Scribner's, 1923.

Miller, G. A., Galanter, E., & Pribram, K. H. *Plans and the structure of behavior.* New York: Holt, Rinehart & Winston, 1958.

Millward, R. Latency in a modified paired-associate learning experiment. *J. verb. Learn. verb. Behav.,* 1964, **3,** 309–316.

Patterson, E. A qualitative and quantitative study of the emotion of surprise. *Psychol. Monogr.,* 1930, **40,** 85–108.

Piaget, J. *Language and thought of the child.* New York: Harcourt, 1926.

Piaget, J. *Judgment and reasoning in the child.* New York: Harcourt, 1928.

Piaget, J. *Les notions de mouvement et de vitesse chez l'enfant.* Paris: Presses Univer. France, 1946.

Piaget, J. *The origins of intelligence in children.* New York: Internat. Univer. Press, 1952.

Piaget, J. *The construction of reality in the child.* New York: Basic Books, Inc., 1954.

Piaget, J. *Six psychological studies.* New York: Random House, 1967.

Razran, G. The orienting reflex. From "The observable unconscious and the inferable conscious in current Soviet psychophysiology: interoceptive conditioning, semantic conditioning, and the orienting reflex." *Psychol. Rev.*, 1961, 68, 109–119.

Ribot, T. H. *The psychology of emotions.* London: W. C. Scott, Ltd., 1911.

Ruckmick, C. A. A preliminary study of the emotions. *Psychol. Monogr.*, 1921, 30, 30–35.

Schlosberg, H. The description of facial expressions in terms of two dimensions. *J. exp. Psychol.*, 1952, 44, 229–237.

Skaggs, E. B. Changes in pulse, breathing, and steadiness under conditions of startledness and excited expectancy. *J. Comp. Psychol.*, 1926, 6, 303–317.

Skinner, B. F. *The behavior of organisms.* New York: Appleton-Century-Crofts, 1938.

Smedslund, J. The acquisition of conservation of substance and weight in children. III. Extinction of weight acquired "normally" and by means of empirical control on a balance scale. *Scand. J. Psychol.*, 1961, 2, 85–87.

Smock, C. D., & Holt, Bess G. Children's reactions to novelty: an experimental study of "curiosity motivation." *Child Develpm.*, 1962, 33, 631–642.

Sokolov, E. N. Neuronal models and the orienting reflex. In Mary A. Brazier (Ed.), *The central nervous system and behavior.* New York: J. Macy, 1960.

Sokolov, E. N. *Perception and the conditioned reflex.* Oxford: Pergamon Press, 1963.

Spitz, R. A. *The first year of life.* New York: Internat. Univer. Press, 1965.

Stanley, H. M. *Studies in the evolutionary psychology of feeling.* New York: Macmillan, 1895.

Strauss, H. Das zusammenschrencken. *J. Psychol. Neurol.*, 1929, 39, 111–231.

Suppes, P., & Ginsberg, R. A. Fundamental property of all-or-none models, binomial distribution of responses prior to conditioning with application to concept formation in children. *Psychol. Rev.*, 1963, 70, 139–161.

Terman, L. M. *The measurement of intelligence.* New York: Houghton Mifflin, 1916.

Tomkins, S. S. *Affect, imagery, consciousness: the positive affects.* Vol. 1. New York: Springer Publishing Co., 1962.

von Restorff, H. Uber die Wirkung von Bereichsbildungen im Spurenfeld. *Psychol. Forschung*, 1933, 18, 299–342.

Voronin, L. G., Leontiev, A. N., Luria, A. R., Sokolov, E. N., & Vinogradova, O. S. (Eds.) *The orienting reflex and orienting-investigating activity.* Moscow: Acad. Pedag. Sciences, 1958.

Warren, H. C. *Human psychology.* Boston: Houghton Mifflin, 1920.

White, S. H., & Plum, G. E. Eye movement photography during children's discrimination learning. *J. exp. Child. Psychol.*, 1964, 1, 327–338.

Wilcocks, R. W. The effect of an unexpected heterogeneity on attention. *J. gen. Psychol.*, 1928, 1, 266–319.

Woodworth, R. S., & Schlosberg, H. *Experimental psychology.* (Rev. ed.) New York: Holt, 1954.

Wundt, W. *Outlines of psychology.* Leipzig: Wilhelm Engelmann, 1901.

Developmental Psycholinguistics

HERMINA SINCLAIR-DE-ZWART

One of the questions a Genevan psycholinguist who works with Jean Piaget hears often is: how does language figure in Piaget's theory? Does his theory of cognitive development provide a framework for the acquisition of language? Does he have an epistemology of language? It is difficult to answer these questions in a straightforward manner; the more so, since the few articles Piaget himself has written on language are almost uniquely concerned with the problem of language as a factor in development, and may seem to be written almost reluctantly (one of them starts off ". . . il aurait fallu me poser cette question à une epoque ou. . . ." 1963); his very early work, *Le langage et la pensée chez l'enfant* (1923) concerns far more "la pensée" than "le langage." On the other hand, it is quite wrong to assert, as many authors do, that Piaget leaves language completely outside his considerations, and that, in fact, his experiments may lose some of their meaning because of this refusal to consider language as a separate, important variable.

To live with, or rather in, Piaget's theories for a number of

315

years may have curious effects on a psycholinguist: from an
initial irritation at the rather off-hand manner in which language
is dealt with in many of Piaget's works and in much of his
experimentation, one reaches the conviction that spread over a
number of works, Piaget has in fact provided the bases for a
general theory of both language-acquisition and of the role of
language as a factor of development. However this may be, the
following is an attempt to explain and elaborate Piaget's views
on language. These views will be presented in two contexts:
language viewed as a factor in cognitive development, and as a
possible theory of language-acquisition.

Piaget's conception of the role of language in cognitive development

In several articles Piaget has been most explicit on this relationship between language and intellectual operations. The two main
points that recur in his writings on the subject are the following:

1. The sources of intellectual operations are not to be found in
language, but in the preverbal, sensorimotor period where a
system of schemes is elaborated that prefigures certain aspects of
the structures of classes and relations, and elementary forms of
conservation and operative reversibility. In fact, the acquisition
of the permanency of objects (elaborated between 6 and 18
months) constitutes a first "invariant." The search for an object
which has disappeared is conducted in function of its successive
localizations: these localizations depend on the constitution of an
elementary *groupe de déplacements,* in which detours (associativity) and returns (reversibility) are coordinated.

2. The formation of representational thought is contemporaneous with the acquisition of language; both belong to a more
general process, that of the constitution of the symbolic function
in general. This symbolic function has several aspects; different
kinds of behaviours, all appearing at about the same time in
development, indicate its beginnings. The first verbal utterances
are intimately linked to, and contemporaneous with, symbolic
play, deferred imitation, and mental images as interiorized
imitations.

The first point is elaborated in many works by Piaget and his co-workers (Bärbel Inhelder in particular). Intellectual operations are actions that have become interiorized and reversible, but they are still actions. The coordination and decentrations of sensorimotor activity are not limited to this first period of life, but are found, in a different form, at work in the constitution of operational intelligence as well. And, as Piaget frequently remarks (1963, p. 72), they are also found in linguistic acts. This may account for a partial isomorphism between language and logic. It is important to bear in mind that already in the sensorimotor period object-permanency is a general acquisition. It would be a contradiction in terms to speak of one specific operation, since an operation is always part of a structured whole, of a system of operations; but in the same way, object-permanency is not to be understood as the permanency of one or of some objects (a toy, the baby's bottle) but of objects in general. Similarly, the *groupe de déplacements* does not mean that the baby can make one specific detour, or return to his starting point in one particular case: these first prefigurations of associativity and reversibility are, again, general. Thought has its roots in action; at the end of the sensorimotor period, and before the appearance of language or of the symbolic function in general, the baby has overcome his initial perceptive and motor egocentrism by a series of decentrations and coordinations. The construction of operations demands a new series of decentrations; not only from the momentary, present perceptive centration, but also from the totality of the actions of the subject.

As regards the second point, Piaget has devoted a whole work to *La formation du symbole chez l'enfant* (1946, English title *Play, dreams, and imitation in childhood*, 1951). This important work cannot be summarized in a few pages, but the main concepts bearing on the role of language in the development of thought may be expressed as follows.

At the end of the sensorimotor period the first decentrations appear in the child's dealings with his *hic-et-nunc* environment; action-schemata appear that permit the child to attain his practical aims, which are limited to the immediate present and to the manipulation of concrete objects within his reach. These spatio-temporal restrictions will slowly disappear with the development of thought. Moreover, the activity of the baby is directed toward success in his manipulations (from the cognitive point of view) and toward personal satisfaction (from the affective point of view). Later on, his activity takes on another dimension: cognitively, immediate success will no longer be the sole aim, but he will search for explanations and will reflect on his own actions; affectively, he will seek not only satisfaction, but also communication; he will want to tell other people about his discoveries, that now become *knowledge of* objects and events rather than *reactions to* objects and events.

One might be tempted to regard language, in the sense of learning to speak one's mother tongue through contact with the persons in one's environment, as the sole or main instrument that causes this transformation. Piaget, however, shows clearly that language is only a symptom and not the source of this change. Retracing the development step by step through careful observation of his own children, he demonstrates that language, despite the fact that later on it becomes most pervasive and takes on the guise of an autonomous capacity, is only part of the symbolic function. The symbolic function can be defined essentially as the capacity to represent reality through the intermediary of signifiers that are distinct from what they signify. The important term in this definition is the word *distinct*. In fact, around six months of age the baby already is capable of treating a partial perceptive datum as an indication of the presence of the whole; even if only a bit of the object is visible, it indicates the presence of the object. But such signals are directly linked to the objects, or are part of the object, whereas distinct signifiers imply a differentiation between signifier and signified, *introduced by the subject himself*. Signals (like the tracks an animal leaves in the snow, or the smell of food, or visible bits of partially hidden objects) are temporally and spatially restricted; the most distinct signifiers (words, algebraic symbols, and such) are free from such restrictions. Using a slightly different terminology, the linguist Bally said that the signal is a signifier only for whoever interprets it; and that a sign (distinct signifier) is a "voluntary act," and also meaningful for whoever uses it.

The child who pushes a small shell along the edge of a box

saying "meow" knows full well that the shell is not a cat and the edge of the box is not a fence. And even if for the child the words "meow" or "cat" are at first somehow inherent in the animal, they are signifiers, and certainly not the animal itself. Piaget introduces a dichotomy in the distinct signifiers themselves: (1) symbols, which like the shell have a link of resemblance with the object or event, and (2) signs (words), which are arbitrary. Symbols, moreover, are usually personal; every child invents them in his play, whereas signs are social. Finally, we may add, symbols are mostly isolated, though within the context of symbolic play they may be loosely associated; signs on the other hand form systems.

According to Piaget, this capacity to represent reality by distinct signifiers has its roots in imitation, which starts very early in the sensorimotor period (around six months of age) and which already constitutes some sort of representation by action. At the end of the sensorimotor period imitation becomes possible in the absence of the model, and evolves from a direct sensorimotor model to gesticulative evocation. First one sees action-schemes appear out of their proper context as representations (for instance, pretending to be asleep); then these representations become detached from the activity of the subject (for instance, putting a doll to sleep). Slowly these deferred imitations become interiorized, and constitute sketchy images, which the child can already use to anticipate future acts. Piaget gives several examples of these action-imitations that announce interiorization: when L. tries to open a box of matches (which is not quite shut), she first manipulates it, but without result; then she stops acting, seems to reflect on the problem and opens and shuts her mouth, several times in succession: she uses a motor-signifier to represent the problem and to find a way of solving it. After this short period of "reflection" she pushes her finger into the small opening and pulls to open the box completely.

A wealth of such observations throws light on the development of the symbolizing capacity, which has many different aspects that are at first inextricably linked in observable behavior. Small children pass extremely swiftly from what looks like pure imitation to symbolic play and to acts of practical intelligence accompanied by words (or onomatopoaeia), but at first these different aspects cannot even be distinguished. Language as seen by Piaget is thus part of a much larger complex of processes that go on during the second year of life; it has the same roots, and in the beginning the same function as symbolic play, deferred imitation, and mental images; it does not appear *ex nihilo* (nor simply from early, prelinguistic vocalizations) but partakes of the entire cognitive development in this crucial period. It is, of course, just as closely linked to affective development; but this aspect of the question has been frequently dealt with by other authors, and the aim of this paper is restricted to the relationship between language and intellectual operations.

In summary, Piaget considers language not to be a sufficient condition for the constitution of intellectual operations, and he has said so, explicitly, in several articles (1954, 1961, 1962, 1963, 1965, 1966). As to the question of whether language (in the sense of the normal acquisition of natural language by the young child) is, if not a sufficient, all the same a necessary condition for the constitution of operations, Piaget leaves the question open as regards the operations of formal logic. He notes (1963, p. 58) however, that these operations go beyond language, in the sense that neither the lattice of possible combinations nor the group of four transformations is as such present in language; they cannot even be expressed in ordinary, natural language. As regards concrete operations, Piaget considers language (again, in the limited sense) not even a necessary condition for their constitution, though he has not explicitly said so. However, he does state:

. . . . the sensorimotor schemata seem to be of a fundamental importance from their very first beginnings; these schemes continue to develop and structure thought, even ∨erbal thought, as action progresses, up till the constitution of logico-mathematical operations, which are the authentic end-product of coordinated action-logic, when the latter can be interiorized and combined into group structures (1965, p. 2254).

Moreover, as regards concrete operations, Piaget quotes experiments with deaf-mute children, which clearly seem to point to the fact that the symbolic function is an obvious necessity for the constitution of these operations, but that the normal acquisition of a natural language is not. A brief summary of experimental data pertaining to the relationship between language and thought can be given and two different kinds of experiments can be distinguished.

(1) The comparison of the reactions of normal children to Piaget-type tests with those of deaf-mute children on the one hand, and blind children on the other. The deaf-mutes have intact sensorimotor schemes, but have not acquired spoken language (or are only at the beginning of an "oral" education), whereas the blind are in the inverse situation. Studies of deaf children have been made by Oléron (1957) and Furth (1966) among others. Their results concur fundamentally, and indicate that deaf children acquire the elementary logical operations with only a slight retardation as compared to normal children. The same stages of development are found as the ones established by Piaget on a normal population. Both Oléron and Furth point out some differences in the reactions of their deaf subjects (particularly in the conservation of liquids). In the case of the conservation of liquids, however, certain difficulties in the presentation of the tests may account for these differences (e.g. in the pouring of liquids, the distinction between the quantity of liquid and the volume of the container is difficult to convey).

Furth notes an interesting difference in the comparative performance of deaf and hearing on "logical symbol discovery" versus "symbol use" tasks. While the deaf are inferior to the hearing on the former, they show equal ability on the use of logical symbols in a structured task. Furth points to several factors that could explain the results: among others, a different approach on the part of the deaf towards problems that call for invention, which may be due to a general lack of social contact. Oléron finds that seriation-tests are only very slightly retarded; that spatial operations are normal, and that classifications possess the same general structures and appear at the same age as with normals, but seem slightly less mobile or flexible (when classificatory criteria have to be changed). Here again, the cause may be more due to a general lack of social exchange and stimulation than to operational retardation.

These results with deaf children are all the more striking when it is considered that the same tests are only solved by blind children, on the average, four years later than by normal. The sensorial deficit of the blind has retarded the constitution of sensorimotor schemes and inhibited their coordination. The verbal acquisitions cannot compensate for this retardation, and action-learning is necessary before blind children reach an operational level comparable to that of the normal and the deaf (Hatwell, 1960).

(2) A second group of experiments, directly bearing on the relationship between language and intellectual operations has been carried out in Geneva by Inhelder in collaboration with the author. These experiments have been described in detail elsewhere (Sinclair-de-Zwart, 1967), and in this paper we shall do no more than briefly indicate their technique and summarize the results. Our aims were twofold: (a) to see whether the profound modification that occurs in the child's thinking with the constitution of the first concrete operations is paralleled by a linguistic development: (b) if the answer to (a) were in the affirmative, to determine whether a child who still lacks a certain concept or operation would show operatory progress after having undergone verbal training aiming to make him acquire expressions used by children who already possess the concept in question.

Consequently, we first chose some Piagetian tasks (conservation of liquids and seriation) that call for understanding and using certain expressions (quantitative and dimensional terms and comparatives). We explored the child's verbal capacities in this domain by first asking him to describe simple situations (which do not touch upon conservation or seriation problems: e.g. we present the child with two dolls, to one of whom we give 4 big marbles and to the other 2 small marbles, and we ask: Is this fair? Are both dolls happy? Why not? Or we ask him to tell us the difference between two pencils, e.g. a short thick one and a long thin one). After this exploration of the child's use of certain expressions, we studied his comprehension, by asking him to execute orders couched in "adult" but simple terms (e.g. "give more plasticine to the boy than to the girl"; "find a pencil that is shorter but thicker than this one").

After dividing our subjects into three groups according to their results on the Piagetian conservation task (total absence of conservation, intermediary stage, and conservation present), we compared their answers in the verbal task. The results can be summarized as follows:

(a) no difference was found among the three groups in the comprehension tasks; in fact, almost all subjects executed all orders correctly; only a very few young children (four years old) had some difficulties in questions of the type: "Find a pencil that is longer but thinner."

(b) striking differences were found between the two extreme groups (no conservation at all and conservation acquired) as regards the description tasks:

Of the children with conservation, 70 percent used comparatives (without adjectives) for the description of different quantities of plasticine, and 100 percent did so for the description of different numbers of marbles: *le garçon a plus que la fille* (the boy has more than the girl).

Of children without conservation, 90 percent used absolute terms (in contrast to comparatives): *le garçon a beaucoup, la fille a peu* (the boy has a lot, the girl has a little).

An interesting point was that 20 percent already used comparatives for discrete units (marbles) whereas they did not do so for continuous quantities (plasticine); and the conservation of discrete units is acquired before that of continuous quantities.

Of the children with conservation, 100 percent used different terms for different dimensions, using two couples of opposites (e.g. *grand petit, gros/mince*, big/little, fat/thin).

Of children without conservation, 75 percent used undifferentiated terms for the two dimensions, i.e. they would use at least one word to indicate two dimensions: e.g. *gros* (fat) for long and for thick, or *petit* (small) for short and for thin.

Of children with conservation, 80 percent described two objects differing in two dimensions in two sentences, coordinating the two dimensions: *ce crayon est (plus) long mais (plus) mince, l'autre est court mais gros* [this pencil is long(er) but thin(ner), the other is short but thick].

Of children without conservation, 90 percent either described only the one dimension, or used four separate sentences, dealing first with length, and then with thickness: *ce crayon est long, l'autre est court, ce crayon* (the first one again) *est mince, l'autre est gros.* (Percentages are approximate; slight variations occurred in different groups of items and with different materials, not described here.)

In a second series of experiments we tried to teach children without conservation the expressions used by children with conservation: comparative terms, differentiated terms and coordinated description of a difference in two dimensions. After this verbal training we again tested their operational level in the conservation task. The results of these experiments were as follows:

It was easy (in the sense that only a small number of repetitions were necessary) to teach the children without conservation the use of differentiated terms; it was more difficult (and about a quarter of the subjects did not succeed) to teach them to use the comparatives *plus* and *moins* in our situations; it was still more difficult to teach them the coordinated structure *long et (mais) mince, court et (mais) gros.*

Even for children who succeeded in learning to use these expressions, operational progress was rare (10 percent of our subjects acquired conservation).

On the other hand, more than half the children who made no clear operational progress, changed their answers in the post-test. Instead of simply using the level of the liquid to decide that there was more to drink in one of the glasses, they now noticed and described the covarying dimensions (higher level, narrower glass); they sometimes explained that the liquid goes up higher in a narrower glass, but this did not lead them to the compensation argument and conservation.

From this first series of experiments we drew the following conclusions:

(a) A distinction must be made between lexical acquisition and the acquisition of syntactical structures, the latter being more closely linked to operational level than the former. The operator-like words (e.g. more, less, as much as, none) form a class apart whose correct use is also very closely linked to operational progress. The other lexical items (e.g. long, short, thin, thick, high, low) are far less closely linked to operativity.

(b) Operational structuring and linguistic structuring or rather linguistic restructuring thus parallel each other. The lexical items are already being used or at least easily learned at a pre-operational level; the coordinated structures and operator-like words are correctly "understood" in simple situations; but the latter are only precisely and regularly used with the advent of the first operational structures. Moreover, the difficulties encountered by the child in the use of these expressions seem to be the same as those he encounters in the development of the operations themselves: lack of decentration and incapacity to co-ordinate.

(c) Verbal training leads subjects without conservation to direct their attention to pertinent aspects of the problem (co-variance of the dimensions), but it does not ipso facto bring about the acquisition of operations.

An additional experiment may be briefly mentioned: in interrogating a group of severely retarded children (age 8 to 15, I.Q. 50 or below) we found that when we used the description patterns of children with conservation for simple orders (*donne plus à la poupee-fille, moins au garçon*), the retarded children were incapable of reacting consistently; but if we used the descriptive terms of our normal nonconservational group (e.g. *donne beaucoup à la fille, et peu au garçon*) their reactions were both correct and consistent. This result illustrated the psychological "reality" of the different descriptive patterns used by normal children.

A second group of experiments dealt with seriation and its verbal aspects, and yielded comparable results.

These Genevan results, together with the results of the research on deaf and blind children mentioned earlier, confirm Piaget's view on the role of language in the constitution of intellectual operations: language is not the source of logic, but is on the contrary structured by logic.

*A possible theory of language acquisition within
the general framework of Piaget's
developmental theory*

No theory of language acquisition has been explicitly proposed by Piaget. We can, however, speculate on the general form that such a theory might take. The problem is complex for several reasons.

In the first place, language, in Piaget's terms (1966, p. 69) is "a ready-made system that is elaborated by society and that contains, for persons that learn it before they contribute to its enrichment, a wealth of cognitive instruments (relations, classifications, and so on) at the service of thought." The knowing person expresses his "knowledge" in this code. As such, language takes the place of symbolization in the relationship knower-symbolization-known. But this code is itself an object of knowing; as such it takes the place of the "known" in the knower-known relationship. Piaget stresses mainly the first aspect; most psycholinguists pay attention only to the second.

A second difficulty lies in the fact that language, though it is a system of signs (in terms of the distinction between signals on the one hand and symbols and signs on the other) that can be used for rational discourse and communication, it need not only be used as such. In fact, linguistic forms can be used as signals "to be reacted to" rather than "to be understood": trivial examples are animal training and verbal conditioning; they can be used as symbols, as in rituals and certain kinds of literature.

Consequently, a theory of the acquisition of language would have to be based on a theory of the developmental changes in the knower-symbolization-known relationship: in other words, on genetic epistemology. On the other hand, it would also have to be based on a theory of the formal properties of language, in other words, on linguistic theory. To understand *how* something is acquired, we first have to know *what* is acquired.

Modern linguistics (since de Saussure) has been concerned with the establishment of systems of elements and procedures for making inventories of elements (segmentation, substitution, association, classification, and so on). For this reason, Chomsky (1964) calls this type of theory taxonomic linguistics.

Taxonomic linguistics was combined with associationist learning theory to produce theories of language-acquisition that left honest observers of young children mystified and that failed completely to account for the fundamental fact of language: the ability to produce and to understand an indefinite number of sentences that have not been previously heard. The comparative ease and rapidity with which young children learn their mother-tongue remained completely mysterious as long as both the learning organism and the verbal behavior to be learned were thought to be as amorphous in structure as associationist theory supposed them to be. Thanks to Chomsky's nontaxonomic theory of language, which aims at a system of rules rather than at a system of elements, our insight into the structural properties of natural languages has so far deepened that it becomes possible to begin to envisage a theory of language acquisition which would be in accordance with the linguistic facts, with the known facts about children's verbal behavior and with the theory of cognitive development in general. Chomsky's theories are most often referred to as "transformational linguistics" or "generative grammar," highlighting two important aspects of his conception of language.

While no attempt is made to summarize Chomsky's far-reaching theory, it seems necessary to underline certain points that have often led to confusion.

A generative grammar is an explicit description of the internalized rules of a language as they must have been mastered by an idealized speaker-hearer. It is adequate insofar as it corresponds to the intuition of the native speaker. However, it is *not* a model of performance; first, the speaker-hearer may not be aware of (or even capable of becoming aware of) the grammatical rules; and secondly, and more profoundly, the grammar assigns a structural description to a sentence, but the derivation of this sentence as made explicit by the grammar does not tell us how a speaker actually (and psychologically) proceeds to produce the utterance.

A generative grammar is said to be descriptively adequate if it meets the criterion of corresponding to the competence of the native speaker. It is said to attain explanatory adequacy if it is linked to a theory of language that deals with the form of human language as such (and not only of the particular language). In this case it contains an account of linguistic universals. It is the universal grammar that deals with the creative aspect of language. General linguistic theory would ultimately provide a theory of the fundamental form of possible human languages and of the strategies necessary for selecting a particular grammar. In this sense, general linguistics belongs to epistemology; in this sense, also, it would give an explanatory model of language acquisition.

A generative grammar contains a system of rules that have three components—syntactical, phonological and semantic. The syntactical rules account for the creative aspect of language. The phonological and semantic components are purely interpretive. The syntactical component consists of a base, which generates deep structures according to certain rules. The basic strings of elements form a highly restricted set; within this set there is a subset of "kernel" sentences. These kernel sentences (exemplified by simple affirmative-active sentences) have played an important role in psycholinguistic experimentation, though often in a confused way. The rules of the base are a very special class of those that are studied in recursive function theory, and may be mostly universal, and thus not part of particular grammars. In addition to the base, the syntactical component contains a transformational subcomponent. These transformational rules are concerned with generating a sentence—with its surface structure—from the base. Elementary transformational rules are drawn from a base set of substitutions, deletions, and adjunctions.

This, necessarily superficial, account of transformational linguistics, points to its deep concern with the creative aspect and epistemology of language. Because of this epistemological position, a psycholinguist who accepts Chomsky's theories of generative grammars for particular languages, cannot at the same time simply reject his, be it tentative, model of language acquisition. His model is still in the nature of a hypothesis; and though many of his fundamental discoveries about language seem to stem from the fact that he considers the problem from the viewpoint of a language acquisition device, not all assumed properties of the device would appear to be necessary to the theory as a whole. The following is a brief discussion of Chomsky's (and his followers') hypotheses about the device and of the points on which a Piagetian psychologist would raise objections.

Katz (1966; following Chomsky, 1957, 1965) who uses the model of a language acquisition device that has as its output the internalized linguistic rules and as its input speech (and, he adds, other relevant data from senses), shows conclusively that such an input is far too impoverished to produce the rules if the device were to be constructed according to empiricist, associationist hypotheses. Up to this point, a Piagetian psychologist cannot but agree. Subsequently, however, Katz develops the rationalist hypothesis that "the language acquisition device contains as innate structure each of the principles stated within the theory of language." Once again, we encounter the epistemological dilemma of structuralism without development or geneticism without structure. But is the choice really restricted to these two extremes? And is it necessary, in order to enrich the internal structure of the learning organism, to postulate innate linguistic structures?

Chomsky's own treatment of the rationalist hypothesis seems at the same time more cautious, more supple and more far-reaching than that given by Katz. Chomsky poses the problem as follows:

A theory of linguistic structure that aims for explanatory adequacy incorporates an account of linguistic universals, and it attributes tacit knowledge of these universals to the child. It proposes, then, that the child approaches the data with the presumption that they are drawn from a language of a certain well-defined type, his problem being to determine which of the (humanly) possible languages is that of the community in which he is placed. Language learning would be impossible unless this were the case. The important question is: What are the initial assumptions concerning the nature of the language that the child brings to language learning, and how detailed and specific is the innate schema (the general definition of "grammar") that gradually becomes more explicit and differentiated as the child learns the language? For the present we cannot come at all close to making a hypothesis about innate schemata that is rich, detailed and specific enough to account for the fact of language acquisition (1965, p. 27).

And

A consideration of the character of the grammar that is acquired, the degenerate quality and narrowly limited extent of the available data, the striking uniformity of the resulting grammars, and their independence of intelligence, motivation and emotional state, over wide ranges of variation, leave little hope that much of the structure of language can be learned by an organism initially uninformed as to its general character . . . . The real problem is that of developing a hypothesis about initial structure that is sufficiently rich to account for acquisition of language, yet not so rich as to be inconsistent with the known diversity of language (1965, p. 58).

From the point of view of developmental psychology, three criticisms can be made:

1. This view of language acquisition fails to take into account the knower-symbolization-known relationship indicated above; it only considers language as the object of knowledge in the knower-known relationship.

2. It assumes tacitly that from the moment the child starts to understand language and to talk, he somehow considers language as a system of signs (as opposed to signals and symbols).

3. No account at all is taken of the structural richness of the learning organism as demonstrated by the acquisitions during the preverbal sensorimotor period.

In other words, there would be agreement on the nature of the output, i.e. the internalized grammar, and also on the need for postulating a structural richness within the acquisition device. But there would be disagreement on the degree of innateness of the structure of the device and on the nature of the input, which would be much richer and more structured than merely speech-samples of a limited and degenerate quality plus (unspecified) "other data from senses."

Much of the need for postulating specific, innate linguistic structures seems to vanish if one considers language acquisition within the total cognitive development and, in particular, within the frame of the symbolic function. This manner of considering language acquisition would moreover be compatible with two facts that seem to be difficult to explain within the theory of innate structures: (1) the time lag between the first manifestations of practical intelligence during the sensorimotor period and the first verbal productions; (2) the particular character of these first verbal productions.

Concomitant with the development of the symbolic function, the child changes from an organism that reacts to objects and events as signals to a being that "knows" objects and events and expresses this "knowledge" by means of signifiers. His knowing, however, is always "acting upon," and the first use of signifiers is only possible in function of the internal richness of coordinated action-schemes. His first verbal productions recognizable as "words" are far from being signs in the sense of belonging to a fully structured system. They resemble far more symbols, which can be loosely associated but are essentially isolated representations of schemes. They share the characteristic of symbols in that they are inextricably entwined in the complex of objects, actions the subject can perform on objects, and symbolic representation of the objects. In Piaget's terms (1946, p. 235), the first words "retain the imitative character of the symbol, either as onomatopoaeia (imitation of the object) or as imitation of words used in adult language, but extracted from this language and imitated in isolation. Especially, they retain the disconcerting mobility of symbols, in contrast to the fixity of signs." And (1946, p. 236) "The first language consists almost solely in orders and expression of desire. Denomination is not the simple attribution of a name, but the expression of a possible action." Examples abound in all recordings of child language; to quote two of Piaget's examples:

(1946, p. 231) J. around 1;6 knows better and better how to take advantage of adults to get what she wants; her grandfather is especially docile in this respect. The term *panana* ("grandpère") is used not only to indicate her grandfather, but also to express, even in his absence, her desires; she points to what she wishes to have and adds *panana*. She even says *panana* to express a wish to be amused when she is bored.

(1946, p. 232) T. at 1;5 uses the term *a plus* ("il n'y en a plus," or something similar, but, of course, *a plus* should not be taken to represent two separate words) to indicate a departure, then to indicate the throwing of an object onto the floor, then it is applied to an object that falls over (without disappearing) for instance when he is playing with building blocks. A little later *a plus* means "remoteness" (anything out of reach), and the game of handing over an object for somebody to throw it back to him. Finally, at 1;7 *a plus* takes on the meaning of "to start over again."

The transition from what Piaget calls *jugements d'action* to *jugements de constatation* takes place soon after: "words" then no longer simply translate sensorimotor action, but describe past actions and events (though usually in the immediate past). At this point begins the slow transition from symbols to real signs, which furnish a re-representation; and at this point the first concatenations of words begin to appear.

Both these facts, the relatively late start of the first verbal productions, and their particular character, seem difficult to reconcile with the theory of innate linguistic structures. The time-lag might conceivably be explained by an allusion to imprinting and critical periods: Katz (1966, p. 276), speaking about the fact that the effortless way in which children appear to acquire a language terminates at about puberty, says, "thus this ability of the child's is much like the abilities of various animals described as imprinting with respect to the existence of a 'critical' period." The peculiar character of the first productions, coupled with the fact that these do not yet show real concatenations of words, might lead a staunch adherent of the theory of innate structures to refuse these verbal schemes the status of linguistic productions. This seems, however, completely unjustified psychologically; whatever their nature, they most certainly prepare the way for further verbal acquisition, and moreover they already have some of the traits of signs: they show a certain detachment from the subject's own actions and a desire to communicate by way of sound-complexes which the other person also uses.

It seems more in accordance with the facts, though less simple, to suppose that the coordination of sensorimotor schemes, which are actively built up during the first 18 months of life, starting from hereditary reflexes, is a necessary condition for language acquisition to become possible, which, like all manifestations of the symbolic function, takes place within a context of imitation. It is true that Chomsky remarks (1965, p. 33), "It would not be at all surprising to find that normal language learning requires use of language in real-life situations, in some way." However, according to him, this would not affect the *manner* in which the acquisition of syntax proceeds. In our view, however, the way in which sensorimotor schemes, coordinated into practical groups, become transformed into operations would determine the manner in which the linguistic structures are acquired. Though it is not possible to make hypotheses about this mechanism detailed enough to account for language acquisition, this approach to the problem seems nearer to the psychological truth. The Genevan research on the parallelism of language-acquisition and operational development of which a few examples have been given, indicates that this hypothesis is at least not in contradiction with the admittedly very few and limited results obtained so far.

One other experiment, which is still far from being completed, also gives some results that seem to run counter to the innate-structure hypothesis. Briefly, the technique is as follows. We give the child a collection of toys, dolls, cars, animals, sponges, sticks, cups, and so on, and we ask him "to act" with these objects a sentence we pronounce, after an introductory period during which the child gives names to the dolls, tells us something about the toys, and such. The sentences used are simple active and passive affirmative ones. We use different kinds of verbs, and "reversible" as well as "irreversible" sentences (reversible: "Peter washes John" or "the red marble pushes the blue marble"; irreversible: "Peter washes his car"). Inversely, we perform an act with some of the toys and we ask the children to tell us what happened. We also try to elicit passive sentences by asking the child to start his sentence with the noun indicating the object of the action performed (We let Peter wash his car and we ask "Now tell us what happened; but I would like you to start this way: the car . . .”). Finally we perform the action and at the same time we pronounce the passive sentence; then we ask whether what we said was correct, and we ask the child to repeat it.

To mention only one of the types of behavior that appear in this experiment, and which we are still far from being able to interpret conclusively, at about four and a half years old several subjects decode a passive sentence into a reciprocal act: “Peter is washed by Mary” is acted so that Peter and Mary both take a sponge and wash each other; “the red marble is pushed by the blue marble” is acted by taking a marble in each hand and making them hit each other, whereas the corresponding active sentence is acted by taking the blue marble in one hand, leaving the red marble on the table and hitting the latter with the blue one. In the items where we try to elicit passive sentences, the children also produce sentences in this way: *“Pierre et Marie se lavent” “La bille rouge et la bille bleu roulent ensemble.”* We also find passive sentences decoded according to active word-order: “Peter is washed by Mary” is acted as “Peter washes Mary.” In these items some children also say that what we ask them is impossible: “you can’t start with Peter, it’s Mary who washes.” It is the reciprocities that intrigue us most; and it seems that they cannot be accounted for by a triggering of innate structures.

Epistemologically, the difference between Piaget and Chomsky seems important, but the two are certainly much nearer to each other than either is to a defender of the empiricist point of view. Moreover, their difference may be less marked than it appears. For instance, Chomsky (1965, p. 202 note 19) warns us that what he is describing as the process of acquisition is an idealization in which only the moment of the acquisition of correct grammar is considered. He adds: “. . . it might very well be true that a series of successively more detailed and highly structured schemata (corresponding to maturational stages, but perhaps in part themselves determined in form by earlier steps of language acquisition) are applied to the data at successive stages of language acquisition.” This seems to indicate that his position is much less extreme than is often thought. However, without knowing more precisely what is meant by “schemata” and "maturational stages" it is difficult to interpret remarks such as these.

It is clear that we are in great need of experimental results. As far as experiments go, approaches starting from either Piaget's or Chomsky's theories would have several points in common. They would share the emphasis put on the creative aspect of language. They would share also the wish to make a clear distinction between performance and competence. Where Chomsky (1964, p. 39) only seems to stress the fact that performance is bound to appear far poorer than an investigation (if this were possible) of real competence would show the latter to be, the Piagetian psycholinguist would add that there is also the opposite danger, namely, that performance can easily induce an overrating of competence. He would assume that the verbal productions of the child may contain prestructures and pseudostructures, just as there are preconcepts and pseudoconservations; the prestructures would be isolated instances of certain syntactic structures, strongly content-bound and context-bound; pseudostructures would be strongly imitation-bound. The prestructures are both important and understandable within a developmental, interactionist theory; they would be hard to explain within the rationalist theory. The main difference between the two approaches corresponds to the fundamental epistemological difference that has been stressed all along in this paper: the Piagetian psycholinguist would always try to study language as part of the symbolic function, within the frame of the total cognitive activity of child rather than as an autonomous "object of knowing."

References

Chomsky, N. *Syntactic structures.* The Hague: Mouton, 1957.

Chomsky, N. *Current issues in linguistic theory.* The Hague: Mouton, 1964.

Chomsky, N. *Aspects of the theory of syntax.* Cambridge, Mass.: M.I.T. Press, 1965.

Furth, H. G. *Thinking without language: the psychological implications of deafness.* New York: Free Press, 1966.

Hatwell, Yvette. *Privation sensorielle et intelligence.* Paris: Presses Univer. France, 1960.

Katz, J. J. *The philosophy of language.* New York: Harper and Row, 1966.

Oléron, P. *Recherches sur le développement mental des sourds-muets.* Paris: Centre National de Recherche Scientifique, 1957.

Piaget, J. *Le langage et la pensée chez l'enfant.* Neuchâtel et Paris: Delachaux et Niestlé, 1923.

Piaget, J. *La formation du symbole chez l'enfant.* Neuchâtel et Paris: Delachaux et Niestlé, 1946. (Translated as *Play, dreams and imitation in childhood,* New York: Norton, 1951.)

Piaget, J. Le langage et la pensée du point de vue génétique. In G. Revesz (Ed.), *Thinking and speaking, a symposium.* Amsterdam: North Holland Publishing Co., 1954.

Piaget, J. *The language and thought of the child.* In T. Shipley (Ed.), *Classics in psychology.* New York: Philos. Lib., 1961.

Piaget, J. *Comments on Vygotsky's critical remarks.* Cambridge, Mass.: M.I.T. Press, 1962.

Piaget, J. *Langage et opérations intellectuelles.* In *Problèmes de psycholinguistique.* Symposium de l'association de psychologie scientifique de langue française, Neuchâtel, 1962. Paris, Presses Univer. France, 1963.

Piaget, J. Langage et pensée. Tome XV. *La revue du praticien,* 1965, **17,** 2253–2254.

Piaget, J., & Inhelder, Bärbel. *La psychologie de l'enfant.* Paris: Presses Univer. France (*"Que sais-je?"* series), 1966.

Sinclair-de-Zwart, Hermina. *Acquisition du language et développement de la pensée.* Paris: Dunod, 1967.

Memory and Intelligence in the Child

BARBEL INHELDER

Introduction

Since the days of Ebbinghaus, a long tradition of research has been devoted to the laws of memory. Against this background our manner of approaching the study of memory may appear somewhat unusual. However, in some respects our work harks back to Bartlett, about whose theories we shall have more to say later on.

In contrast to the strict behavioristic tradition, we were mainly interested in the internal mechanisms of transformations between stimulus and response. We did not follow the experimental tradition of varying the spatio-temporal and meaning constellations of the stimuli to discover new laws or the optimal conditions for memory performance. Instead, we attempted to state hypotheses concerning the transformations within the "black

This paper is a preliminary sketch of several years of research conducted in Geneva, the results of which were recently published in *Mémoire et intelligence*, J. Piaget & B. Inhelder, in collaboration with H. Sinclair, Paris: Presses Univer. France, 1968. I would like to thank Hans Furth and Morris Sinclair for their help in translating this article from the French.

337

box" and focused our attention upon unobservable events. However, we hope we avoided falling into subjective mentalism, for indeed unobservable transformations can be objectively studied as a function of factors that depend on general development. Perhaps, after the manner of G. Miller, we should label ourselves "subjective behaviorists." Our previous studies on the genesis of the operations of thought have demonstrated that it is possible to study the results of thinking activities in an objective fashion. From the progressive and coherent modifications of these activities as a function of age, laws of internal transformations can be inferred.

These internal mechanisms seem closely linked to what one usually calls the processes of encoding and decoding. We were particularly interested in the code as such. If the structure of the code remains the same, one would expect memory to stay intact or to deteriorate in proportion to its complexity and especially to the passage of time. Such assumptions seem to be implied by those who hold that memory in general, and memory images in particular, are copies of reality. If on the contrary the structure of the code changes in the course of, and perhaps as a function of, the evolution of thinking operations, some initial hypotheses about the functioning of the internal mechanism of transformation become possible.

If we are right in supposing that the structure of the mnemonic code varies with the passage of time, it remains to be seen whether this modification is dependent on specific mnemonic laws or rather on the developmental changes in the cognitive structures. The laws of development proper to the cognitive structures were known to us from previous research. This approach to the problem naturally influenced the choice of experimental situations.

We presented children between the ages of three and twelve years with a great variety of configurations that they were asked to memorize. Most of the configurations were the (static) end result of operational transformations (classifications, seriations, numerical and metric correspondence, and so on). There were also spatial configurations, the product of spatial operational activity. Finally, some configurations were presented that embodied the outcome of physical process: understanding the causal sequence of these processes follows readily analyzable developmental lines. A number of situations involved random elements. Our purpose was to observe qualitative differences of behavior according to age levels and to throw some light onto the process of memory organization.

Even if, in these processes of mnemonic organization, we discovered many regularities dependent on the development of operativity, we had no intention of equating memory with intelligence as a whole. In a broad sense, memory is the apprehension of that which has been experienced or acquired in the past and implies the conservation of schemes of intelligence as well as conservation of biological mechanisms. But we proposed to study memory in the strict sense and this memory is limited to types of behavior such as recognition, reconstruction, and particularly evocation of particular events located in the past. It is clear that mnemonic evocation, which is our particular concern, is possible only by means of memory images or of recall based on figurative or semiotic mechanisms. It should be noted that the memory image in the mnemonic evocation is distinct from the reproductive or anticipatory image in general. The former is accompanied by a localization in the past that manifests itself through an impression of something that has already been experienced or perceived, and not of something that is merely known.

In this connection it is useful to recall the distinction introduced by Piaget between the operative and figurative aspects of cognitive functions. Operative aspects (actions or operations) bear on transformations of reality, and consequently, action schemes depend on the operative aspects. Figurative aspects on the other hand (perception, imitation, image) are limited to the representation of states without reference to the transformations that result in those states. This distinction will be frequently used as we describe some of the surprising results of our experiments. If one presents the child with such simple configurations as, for instance, a series of lengths to be memorized, the memory performance seems to be determined not merely by the figurative presentation but equally by the operative schemes that influence the way in which the child understands the configuration. The distinction between operative and figurative is essential for understanding the distinction between a *scheme* and a *schema*. A *scheme* indicates the general structure of actions and operations (e.g. the scheme that permits one to arrange elements in an ordered series). A *schema*, by contrast, is merely a simplified imagined representation of the result of a specific action; this term can therefore be applied suitably in the figurative field. A model can unite the two: it is a schema insofar as it is a simplified representation, but it is a scheme as a means of generalization.

Our general problem is that of the relations between memory and schemes of intelligence, thus between memory in the strict sense and in the broad sense since memory in the broad sense includes schemes. More specifically, is the conservation of memory images possible without the functioning and the support of schemes? Some examples of our memory experiments may clarify this question.

Memory of a serial configuration

This particularly simple experiment will exemplify our preliminary working hypotheses and the general procedure of most of our studies.

Children of three to eight years of age were shown a configuration consisting of ten sticks of 9 to 15 cm. in length. The sticks were arranged in a series from the smallest to the longest. The children were told merely to look carefully at the sticks in free vision to remember them later. There was no particular time limit. After a week they were asked first to indicate by gesture what they remembered and then to make a drawing. On this and the following occasion there was no new presentation of the model. Six to eight months later the children were asked to draw again from memory what they had seen previously. A special group was also asked to describe the series verbally.

A series of coordinated experiments with comparable groups of subjects allowed us to draw conclusions with regard to the level of memory organization and the level of operational and linguistic development. In a modification of the experiment, to be described later, we arranged the sticks in the form of the letter "M" and compared mnemonic evocation with recognition.

After the children finished their memory drawings, they were given sticks and asked to make the seriation themselves so that their level of operativity could be determined. On the basis of their performance and the criteria established previously (Inhelder & Piaget, 1964), the children were assigned to one of the four groups in Table 1. At the third stage the child uses an empirical trial-and-error method, whereas at the fourth he is clearly operational.

Table 1   Seriation

Distribution of subjects (in percentages) by memory types and operational stages

OPERATIONAL STAGES	MEMORY TYPES		
	1	2(a-d)	3
Preoperational	83	17	0
Transitional	0	65	35
Empirical seriation	0	27	73
Operational seriation	0	0	100

With regard to memory performance, while there was no clear-cut separation without overlap, the drawings could be divided reasonably into a sequence of types of organization (Fig. 1). (1) The youngest subjects, three to four years of age, drew a number of sticks lined up, but the length of the sticks was more or less equal. (2) The drawings of children in the next age group, four to five years, showed one or other of the following features: (a) The sticks were paired, a large one with a small one; (b) All the sticks were divided into two classes, one big, one small; (c) Sticks were arranged in threes or fours, in groups of small-, big-, and middle-sized sticks; and (d) Starting with five years of age, the children generally succeeded in drawing a correct seriation but which comprised only a few elements. (3) Starting with six to seven years, correct serial configurations were frequently drawn.

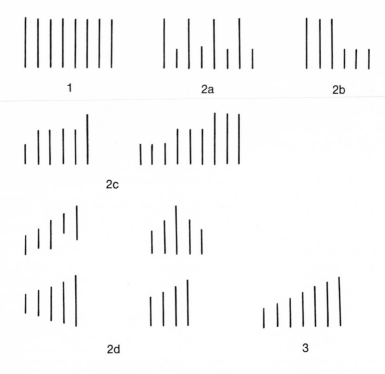

Figure 1   Three types of memory reproduction of a size graded seriation.

These types of drawings correspond closely to what the children did when they were asked to make a series with the sticks. The drawings are also similar to what children drew when they had not seen a series beforehand and were asked to imagine what a number of sticks would look like when put into order.

The drawings relate also to the manner in which children describe the seriation verbally (Sinclair, 1967). In fact, the verbal descriptions also fall into four distinct patterns: (1) Only two descriptive terms are used, the adjectives *long* and *short* (or equivalent words). The children say either: "This one is short, this one is short, this one too, this one too, this one is long, this one is long," dividing the sticks into two groups, short sticks and long sticks.

Or they say: "This one is short, this one is long, this one is short, this one is long," describing successive pairs of sticks.

(2) Three or more terms are used, and sometimes a different label is attached to each of the sticks: "Tiny, very short, a bit short, middling long, long, very long."

(3) Only two terms are used, but with the addition of one comparative: "short, longer, longer, longer." The characteristic of this pattern is that when the child is asked to immediately give a second description, starting at the other end of the series, he is incapable of describing the sticks he has just called *longer* as *shorter*; and he falls back into pattern 2.

(4) The description of the series from the shortest to the longest is the same as in pattern 3, but now the child can also reverse his pattern and use a second comparative: "short, longer," "long, shorter." It seems that memory images are linked to operational schemes and that schemes control the images and dominate the model perceived. Table 1 summarizes the distribution of subjects by memory types and operational stages.

A second result is even more striking. After an interval of six to eight months, most of the children (74 percent of the group as a whole and 90 percent of children between five and eight years) made drawings that showed progress relative to the first drawing. This progress was always gradual; that is to say, subjects progressed from one substage to the next.

How can these results be interpreted? It is clear that the memory image is not a simple residue of the perception of the model, but rather a symbol that corresponds to the schemes of the child. What seems to happen is that the child interprets the seriation as a possible result of his own actions. During the interval between the first and the second evocation, the schemes themselves evolve because of their own inherent functioning through the spontaneous experiences and actions of the child. According to our hypothesis, the action schemes—in this particular case, the schemes of seriation—constitute the code for memorizing: this code is modified during the interval and the modified version is used as a new code for the next evocation. At each stage, the memory image is symbolized according to the constraints of the corresponding code.

The first results of this experiment seemed too good to be true. We therefore attempted to check our hypothesis about the transformations of the code by means of a more complex configurational situation.

Here we used a double seriation in the shape of the letter "M" of sticks placed vertically in symmetrical order (Fig. 2). The children were to draw the configuration from memory after one week and again after two and one-half months. Once more, the results were found to be in good agreement with the operational activity of the subjects and there was progress in the type of mnemonic representation in gradual fashion, from one substage to the next (Fig. 3 a, b, c). When the children were presented with a set of drawings corresponding to the various substages (and the correct model), recognition was better than evocation, but was still far from perfect, especially among the younger children. Here also there apparently was assimilation to schemes according to the operational level of the subject. The progress from the first evocation to the second was less marked than in the case of the simple seriation (38 percent as against 74 percent). But this difference seems to confirm our hypothesis of an evolution of the code in accord with operational development. If the code were fixed, one might suppose that the memory would show greater deterioration the greater the interval of time. On the contrary, progress was more evident after the longer delay and this can be interpreted as being due to a further development of schemes. It can also be suggested that the improvement of memory is in direct proportion to the simplicity of the underlying operational activity. A more difficult model, as in the case of the "M," would then give results that are qualitatively similar but quantitatively less marked. The essential fact is that for the configuration "M" too, the code changed in the course of the retention period.

Memory of horizontal levels of liquid

In most memory experiments with children, one does not deal with modifications of a single scheme but with a whole group of converging schemes. For example, there might be present pre-operational schemes and empirical regularities that would lead to solutions that are close to the preinferences (or unconscious reasonings) that Helmholtz attributed to perception. Pavlov con-

Figure 2   "M" variation of a size graded seriation used as a standard for memory reproduction.

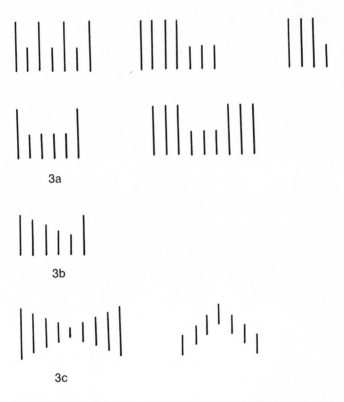

3a

3b

3c

Figure 3   Three types of memory reproductions of the "M" variation of a size graded seriation.

sidered this idea to be one evidence of Helmholtz's genius.

A particularly striking example, among others, was furnished by the memory of horizontal levels of water in an inclined decanter. Our previous research on the representation of space (Piaget & Inhelder, 1956) had shown that the notion of horizontality is acquired relatively late (around nine years of age). This was observed in situations where the child was required to anticipate the direction of the water level in a decanter that was presented first vertical, then lying down, then turned upside down, and finally inclined at 45°. The decanter was covered with a cloth so that the water level was not visible. Before the child succeeds in utilizing natural systems of reference and constructing coordinates that permit him to establish interfigural relations, he does not draw horizontal water levels but levels that are inclined or parallel to the base or the side of the decanter or that adhere to the angles of the decanter. At this stage, the child obviously cannot establish interfigural relations.

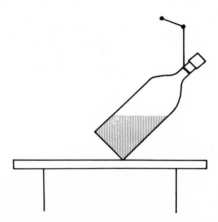

Figure 4   Figure used as standard for memory reproduction of water level
            orientation.

For the memory experiment, two situations were presented. In one situation, children were shown the drawing of a bottle inclined at 45°, and one-quarter of which was filled with colored water. The horizontal water level was parallel to an external line of reference (Fig. 4). After one hour, after one week, and after six months the children were asked to draw what they remembered of the presentations.

On the occasion of the first and second evocations, several memory types were found which shows once more that memory does not conform to the perceptual configuration of the model but rather to the manner in which the model was assimilated to the preoperational schemes of the subject. In fact, the series of memory types corresponds to a compromise between a symbolization of schemes and empirical inferences. Memory types as a function of age and operational level can be characterized as follows. At the lowest level, between five and seven years of age, there was a preponderance of drawings (71 percent to 87 percent) that depicted straight or inclined bottles with the liquid placed either against the side or parallel to the inclined base (Fig. 5). Then there were solutions of a somewhat superior type: bottles were inclined and water levels were still not horizontal, but no longer parallel to the base or to the side. Next, there was a series of characteristic compromises such as drawings of a vertical bottle with an inclined surface of water, or of an inclined bottle that was completely filled with water. Finally, the model was correctly represented.

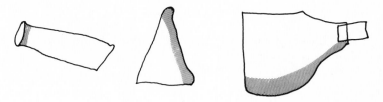

Figure 5   Memory reproductions of water orientation standard (Fig. 4).

After one week's interval the children reproduced with very little deviation the drawing they had made after one hour. After six months there were some modifications: 30 percent of children progressed, 12 percent regressed, and 58 percent remained stationary. In general, correct drawings after one week remained correct after six months.

While the first experimental situation reflected mainly pre-operational schemes, the second situation revealed compromise solutions in which preinferences based on empirical probabilities were evident.

The drawing to be memorized depicted three objects (Fig. 6). One of these was a bottle, partially filled with colored liquid, lying on its side, another was of a car in a normal position, and the third was another bottle turned upside down and partially filled with liquid. The water level could thus be related not only to a base line but also to the car which moreover had a horizontal colored strip along the lower part of the body.

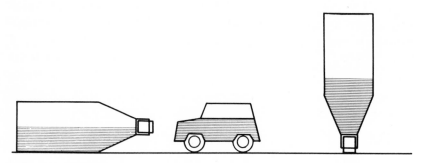

Figure 6   Figures used as standards for memory reproduction of water level
             orientation.

We wanted to know whether the children would recall the prone bottle as it was in the model, or whether the fact that in real situations bottles are seldom lying on their sides or standing upside down would interfere with the memory image of the model as it was perceived. It should again be noted that we simply took only the children's drawings as data and did not ask any questions. If the child modified the position of the bottles, would he nevertheless recall the horizontal water level? A horizontal level was of course strongly suggested by the little car with its horizontal colored strip: a car is seen only exceptionally in any but a horizontal position.

The memory drawings of the children of five to six years of age appeared at first sight rather fantastic (Fig. 7). Nonetheless their spontaneous commentaries indicated that they really believed they had seen what they drew and that they did not think their drawings of the water level unrealistic. "That is easy," said a six-year-old child, "I should draw some bottles and a car; I remember because I've been thinking." Some children remembered the upside-down bottle correctly and failed only with the water level of the bottle on its side, but others turned the upside-down bottle right-side up which in itself is perhaps not very surprising, but they also drew the liquid as if it were sticking to the side. The reason for such a performance seems obvious. First, they drew the bottle in an upright, i.e. its most probable position; second, they drew the water parallel to the side since they remembered the side as close to the water level; and, third, from these premises, they made the inference that a vertical wall required a vertical orientation of the water level.

Figure 7   Memory reproductions of water orientation standards (Fig. 6).

Memory for numerical and spatial correspondences

As operativity develops, modifications of the memory code may lead to surprising, though not fortuitous, deformations. When two or more schemes are in active conflict because of nonsynchronous development, interesting memory types emerge. Such conflict can be brought about, for example, by the following

situation. The child was shown four matches placed in a horizontal broken line and another four matches directly underneath,
arranged in a flattened "W" so as to avoid suggesting the letter of
the alphabet (Fig. 8). This configuration of matches could be
assimilated by the child either as the result of a numerical or as
that of a spatial relationship.

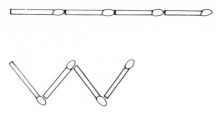

Figure 8   Figures used as standards for memory reproduction of length and
            number.

Previous research on the spontaneous development of geometrical notions indicated that these two systems, numerical as
against spatial, produce antagonistic results before becoming
coordinated in the thinking of the older child (Piaget, Inhelder,
& Szeminska, 1960). In fact, when the child establishes numerical
equivalences by a one-by-one correspondence, he is still at a
level at which he estimates the equality of spatial extensions by
the coincidence or noncoincidence of the extremities of lines, so
that "to pass" or "to go beyond" means to the child "to be
longer." This characteristic of preoperational thinking is moreover reinforced by the particulars of the mental image at this
level. We have noted in our study of the mental image (Piaget &
Inhelder, 1966) that boundaries play a predominant role in the
formation of such structures.
    An analysis of memory drawings of the matches as a function
of age and operativity suggested five successive types. Type 1: a
double line-up of a great number of matches without any numerical or figural correspondence. In type 2 (an interesting intermediary form) the coincidence of extremities dominates over numerical
correspondence; the child draws one horizontal line-up of
matches and another one in a zig-zag fashion, several times re-

peated, such that the extremities of the line-ups coincide. Type 3 shows the conflict at its height in a false solution that respects the numerical correspondence but in which the length of the matches in the second line is exaggerated so as to achieve a topological coincidence with those in the first. In type 4 the conflict is attenuated; the matches in the straight line go beyond the matches in zig-zag, but the number of the segments in the two lines is not the same. Finally, type 5 achieves the correct solution (Fig. 9).

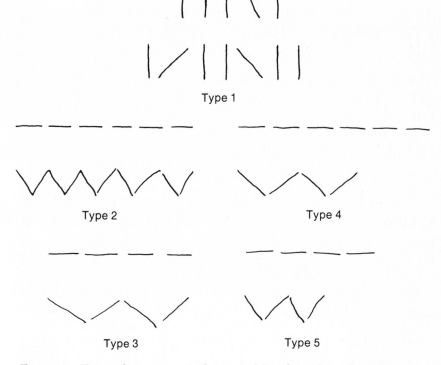

Figure 9   Types of memory reproductions of lengths and numbers (Fig. 8).

The evocation of the matches six months later shows considerable deterioration. The drawings, far from being faithful to the model, were organized by the dominating tendency to equalize the extremities. Apparently the developing schemes accentuated the conflict between the numerical and the spatial systems before the schemes were sufficiently developed to surmount the conflict.

It is noteworthy that the conflict does not reside in the configurations as such, but in the assimilatory schemes with which the child responds to the configurations. In fact, the memory drawings of a figure using continuous lines, resulted in hardly any deformations and then only with the youngest subjects. Yet the same figure, arranged in broken lines by means of matches, produced types of deformations similar to those of the main experiment (Fig. 10).

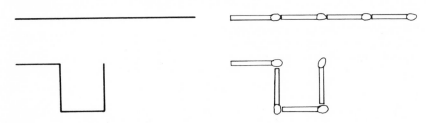

Figure 10   Figures used as standards for memory reproduction of length and number.

As with previous experiments, one may assume that in the memory performance preinferential processes intervened that are midway between perception and conceptual elaboration. It seems that children of a preoperational level apprehend the numerical correspondence. But they do not yet possess the scheme of spatial conservation that would enable them to understand that a line twisted into a zig-zag remains of the same metrical length as it was before transformation. It was as if the children made a memory preinference as follows: If the two lines are equal by numerical correspondence of their elements, their extremities must coincide.

It is difficult to state exactly at which moment such preinferences are made. We have frequently noticed immediate quasi-deformations, and are accordingly inclined to believe that there occurs a kind of deforming conceptual assimilation already in the presence of the model, and that this deformation becomes manifest in memory. Previous research has shown that the image represents an object by means of its "concept" as much as or even more than by means of its "perception."

Memory of a situation involving causal relationships

We have so far discussed memory situations related to configurations that are apt to activate the subjects' operative schemes; other experiments concerned the evocation of a sequence of events or states that become comprehensible only when they are seen as the result of a causal process. In fact, causality can be considered as a system of actions and operations that are attributed to the objects themselves. One could therefore expect that, just as before, the schemes of the child would intervene in memory according to his level of comprehension.

We used models that permitted the child to notice a causal process, for instance, the transmission of movement by means of balls rolling down an inclined plane, or the movement of objects through a system of levers. There were also some static situations that could be encoded either as spatial configurations or as the result of causal processes. The following experiment is an example.

The child was shown two U-shaped tubes (Fig. 11). In the one, A, the water was at the same level in both branches, the other, B, showed a higher water level in the right branch, which was closed by a cork.

We knew from our previous investigations (Inhelder & Piaget, 1958) that the physical comprehension of the phenomenon of communicating vessels only starts at eleven to twelve years of age with the beginnings of formal operational thinking. The event that was indicated in B could hardly be understood before the age of fourteen to fifteen years. Nevertheless, well before this age the observation of the uneven levels in B compared to the even levels in A could suggest an interesting problematic situation to the child and the cork in B could indicate a causal influence.

Figure 11   Figure used as standard for memory reproductions of water levels.

We used an essentially similar procedure as before with some slight modifications. The child was first told to look carefully at what he was going to see so as to remember it afterwards. Then the actual physical model was shown to him for 45 seconds. Immediately afterwards the child was asked to draw what he could remember and to accompany the drawing with a verbal description. No questions of any sort were asked and no mention was made of any further memorization. One week later, and again six months later, the child was asked to draw what he remembered. Finally, one week after his last memory performance, a recognition procedure was used. For this purpose we utilized drawings representing different ways in which children of various ages had represented the model. One of the drawings was of course the correct one. In the course of this experiment we realized that the drawing furnished by the children corresponded more closely to the manner in which they became conscious of the existence of a problem than to the manner in which they solved the problem. Subsequently we worked with some control groups with whom we attempted to modify the memory performance through situations and questions that facilitated awareness of the problem. These children would first watch the tubes being filled from cups that obviously contained equal amounts of liquid, and they would be asked such anticipatory questions as: "What would happen if I remove the cork in B?" "What would happen if I put a cork in A?"

The overall results of this experiment provided many interesting insights into the types and modifications of the schemes as a function of the development of the child and of the child's discovery that there *was* a problem. With a group of children mainly between four and nine years of age, we distinguished five types of memory performance (Fig. 12): (1) No differentiation between the container and its content; (2) differentiation between container and content, with four even water levels but no indication of the cork; (3) tube A is drawn just like tube B with the water levels in the two branches of both tubes clearly differentiated; (4) differentiation between the drawing of the water in A and B but the water level in the right branch of B does not reach the top, nor is the cork indicated; hence one cannot assume that there is a causal comprehension of the situation; and (5) a correct memory drawing.

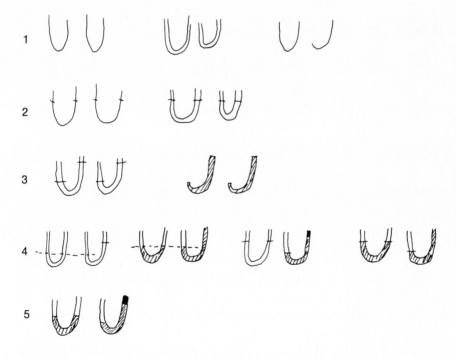

Figure 12   Types of memory reproductions of water levels (Fig. 11).

Table 2 summarizes the percentage distribution of memory types after one week as related to age. It is particularly striking that even at the age of eight and beyond, a correct drawing of such a simple constellation as two U-shaped tubes is provided by no more than 25 percent of the children. Analysis of the changes of memory from one evocation to another indicated an uneven progress, depending on level of development and memory type. In fact, after the immediate memory and the evocation after one week, 17 percent of the group improved, whereas at age six to seven as many as 39 percent improved. The difference seems to be related to the fact that children of this age group begin to be intrigued by the phenomenon that they assimilate to a problem of physical causality. Here, by way of illustration is what a six-year-old child whose memory became better with time said during immediate evocation: "This water level is funny because it is not like the other. It must be because of the cork." A week later he said: "I still don't understand that." Probably he became aware of a problem at the occasion of the evocation rather than at the moment when he perceived the model.

Table 2   U-shaped tubes

Distribution of subjects (in percentages) by memory types and age-groups

AGE	MEMORY TYPES				
	1	2	3	4	5
4-5	45	36	9	9	0
6-7	11	27	11	33	16
8 and beyond	0	5	10	60	25

When a child recognizes that his drawing does not quite meet the model, he often will verbally express his dissatisfaction with the drawing. Recognition implies some rather elementary sensorimotor schemes and develops long before the formation of representational images. Moreover, schemes of recognition are more faithful than schemes of evocation. Even a partial recognition could therefore be sufficient to create the impression that "something is not quite right." This would motivate the child to improve his evocation. If the child in the interval between successive memory performances acquires schemes that enable him to understand the phenomenon better, then one can expect progress.

We observed that progress after six months was marked particularly by an increase of type 3 memories. Children at that stage recall that there are unequal water levels, but they easily forget the difference between tubes A and B. At the same time we observed some deterioration of memory in children who initially had made fairly adequate drawings. The deterioration was probably due to the child's lack of causal comprehension. Interestingly enough, the conditions that were introduced to help the child notice the problem facilitated the second recall, so that we obtained about 80 percent correct solutions.

There is, therefore, no justification for postulating a memory of a previous memory as a simple, automatic preservation of the first memory within the second. Rather, the memorizing of a previous memory is modified according to what the child has learned and understood during the interval.

Memory of a configuration involving arbitrary combinations

Traditionally, studies of memory have been conducted in such a manner as to maximize the singular, the fortuitous, if possible the senseless, e.g. nonsense syllables. It was argued that memory would reveal itself the purer the more completely it is deprived of any significance. In actual fact, memory is never like this in real life. Yet it seemed of interest to investigate the memory of a configuration that is in part arbitrary. Strictly speaking, each configuration is always the outcome of some previous action, hence the result of a transformation. However, the transformations correspond only rarely to simple operations. The models that were used in the present experiments provided a mixture of elements some of which lent themselves readily to a reasoning process, whereas others did not.

In one of these experiments children were presented with a

model of eight regular (cut-out) figures in the sequence triangle, circle, square, oval, triangle, circle, square, oval. On these figures were pasted black strips in a rather irregular fashion from an operative viewpoint yet with some figural regularities (Fig. 13). For each pair of identical figures there was a short interior strip on one of them and a long one continuing beyond the frontiers of the figure on the other. The strips were vertical in four cases and horizontal in four cases. But there was no relation between the length of the strips and the directions from one element in the series to the next. Consequently there were three regular features to be noted: (1) Pairs of figures; (2) Contrast of short and long strips; and (3) Contrast of horizontal and vertical strips.

Figure 13   Figures used as standards for memory reproduction of enclosed and overlapping lines.

How would children of different operational levels retain the figures? Would they use methods of perceptual encoding or conceptual schematizations? The children were divided into two groups. One group, but not the other, was led toward some general conceptual organizing activity by being asked during the presentation session to classify the figures. What effect would this activity have on memory? In other respects the procedure was as before with evocations after one week and after six months. We also investigated memóry reconstruction from the choice of a variety of figures and strips. Furthermore, after the second evocation, we proceeded to a new presentation of the model and asked for a third evocation and reconstruction one week later. This was a kind of mnemonic relearning.

From a great variety of suggestive results we here select two for discussion. First, when the model includes an inextricable mixture of elements some of which can and some cannot be readily assimilated to schemes of classification, the child appears to proceed as follows: For the first elements he will utilize schematizations that correspond to his operative level of classification and he will simplify, often in a deforming manner, or leave out the second elements. An illustration of these procedures is furnished by the developmental sequence of memory behavior that we can present here only in a summary fashion.

For the total group of children between four and nine years of age, we could distinguish four types of memory performance (Fig. 14).

1. The youngest children retained only some isolated forms without any discernable systematization; no pairing or contrasting of shapes or strips was evident.

2. There was a beginning of schematization that became manifest by some pairing, which however was not systematic. For

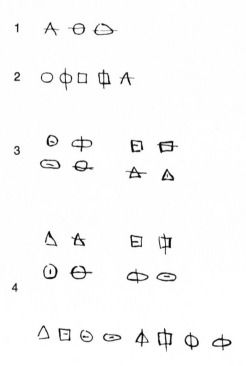

Figure 14   Four types of memory reproductions of enclosed and overlapping lines (Fig. 13).

example, one or two pairs would be noted based on a simple contrast between the length or the orientation of the strips.

3. In this group there was the beginning of a coordination between the contrasting attributes within a pair. For example, there were at least two pairs each with a single contrasting attribute or at least one pair with double contrasting features.

4. This last class showed a generalization of pairs together with the double contrasting features.

When memory levels were compared with levels of classification we noticed a convergence, but there was no direct influence on memory drawings of the previous classifying activity. In fact, while there were some striking correspondences in the manner of general schematizations, the particular content in which schematization was expressed was not identical in detail. The behavior of children at superior levels who can take account of all the three regular attributes at the same time constitutes an exception. The schematization of the nonclassifying children was similar to the classifying children except that in the former it occurred at a somewhat more advanced age level. Hence the previous classifying activity seems to have less to do with establishing classifying schemes in memory than with activating a schematization inherent in the spontaneous development of the child.

A second noteworthy result relates to the clear advance of reconstructions over evocation, as noted also in many other experiments. In fact, for the total population we observed improvement for 50 percent of the subjects, and on relearning even in 70 percent. This raises an interesting question. Why is reconstruction so clearly better than evocation in a situation that is rather close to those that were employed in traditional investigations of rote memory? Obviously it is not sufficient merely to have figures and strips some of which are identical to the perceived model to remember the combination originally presented. It should be noted that reconstruction is an action and, according to our working hypothesis, an action presupposes the utilization of schemes. Moreover, the conservation of an operative scheme is easier than the conservation of a figurative schema since a scheme is conserved by its own functioning. But why during the reconstruction of an action are schemes progressively more easily organized than during evocation as an image or a drawing? Various experiments, the above-mentioned especially, indicate that during encoding, the perceived input is assimilated to a totality of schemes. In memorizing the particular figures and strips, schemes of similarities and differences of length and direction were involved. In the case of a simple evocation, these schemes probably are present but are not always actively applied. The quite fragmentary memory image of these elements is not sufficient to make the schemes active. On the other hand, reconstruction through manipulation of the elements activates the schemes directly and they in turn determine the emergence of the memory image.

Conclusions

Admittedly, it is rather ambitious to want to contribute something new in a field that has been so extensively worked over as has memory. It should be emphasized again that our investigations of memory were limited to the relations between memory and the general structure of intelligence. We hope to have clarified some points that have general implications for memory and thinking behavior.

Thus the developmental study of memory in its relation to intelligence, of which we have here sketched some characteristic results, seems through a converging number of facts to support the initial hypothesis. We hypothesized that the mnemonic code, far from being fixed and unchangeable, is structured and restructured along with general development. Such a restructuring of the code takes place in close dependence on the schemes of intelligence. The clearest indication of this is the observation of different types of memory organization in accordance with the age level of a child so that a longer interval of retention without any new presentation, far from causing a deterioration of memory, may actually improve it. In fact, such progress is due to and makes evident the general progress of intelligence during the interval concerned.

This hypothesis should not be taken to mean that any kind of memory encoding in situations related to operativity will lead to progress with a sufficient interval of time. The progress observed occurred in relatively simple memory situations in which quite general schemes sufficed as a support for the child's memory. In addition, these schemes were in a state of active evolution during the ages under study. When conflicting schemes exist side by side, as is frequently the case in everyday situations, and especially when the situations are fortuitous, the schemes of the subjects, as we have seen, can play a twofold role. They can bring about deformations or adaptive simplifications. Hence we are far from asserting that memory is always making progress. Our main assumption is that the figurative schemas of memory —from perceptual recognition to image evocation—are not by themselves sufficient to explain memory. They need the support of operative schemes, on which the element of comprehension —which is nearly always present in memory behavior—depends.

At this point, we would again like to emphasize that our work in memory is in the tradition of the great Bartlett (1932). In fact, our terminology, and, at a deeper level, the ideas that have directed our research are no doubt reminiscent of his highly original approach to these problems. Bartlett used the term "schema" proposed by Head, though he expressed his dislike for the word. According to him a more dynamic term, such as active developing patterns, or organized setting, would be more appropriate. Such schemata or patterns are always active in well-adapted reactions of the organism according to Bartlett. Head's schemata were primarily conceived as applying to functions of afferent sensibility; Bartlett went much further and saw in the schemata the explanation of many facts of memory. It is hardly necessary to emphasize in this context that Bartlett's term schema is coextensive neither with our term *scheme* nor with our *schema*, though it is nearer to *scheme*. Bartlett encounters a difficulty in the fact that each of these schemata possesses its own natural and essential time order, in which the "last preceding member" of a series dominates. The iterative and circular character of motor habits poses no problem here; but it is obvious that in many facets of memory, especially those of the kind we have explored, the individual succeeds in "breaking up" the temporal order. As an explanation of this "breaking up" Bartlett very tentatively proposes a kind of general attitude of the subject toward new experiences, this attitude being determined by the schemata. Perhaps we have contributed in some measure to the solving of Bartlett's problem.

To sum up, memory cannot be dissociated as a separate ability from the functioning of intelligence as a whole. The problem of the relation of memory and intelligence remains to be analyzed in greater depth and with greater precision than in our preliminary investigations.

The observed developmental dependence of memory on the encompassing structures of the child suggests two rather general implications. First, our results reconfirm the importance of operative structures. These structures not only control strictly logical behavior but also become manifest as determining factors in many different fields; this has been shown in experiments on perception, on mental image, on learning, and now also on memory. Second, even in the field of biological memory it seems that it is no longer appropriate merely to speak of traces or engrams. There is always an underlying structure that contributes to the integration of memory acquisition. These structures may well depend on the integrity of RNA or DNA or on some other factor. But whatever role may in the future be assigned to such biochemical factors, a process of structuration will no doubt always be present in mnemonic organization.

References

Bartlett, F. C. *Remembering.* London: Cambridge Univer. Press, 1932.

Inhelder, Bärbel, & Piaget, J. *The early growth of logic in the child (classification and seriation).* New York: Harper, 1964. (Original edition, 1959.)

Inhelder, Bärbel, & Piaget, J. *The growth of logical thinking from childhood to adolescence.* New York: Basic Books, 1958. (Original edition, 1955.)

Piaget, J., & Inhelder, Bärbel. *The child's conception of space.* Humanities Press, 1956. (Original edition, 1948.)

Piaget, J., Inhelder, Bärbel, & Szeminska, Alina. *The child's conception of geometry.* New York: Basic Books and Harper, 1960. (Original edition, 1948.)

Piaget, J., & Inhelder, Bärbel. *L'image mentale chez l'enfant*. Paris: Presses Univer. France, 1966.

Piaget, J., Inhelder, Bärbel, & Sinclair, H. *Memoire et intelligence*. Paris: Presses Univer. France, 1968.

Sinclair, H. *Acquisition du langage et développement de la pensée*. Paris: Dunod, 1967.

Some Implications of Ontogenetic Changes in Perception

ROBERT H. POLLACK

The major thesis of this chapter is that ontogenetic changes in visual perception may not be accounted for by a single mechanism based upon a principle of development. It is necessary, at the outset, to define the notion of development that will be applied throughout this paper. The viewpoint held earlier (Pollack & Chaplin, 1963) that development is simply change in behavior through time, is no longer considered useful because it encompasses too many behaviors shown by analysis to be underlain by different organismic mechanisms. Rather, the orthogenetic principle proposed by Wapner and Werner (1957), that behavior becomes more differentiated and hierarchically organized, appears to handle the data better. Implied in such a prin-

The research for this chapter was supported in part by Research Grant No. HD 01433, awarded by the National Institute of Child Health and Human Development.

I wish to acknowledge the invaluable suggestions of my colleague, Dr. Helen Streicher, and the painstaking editorial assistance of Dr. Streicher, Miss Peggy Wild, and Miss Dorothy Jean Carter.

ciple is the notion that similar behavior at different times in the life cycle is governed by discrete organizing principles that differ in complexity and hierarchization. If this viewpoint is adopted, then those ontogenetic changes in behavior that are the result of practice or of deterioration due to organic aging cannot be regarded as developmental, since they occur without any concurrent shift in underlying organization. The argument to be presented here is that there are two major mechanisms of ontogenetic change in visual perception during childhood, receptor aging and the orthogenetic principle. These produce three observable courses of change with age: (1) a decrease in phenomenal magnitude due to organic aging, (2) an increase due to development, and (3) a decrease followed by an increase due to the replacement of the aging mechanism by development.

In contrast to the above, Piaget (1967), in a succinct summary, offers a single explanatory principle for age changes in perception. This is the law of relative centrations. The empirical ground for the theorizing of both Piaget and myself is the visual illusion, with extensions into aftereffects and the constancies. There is a class of illusion phenomena, called primary or Type I illusions, which decline in magnitude steadily through childhood. These illusions are produced partially by virtue of their physical structure and partially by the observer's mode of viewing. If he tends to view the whole figure, or a part of it, with a single glance or with relatively few glances (centration), he will not, according to Piaget, make the necessary number of comparisons of the figural parts to reduce or eliminate the distortion produced by the configuration of the figure. Since centration as a mode of viewing gradually gives way to decentration, or successive looks presumably integrated in some way, the Type I illusion gradually diminishes and greater accuracy of perception results. For Piaget (1958), pure perception gradually gives way to developmentally higher perceptual activity. Support for increasing decentration has come from work on eye movements in children and adults (Piaget & Vinh-Bang, 1961).

There is, however, a second category of illusory phenomena, secondary illusions or Type II, which show an increase in magnitude as a function of age. Because of the structure of the configurations and the way they are presented, with their parts separated by distance or by time, they produce relatively smaller illusions in young children than in their elders. The young child has not yet learned to make comparisons of distant objects or of objects presented in temporal succession, whereas such comparisons and contrasts are an adaptive mode of perceptual activity for the adult. But we should let Piaget speak for himself:

> In sum, in addition to the "primary" effects which stem from the law of relative centrations, there is a whole body of perceptual activities—transports, comparisons at a distance, transpositions, anticipations, etc.—which, in general, lead to the attenuation of primary errors but can provoke secondary errors when they relate elements at a distance giving rise to contrasts, etc. In other words, they give rise to illusions which would not be produced without the establishment of distant relationships.
>
> It must, however, be understood that these perceptual activities in a sense stem from the primary effects, since the "encounters" and "couplings" associated with them are due to centrations and decentrations which constitute activities in themselves. At all levels perception is active and cannot be reduced to passive reception. As Karl Marx said in his objections to Feuerbach, sensibility must be considered as "the practical activity of man's senses" (1967, p. 141).

For Piaget, then, the same mechanism underlies all age changes in perception.

Before I go on to outline my own position, which bears certain similarities to that of Piaget as well as some fundamental differences, I wish to point out some contraindications for this single mechanism theory. As the reader may suspect, the contraindications have me convinced, but the racing researcher, clinging to a promising theoretical lead of his own, is not easily discouraged and plunges on until the constraint of negative data eventually stops him.

First, although phenomena that fall into Piaget's Type II appear to be correlated with intelligence (Spitz & Blackman, 1959; Prysiazniuk & Kelm, 1963; Gaudreau et al., 1963; Pollack, 1964a), Type I phenomena do not (Spitz & Blackman, 1958; Gaudreau et al., 1963; Pollack, 1963c, 1964a, 1965c). Second, despite the necessity, in Piaget's system, of allowing time for eye movements during stimulus presentation, even tachistoscopic studies of the Type I illusion (Pollack, 1963c, 1964a) show an ontogenetic decline. I propose, therefore, that Type I and Type II phenomena represent two distinct ontogentic courses. Type I phenomena reflect a nondevelopmental age change dependent upon factors of physiological aging, such as reduced pupil size, increased lenticular density, and increased retinal pigmentation. All of these serve to render the visual receptor system less sensitive to those variables that underlie configuration: figure-ground contrast, intercontour distance, and contour orientation. Thus, increasing perceptual veridicality is an accidental by-product of reduced receptor efficiency rather than the product of a developing cognitive structure making use of past experience (Weale, 1963; Pollack, 1963c). Paradoxically, the ontogenetically increasing nonveridicality of Type II phenomena is related to intellectual functioning and represents the emergence of the higher-level activity of organizing sense data.

According to Piaget, then, developmental changes in Type I and Type II phenomena take place for the same reason. The child's increasing ability to take successive looks at his environment, to compare his partial percepts, and to integrate over time the perceptual information he gathers, is the major mechanism accounting for this developmental change. This growing ability is described by Piaget as a crude form of intellectual behavior —crude only because stimulus factors impose irreversible restraints upon the judgments that can be made about them. Therefore, Type I illusion phenomena, determined largely by the stimulus configuration seen in a single glance, become less apparent as the child becomes more proficient in his perceptual activity. He gains accuracy because successive comparisons of the parts of the configuration in some way counteract the illusory effect. In the case of Type II illusion phenomena, however, the illusory effect is produced, rather than diminished, by successive comparisons of the parts of the configuration. The young child who does not integrate his percepts through time is relatively unaffected by the succession of stimulus configurations and perceives more accurately. The adult is deceived by his own higher-level capacities.

If Piaget were correct, both developmental sequences should be significantly related to intellectual capacity. As stated above, such is not the case. Despite the sparseness of the data collected so far, there is little indication of a strong relationship between intelligence and the magnitude of Type I phenomena. Such a relationship does exist with Type II phenomena. Furthermore, the tachistoscopic presentation of Type I phenomena should eliminate the developmental trend toward veridicality since eye movements are severely restricted. Piaget, Matalon, and Vinh-Bang (1961) have found no such disappearance with the Delboeuf illusion, nor has Pollack (1963c, 1964a) with the Mueller-Lyer illusion.

It is proposed, therefore, that the mechanisms underlying the two types of phenomena are different. The present investigator argues that Type I phenomena and their development can be accounted for in terms of stimulus factors in interaction with a more or less efficient receptor system, without appeal to intellectual functioning or learning experiences. On the other hand, Type II phenomena represent the integration over time of traces of past interactions with an ongoing interaction. These temporal integrations must involve higher-level associative functions that probably are related to intelligence and to learning experience.

To demonstrate the differences between mechanisms, it is necessary first to list and describe the operation of the stimulus determinants of the Type I interaction. Their operation has been exhibited with fixation effects, aftereffects, and geometric illusions. As long ago as 1937, Gibson (1937) demonstrated that prolonged visual exposure to a given stimulus results in adaptation to that stimulus; that is, there is a loss of sensitivity to the quality presented, whether it is brightness, contrast, saturation, tilt, curvature, or motion. The removal of the adapting stimulus results in a negative aftereffect or a successive contrast effect. The stronger the initial adaptation, the stronger the aftereffect is. In general, such a relationship would be expected to hold, with the stipulation that the introduction of successive stimulation brings with it the complicating factor of temporal integration (Hearnshaw, 1956). Koehler and Wallach (1944), in their monograph on figural aftereffects, listed and crudely demonstrated the operation of some of the possible stimulus variables that affect the level of adaptation and thus the magnitude of the effect. The critical variables were duration of exposure, figure-ground contrast, and intercontour distance. The major quantitative confirming studies of these variables were performed by Hammer (1949) on duration; by Pollack (1958), Oyama (1961), and Graham (1961) on figure-ground contrast; and by Fox (1951) and Pollack (1958) on intercontour distance. In summary: (a) duration of exposure (fixation) increases the magnitude of fixation effects and aftereffects up to a maximum at 90 sec.; (b) the greater the contrast between the inspection or inducing figure or line and its background, the greater the aftereffect; and (c) as intercontour distance increases, the aftereffect will increase to a maximum and then decline (distance paradox). Later, George (1962), Pollack (1963b), Pollack and Chaplin (1964), and Pollack (1964a) introduced the variable of intercontour orientation, demonstrating that parallel contours phenomenally attract each other during inspection, while intersecting contours repel each other.

The operation of all of these variables depends upon the sensitivity and efficiency of the visual receptor system. If it could be shown, first, that sensitivity declines through childhood, and second, that such a decline is correlated significantly with the magnitude of Type I phenomena, then an explanation of these phenomena and their development could be given without appeal to intellectual operations or learning experiences. This explanation would fit the developmental facts as they are now known. The author's investigation of contour detectability thresholds in childhood (Pollack, 1963c) offers confirmation for this view. Both sensitivity to contour as produced by brightness contrast and the magnitude of the Mueller-Lyer illusion were found to decline between ages 8 and 12, yielding a significant product-moment correlation of −.49 between detection threshold and illusion magnitude (see Fig. 1). Intelligence was found to play no significant role. This loss of sensitivity might be due either to permanent adaptation of the retina as a result of increasing exposure to patterned stimulation, or to the fact that less light reaches the retina as the organism ages. Weale (1961a,

1961b) has shown that lenticular density and pigmentation increase with age while pupil size decreases. Retinal pigmentation
also increases with age. The pinpointing of the mechanism involved requires physiological investigation rather than behavioral research, but some indirect evidence will be presented
later.

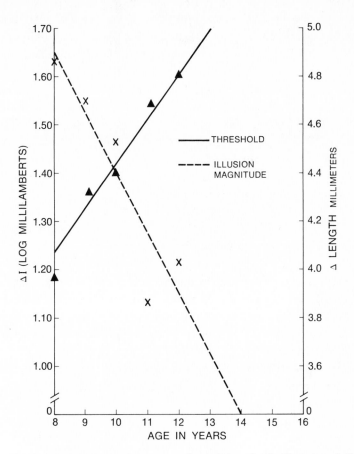

Figure 1   Linear trend lines for contour detectability thresholds (o) and illusion
magnitudes (+) as a function of age.

The importance of the unique role of succession to the kind of
phenomenon obtained and its ontogentic development was

demonstrated by Piaget et al. (1942) and by Piaget and Lambercier (1944) in comparing the Delboeuf illusion with the
Usnadze effect. Pollack (1963b) obtained similar results comparing fixation and aftereffects. In both cases, the illusory effect was
reversed when presentation of the figure was altered from simultaneous presentation of all figural parts to successive presentation of adjacent parts. Furthermore, Piaget and his co-workers
demonstrated that the introduction of succession reversed the
ontogenetic trend of the illusions obtained, as stated above.
Ikeda and Obonai (1955) and Adam, Gibb & Freeman (1966)
demonstrated an abrupt shift in the direction of illusion when
two stimuli become far enough separated in time to be perceived
as successive rather than simultaneous. As part of a program of
investigation, the author (Pollack, 1964a) converted a Type I
illusion (Mueller-Lyer) into a Type II illusion by altering the
mode of presentation from simultaneous to successive. This was
done by presenting the oblique inducing lines before presenting
the main line. It was predicted that the classical illusion would
reverse in direction, that the new illusion would increase rather
than decrease in absolute magnitude, and that a positive correlation with intelligence would be obtained. All three predictions
were confirmed (see Fig. 2).

The long-range research program just mentioned was designed
to investigate the problem area. The initial objectives of the
effort were:

1. To study the properties of Type I phenomena and to isolate
   their stimulus determinants;
2. To locate the boundary between Type I and Type II phenomena and to discover the nature of the transition between
   these types; and
3. To examine the properties of Type II phenomena and to discover the characteristics of the intellectual activity with
   which they are related.

Type I phenomena

To extend the inference,·drawn from the contour detectability
study by Pollack (1963c), that receptor sensitivity declines

throughout childhood as age increases, a study of hue detectability was undertaken (Pollack, 1965a). The experiment was designed as a discrimination task to determine the threshold for
detection of a difference between two neutral gray samples of
reflected light as a function of the addition of some hue to one of

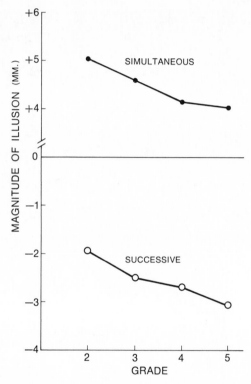

Figure 2   Magnitude of simultaneous and successive illusions as a function of
age level.

them. Lightness was held constant within standard Illuminant C
illumination, and the complicating factor of color naming never
entered into the situation. The subjects ranged in age from seven
to twelve years. (For apparatus details, see Pollack & Magerl,
1965.)

Unlike the contour detectability study, the results of this experiment showed no age effects (see Fig. 3). It appears as if

receptors underlying the perception of contour, as determined by brightness contrast, follow a different course of aging than those underlying the perception of saturation. Curiously, however, at all ages the purple-blue and green samples were more difficult to detect than the yellow-red sample. This second finding has been followed up in a study of the limits of visual acuity as exhibited by the perception of minimal separation of horizontal colored bars on a neutral gray background of equivalent lightness. Red (Munsell 5 R 5/12) and blue (Munsell 7.5 PB 5/12) pairs of bars on a gray (Munsell 5/-) ground were employed. The visual angular dimensions of the bars were 4′ × 1′ on an 8.3′ × 8.3′

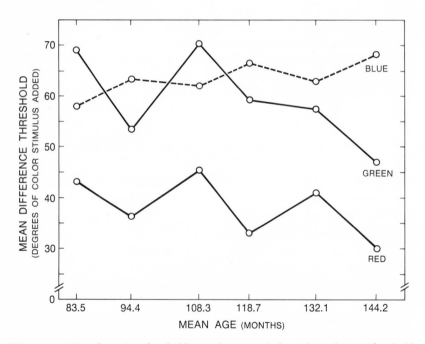

Figure 3   Hue detection threshold as a function of chronological age. Threshold measures are given in terms of mean degrees of hue added to gray on the variable color wheel.

square field. Separations varied from 5″ to 60″ in 5″ steps. All stimuli were illuminated by Illuminant C.

Two adult subjects were employed and both showed significantly finer acuity with red than with blue bars. The means were 18.58″ and 26.94″ for the red bars and 46.88″ and 40.50″ for the blue bars for the two subjects respectively. This line of research is being continued by an associate, Eugene Skoff, with children age six through fourteen with a task that combines contour and hue detection in a single stimulus situation. Thus far, only the hue difference appears clear. The possibility of age trends still awaits analysis. Separation acuity of black bars on a white ground is also being studied over this age range so as to discover whether age changes in contour detection influence the minimum perceptible separation of suprathreshold bars. If no such effect is demonstrated, the lightness of the background will be varied systematically to approach threshold conditions. Exposure time will be varied as well, since it has been found that parallel bars tend to exhibit irradation with longer exposure times and thus to fuse phenomenally. Speed of fusion would be an indirect measure of receptor sensitivity and would be expected to be more rapid in younger subjects.

Type I–Type II boundary

Work on this problem began inadvertently some years ago with an attempt to test Koehler and Wallach's (1944) hypothesis that figural aftereffects should decline with age. Pollack (1960) studied the frequency of occurrence of two types of displacement aftereffects following short (10 sec.) exposures to an appropriate inspection figure (IF) as a function of the chronological age. The frequency of both effects did indeed decline between the ages of four and ten (see Fig. 4), but unexpectedly increased again thereafter. These results suggested that the inflection in the curve after age ten was due to a change in the process underlying the production of aftereffects. In other words, the inflection represents development. It was suggested, further, that early decline in the frequency of aftereffects is due to a loss of receptor sensitivity, resulting in the decrease in duration of an afterimage-like process following fixation of IF. That is, early in life the child makes a simultaneous comparison between the afterimage of an adapted-to IF and a subsequently presented test figure (TF), which produces the phenomenon of displacement. Later on, some sort of successive comparison process replaces the earlier simultaneous process and the aftereffect increases once more. The inflection of the curve is presumably produced by a lag in the effective onset of the second, more complex process.

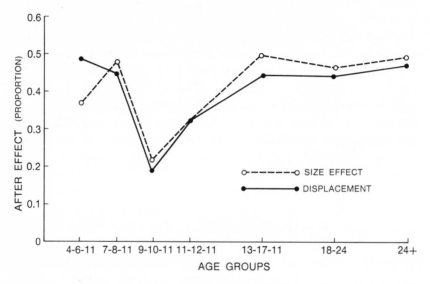

Figure 4   Graph of proportions of frequencies of normal displacements at each age level for the two stimulus figures.

If this reasoning is correct, then phenomena resulting from stimuli that are not detected as successive should behave as though they are of Type I. Those stimuli perceived as continuously changing rather than successive might well indicate a shift from Type I to Type II phenomena somewhere in the age range.

Two experiments (Pollack, 1965b, 1965c) on backward figural masking were carried out. Backward masking was chosen because this situation involves a discrete succession of stimuli that are experienced as simultaneous whether or not the target is detected. The first experiment was carried out with two adult subjects to make sure that two of the psychophysical variables, figure-ground contrast of the target and contour orientation of the target and mask, were potent in this particular situation. If they did indeed influence the amount of masking in a systematic fashion, the assumption could be made that backward visual masking is a Type I phenomenon. The results (see Figs. 5 & 6) showed clearly that both variables were operative. Masking occurred only when the target exhibited distinctly less contrast with its ground than did the mask, and was greatest when the contours of the mask and target were parallel and without angles. In the second experiment, the conditions that produced the maximal amount of backward masking were presented to children ranging in age from seven to ten years. The interstimulus interval permitting masking declined steadily as a function of increasing chronological age (see Fig. 7). Correlation with chronological age was higher than with mental age, and there was no correlation with IQ when age was held constant. Back-

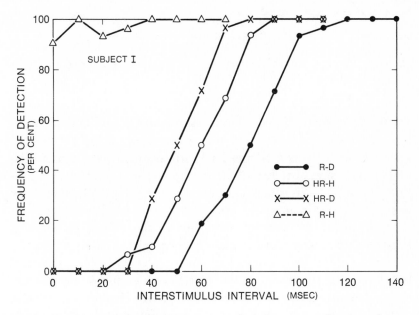

Figure 5   Percent detection of inner or masked figure as a function of inter-stimulus interval for S I.

ward figural masking, therefore, exhibits the characteristics of
Type I phenomena.

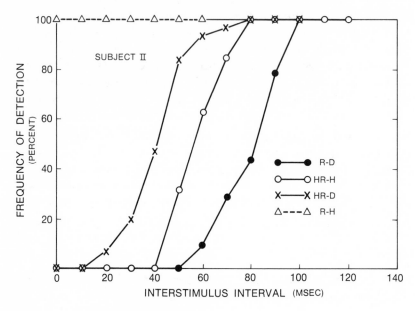

Figure 6   Percent detection of inner or masked figure as a function of inter-
            stimulus interval for S II.

The next series of experiments dealt with the phenomenon of
apparent movement. Apparent movement was chosen because, as
in the case of backward masking, stimuli are presented in discrete succession. In this situation, however, a spatial displacement occurs at the same time and is experienced phenomenally
as a continuous change of position across a visual field.

Once again, the strategy of studying the effects of stimulus
variables upon a particular phenomenon was preliminary to the
examination of its ontogenetic course. As was the case with
backward figural masking, the first variables investigated were
those of figure-ground contrast and contour orientation (Pollack,
1966a). To maintain as close a correspondence with visual masking as possible, the dependent variable measured was the tempo-

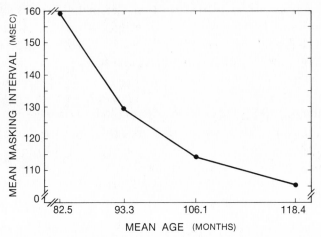

Figure 7   Mean interstimulus interval for backward figural masking as a function of chronological age.

ral range of apparent movement, namely, the range of interstimulus intervals over which subjects reported a single figure as moving. This measure, obtained by subtracting the simultaneity-to-movement threshold from the movement-to-succession threshold, was analogous to that employed in the masking studies; that is, the range of interstimulus intervals over which the initial figure in the sequence was masked.

As in the masking experiment, two trained adult subjects were employed. The stimuli were white, light gray, and mid-gray squares on a black background. Each square subtended a visual angle of 56′22″. The interstimulus distance subtended a visual angle of 39′40″. Variation along the dimension of contour orientation was provided by having the squares presented horizontally under one condition and tilted 45° under the other, so that the phenomenally experienced shapes were diamonds. All stimuli were presented tachistoscopically. The first figure appeared to the left of the center of the visual field, the second to the right. During the interstimulus interval, a plain black background was visible. Each figure was presented for 50 msec., and the interstimulus intervals varied from zero to 150 msec. in 10-msec. steps. The method of limits was employed throughout. The subject was simply asked to report "two" when he saw either two figures presented successively or two figures presented simultaneously. He reported "one" when he perceived a single figure moving from left to right across the visual field.

The results were clear-cut. Each subject showed a significant decrease in the temporal range of apparent movement as the figure-ground contrast level was decreased (see Figs. 8 & 9). Furthermore, the temporal range of apparent movement was significantly greater when the figures were parallel to each other (i.e. square orientation), than when their projections would have intersected each other (i.e. diamond orientation). The results were therefore parallel to those obtained for backward figural masking.

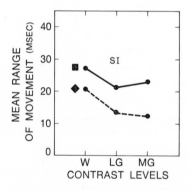

Figure 8   Range of interstimulus intervals permitting detection of apparent movement as a function of figure-ground contrast of initial stimulus for S I (male).

The second experiment was carried out to study the effect of the duration of the initial stimulus on the temporal range of apparent movement (Pollack, 1966b). The reason for this study was that previous work in the area had dealt with transmitted rather than reflected light and with figures having no sharply articulated contours. It was felt that since articulated contours require time to build, one might expect the equivalent of a microgenetic sequence in the effect of the duration of the ini-

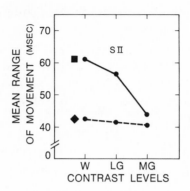

Figure 9   Range of interstimulus intervals permitting detection of apparent movement as a function of figure-ground contrast of initial stimulus for S II (female).

tial stimulus. That is, as stimulus duration was increased from zero to a certain time, the temporal range of apparent movement would increase as a function of the buildup of contour. Once beyond this point, however, adaptation processes would take over and the temporal range would begin to decrease.

The square white figures of the previous experiment were used again. The duration of the second stimulus was always 50 msec., and that of the initial stimulus was varied (50, 150, 1000, 2000, 5000, 10,000 msec.). As before, two trained adults served as subjects.

The results were quite clear. The temporal range of apparent movement increased as the duration of the initial stimulus was increased from 50 to 150 msec. From this point onward, the temporal range of apparent movement decreased as the initial stimulus duration increased (see Fig. 10).

The results of these two experiments indicate that the phenomenon of apparent movement is dependent upon the same stimulus variables as are other Type I phenomena. Consequently, it was expected that with young children, one would obtain results comparable to those obtained with other Type I phenomena (Pollack, 1966c). This phenomenon was expected to decrease with age up to a point and to be relatively unrelated to intelligence. As the children grew older, they would tend to make use of the stimulus trace of the first stimulus to mediate apparent movement. One could then expect that beyond a given age level, the temporal range of apparent movement would again begin to increase. In other words, as the persistence of the initial stimulus declined as a function of aging in the receptor system, a new analogous process making use of the stimulus trace would replace it.

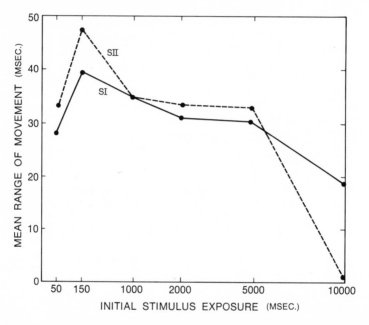

Figure 10   Temporal range of apparent movement as a function of initial stimulus duration.

The stimulus conditions optimal for producing the greatest temporal range of apparent movement were employed, namely, white squares with an initial stimulus duration of 150 msec. The subjects were 72 children, ranging in age from six to eleven years.

As expected, the temporal range of apparent movement decreased between ages six and nine but increased again beyond age nine (see Figs. 11, 12). Analysis of the simultaneity-to-movement and movement-to-succession thresholds indicated that most of the variation in the range of apparent movement was contributed by the movement-to-succession threshold. Correlation with IQ was nonsignificant for the seven- to nine-year-old children, but positive and significant for the ten- and eleven-year-olds. The pattern of results obtained in this experiment was very similar to that obtained in the earlier (Pollack, 1960) study of the frequency of occurrence of figural aftereffects after brief inspection.

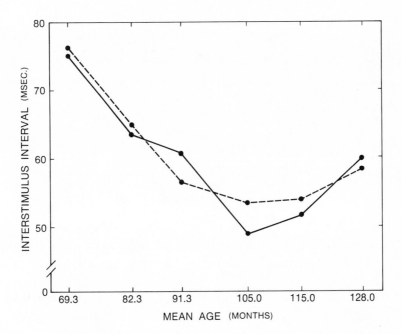

Figure 11   Mean range of interstimulus interval times permitting the report of apparent movement as a function of age. The solid line represents empirical data; the dotted line represents the curve of best fit.

The inflected ontogenetic curve and the pattern of correlation with intelligence seem to indicate that an underlying developmental change takes place to reverse the ontogenetic trend.

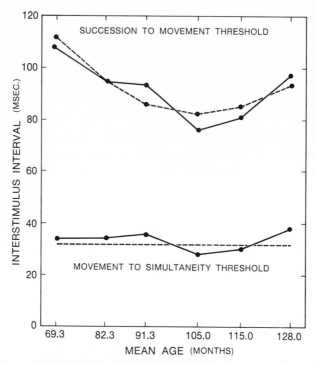

Figure 12   Mean succession to movement and movement to simultaneity thresh-
             olds as a function of age. The solid lines represent empirical data;
             the dotted lines represent the curves of best fit.

Further evidence for such a developmental change is given by
the changing pattern of intelligence-test correlations with the
phenomenon under study. It appears that the borderline between Type I and Type II phenomena is defined for adult
subjects by a critical interval of temporal succession of stimulus
patterns. This succession borderline was demonstrated conclusively by Ikeda and Obonai (1955) and later by Adam, Gibb &
Freeman (1966), who gradually increased the delay of onset of
one of the Delboeuf concentric circles until the usual illusion
reversed its direction. It is also possible that the succession
boundary may be given in terms of spatial separation of contours
as well as temporal succession of adjacent contours. Experiments
by Sutherland (1954) and by Day and Logan (1961), compar-

ing fixation effects with small and large figures, seem to support this possibility. In both these studies, the fixation of a small circle resulted in shrinkage of that circle—a finding that is quite analogous to the expectation of contour attraction discussed earlier (Pollack, 1964b). Large circles, on the other hand, appeared to increase in size following fixation. This reversal may have been due to the introduction of an element of temporal succession into the stimulus situation, since not all parts of the large circles could be fixated simultaneously.

These phenomena, because of the particular form of stimulus presentation (i.e., fairly rapid succession), illustrate the changing interplay of the ontogenetic processes which underlie Type I and Type II phenomena. The Type I process, which depends upon the interaction of the variables of relative intensity, duration, and contour orientation within the proximal stimulus, gradually declines with age as a function of decreasing receptor sensitivity. The effects of this loss of sensitivity are twofold. First, the strength of the interaction among these variables is reduced, thus decreasing the magnitude of Type I phenomena; second, stimulus persistence in the receptor system is also reduced, thereby diminishing the magnitude of phenomena that depend upon the perceived simultaneity of stimuli presented in rapid succession. As the Type I process is declining, the Type II process is progressively developing. This process, which involves the registration of stimulus traces and their integration with later stimuli in the series, becomes more manifest as the child grows older. Essentially, the child learns to compare the registered traces with new stimulation and begins to view the world in terms of sequences of stimulus events. When the succession of stimulus events is long enough, but is still relatively short, the transition between these two basic processes can be observed. The indices of this transition are the inflected ontogenetic curve and the change in the pattern of correlation between the magnitude of the perceptual phenomenon and other cognitive abilities as measured by intelligence test scores.

Since the phenomena themselves change in their magnitudes only and not in their qualities, despite the probable fact that they are underlain by different processes at different developmental stages, it would appear that the Type I process serves as the primitive lower-level analogue to the higher-level Type II process that follows it in time. Consequently, the proper and rapid development of the skills necessary to put the Type II process into operation as the dominant form may depend heavily upon whether the child has a good deal of exposure to Type I situations in which stimulus persistence is strong and readily apparent. Deprivation of the stimulus persistence due to some kind of reduced efficiency of the receptor system may therefore retard the development of the Type II process. This possibility will be discussed later.

Type II phenomena

Thus far, our experiments with Type II phenomena have been limited to an exploration of intersensory phenomena, which may or may not follow the rules governing the usual kinds of Type II events. We assume that intersensory phenomena belong in the Type II category because perceptual behavior resulting from stimulation in more than one sense modality must be mediated by some form of central integration of sensory information. Wohlwill (1960) reported an increase with age in the magnitude of the size-weight illusion, suggesting that this phenomenon is Type II. Whether or not intersensory integration is related to higher levels of cognitive activity remains unknown, however.

Our first study of Type II phenomena in children (Pollack, 1967) dealt with the effect of fixation upon the perceived distance of a three-dimensional object. It had been found earlier (Pollack, 1963a) with adult subjects that the phenomenal distance of a horizontal three-dimensional rod tended to increase following fixation. This displacement was explained in terms of sensoritonic theory. It was proposed that fixation of a three-dimensional object in a fixation plane is dependent upon maintenance of the degree of convergence necessary to keep a single sharply-focused image. Since this produces a certain amount of strain, and since instructions do not permit the subject to relax his muscles directly, it was hypothesized that relaxation, or counteraction of muscular activity, occurs vicariously by displacement of the figure away from the subject. A series of experiments (Pollack, 1963a), which will not be described here, supported this explanation. Adult subjects did indeed counteract the strain of convergence by displacing the objects away from themselves. In studying the effect of body tilt upon perception of the vertical, Wapner and Werner (1957) found, however, that young children tend to assimilate to the muscle activity produced by the tilt rather than to counteract it. Whereas adults adjusted the vertical in a direction opposite that of the body tilt, young children adjusted the vertical in a direction identical to the tilt. Evidence from their research indicates that the transition from assimilation to counteraction occurs early in adolescence. Assuming that this ontogenetic trend is transposable to the perception of objects in the third dimension following fixation, there is no guarantee that the age of transition will be the same for the two phenomena. Indeed, we find from Wohlwill's (1963) report on the perception of size and distance as a function of chronological age that a shift from under-constancy to over-constancy occurs at about age seven. It may be that the transition to overestimation of distance and probably, therefore, overestimation of size, is due to a change in mechanism: from (1) assimilating to convergence—bringing objects of a given retinal size closer and thus estimating their size as smaller, to (2) counteracting convergence—displacing objects away from oneself and therefore estimating their size as larger. Thus, one might expect the transition age to be the same as that from under- to over-constancy, namely, about seven years of age.

In evaluating the relationship between perceived distance as a function of fixation and higher-level cognitive processes, one must take into account earlier work on the relationship between size-distance judgments and intelligence. Jenkin and Feallock (1960) studied this relationship, comparing samples of normals and retardates matched for chronological age, and found no differences. It appears that although such perception must require central integration of information from more than one sense modality, vision and proprioception, this may not occur on the

same level as the integration of information through time. The
shift might be due to an underlying cognitive developmental
change, but it may also be due to an attitudinal change in the
mode of perception from assimilation of extraneous bodily stimulation to counteraction of such stimulation. The introduction
of counteraction may represent an attempt on the part of the
child to maintain the stability of his perceptual world by
compensating for stimulus forces. Assimilation, however, represents a state in which the child defines the dimensions of his
perceptual space in terms of the ongoing stimulation and adjusts
these dimensions in the same direction as new stimulation
occurs. Once a shift from assimilation to counteraction has taken
place, there is no further need for any change, except perhaps in
degree. Whereas the continued sharpening of contrast between
temporally separated stimuli improves the contrast mechanism,
and thus the ability to make subtle comparisons between stimuli,
the exaggeration of counteraction serves no such purpose. Exaggeration of counteraction, in real life, produces a distortion as ill-
adaptive as the distortions produced by assimilation. Therefore,
the dual possibility exists that the assimilation-counteraction
shift is a fairly low-level cognitive shift, and that once it is made,
no further progress is evident. If such were the case, then correlation with intellectual ability should be minimal. In an empirical investigation (Pollack, 1967), subjects were asked, first, to
adjust one of two three-dimensional vertical rods, objectively
placed one meter from the eyes, so that the two rods appeared to
be at an equal distance from the subject. The subjects then fixated
a point midway between the two rods for a 30-sec. period during
which only one rod was visable. At the end of the fixation period,
the other rod was brought back into view, and the subjects again
adjusted it so that both rods appeared to be at the same distance.
These subjects ranged from six to thirteen years.

Only the six-year-olds assímilated. Their adjustments of the
nonfixated rod indicated that they perceived the rod as having
moved toward them during the fixation period. All other age
groups tended to displace the rod away from themselves following fixation (see Fig. 13). The transition point between the two
modes of responding appears to be about age seven, which is the

same point at which Wohlwill reports a shift from under- to over-constancy of size and distance judgments for near objects. Correlation with chronological age was significant, but correlation with intelligence test scores was not. The results therefore confirmed our own expectations and earlier findings in the literature.

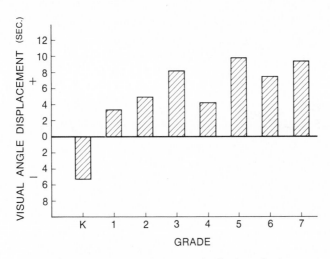

Figure 13   TF displacement as a function of school grade (positive values indicate displacement of TF away from S; negative values indicate displacement toward S).

The next study undertaken dealt with a situation in which muscular activity and visual stimulation could be observed to operate separately, presumably in cooperation with and in opposition to each other. The phenomenon investigated was the subjective median plane (SMP), or the straight-ahead. Visual stimulation was provided by an illuminated square subtending a visual angle of 2°12′ at 5 m. viewing distance. The subject raised one laterally extended arm to shoulder height for 15 sec. to induce muscular stimulation. Eight stimulus conditions were presented: (1) left extent (i.e. right edge of square set at the apparent straight-ahead), (2) right extent (i.e. center of square set at the apparent straight-ahead), (3) left arm raised, (4) right arm raised, (5) left extent–right arm raised, (6) left extent–left arm raised, (7) right extent–left arm raised, and (8) right extent—right arm raised. All measurements were deviations from a previously established SMP obtained by having the subject set the center of the square straight ahead in the absence of muscular stimulation. Twenty subjects (10 boys - 10 girls) at each of nine age levels ranging from six to fourteen years were employed over all conditions.

Initially the data were examined for sex differences. Since none were found, boys' and girls' scores were pooled. Analysis of variance revealed a significant main effect for stimulus conditions and a significant interaction between conditions and age. The main effect for age was cancelled by presenting stimuli both on the left and on the right. Single classification analyses of variance were run alone for both extent effects and arm-extension effects. The patterns obtained for extent were similar to those reported by Wapner and Werner (1957). The effect of asymmetrical extent was to shift the SMP in the direction of stimulation. As age increased this effect diminished (see Fig. 14). Product-moment correlation produced a coefficient of $-.25$ ($p. < .01$) between chronological age (CA) and extent effect. Partial correlation holding mental age (MA) constant revealed that CA alone accounted for the relationship. Thus, extent effect fits into the Type I category on all counts.

The effect of arm extension on the SMP of the center of the square was more complicated. The six- and seven-year-olds tended to set it in the direction of stimulation, whereas the older children tended to set the SMP in the direction opposite that of stimulation. Thus, the results are similar to those obtained in the fixation experiment discussed earlier. The transition age for the shift from assimilation to counteraction is also the same (about age seven). In this case, however, analysis of variance indicated a more continuous age effect. Even this appears to stabilize by age nine (see Fig. 15). Once again correlation with CA was significant ($r = .24$, $p < .01$), and partial correlation demonstrated that CA was the major variable correlated with magnitude of effect. In light of the earlier fixation experiment (Pollack, 1967), these results were as expected; they showed a lower kind of

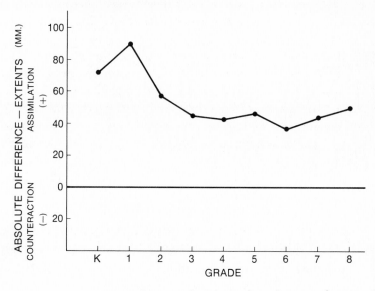

Figure 14   Spatial extent effect on subjective median plane as a function of age.

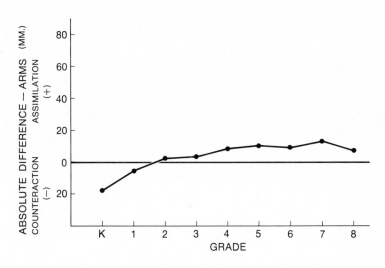

Figure 15   Lateral arm extension effect on subjective median plane as a function of age.

Type II phenomenon in which assimilation to muscular stimulation shifts to counteraction of stimulation, but without regard to
higher-level cognitive ability.

Interesting and unexpected results were produced by analysis
of the conditions in which extent and muscular involvement
were combined so that they would be expected either to summate or to cancel each other. With a shift from assimilation to
counteraction of the effects of arm extension, it was expected
that the youngest children would show a greater left deviation
with a combination of left extent–left arm raised, while the
effects of left extent–right arm raised would tend to nullify each
other. With older children this pattern would be reversed. A
glance at Fig. 16 makes it apparent that this did indeed occur,
but without a significant age trend. It is curious that the effect of
extent appears to dominate completely that of arm extension
when the two are presented in combination. A similar experiment with adults (Pollack, 1961) indicated that the dominance

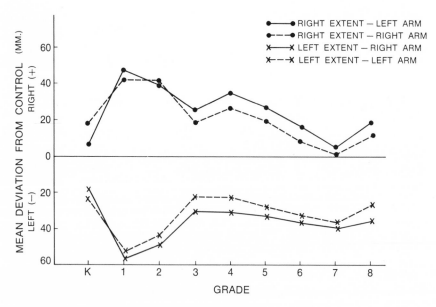

Figure 16   Shifts in the subjective median plane (SMP) resulting from the
interaction of visual and muscular stimulation as a function of age.

of the visual stimulus comes to an end somewhere in the age scale, perhaps further on into adolescence. Future investigation will extend this analysis through the high school years.

In their work on the effects of body tilt on the perceived verticality of a rod, Wapner and Werner (1957) found that the transition from assimilation to counteraction did not occur until mid-adolescence. The rod, however, was not placed in a perfectly vertical position while the body was tilted. Consequently, some asymmetrical visual stimulation was always present, making dominance by visual stimulation possible. It may well be that our planned experimentation will yield results similar to those of Wapner and Werner. Whether or not this relatively late differentiation of visual and muscular stimulation effects is related to higher cognitive functioning remains to be seen.

Intelligence and perceptual development

Despite the fact that a number of workers in the field subscribe to the existence of a general intelligence factor, it is a truism to state that behavior labeled as intelligent is multifaceted and multidetermined. With this truism firmly in mind, I propose to deal with only one facet of intelligence—that which is concerned with the integration of information received by the sensory apparatus over short periods of time. Temporal integration is Hearnshaw's term. He defines it as "the formation of contemporaneous patterns of action and meaning when the units from which these patterns are constituted are serially ordered and in temporal succession" (Hearnshaw, 1956, p. 5). His examples deal with a series of visual presentations of verbal or configurational material whose variation within the series can be predicted only by keeping in mind their past relationship to one another and to the present.

From Hearnshaw's description, it might appear that two main variables are involved in temporal integration: first, immediate memory; and second, a set toward viewing the world as a series of successive events that cohere in an ordered pattern. In examining these variables, let us now shift our attention from Hearnshaw to

Ellis. Ellis (1963) proposed a mechanism to account for the poor performance of retardates in tasks that involve sequences of events or delays. He suggested that sensory activity leaves an immediate stimulus trace that persists for a short period and that influences subsequent behavior. The poor performance of the retardate is supposedly due to a failure to register stimulus traces adequately. In other words, short-term memory is impaired. For Ellis, then, the establishment of the stimulus trace depends upon prior stimulation in interaction with some aspect of intelligence. Although this position takes adequate account of the first variable believed to be involved in temporal integration, immediate memory, it does not handle the other.

However, let us examine two perceptual studies by Spitz and Blackman (1958, 1959) in which retardates and normals were compared. We find that these groups did not differ with respect to the magnitude of a simultaneously presented geometrical illusion (Mueller-Lyer), but that the retardates showed significantly smaller figural aftereffects when the inspection (IF) and test figures (TF) were presented sequentially. Presumably, the failure of retardates to exhibit larger figural aftereffects is due to their inability to register adequate stimulus traces of IF as it appears at the end of the fixation period.

As a consequence of such an explanation, one could predict that as normal children grow older, they will report figural aftereffects more frequently under an inspection condition of short duration. As indicated earlier, this is the case beyond age ten (Pollack, 1960), but between ages four and ten, the frequency of aftereffects decreases. Obviously another factor is involved at the earlier age levels. Most probably, persistence of stimulus activity is greater in younger children, so that their so-called aftereffects are produced by a simultaneous contrast between an afterimage of IF and TF, rather than by a comparison between TF and a trace of IF. Therefore, stimulus duration must be taken into account in examining phenomena involving physical succession, especially in younger children.

Let us consider the other proposed variable underlying temporal integration, or a set toward viewing the world as a series of successive events. A study comparing normal achievers and low achievers in a lower-class Negro school in Chicago is currently being conducted at the Institute for Juvenile Research. A social anthropologist, Daniel Scheinfeld, working on the project has, on the basis of his observations, adopted the viewpoint that those who are below average in their school performance tend to treat each new occurrence as isolated from the past rather than to organize their world as a sequence of events. This observation suggests that the middle-class mode of viewing the world in terms of temporal succession is not universal in American culture. Indeed, the lower-class Negro child may receive no reinforcement in his home environment for sequencing his life. Some experimental evidence for class differences in perception of sequences can be found in a paper by Birch, Belmont, and Karp (1965). They demonstrated that with long time intervals, auditory time errors were similar for middle- and lower-class groups. With short intervals, however, the lower-class group showed positive rather than negative time errors. It seems possible that the instructions, which directed an unfamiliar focusing upon prior stimulation, led to exaggeration of the first stimulus for the lower-class group, adding factors other than stimulus trace alone to the second stimulus.

If perceptual development itself is now considered in its relation to intelligence, confrontation with the work and theories of Piaget is unavoidable. Piaget and his co-workers, dealing largely with illusions, developed a typology of phenomena based initially on changes in illusion magnitude as a function of increasing chronological age. Mechanisms for the various sequences were developed, resulting in a theory that is attached as an appendage to Piaget's general theory of cognitive development. Perceptual theory looks like an appendage because perception itself is accorded second-class citizenship in the population of psychological activities (Piaget, 1958). Its continued bondage to ongoing stimulation and its dependence upon such external factors as stimulus configuration, renders perception inferior to the lofty cognitive operations that employ manipulable schema.

Essentially, Piaget divides perceptual phenomena into three types: Type I phenomena, typified by standard simultaneously-presented geometrical illusions that decline in their effect as age

increases; Type II phenomena, typified by illusions whose parts
are presented in succession or in different sense modalities and
that increase with increasing age; and Type III phenomena,
similar to Type II except that they increase with age to a point
and then decline. According to Piaget, there are two ways of
perceiving, and these tend to be related to two determinants of
percepts. The ontogenetically earlier type is called centration,
which refers to looking at a visual display *in toto*, in a single
glance. It ranges from fixation to close inspection of spatially
adjacent areas. Things centrated upon are usually overestimated.
The second type of perceiving is called decentration and involves
successive looking, or successive centrations, usually upon various parts of a display. When centration is dominant, the major
determinant of perception is what Piaget calls "field forces," or
more familiarly, configuration. As the child grows older, decentration becomes dominant and perception becomes a matter of
"perceptual regulations" in which various parts of the display are
isolated in successive centrations and compared with one another. "Perceptual regulation," in contrast with pure perception,
which is implied to be innate, are given the status of low-level
intelligent behavior.

The stimuli for Type I phenomena are presented in such a
way that centration is favored, thus making distortions greater in
magnitude at earlier age levels. With age, the child becomes
more accurate in his perception precisely because he decentrates
more and more and makes successive comparisons of the parts of
the figure. He also isolates inducing lines from comparison lines
in illusions (e.g. Mueller-Lyer). There is some evidence that the
number of eye movements and their directedness increase with
chronological age (Piaget & Vinh-Bang, 1961).

Type II phenomena are usually presented in such a way that
perception must occur by decentration. That is, parts of the total
display are presented successively, as in the Usnadze effect
(Piaget & Lambercier, 1944), or in different sense modalities.
Since such phenomena are produced by comparison itself, they
appear less noticeable at earlier age levels and increase steadily
with age. It is interesting to note that, almost paradoxically,
perception of this type becomes less accurate as the child grows
older.

Type III phenomena represent more complicated shifts in modes of perceiving that involve alternation of perceptual regulations and will not be discussed here.

As can be readily seen, Piaget provides a single mechanism— the introduction of perceptual regulations accompaning decentration—to account for ontogenetic changes. Furthermore, the mechanism is developmental in nature; that is, a higher order of functioning replaces a lower order. The higher order is said to be related to intelligence. Finally, the demonstration of ontogenetic changes appears to require that time be allowed for eye movements so as to permit the appropriate decentrations.

From Hearnshaw, we see that the mode of perceiving events in sequence provides patterns whereby the immediate past affects the present. Ellis fleshes out temporal integration with a hypothetical construct, the stimulus trace, providing a vehicle for the continuity that Hearnshaw postulates. Piaget, with his notion of decentration, adds the attention factor, which allows for succession even with repeated exposures of the same stimulus configuration and thus provides a means for isolating and comparing different parts of the perceptual field. I believe that we now have a framework for investigating the development of cognitive intelligence through perception.

There are advantages to such a perceptual approach, the greatest of which is the fact that it is amenable to controlled laboratory experimentation. Both stimuli and responses can be defined with relatively more precision, independent of external extraneous influences and under fixed background conditions. There are no effects of specific content experience, no specific skills required, and nothing that resembles a test or school work, for example. In addition, should it be shown that temporal integration is an ability necessary to the success of cognitive functioning, perceptual situations offer a precise, efficient mode of intervention designed to develop the ability to integrate information over time.

Once the basic work on ontogenetic perceptual changes is completed, application of the above gross and tentative theoretical structure will begin. One step will be a study to determine just what aspects of the tasks in our tests of intelligence correlate with the magnitude of Type II phenomena. Presumably, highest correlations will be obtained for tasks that involve temporal sequencing, like number series and series that require that a relationship be kept in mind while two cognitive stimuli are compared, as in analogies. Another step will be the introduction of perceptual sequential experience in which young children are required to make comparative judgments of size, for example, with interstimulus intervals gradually increased. The object of such intervention is to note the occurrence of transfer to traditional Type II phenomena to see whether the normal ontogenetic trend can be accelerated and with what degree of permanence. If positive results are obtained, the effects of sequencing experience on more abstract cognitive tasks will be studied.

Despite its low probability of success, the manipulation of perceptual experience through precise variation of experimentally controlled stimulus conditions to influence so-called higher-level cognitive activities is a most exciting prospect. Three aspects of temporal integration were discussed above. The present approach is directed neither toward the registration of stimulus traces, which may depend primarily on biochemistry, nor toward the basic capacity to make successive comparisons, but rather toward the set to view the world sequentially. In Piaget's terms, the object of intervention would be to convert centrators into decentrators by manipulating the ontogenetic course of perception. As mentioned earlier, world view may be conditioned by such all-pervasive complicating factors as ethnic and social class variables. Some of these will be described in the next section.

Ethnic and social class factors

Earlier we discussed the transition from Type I to Type II processes (Pollack, 1960, 1966c), and the idea of temporal integration was set forth to show the perception-intelligence relationship. Both topics raise a number of "what if" questions. What if early stimulus persistence is a necessary precursor of the next developmentally more complex process? What if deprivation of intense stimulation, and therefore lessened stimulus persistence, occurs in certain individuals?

Let us keep these questions in mind as we look at background material from cross-cultural studies. Segall, Campbell, and Herskovitz (1963, 1966) studied responses to some of the geometric illusions, comparing white Northwestern University students and white South Africans with members of 13 other societies. In the case of the Mueller-Lyer illusion and the Sander parallelogram —both primary illusions—the non-European groups showed less susceptibility, smaller illusions. They found, however, that the children of these groups generally experienced larger illusions than their elders, showing the same ontogenetic pattern as European groups. Since the differences among groups were explained in terms of a lack of experience in a carpentered environment with its rectangular cues to perspective, the age trends are mystifying to say the least. The fact that all of the non-European groups had more darkly pigmented skins seems to have evoked no notice.

When once asked to comment on these results, I mentioned that physical factors might well provide alternative hypotheses to learning experience. In the course of my examination, I rated the non-European groups on the basis of nearness to the equator, amount of sunshine, and density of forest cover, and found an inverse correlation between these as a complex and the magnitude of illusion. No such result has come from a correlation of carpentering with magnitude. The latest piece of nonconfirmatory evidence comes from Jahoda (1966) who studied three Ghanian groups and found that although one group had a considerably more carpentered environment than the other two, this group exhibited the same small illusion magnitudes.

At this point, psychophysical work by Wald (1945), Ishak (1952a, 1952b), Fitzpatrick (1964), and Eckardt (1966) becomes quite relevant. Wald, working with aphakic eyes, found that blue and violet light was absorbed by the yellow macular pigment, thus reducing sensitivity in the central area of the retina—the area of clearest form perception. Wald found that up to 60 percent of the light of wave length 430–490 nanometers incident on the retina was absorbed. Ishak found, first, that macular pigmentation was darker in Egyptians than in Englishmen and other Europeans, and second, that visual sensitivity in the Egyptians, especially in the green and blue spectral areas, was deficient when compared with the standard visual sensitivity curve.

Fitzpatrick (1964) worked with white American subjects who were rated on the depth of their macular pigmentations with an ophthalmoscope. Five of the most lightly pigmented subjects were compared with five of the darkest with respect to thresholds for lights of various wave lengths. A significant difference in sensitivity of .2 log units to blue light was found in favor of the lightly pigmented subjects. Finally, Eckardt (1966) found a significant mean decrement in sensitivity to blue and violet light in five Negro subjects as compared with five white subjects. These findings raised more "what if" questions. What if skin pigmentation and retinal pigmentation are strongly correlated? What if deeper retinal pigmentation reduces sensitivity to patterned stimuli and reduces stimulus persistence? What if the developmental shift to trace integration in such individuals is delayed because stimulus-persistence experience is less intense? Let us look at the results of two preliminary experiments (Silvar & Pollack, 1967; Pollack & Silvar, 1967).

An experienced ophthalmologist examined the maculae of 14 Negro and 26 white children ranging in age from eight to thirteen and residing in one of Chicago's few integrated middle-class suburbs. Retinal pigmentation—yellow—was rated at the maculae on a four-point scale from very dark to very light. It can be seen from Table 1 that the results were as expected. Collapsing

Table 1   Macular Pigmentation Ratings by Race

	Light		Dark	
	1/1	1/2	2/1	2/2
Negro	0	1	9	4
Caucasian	7	17	2	0

the extreme categories to permit chi-square analysis statistically demonstrated the obvious. Next, all of the Negroes and 21 of the whites were examined to discover the magnitude of the Mueller-Lyer illusion under bluish illumination (see Fig. 17). The results, again, were surprisingly clear. The children with darkly pigmented maculae had a mean illusion magnitude significantly smaller than those with light pigmentation. Biserial correlation yielded a coefficient of −.745. Certainly, these results are uncontaminated by any factor of cultural diversity, especially with respect to a carpentered environment.

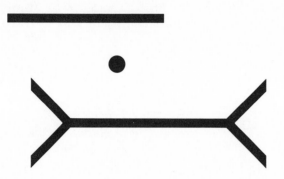

Figure 17   Portion of Mueller-Lyer figure presented tachistoscopically in blue light.

On the basis of these two very rough preliminary experiments, two of the "what if" questions seem to have been answered in the affirmative. The others will be examined as soon as my experimental schedule permits.

The results of the above experiments make clear the direction of future research. First a study comparing Negro and white subjects using illusion figures articulated solely in terms of hue contrast across a range of colors will be carried out. Second, stimulus persistence, using afterimage duration as the dependent variable, will be studied as a function of retinal pigmentation, age, and social class. Third, methods to correlate skin pigmentation with retinal pigmentation will be sought. The general pattern of future experimentation and the expected results are presented in Table 2.

If pigment differences are a factor in perceptual development, they can be remedied in educational experience as easily as acuity defects and color blindness, either by altering the hues of

Table 2   Experimental Plan and Expectations in Studying Class and
           Ethnic Differences

CLASS	TYPE I	PHENOMENON TYPE II	TRANSITION FROM I TO II
Middle-class white	Normal	Normal	Normal
Middle-class Negro	Smaller magnitude with short-wave stimuli	Normal	Possible delay due to lowered intensity and persistence of short-wave stimuli
Lower-class white	Normal	Decrement due to lack of set to view world sequentially	Decrement due to lack of set to view world sequentially
Lower-class Negro	Smaller magnitude with short-wave stimuli	Decrement due to lack of set to view world sequentially	Delay due to lack of set to view world sequentially and lowered intensity and persistence of short-wave stimuli

the stimuli or by increasing their contrast levels. Class differences
due to differing world views will be much harder to reduce. The
research and theoretical prospects, however, are exciting and
will be followed up, I hope with vigor and enthusiasm, even
though one must entertain some doubts concerning the durabil-
ity of the preliminary theoretical framework set forth in this
chapter.

Summary

A study of the literature has led the author to conclude that
there are two processes underlying age changes in perception.

One of these involves a progressive loss of receptor sensitivity due to physiological aging. This process is essentially nondevelopmental because it involves neither a differentiation nor an integration of sensory and cognitive functions. The other process is developmental in that the age changes are related to central cognitive functions which have differentiated and appear to have become integrated in a complex fashion.

Those phenomena showing nondevelopmental age changes (Type I) are not correlated with intellectual ability, but appear to be related directly to receptor efficiency in responding to stimulus variables such as intensity, contrast, duration, and orientation. When the phenomena under study are illusions, age changes reflect a shift in the direction of smaller illusions, but the improved "accuracy" appears to be merely a by-product of a decline in receptor sensitivity.

Those phenomena showing developmental age changes (Type II) are correlated with intellectual ability and are not so closely related to classical stimulus variation. When the Type II phenomena studied are illusions, there is an apparently paradoxical progression toward greater illusion magnitudes as age increases. Presentation of such phenomena usually involves a sequence of discrete stimulus events which the subject registers as traces which are then centrally compared and contrasted. Thus, the illusion is produced by the appropriate sequencing of certain qualities of stimulus events designed to maximize contrast and produce an illusory distortion. The better able the subject is to register and integrate traces, and to view his world as a sequence of related events, the larger his "error" will be. The mechanism that is highly adaptive for complex cognitive activity appears to be paradoxically maladaptive in perception.

The viewpoint expressed here is in essential agreement with that of Piaget with respect to Type II phenomena, with perhaps greater emphasis on the relationship to intellectual functioning than Piaget would be willing to assume. There is complete disagreement with respect to age changes in Type I phenomena. Piaget places his emphasis on change due to successive comparison of parts of a simultaneously-presented stimulus complex (decentration) designed to break down the effects of single-

404 RESEARCH PERSPECTIVES

glance viewing (centration) of a configuration. The current study on the effects of psychophysical variables suggests to the author that the condition of the receptor system, and thus its sensitivity, is a more important variable. If these physical factors are predominant, a single-process theory accounting for all age changes in perception is untenable.

An ongoing research program designed to isolate Type I phenomena, to find the point of transition from Type I to Type II phenomena, and to study the nature of trace integration in Type II phenomena, has been described in some detail. The importance of such complicating variables as social class and race have been discussed in light of preliminary research, and an outline of future research has been presented.

References

Adam, June, Gibb, Margaret, & Freeman, I. Effects of luminance contrast factors upon figural aftereffects induced by short fixation periods. *Precept. mot. Skills*, 1966, **22**, 535–541.

Birch, H. G., Belmont, I., & Karp, E. Social differences in auditory perception. *Percept. mot. Skills*, 1965, **20**, 861–870.

Day, R. H. & Logan, J. A. A further investigation of apparent size and retinal size as determinants of the figural aftereffect. *Quart. J. exp. Psychol.*, 1961, **13**, 193–203.

Eckardt, Rudolph A. Foveal luminosity functions of five Negroes in relation to macular and skin pigmentation. Unpublished doctoral dissertation, Fordham Univer., 1966.

Ellis, N. R. The stimulus trace and behavioral inadequacy. In N. R. Ellis (Ed.), *Handbook of mental deficiency*. New York: McGraw-Hill, 1963. Pp. 134–158.

Fitzpatrick, Gladys. An investigation of the role of macular pigmentation in spectral sensitivity to the short wave lengths. Unpublished doctoral dissertation, Fordham Univer., 1964.

Fox, B. H. Figural aftereffects: 'satiation' and 'adaptation.' *J. exp. Psychol.*, 1951, **42**, 317–326.

Gaudreau, J., Lavoie, G., & Delorme, H. La perception des illusions de Müller-Lyer et d'Oppel-Kundt chez les déficients mentaux. *Canad. J. Psychol.*, 1963, **17**, 259–263.

George, F. H. Acuity and the statistical theory of figural aftereffects. *J. exp. Psychol.*, 1962, **63**, 423–425.

Gibson, J. J. Adaptation with negative aftereffect. *Psychol. Rev.*, 1937, **44**, 222–224.

Graham, E. Figural aftereffects as functions of contrast, area, and luminance of the inspection-figure. *Psychologia*, 1961, **4**, 201–208.

Hammer, Elaine R. Temporal factors in figural aftereffects. *Amer. J. Psychol.*, 1949, **62**, 337–354.

Hearnshaw, L. S. Temporal integration and behavior. *Bull. Brit. psychol. Soc.*, 1956, **9**, 1–20.

Ikeda, H., & Obonai, T. Studies in figural after-effects: IV. The contrast-confluence illusion of concentric circles and the figural after-effect. *Jap. psychol. Res. J.*, 1955, **2**, 17–23.

Ishak, I. G. H. The photopic luminosity curve for a group of fifteen Egyptian trichromats. *J. optical Soc. Amer.*, 1952, **42**. 429–433 (a)

Ishak, I. G. H. The spectral chromaticity coordinates for one British and eight Egyptian trichromats. *J. optical Soc. Amer.*, 1952, **42**, 534–539. (b)

Jahoda, Gustav. Geometric illusions and environment: a study in Ghana. *Brit. J. Psychol.*, 1966, **57**, 193–199.

Jenkin, N., & Feallock, Sally M. Developmental and intellectual processes in size-distance judgment. *Amer. J. Psychol.*, 1960, **73**, 268–273.

Koehler, W., & Wallach, H. Figural aftereffects: an investigation of visual processes. *Proceedings of the Amer. Philos. Soc.*, 1944, **88**, 269–357.

Oyama, T. The illusion of concentric circles as a function of hue and brightness. *Hokkaido Rep. Psychol.*, 1961, **6**, No. 3.

Piaget, J. Assimilation et connaissance. In B. Mandelbrot, A. Jonkheere, & J. Piaget, *La lecture de l'expérience*. Vol. 5. *Études d'épistémologie génétique*. Paris: Presses Univer. France, 1958. Pp. 49–108.

Piaget, J. Problems of genetic psychology. In D. Elkind (Ed.), *Six psychological studies*. New York: Random House, 1967. Pp. 116–142.

Piaget, J., & Lambercier, M. Recherches sur le développement des perceptions: V. Essai sur un effet d' "Einstellung" survenant au cours de perceptions visuelles successives (effet Usnadze). *Arch. Psychol., Genève*, 1944, **30**, 139–196.

Piaget, J., Lambercier, M., Boesch, E., & Albertini, B.V. Recherches sur le développement des perceptions: I. Introduction à l'étude des perceptions chez l'enfant et analyse d'une illusion relative à la perception visuelle de cercles concentriques (Delboeuf). *Arch. Psychol., Genève*, 1942, **29**, 1–107.

Piaget, J., Matalon, B., & Vinh-Bang. L'évolution de l'illusion dite "verticale-horizontale" de ses composantes (rectangle et équerre) et de l'illusion de Delboeuf en présentation tachistoscopique. *Arch. Psychol., Genève*, 1961, **37**, 23–68.

Piaget, J., & Vinh-Bang. Comparaison des mouvements oculaires et des centrations du regard chez l'enfant et chez l'adulte. *Arch. Psychol., Genève,* 1961, **38**, 167–200.

Pollack, R. H. Figural aftereffects: quantitative studies of displacement. *Austr. J. Psychol.,* 1958, **10**, 269–277.

Pollack, R. H. Figural aftereffects as a function of age. *Acta Psychol.,* 1960, 17, **5**, 417–423.

Pollack, R. H. Apparent median plane shifts with asymmetrical stimulation and fixation. *Austr. J. Psychol.,* 1961, **13**, 195–205.

Pollack, R. H. Application of the sensoritonic theory of perception to figural aftereffect. *Acta Psychol.,* 1963, **21**, 1–16. (a)

Pollack, R. H. Contour detectability thresholds as a function of chronological age. *Percept. mot. Skills,* 1963, **17**, 411–417. (c)

Pollack, R. H. Effects of temporal order of stimulus presentation on the direction of figural aftereffects. *Percept. mot. Skills,* 1963, **17**, 875–880. (b)

Pollack, R. H. The effects of fixation on the apparent magnitude of bounded horizontal extents. *Amer. J. Psychol.,* 1964, **77**, 177–194. (b)

Pollack, R. H. Simultaneous and successive presentation of elements of the Mueller-Lyer figure and chronological age. *Percept. mot. Skills,* 1964, **19**, 303–310. (a)

Pollack, R. H. Backward figural masking as a function of chronological age and intelligence. *Psychon. Sci.,* 1965, **3**, 65–66. (c)

Pollack, R. H. Effects of figure-ground contrast and contour orientation on figural masking. *Psychon. Sci.,* 1965, **2**, 369–370. (b)

Pollack, R. H. Hue detectability thresholds as a function of chronological age. *Psychon. Sci.,* 1965, **3**, 351–352. (a)

Pollack, R. H. Effect of figure-ground contrast and contour orientation on the temporal range of apparent movement. *Psychon. Sci.,* 1966, **4**, 401–402. (a)

Pollack, R. H. Initial stimulus duration and the temporal range of apparent movement. *Psychon. Sci.,* 1966, **5**, 165–166. (b)

Pollack, R. H. Temporal range of apparent movement as a function of age and intelligence. *Psychon. Sci.,* 1966, **5**, 243–244. (c)

Pollack, R. H. Changes in the effects of fixation upon apparent distance in the third dimension. *Psychon. Sci.,* 1967, **8**, 141–142.

Pollack, R. H., & Chaplin, Mary Rose. Perceptual behavior: the necessity for a developmental approach to its study. *Acta Psychol.,* 1963, **21**, 371–376.

Pollack, R. H., & Chaplin, Mary Rose. Effects of prolonged stimulation by components of the Mueller-Lyer figure upon the magnitude of illusion. *Percept. mot. Skills,* 1964, **18**, 377–382.

Pollack, R. H., & Magerl, G. E. A binocular viewing apparatus for sensory threshold studies in children. *Percept. mot. Skills,* 1965, **20**, 127–130.

Pollack, R. H., & Silvar, S. D. Magnitude of the Mueller-Lyer illusion in children as a function of pigmentation of the Fundus oculi. *Psychon. Sci.*, 1967, 8, 83–84.

Prysiazniuk, A. W., & Kelm, H. Visual figural aftereffects in retarded adults. *J. abnorm. soc. Psychol.*, 1963, 67, 509.

Segall, M. H., Campbell, D. T., & Herskovitz, M. J. Cultural differences in the perception of geometric illusions. *Science*, 1963, 139, 769–771.

Segall, M. H., Campbell, D. T., & Herskovitz, M. J. *The influence of culture on visual perception.* Indianapolis, Indiana: Bobbs-Merrill, 1966.

Silvar, S. D., & Pollack, R. H. Racial differences in pigmentation of the Fundus oculi. *Psychon. Sci.*, 1967, 7, 159–160.

Spitz, H. H., & Blackman, L. S. The Mueller-Lyer illusion in retardates and normals. *Percept. mot. Skills*, 1958, 8, 219–225.

Spitz, H. H., & Blackman, L. S. Studies in mental retardation: I. A comparison of mental retardates and normals on visual figural aftereffects and reversible figures. *J. abnorm. soc. Psychol.*, 1959, 58, 105–110.

Sutherland, N. S. Figural aftereffects, retinal size, and apparent size. *Quart. J. exp. Psychol.*, 1954, 6, 35–44.

Wald, George. Human vision and the spectrum. *Science*, 1945, 101, 653–658.

Wapner, S., & Werner, H. *Perceptual development.* Worcester, Mass.: Clark Univer. Press, 1957.

Weale, R. A. Notes on the photometric significance of the human crystalline lens. *Vision Res.*, 1961, 1, 183–191. (a)

Weale, R. A. Retinal illumination and age. Illum. Eng. Soc., London. *Transactions*, 1961, 26, 95–100. (b)

Weale, R. A. *The aging eye.* Great Britain: Adlard & Son, Ltd., New York: Harper & Row, 1963.

Wohlwill, J. F. Developmental studies of perception. *Psychol. Bull.*, 1960, 57, 249–288.

Wohlwill, J. F. The development of "overconstancy" in space perception. In L. P. Lipsitt & C. C. Spiker (Eds.) *Advances in Child Development and Behavior* 1. New York: Academic Press, 1963, 265–312.

Stimulus and Cognitive Transformation in Conservation

HARRY BEILIN

Adult behavior and thought have provided the principal sources for understanding the nature of the "real" world since only in adulthood is a sophisticated characterization of natural phenomena possible. Analyses of mature behavior and thought might have been expected, as a consequence, to have resulted by now in a cohesive and verifiable conception of human cognition. This is far from the case. An undue concentration on adult thinking, reasoning and problem solving has resulted in only limited yields from what should be a rich soil. The relatively recent work of Piaget and his associates has changed that. Just as the contrast between preliterate and literate societies provided social anthro-

The research upon which this paper is based was supported in part by research grants from the United States Public Health Service, with National Institute of Mental Health grants M-5681-01-02, and National Institute of Child Health and Human Development grants HD 00925-03-04.

This paper was prepared in 1966–67 while the author was Visiting Scholar in the University of London Institute of Education. He is grateful to the Institute for making their facilities available to him, and to Professors R. S. Peters and P. H. Hirst, in particular, for many stimulating discussions.

pologists with a significant intellectual instrument for the analysis of sophisticated social behavior and organization, so has the contrast between the child's knowledge and that of the adult's, as presented by the Genevans, provided a significant analytic instrument for the understanding of human cognition. One of the striking instances of this is provided by the study of conservation. The young child's conservation capacities stand in such contrast to those of the older child's and adult's that research investigations throughout the world have been stimulated into an attempt to elucidate their nature. The very considerable interest in the phenomenon, aside from its novelty and incongruity, is that it appears to offer some important possibilities for understanding the general character of cognition and cognitive development.

As a starting point, conservation may be said to involve the ability to retain one of a series of physical concepts in the face of the transformation of elements related to that concept. The "area" concept for example, to be conserved requires maintenance of the concept (i.e. area remains invariant) while a related attribute, the physical pattern, is transformed, although the total area itself remains the same. In direct response to reality, particularly where reality is a highly industrialized world with almost constant activity and change, the development of invariant concepts may have considerable adaptive significance. As Piaget implies (Piaget, 1952), a highly developed technology can evolve only with the ability to conserve since most rational thought is dependent upon it.

If it is granted that conservation represents the development of a conceptual phenomenon that is at least in some ways unique, it is an open question as to whether the processes by which it develops are unique or are those of general concept formation. Some of my own research relates to the nature of the processes required in conservation and will be reviewed here for its bearing upon cognitive development.

Experimental method in the study of conservation

Methodological problems have been recognized as a major difficulty for research on cognition. Piaget, for one, has been vigorously reproached for his research methods, but in one important sense, unfairly. The formal and empirical discoveries produced from his research are not likely to have been possible at this time without this particular style of data collection. The "clinical method" with its open-ended, pragmatic and exploratory quality superimposed upon an experimental attitude, permits the pursuit of suggestive and intriguing leads from the child's behavior. At the same time, it cannot be denied that the method has its limitations, particularly in the degree to which one may make causal inferences from data so obtained. The general lack of experimental control associated with the varying nature of interrogation, the method's asset as an exploratory device, is its greatest liability for making psychological generalizations. My own decision to use experimental methods where possible was based upon the desire to limit the use of language where such use could confound the study of other processes, as well as for the usual controls upon the operation of irrelevant variables. A further and equally important reason was the conviction that experimental methods do not of necessity preclude the use of exploratory methods. At the end of an experimental trial series, it is usually possible to include an interrogation that permits the collection of verbal (phenomenal) reports unless of course additional experimental tasks are to follow. One important difficulty with experimental methods, however, is that they do not always permit the development of adequate analogues to the "clinical" procedures. Conservation problems are an example in that there are ready analogues for some kinds of conservation but not others. An indirect analogue may also provide a different kind of information from one that is direct, principally because different processes may be tapped by such indirect methods. This is relevant to the present discussion, for in seeking an experimental analogue to area conservation we were at first surprised by results that were

strikingly different from those obtained with experimental analogues to length and number conservation. The differences, however, led us to examine more closely the processes involved in
conservation.

Area conservation

Piaget employed two methods for testing area conservation
(Piaget, Inhelder, & Szeminska, 1960). In one, the child was
shown two identical rectangular pieces of green cardboard,
which were described as "meadows." A wooden cow was placed
on each meadow. Houses of identical size and shape were then
placed one by one on each rectangle and set so that the house
arrangements were equivalent. The arrangement on one of the
meadows was then changed and the child was asked whether the
areas in each were still "the same" (i.e. whether the cow had
equal amounts of grass to eat in each meadow). The solution
was based in part upon subtracting smaller congruent areas
from larger congruent areas.

In a second method, one of two congruent areas was cut with
scissors and the severed part moved to another section of the
figure. The conserving child was identified as the one who
asserted that the areas were the same, even though the patterns
looked different as a result of the translocation of a part of the
figure.

Our analogue was developed for the second method (Beilin,
1964). For this purpose equipment, called the Visual Pattern
Board (VPB), was built consisting of two pieces of apparatus—a
display panel and a control box. The display panel contained a
milk white plexiglass screen laid off in a 12 x 12 matrix of 2 x 2
inch squares. The squares were separated by black adhesive
plastic. Behind each plexiglass square was a lamp and each of
the 144 lamps was connected through a cable to individual contacts in the control box. With the insertion of a prepatterned
template it was possible to program various patterns of lighted
squares against a field of unlighted squares. In this way one
could present in a reliable fashion either one or more patterns on

a single display panel or one could use two VPBs, as we have done in most of our studies. We have also found, in an unpublished study, that a printed pattern series offers a reasonably good approximation to results obtained with the VPB.

The experiments

EXPERIMENT I

In our first study (Beilin, 1964) we were interested in contrasting conservation performance with base-line judgments of the equality and inequality of area patterns. The usual conservation task, as already indicated, requires the judgment that equality of areas is maintained in the face of physical transformation. Conservation presupposes, however, that a child has an adequate concept of equality and inequality. If a child did not conserve, it would have to be shown that it was due to some feature other than lack of knowledge of equality and inequality (i.e. identity). To substantiate this assertion we tested the child with three stimulus series. In the *equality* series, he was shown two patterns equal in area whose configurations were the same (in 2 x 2 and 3 x 3 arrangements) as is shown in Figure 1. In another series, one which ultimately came to be known as the *quasi-conservation* series for reasons to be described, two patterns equal in area were also shown, but the match pattern had a different configuration from the standard. The areas were to be judged as equal even though the patterns were different. It was thus considered an analogue of the classic conservation task in that the concept of equality had to be achieved in the face of a stimulus array that was different in a related attribute. A third series of patterns represented area *inequality*, in that the match pattern was either one square larger or smaller than the standard. The areas appeared unequal and were unequal. The three stimulus sets, then, provided the child with the opportunity to judge the equality of two areas that appeared the same and were the same (equality), to judge another series that appeared different but were in fact the same (quasi-conservation), and still another

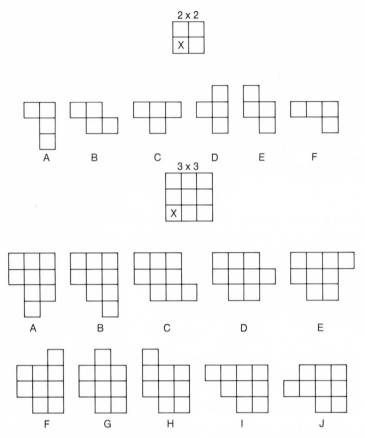

Figure 1　　Standard and match patterns for 2 x 2 and 3 x 3 groups. Square unit "X" of standard is systematically rotated around units on periphery to make each match pattern. Standard and match constitute a "pattern-pair." (From Beilin, 1964.)

series in which the pattern-pairs appeared different and were different (inequality).

The children studied ranged in age from a mean of 68.6 months to 116.6 months. There was one subsample of middle-class kindergarteners (N = 170), but the remainder (N = 146) were lower-class children distributed over the kindergarten through the fourth grade.

The data, as represented in Figure 2, show that for the equality and inequality judgments in the veridical condition (where areas were what they "appeared"), practically all of the children at the kindergarten age were correct when judging 2 x 2 patterns (93 percent). They were only slightly less successful with the more difficult 3 x 3 patterns, and there was less success with the equality (77 percent) than the inequality concept (88 percent). Compared with these, the quasi-conservation judgments were most difficult to make. Very few kindergarten subjects (3.5 percent) could respond correctly on all trials in a series. By the

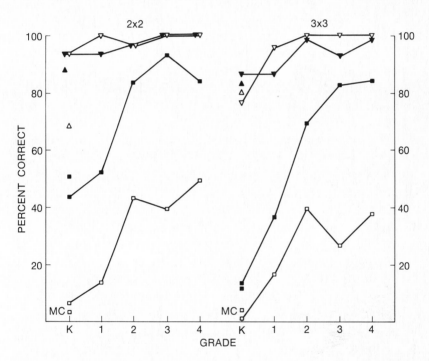

Figure 2   Percentage of lower-class children giving wholly correct equality (▽) inequality (▼), categorical (■), and quasi-conservation (□) responses by grade and by free-standing symbols. (From Beilin, 1964.)

fourth grade only 50 percent succeeded with the 2 x 2 patterns and only 38 percent with the 3 x 3 patterns. The difficulty, then, in making quasi-conservation judgments was not based upon an inability to understand the concepts of equality or inequality, or their associated verbal labels.

Judgments were also sought within the *inequality* series as to whether a match pattern was larger or smaller than the standard. In this instance there was considerably more confusion than with the equality and inequality judgments themselves. Subjects responding correctly on 3 x 3 patterns ranged from 11 percent at the kindergarten level to 85 percent at the fourth grade level. Although substantial numbers of subjects could judge inequality correctly they could not judge the direction of the inequality. This was a function either of a lack of knowledge of the class characteristics of the terms "larger" and "smaller," or a confusion in labelling, i.e. in assigning the correct verbal label to the judgment of the relation. It is unlikely that either of these alternatives is influencing the quasi-conservation judgments, however, as is indicated by the disparity in the number of subjects who respond correctly in each condition.

Where the subjects seriously fail, then, is in the condition of equality where the appearance of the patterns ostensibly suggests inequality. These results support the Piaget findings in demonstrating age differences in the development of an invariant concept and provide evidence that this development is not a function of the lack of knowledge of the concepts of equality and inequality nor a lack of understanding of the verbal terms with which these concepts are identified. There is an important way, however, in which these data differ from those of Piaget. Performance is not as good as one would predict from the Piaget norms. Even though these results are in the main from a lower-class sample, the proportion of subjects who succeed in the task is far lower than obtained by other investigators measuring conservation in lower-class children, even with the "easiest" type of conservation (Almy, et al., 1966). In Almy's study, for example, 47 percent of a *second* grade sample of lower class children performed successfully with a number conservation task; by contrast, only 48 percent of our *fourth* grade class was successful.

An analysis of this invariance task gives a clue as to why the performance differed so. In the traditional conservation task two areas that are at first congruent, both in outline and area, are judged by the child, and then one of the pattern arrangements is changed in full view of the subject. In our task the judged areas are static. The difference between the classic conservation task and ours, which for the sake of differentiation we call a quasi-conservation task, is in the role of the stimulus transformation. It seems reasonable to expect that pattern transformation would create difficulty for the child since it introduces a change in appearance that may be confusing in relation to the judgment required. The fact is that, in contrast to the quasi-conservation or static condition, transformation in the classic conservation case appears to be facilitating judgment of equality. If transformation functions in this manner, its nature is still far from clear. To determine the source of the inhibited performance in the quasi-conservation task and acquire some understanding of the role of transformation we undertook a further study.

In the first investigation (Beilin, 1964), it was inferred that for the subject to arrive at a correct judgment of area equality it was necessary for him to achieve such a judgment from an infralogical analysis of the stimulus data. Taking a cue from the Piaget description of the relevant processes in qualitative area measurement, it was proposed that in the quasi-conservation task, with the stimulus materials as we presented them, equality could be judged by using either an "iterative" or "translocative" method (a variant of the method of superposition). With iteration the subject utilizes a count of the boxes in the respective patterns, and says in effect, "The number of boxes here is 'x,' and the number of boxes here is 'x,' therefore they are equal." This method presupposes that the size of the boxes is understood to be the same. Even more primitively, the child need not count but can achieve the same understanding by a one-to-one correspondence method, matching box for box. This is a somewhat easy method when there are four boxes, it is less easy when there are nine. The second method, the translocative, involves the inference of area equality from the recognition that if one of the boxes were moved to another location the patterns would appear equal. The utilization of these strategies requires an "active" subject, one who has reason to invoke them. Considering for the moment only the older subjects of the first study, we assumed that the majority of those who failed the quasi-conservation task did so in spite of having the infralogical strategies or methods of solution available to them, but for some reason not using them. This assumption was based on the data of other investigators and ourselves on the success of younger children in conservation and in tasks of qualitative measurement (Beilin & Franklin, 1962). We assumed further that the quasi-conservation task by its nature would not lead to evoking these strategies, even when the experimenter asked a direct question concerning the equality of the figures. Instead, some kind of "suspiciousness" or special attention was necessary in the subject to trigger these methods of analysis.

EXPERIMENT II

The second study (Beilin, 1966) was designed as a training experiment to test these assertions. One experimental variable was introduced to test the possibility that the ability to respond adequately in the quasi-conservation task was due to the lack of attention to relevant features of the stimulus, and to a too-ready acceptance of an inference based upon incomplete or incorrect information. This method used a feedback procedure in which the subject was given information of the correctness or incorrectness of his response. It was hypothesized that notification of an incorrect judgment would lead the subject to "question" his own inference of area inequality ostensibly made on the basis of a perceived difference in pattern arrangements. Further, he would be led to use an infralogical strategy already available to him and thus be led to produce a correct judgment of area equality.

An alternative training approach was based upon the supposition that the lack of ability to judge correctly was due to the Ss' lack of available solution strategies. Since the only solution strategies shown to be used in the first study were the iterative and translocative, we included related training procedures in the second experiment. The principal iterative training method (there were two) utilized two patterns made of flat masonite blocks that were placed before the child in each trial. He was asked to count the number of blocks in each pattern but was not asked whether the patterns were equal. For the translocative training method, two patterns were also set before the child, and he was instructed to make his pattern look like the *E*'s by moving only one block in the pattern.

The *S*s of this study were mainly lower-middle-class first and second grade children (N = 118 in each grade). The study utilized a pretest-training-posttest design, and the only subjects trained were those who did not reach the criterion for successful pretest performance.

The results were clear-cut. Only one posttest group had a significantly greater number of conservers than the control. This was the feedback group, where 19 of 33 subjects met the conservation criterion after training, whereas only four of the control group of 33 subjects reached the same criterion. This study also showed that 97 percent of the subjects who gave a classifiable verbal report used either an iterative or translocative strategy. In this study, where only 3 x 3 patterns were used the proportion of translocaters to iterators was about two to one. In the first study, when 2 x 2 patterns were used the preferred strategy was iterative and with 3 x 3 patterns the preferred solution strategy was translocative. In the second study, there was a significant grade (age) effect, with a larger number of conserving subjects in the second grade than the first.

The results of this experiment confirmed that the basis for improved performance was not that the subjects in some way had acquired a set of strategies previously unavailable to them, but suggested rather that when confronted with the incorrectness of their prior inferences, *S*s began a covert search for the appropriate strategy to deal with the perceived stimuli. The strategy utilized from among the available alternatives was not haphazard, either. It was achieved with some efficiency in that the apparently easier way of processing the data was utilized. With the more complex (3 x 3) stimuli the translocative method was easier for the child than the iterative method. (We have informally observed that adults perform the same way in this procedure.) With 2 x 2 patterns, on the other hand, where it is easier to count, the method of choice is the iterative. This parsimony in strategy choice is an instance of *cognitive efficiency* and is akin to a principle of least effort.

It would seem further that utilizing an appropriate strategy is not one in which appropriate ways of analyzing or integrating data are automatically employed. An intervening attention or orientation process is necessary, although attention or orientation alone does not seem to be sufficient for correct judgment either. An additional feature, a quality of "suspiciousness" is needed to induce the type of analysis evident in the second experiment. This process may be identified as *analytic-orientation* and distinguished from other nonanalytic types of set.*

Before considering what these data suggest for an understanding of the process of conservation there were two questions which suggested further investigation.

Is quasi-conservation confined to area invariance or is it associated with other physical attributes? Second, what is the relation of conservation to quasi-conservation performance in the same subjects? It was necessary to ask this since our prior data on conservation and quasi-conservation came from independent groups. To satisfy ourselves on both points a third study was designed to answer both questions.†

EXPERIMENT III

A technique for the measurement of *number* quasi-conservation was available from a study in which the distinction between classic conservation and quasi-conservation was not made (Zimiles, 1966). The basic procedure involved the presentation of two rows of counters, identified as "dots," that were fixed against a background of a different color (i.e. white counters against a blue background). The S was required to judge whether the rows were the same in number. There were three experimental series. One consisted of five stimulus cards. On each card there was an unequal number in each row and the counters were spaced so that the rows were also unequal in

---

* Although analytic-orientation may be related to other kinds of expectancy (Gibson, 1941), its distinctive feature is that it is followed by an appropriate problem solving or reasoning process. Its operation has the implicit logic of the statement "appearance may be deceiving."

† Mr. Edwin Cooperman and Mrs. Marilyn Pelz Cooperman carried out this research while participating in a graduate seminar at Brooklyn College.

length, as judged from the beginning to terminal counter. Another five-card set consisted of cards in which there was an *unequal* number of counters in each row, but the beginning and terminal counters were aligned so that the lengths they covered were equal. Zimiles refers to this type of series as a test of the "conservation of inequalities." The *quasi-conservation* test series utilized ten cards in which the two rows of counters were numerically *equal,* but one row was extended relative to the other so that they covered unequal lengths on the card. The question asked the subject in each trial was whether the two rows had the same or a different number of white "dots." The subject was informed after each response as to whether he was correct in his judgment. Prior to the experiment, subjects were tested to determine whether they could count to a number equal to the maximum number of counters used in the test as well as for their ability to respond reliably to questions concerning inequality and equality of number in displays of red chips placed before them.

The number *conservation* task in this study was one used in another investigation (Beilin, 1965). The apparatus held three rows of red-topped corks. The center row was secured to a stretching and contracting frame so that the corks could be made to align or misalign with the rows of corks on either side of it. There were two parts to a trial. In the first part, the corks in the center row (e.g. 6) were aligned with the corks in the row to which it was equal in number (i.e. also 6). In aligning it so, it was at the same time unequal in number and not aligned with the corks in the row on the other side of it (e.g. 4). The subject was instructed to identify the row that was "like" the middle one by pressing a buzzer-activating-button next to that row. After this was done, the center apparatus was then adjusted so that the center row became equal in length to the decoy row (i.e. the one with 4 corks). The subject was again asked to indicate which row was "like" the center row. If he chose the "6" row, the choice was presumed to be based upon the use of a number concept. If the "4" row was chosen it was presumed to be based upon the perceptual alignment of the rows or some other non-relevant hypothesis. On the first trial the subject learned from the buzzer reinforcement whether his basis for choice was correct. A child who chose incorrectly because he did not equate "like" with "in respect to number" could then switch to the correct base. A conserver was one who, after the transformation from the first part of the trial to the second, consistently chose on the basis of number.

In the study each subject was tested for conservation and quasi-conservation ability in both number and area tasks. The results confirmed that the conservation tasks were performed more successfully than the quasi-conservation tasks. Of 80 subjects, 26 met criterion (eight of ten trials correct) in the number conservation task, 7 in the number quasi-conservation task. On the other hand, of the same 80 subjects, 18 met criterion for the area conservation task, whereas only 13 did in the area quasi-conservation task. The relative difficulty of quasi-conservation is seen further from the number tasks for which 16 subjects passed the conservation but failed the quasi-conservation task; 2 did the reverse. On area, 9 subjects passed the conservation but failed the quasi-conservation task, while 5 did the reverse. The number of subjects who passed both area and number tasks in the quasi-conservation series was 4, whereas 15 passed both in the conservation series. There were only 2 subjects of the entire sample of 80 kindergarteners who passed all four tasks. There is, then, much greater convergence in performance on the conservation than the quasi-conservation tasks. Transformation in the classic conservation task not only leads to better performance (i.e. more correct identity judgments) but also provides impetus to invoking the kinds of strategies that overcome the difficulties represented by the different class properties of area and number.

One issue in regard to which we may offer some data may be dealt with parenthetically, namely, the relationship of number quasi-conservation to what Zimiles refers to as the "conservation of inequalities." If the latter capacity is a conservation phenomenon as Zimiles implies, it should bear a close relationship to quasi-conservation performance as we have tested it—*quasi-conservation* rather than *conservation* performance, because the Zimiles "conservation pictures" contains items in which no transformation is made.

For number judgment in the classic *inequality* case, the number of counters in one row is compared with another which has a larger or smaller number, and is laid out so that it appears longer or shorter than the standard row. By contrast, in the "conservation of inequality" case the rows are unequal in number but are laid out so that the beginning and terminal counters were aligned and the internal counters equidistantly spaced. Quasi-conservation of number is tested in the manner we described for the third study.

In the study we are reporting there were five "classic inequality" trials and five "conservation of inequality" trials. The pass criterion in each case was four out of five correct. The data show that "conservation of inequality" performance is at a point between meeting criterion for classic inequality and that for quasi-conservation. Twenty of 80 Ss tested who passed the classic inequality items failed the other two. Another 20 passed the classic inequality plus the conservation inequality but failed the quasi-conservation task, and 11 passed all three tasks, while 21 failed all. Looked at another way, 51 subjects passed the base classic inequality items; 31 passed conservation of inequality as well as the classic inequality items, and 11 subjects passed all three tasks. This clear progression suggests three levels of difficulty, which may reflect the function of three different processes. The conservation of inequality task is apparently more easy than the quasi-conservation task and more difficult than the classic inequality. That conservation of inequality should be more difficult than classic inequality is obvious, but why it should be easier to solve than the quasi-conservation task is not readily apparent, if as a "conservation" task the same type of operations are necessary. It would be of interest to know whether the same relationship holds for classic conservation tasks where the transformations are made by the experimenter or the subject himself.

EXPERIMENT IV

It was an assumption of the second experiment that feedback training did not initiate new learning—that it only led to the use of problem solving strategies already in the child's repertoire. To ensure that feedback did not lead to the creation of new schemata a further experiment was devised in which the training procedures of the second study were used with a younger sample, a smaller percentage of whom could be presumed to have the appropriate measurement strategies in their repertoires.*

A pretest-training-posttest design was again used with 60 kindergarten children in a middle-class school. There were three training groups and a control. The training groups, identified by treatment procedure, were feedback, translocation, and translocation plus feedback groups. The control received an additional repetition of the pretest. The feedback and translocation procedures were the same as in the prior study. The translocation plus feedback group was a new one to test whether the addition of methods would produce a substantial improvement in performance. The criterion for conservation performance was 8 of 10 quasi-conservation trials, and 8 of 10 inequality trials correct. The results indicated that from pretest to posttest only two kindergarten subjects became conservers, one in the feedback group and one in the feedback plus translocation group. Where the number of correct trials are considered, irrespective of whether the criterion was reached, there was a significant change only in the feedback group (pretest $\overline{X} = .60$, posttest $\overline{X} = 2.80$, $p < .05$). In spite of this increase in correct *equality* responses there was a significant *decrease* in the *inequality* responses for the feedback group. To be certain that the poorer inequality performance after feedback training was not peculiar to this experiment, the relevant data of the second experiment were analyzed and the same result was obtained. For the second grade subjects the decrease in mean was significant ($p < .05$); at the first grade level p was $< .10$. What these data suggest is that feedback creates a state of response disorganization for some subjects. For these subjects, two possiblities exist. Either, the disorganization due to feedback leads to the utilization of another more appropriate strategy, or it leads to disorganization that is nonadaptive with resulting increased random response. Random response led

* Mr. Steven Rubin carried out this research while participating in a graduate seminar at Brooklyn College.

to a reduction in accuracy in inequality judgments, which before feedback were judged substantially correctly; at the same time it led to a slight improvement in equality (conservation) judgments, which prior to that were judged substantially incorrectly. In older children, random response following feedback is more likely to be superseded by the use of logical strategies and thus to successful performance in both the quasi-conservation and inequality tasks. In younger kindergarteners, who apparently do not have the strategies available to them, feedback leads to disorganization rather than to the adaptive use of infralogical analysis. The reason strategy training does not lead to improved performance with the younger subjects may be due to a limitation in the method of training or to maturational and experiential limitations of the subjects.

That infralogical strategies are used to achieve correct quasi-conservation performance gets confirmation from the S's verbal reports. Practically all older children who were conservers were able to verbalize the use of a strategy. A further finding, seen also in the prior experiment, was that a number of subjects (four on pretest, eight on posttest) reported the use of an iterative or translocative strategy but were unable to use it successfully in actual performance. Other research (Beilin, 1965) has shown that although verbal rule-instruction methods may lead to superior conservation performance than is achieved through the use of nonverbal and nonrule training methods, the presence of a verbal rule whether generated spontaneously by the subject or provided to him through an experimental procedure will not ensure correct conservation performance. Some other "elements," in addition to strategy or infralogical operation availability, are apparently necessary for conservation. The now extensive literature on training and instruction in conservation has not led to a clear identification of what these elements or processes may be.

Conservation and quasi-conservation

Piaget makes the sweeping assertion that conservation is a necessary condition for all rational activity. The origin of conservation abilities was previously related by Piaget to the (primitive) per-

ceptual schema of the permanent object. A recent statement
(Piaget, 1968) which summarizes new work on the development
of identity and also serves to refute Bruner's (1966) position vis-
à-vis the place of identity in conservation, modifies this view.
The new view is that the schema of the permanent object is
associated not with conservation but with identity. It is seen as
an instance of the dissociation of permanent from variable
qualities. He describes further a developmental sequence for
knowledge of identity in which preoperative identity, which
deals with single *qualitative* invariants, yields to an intermediate
stage, which in turn evolves into operative identity. Operative
identity is the only kind of identity that acts in conjunction with
the operations of conservation. Piaget still holds that reversible
operations represent the key elements in conservation. Conservation is achievable only through "reversibility by inversion" (a
return to the original condition) or "reversibility by reciprocity
or compensation."

Since conservation by *definition* for Piaget involves *quantitative* invariants, conservation is not possible without a composition of certain transpositions (i.e. quantitative variations that
take the form of compensations of relations (higher x thinner =
the same amount), or of an additive composition (nothing
added, nothing taken away = the same amount). Preoperative
identity, on the other hand, involves single *qualitative* invariants
without quantitative composition. The child, for example, recognizes that the water remains the same (i.e. is the same water)
when poured from one vessel to another but he does not know
that the quantity of the water has not changed. Piaget criticizes
Bruner's (1966) experiment for not employing the proper controls to demonstrate this. The emphasis in Piaget's view of
conservation, as indicated in this exposition, is on the role of
infralogical and prelogical operations. In accounting for the
maintenance of a quantitative invariant in the face of object
transformation, the psychological problem, in Piaget's view, is
one of identifying the processes by which the concept is
achieved and maintained, particularly when such concepts are
ultimately associated with identity.

There is a related philosophic problem in establishing the

logical meaning of identity. In conservation studies the assumption is usually made, often as a starting point, that the child is capable of "knowing" the nature of an identity. This is usually tested by having him report that two objects which "appear" the same "are" the same. These responses are made as a rule to questions about the "amount" of clay, the "number" of dolls, or the "lengths" of string. Since conservation involves the maintenance of an identity concept, it is implied that the child must have the concept prior to being able to maintain it under specifiable conditions. Logically, to assert an identity means that one can state the proposition "if and only if 'p,' then 'p' " (the law of identity). Such a statement is predicated upon a clear delineation of the category "p." Assume that "p" is "area," then establishing the truth of the statement that two areas are identical or that one area is identical to itself requires that one is able to delineate the defining properties of the term "area." * If, on the other hand, one were referring to "this object" rather than "this area," the definition could be more primitive. An ostensive definition achieved through "pointing" to the object could be sufficient, since it could be reasonably assumed that the connection between the operation of pointing and the reference term would be understood by everyone.

When one is dealing with a conceptual term such as "area" or "number" an ostensive definition is not sufficient. Unless we are treating area as "this object" the difficulty in defining area in logical terms may not be any more simple than that in defining number. Recall the historical difficulty in defining number, a difficulty that Piaget at least holds was not solved by Russell, who defined it in set or class terms independent of the notion of order or position and predicated it upon the use of a one-to-one correspondence method of measurement. The fact that Piaget argues that the Russell definition of number is not logically adequate only points up the complexity of knowing how to establish logical identities, particularly when the identity is other than that of an object to itself. To make logical statements of

---

* I am not implying, of course, that the child has to be able to state these propositions.

identity requires a lexicon of conceptual terms such as "number," "area," or "object" and a syntax for relating these terms. When the terms used in logical statements are those of a common language many difficulties are likely to arise from ambiguities acquired through extensive usage. This is the case with the terms "identical" and "same" when dealt with as common language terms. In the common language "identical" is equated with "same." The use of both terms is primarily adjectival. They are usually used in relation to the attributes or properties of things and states, so that we may properly say, "they are the same amount," or "the same length," or "the same in length" with the implication that "amount" and "length" are also definable in common language terms. Even in the common language, however, these terms are of a different type from those represented by such statements as "this is the same object that I saw before," or "this is the same object he is talking about."

Although the question of whether one can make reference to an object without referring to its properties is a difficult one, it would still appear that both in common language and in logical terms one can make a distinction between the conceptual use of "identical" and "same," and a more primitive notion of these. While the distinction is being made between primitive identity and identity related to the use of abstract conceptual terms there is an intermediate sense in which identity is intimately associated with the definition of "concept" itself. The notion of identity is implicit in the definition of the term concept, since having or forming a concept is predicated upon the recognition that all members of the class or category to which the concept refers are identical in regard to the attribute that defines the class and nonidentical with those outside the class.

The psychological events parallel those of logic and common-sense. As a start, one may ask in common-sense fashion, "When are things said to be the same?" and reply that people tend to say they are the same when, first, they appear to be the same. This is not taken as an adequate criterion since it is sometimes recognized that things appear to be the same when they are not, as in the case of illusions. Things are also said to be the same from one time to another when nothing has apparently been added or taken away from an object or situation. This is not an infallible criterion either, as is clear from the example of dough used in baking bread which may change ("rise") although nothing has been added or taken away from the dough. Finally, things are said to be the same when people agree they are the same. Here the object or its character is compared with a common standard held by different persons. This use is characteristic of those conditions where judgments are esthetic or attitudinal and where precise definition is not possible, but where the introduction of "merely" counting or using another common standard may sometimes be of help in making a judgment. In connection with these common-sense definitions of identical and same, the psychological question is one of determining what processes make such judgments possible in conditions when "it appears so," "when nothing is added or taken away," and when one, for example, "merely" counts. As already noted, Piaget's evidence supports the view that two processes make it possible for a child to maintain quantitative invariants, or to put it another way, to make the inference of identity. These operations are "reversibility by inversion" and "reversibility by reciprocity of compensation," the latter requiring a process of logical multiplication.

The difficulty in being able to conserve is related to one of the common-sense criteria for establishing an identity. The tendency to ascribe identity on the basis of things "appearing the same" leads to difficulty because one attribute, usually a visually salient one, does not appear the same (and in fact is not) when the object is transformed. In the condition to which conservation refers, one attribute is transformed and the other is not. The one that is changed is related to some obvious physical property (i.e. form, location). The attribute that is invariant is usually a conceptual attribute (mass, volume, number) and a higher order concept than the dimensional attribute that undergoes change (e.g. length, width). Although the dimensions that undergo change are also identifiably conceptual, they have a perceptual component which is "immediately" experienced. The judgment of identity of the conceptual attribute that is conserved, however, must be *inferred* from more primitive data. Although there is a primitive perceptual identity associated with the constancy of the object, this concept of identity is not of the same type or order as the inferred identity associated with the conceptual attribute, and it is to this latter class that Piaget's conservation ability refers. While it may be easy for a child to respond to the perceptually changing attribute, he may be quite incapable at the same time of responding to the conceptual identity. The difficulty in conservation is the difficulty in thinking at the level of these abstract concepts and employing inference or concept forming processes related to them. In Piaget's terms it would be related to the ability to employ the appropriate reversible operations.

On logical grounds alone, then, with conservation defined in conceptual terms, a perceptually based identity could not be the only necessary condition to conceptual invariance. Although it is Piaget's contention that the ability to arrive at the conservation inference is possible only through the utilization of reversibility and logical multiplication operations, Bruner and his associates (Bruner et al., 1966), have attempted to demonstrate that it is possible to maintain an identity concept through shielding the changing dimension and forcing attention on the unvarying nature of the object itself. What the child arrives at, however, is what Piaget and others refer to as pseudo-conservation, an identity mantenance that is not based upon a conceptual inference but on a more primitive concept. For some learning-experiment subjects this pseudoconcept may be the basis for invoking the processes that lead to conceptual invariance, but for others, particularly younger subjects, proper transfer or time delay methods would expose the responses as pseudoconcepts. In a criticism of the Bruner-Frank experiment (Bruner, 1966), Piaget points out that simply asking the child to pour "the same amount of water" into both a *wide* and a *narrow* glass would demonstrate the child's inability to conserve. The reason the Bruner-Frank shielding method works is that it enables the child to utilize commonsense criteria for "same" judgments. The shielded volume does not appear any different, and additionally, the nothing-added, nothing-substracted notion can also be brought to bear. It is also possible to induce conservation in an analogous fashion, by teaching children a verbal rule for conservation as we have done (Beilin, 1965). In this instance the child has a model, an algorithm in effect, for solving a conservation problem. There is little assurance, however, that the achievements made through the use of such algorithmic (or screening) methods are conceptual in nature or require the use of an appropriate inference-generating system.

In fact, the evidence seems to suggest they are not, except for a minority of subjects. A number of investigators have attempted to test whether the infralogical inference-producing processes, such as compensatory and inversion reversibility are necessary for conservation. Without an extensive review of these studies here, one could reasonably claim that the results, as they point to the necessity of the two Piaget schemata, are equivocal. Neither compensatory training nor reversibility training invariably leads to conservation (although the latter, in some studies, seems to be more efficacious). Training through verbal procedures embodying rules which directly embody neither reversibility nor compensation, but only the common-sense criteria mentioned above, may also lead to conservation (Beilin, 1965), but it is questionable whether what is achieved is true conservation.

What we hold, in essence then, is that the problem in conservation is not with the "identity concept" but with conceptually represented physical attributes which entail identity. The difficulty for the child is one associated with the lack of appropriate inference-generating equipment necessary to making appropriate infralogical judgments.

The experimental data presented in this paper have relevance to the sufficiency of conservation operations and the role of certain situational elements. Transformation is obviously an integral part of what is meant by conservation. The function of transformation has previously been given little attention, however. Since concept invariance must occur "in the face of" object transformation, there has been a tendency to interpret transformation as an impediment to invariance. In one sense this is true, for without the transformation's being carried out it would not be possible to differentiate those who can from those who cannot conserve. Involving transformation in the maintenance of a conceptual identity extends the psychological meaning of such invariance concepts, however. It implies that truly having such a concept entails the ability to maintain it in the face of conditions that suggest a lack of the concept. Some concepts may logically entail this condition, but it is not clear that all do. "Number" is an example where it may, if one accepts the Russell interpretation of the logical status of the number concept. With number (as a class or set) based upon a one-to-one correspondence method, and the assumption explicitly made that the order or transformation of the elements of the set is of necessity irrelevant, then, the concept of number must be maintained even with relocation of the elements in the set. Piaget, of course, disputes this type of definition. Irrespective of the merits of his case, the possibility exists that the logical definition of the concept entails maintenance in spite of transformation of the elements. Whether other conceptual terms such as area and mass have the same entailment is not entirely clear but on superficial examination it seems that they would (i.e. since any area is equal to more than one multiplication of length and width). If the logical status of these concepts entails maintenance irrespective of change, then conservation statements are redundant. If the nature of these concepts has not been conceived in this way in the past, Piaget's introduction of the conservation problem certainly provides them with the basis for such a status and also extends the psychological definition of these concepts.

In any case, the transformation, while it creates a problem for the child, at the same time may do two positive things: it can provide information necessary to maintaining identity, and it can alert the child to the nature of the information. The data reviewed here suggest that the information feature of transformation is not crucial. What happens may be described as follows: The child ostensibly has (or is capable of achieving) a notion of identity, at least a primitive one associated with the constancy of the object, and thus is able to recognize two objects as the same when they appear the same. When one of the objects is transformed, however, the child may again in a primitive way see that the objects no longer appear the same. The first and simplest inference he can make is that the two objects are no longer identical (or that the object transformed is no longer identical to the one he saw before), and he would be right since they are no longer identical in appearance. If the child is asked, "Are they the same?" the question is ambiguous since "the same" can apply to both the attribute changed and the attribute that has not changed.

When we specify the conceptual attribute (for example, area) either by labeling it or through a reinforcement procedure which provides equivalent information (as is done in Beilin, 1965), then the child is forced to attend to the conceptual attribute. To make a judgment of identity in these circumstances requires some kind of cognitive "apparatus" to permit this induction. Leaving aside the specifications of this apparatus, it is clear from the data that mere possession of it is not sufficient to ensure that a conservation judgment will be made. Some kind of triggering or initiating mechanism is necessary to set these operations into motion. To account for our data we posit the existence of an analytic-set that activates the individual's cognitive apparatus and permits him to analyze the information inhering in the stimulus events. This set keeps the individual on the alert for particular kinds of information, and permits the stimulus transformation to activate solution strategies (or schemata) already available to the child.

Invoking these solution strategies makes it possible for the child to produce two inferences, one related to the attribute that changes, one to the attribute that is invariant. The character of the question asked the child determines which of the attributes is "chosen." If the relevant solution strategies are available to a child, then it is highly likely that the conserving response can be experimentally produced through activating these processes. In the case of area quasi-conservation, where a translocative or iterative strategy is in the child's repertoire, triggering can be achieved through the use of a feedback procedure that makes clear to the subject the inadequacy of his common-sense non-identity inference. Achieving the identity concept is possible also, as previously indicated, by the Bruner-Frank shielding procedure.

If, however, the child has no schemata or solution strategies to invoke, when the distracting elements are once again made evident, the judgment falters, as is the case with the Bruner-Frank four-year-old Ss and even with a number of older ones. When feedback was administered to younger children in the quasi-conservation task, no increase in conservation was evident either, supporting the conclusion that an analytic-set is in itself not sufficient for conservation and that some inference-generating procedure is required. That a number of Ss in our studies were able to show through their verbalizations that these inference strategies were available to them and yet were unable to succeed in their use suggests that verbal strategies in themselves are not sufficient for conservation. It was shown further that even combined analytic-set and strategy training in young children was not sufficient to induce conversation performance. If this latter finding is sufficiently reliable then we must recognize that the apparently "simple" conservation phenomenon is still far from being completely accounted for without recourse to explanations of genetic programing.

The role of transformation in the studies reviewed here requires differentiation of two significant aspects of transformation, stimulus transformation and cognitive transformation. Although the child in natural learning situations comes to respond to a variety of stimulus transformations that create conservation problems for him, he may or may not use the stimulus transformation as a cue for ideational transformation, that is, perform a backward or reverse transformation of the stimulus to the original state or use the transformation as the cue for logical multiplication. The quasi-conservation experiments suggest that there may be a variety of real-life situations in which no stimulus transformation occurs but where, analogous to the classic invariance case, an identity concept must be achieved even though the appearance of stimulus elements suggest nonidentity.

Such is the case where two patterns (i.e. areas or number arrays) appear different with respect to one of their attributes. The form or pattern of the array differs while, at the same time, they are identical in a conceptual attribute. A potential response conflict exists involving the choice between an inference of "different" (nonidentity), and that of "same" (identity) in a manner analogous to the classic invariance task. In this static condition one cannot ask how the stimulus "might have been" since it never "was." No recourse to reversibility is possible, but an analogous process does exist, that of "forward transformation" in which the patterns can be ideationally rearranged in anticipation of an actual or hypothetical rearrangement.

Forward transformation is a more significant type of transformation than reverse transformation since it is the basis of many kinds of problem solving. It is apparently more difficult to initiate, however, than backward or reverse transformation. Carrying out the forward transformation in the quasi-conservation problem becomes the basis for generating an identity inference. The forward transformation inevitably means involving a compensation procedure with the dimensions of length and width and so the transformation is inextricably involved with logical multiplication. In our experimental procedure the dimensions were made discontinuous as a result of partitioning of stimulus patterns. The partitioning led to the possibility of using a more primitive counting procedure as the basis for making an inference of identity, a situation that did not exist in continuous area conservation. As was seen, however, when the number of "boxes" became large for the child, as in the 3 x 3 patterns, he moved to the use of the translocational procedure if such a strategy were available to him.

Successful response in the quasi-conservation task is much more difficult than in the classic conservation task. The difference, as we have suggested, highlights the role of the analytic-set which triggers an internal transformation process that gives rise to some kind of conflict among inferences. No conflict exists on the stimulus side of the equation per se. Conflict results only from the subject's disposition to analyze the data of his experience in such a way as to generate inferences which are in conflict because of their logical incompatibility (i.e. "the objects cannot be both identical and nonidentical at the same time").

In regard to the analytic-set, it is more reasonable to assert that the child must first be able to recognize the possibility of a problem than that the child thinks only in response to problems. To avoid the obvious difficulty of an infinite regress (in explaining the analytic-set only on the basis of having encountered prior problems, and so on) one need only posit that the child learns certain logical rules prior to encountering problems or learns such rules in response to problems that are programmed for him by adults. The rule that two objects cannot be both same and different at the same time with regard to a single property would seem to require such learning. The likelihood of a child's achieving such an insight solely through his own actions in relation to objects seems slight. It is much more likely that they are learned through adult intervention. At the same time it must be granted that adult provision of verbal rules is not always as successful as learning rules by other means. An example is provided in a study of children's inferences about water levels (reflecting an understanding of horizontality and gravity) in which incorrect performance was more easily corrected by a confrontation with visual reality than by a verbal statement of the water level principle (Beilin, Kagan, & Rabinowitz, 1966). This suggests that verbal rule learning is not necessarily the only basis for acquiring appropriate analytic-sets. In this experiment, however, learning the rule was achieved through a type of adult programming, and there is no assurance that a similar achievement would occur spontaneously in a child's experience.

The quasi-conservation task, then, is one in which greater self-initiated cognitive activity is required than in classic conservation. In both classic conservation and quasi-conservation tasks it is clear that the nature of the stimulus, whether static or transformed, is not in itself sufficient to lead to correct inferences concerning the stimulus.

In general, there are two kinds of conservation conditions with which the child may have need to cope. The classic conservation condition is one in which there is an active stimulus transformation carried out by others or by the child himself which is identified as constituting a class of events leading to dynamic object invariance or *transformational invariance,* and another class of events in which an identity judgment is required in the face of stimulus conditions which support nonidentity and where the stimuli are in a static condition. This latter class may be identified as static object invariance or *fixed state invariance.*

References

Almy, Millie, Chittenden, E., & Miller, Paula. *Young children's thinking.* New York: Teachers College Press, 1966.

Beilin, H. Perceptual-cognitive conflict in the development of an invariant area concept. *J. exp. Child Psychol.,* 1964, **1,** 208–226.

Beilin, H. Learning and operational convergence in logical thought development. *J. exp. Child Psychol.,* 1965, **2,** 317–339.

Beilin, H. Feedback and infralogical strategies in invariant area conceptualization. *J. exp. Child Psychol.,* 1966, **3,** 267–278.

Beilin, H., & Franklin, I. C. Logical operations in area and length measurement. *Child Developm.,* 1962, **33,** 607–618.

Beilin, H., Kagan, J., & Rabinowitz, R. Effects of verbal and perceptual training on water level representation. *Child Developm.,* 1966, **37,** 317–329.

Bruner, J. S. On the conservation of liquids. In J. S. Bruner, Rose R. Olver & Patricia M. Greenfield (Eds.), *Studies in cognitive growth.* New York: Wiley, 1966. Pp. 183–207.

Gibson, J. J. A critical review of the concept of set. *Psychol. Bull.,* 1941, **38,** 781–817.

Piaget, J. *The child's conception of number.* London: Routledge and Kegan Paul, 1952.

Piaget, J. *On the development of memory and identity.* Worcester, Mass.: Clark Univ. Press, 1968.

Piaget, J., Inhelder, Bärbel, & Szeminska, Alina. *The child's conception of geometry.* London: Routledge and Kegan Paul, 1960.

Zimiles, H. The development of conservation and differentiation of number. *Monogr. Soc. Res. Child Developm.,* 1966, **31,** No. 6.

Problems in Research on
Culture and Thought

JACQUELINE J. GOODNOW

When we consider intellectual growth or style in different cultures, we are confronted by three requirements. We need to obtain, by combining results from several studies, some picture of skills common to people from many backgrounds, as well as skills that differentiate among them. At the same time, we need to find the features of milieu that may account for the similarities and differences in skills. And finally, the thorniest requirement of all, we have to ask as we transpose a task from one culture to another, whether the same answer means the same thing in both worlds.

For each of these requirements there is interesting new material, some of it in recent milieu studies, and some of it in studies

I take this opportunity to express again my appreciation of several stimulating discussions with Bärbel Inhelder, Magali Bovet, and Mimi Sinclair, discussions often marked on my part by surprise and on theirs by a warm-hearted tolerance for the things I might have known but did not. They are not responsible for any remaining errors in my grasp of Piaget's position. To Magali Bovet, in particular, I am indebted for many prepublication details of her continuing work with Algerian children, and for an especially happy exchange of ideas about milieu effects. All references to her work are based on this personal communication.

of how the child arrives at various answers on Piagetian tasks, regardless of milieu. I should like to draw some of this material together and to show that for each requirement the work of Piaget and his colleagues is invaluable, both directly and as a powerful source of ideas, extending and challenging our knowledge of how we come to think as we do.

We may begin by grasping the thorn, asking about the comparability of results from persons with varying backgrounds.

Transposing tasks and comparing answers

Any time we take a task from one culture to another, we must look as closely as possible at what the task demands and what the subject's answer may mean. We may need to change the stimuli or the response we ask for, always hoping the task will remain the same. And even if we make no changes in the original procedure, we may be surprised by new definitions of the task or new ways of solving the problem. In fact, many of the persons who have had to deal with cross-cultural material end by feeling that the greatest deterrent and the greatest reward in milieu studies consists in discovering what lies behind the subject's response (Wallace, 1965).

Either to adapt tasks or to compare results, then, we must make progress with the analysis of tasks and responses. Suppose we take for the moment only the problem of comparing results, and narrow that down to some varying results with Piaget's conservation tasks. Price-Williams finds that all the unschooled Tiv children he tested in Nigeria could cope, by age eight, with tasks for conservation of amount, i.e. could say that the amount of something remained the same despite changes in its shape (Price-Williams, 1961). This is a considerably higher level of achievement than what Greenfield reports for unschooled Wolof children in Senegal (Greenfield, 1966) and compares very favorably with the performance of Western schoolchildren. It looks as if there may be some particular difference between the worlds of the Tiv and the Wolof. But it may also be that the judgments by the two groups are not strictly comparable either with each other or with those made by Genevan children. By comparability I mean not simply a difference in the way a task is given, but a difference in the way the several groups of children arrive at their answers. Differences of the latter kind are the significant ones. They enlarge our understanding of a task, and they offer some very useful pointers on where the cultural differences may lie. Before we take these steps, however, we have to know how one goes about comparing one answer with another or one basis for an answer with another.

What, for example, are the several bases or routes by which a child may give a judgment of equality on a conservation task? Conservation of liquids will provide a specific instance. A child pours two equal amounts of water into two unidentical glasses so that the water levels are different from one another. He says, when we ask him, that the amount of water is still the same in each glass. Is this answer based on simply remembering that the two amounts were equal before, paying no heed to the differences in water level? Is it based on the child's own act of pouring, on the feeling in his hands of having poured out all the water or equal amounts of it? Is it based on a grasp of a general principle, a grasp that allows the child to know not only that the amount remains the same but also why it remains the same? In another vein, what features of the experimental situation make a difference? Is the answer the same if we obtain it in a situation where the child does not see the uneven water levels or where someone else does the pouring?

One of the advantages to using Piagetian tasks for milieu studies is that questions like these have already been given a great deal of thought, both in Geneva and in other centers. In fact, it is rare to find so much material on ways of determining the basis for response and for distinguishing one kind of response from another. Moreover, the methods, and the distinctions drawn, hold for a wide variety of tasks, so that one does not have to shift rationale with every change in task. There is a drawback, however. There is as yet no simple and readily available statement of what the criteria are for comparing one kind of answer with another. This is a serious drawback. It makes it very easy for misunderstandings to occur about the comparability of results.

And it makes many of the task procedures seem rather arbitrary, when in fact they are meaningfully built around various criteria for determining the basis of an answer.

Eventually we may expect to see from Geneva a full statement of the critical procedures for various tasks and the critical differences among answers. Certainly, the written material on such points is beginning to accumulate, although in a scattered form (Leone & Bovet, 1966; Inhelder et al., 1966; Smedslund, 1963). As Elkind (1967) comments in another context, however, much of what is written in Geneva is, or was, written for an audience that already had direct contact with work at Geneva. In such a setting, the need for a set of written rules and cautions is not obvious. The stress falls instead on direct training in the use and interpretation of tasks.

Before a full statement or the opportunity for training is available, what can we determine about the differences among answers that are critical from Piaget's point of view? (These are the differences we need to know if we are to compare our results with Genevan results.) This is not the place to try to cover all the distinctions that are drawn. Out of the large and ingenious array, however, I have chosen three. These three are particularly important for studies of the effects of milieu or of special experience and training. They are all the more significant for not being the distinctions that many of us who use Piaget's tasks, or our own versions of his tasks, would make first or would make in the same way.

The three differences among answers are as follows:

1. Differences in the extent to which an answer is tied to a specific situation, as against having a general base and applying to several situations.

2. Differences in the extent to which a judgment needs some perceptual prop.

3. Differences in the child's use of "thought" and "action" in arriving at a judgment.

The procedures and problems related to these three distinctions are discussed here in the kind of language one might use if the Piagetian tasks had been developed away from Geneva, from a background of equivalence, discrimination, or learning studies.

This language, I am aware, does not always fit well with the language that would be used in Geneva. My aim, however, is not to attempt an account of the Genevan position in its own terms. Rather, it is to describe, in terms more familiar to experimental psychologists, why some Genevan task designs and task procedures take the form they do; to describe, in effect, the Genevan analysis of responses from the outside.

DIFFERENCES IN THE GENERALITY OF A JUDGMENT

In Genevan work, there is often the statement that one important way of distinguishing among answers is in terms of whether or not the judgment can be transferred to other stimuli (Leone & Bovet, 1966). What kind of transfer, and to what other stimuli? When we ask these questions, we find that Genevan forms of transfer have some special features. First, there are several ways to check the generality or specificity of judgment. I have found it helpful to separate these from one another.

1. Will the behavior hold up if we use the same kind of task and the same material, and simply extend the range of forms this material may take? In testing for conservation of amount, for example, one may always use clay but in a variety of shapes—pancake, sausage, halves, or many small pieces—rather than rely on any one change in shape.

2. Can the behavior be extended to other material, within the same kind of task? Within a task for conservation of amount, for example, one may shift from clay to liquids, or from continuous to discontinuous material such as beads.

Up to this point, the checks on generality are ones that would be familiar in any experimental procedure. They are common ways of asking whether a judgment is based on a general principle or on a highly specific stimulus situation. With the next check, however, the Genevan position becomes more unique.

3. Is the judgment based on some particular principles? Is it based on a grasp of such principles as reversibility and compensation? It is possible, for example, for the child to meet the second criterion but not to have a grasp of compensation. Working with clay, for instance, he may know that the amount of clay

remains the same after a change into a sausage shape but may
not know that this is because a change in one property, the
length of the piece, is compensated for by a change in another,
the thickness of the piece. Such a gap is most likely to appear if
we ask the child to carry out a "spontaneous composition," to
make, for example, a piece of clay that would be longer but still
have the same amount as the original. The child may fail this
task but still be able to say that the amounts remain the same in
the standard procedure for a conservation task. Or he may be
able to carry out the composition task but still maintain that the
amounts are unequal in the usual conservation procedure. Such
discrepancies in what the child can do have prompted Bruner to
wonder whether compensation is a necessary basis for conservation
judgments (Bruner et al., 1966). In Geneva, the same discrepancies prompt the argument that conservation judgments by definition are based on a grasp of compensation. Without such a grasp,
the child makes a judgment of equality, but does not make the
conservation judgment that the tasks, in their role as indices of
operational thought, were initially designed to measure (Inhelder et al., 1966).

4. Can the judgment be extended to other kinds of task? Such
extensions can be used as another check on whether the child's
judgment is based on some particular principles, on the operations that form a *structure d'ensemble*. Kohnstamm, for example,
has used a form of training for the class inclusion task that results in a sharp increase in the number of correct answers. This
increase is maintained in the face of a change of stimuli, a
change in experimenters, and a period of weeks (Kohnstamm,
1963). But, Leone and Bovet point out, what is not demonstrated is a transfer to any other task (conservation, for example) that demands the same underlying operations (Leone &
Bovet, 1966). Until such transfer is demonstrated, it cannot be
claimed that the child's judgments are the same as those classed
as fully operational on Genevan standards.

Why should we distinguish among these several checks on
generality? The simplest reason is that "transfer to other stimuli"
sounds like a procedure we all know well. In fact, it has some
special meanings in Genevan usage. As these meanings become

clearer, we shall run less risk of working at crosspurposes and of finding that results obtained in Geneva and outside of Geneva are regarded as not comparable.

DIFFERENCES IN THE NEED FOR STIMULUS SUPPORT

Closely allied to the dimension of generality-specificity is a dimension in terms of the need for some perceptual prop, some *facilitation situationelle,* to use a term from Leone and Bovet (1966). In a general sense, both dimensions refer to the extent to which the child can arrive at a correct answer only if the stimulus situation is structured in a certain way, either because he first learned to make this kind of judgment with that kind of situation, or because the arrangement of the stimuli somehow suggests the correct answer, or because the physical presence and arrangement of stimuli make it possible for him to solve the problem on an intuitive or perceptual basis rather than a logical one. *Facilitation situationelle* appears to be predominantly a concern with the latter two possibilities.

To explore the child's reliance on perceptual props and the possibility of a "perceptual" solution, there are three commonly used techniques: exceeding the perceptual span, changing the perceptual availability of a stimulus, and breaking up any match between perceptual and logical relationships.

In the first technique, the stimuli are objects, but they are multiplied so that they exceed the child's perceptual grasp or perceptual span. In testing for conservation of liquids, for example, the child may be able to say that an original amount of water remains the same when it is poured into two small jars, because he can almost see in his mind's eye the two jars poured back into one. The same child may well have difficulty if the original amount is poured into six small jars.

The second technique is to change the perceptual availability of the stimulus. We may simply shift from objects to words. Or we may screen the child from some part of the stimulus. In a task for construction of a series, for example, the child may be allowed first to complete a series with all sticks in full view, i.e. the sticks he has already placed and the sticks yet to be placed.

As a check on his grasp of the idea of a series and his ability to dispense with perceptual guidelines, he may be asked to hand sticks to the experimenter, so that the experimenter may make the series. In such a case, the child sees only the sticks yet to be placed, the experimenter keeping his sticks behind a screen.

The final technique is the most provocative. The aim is to leave the stimuli in full view, but to avoid any simple correspondence between the perceptual and the logical relationships. In any classification task, for example, instances that are to be placed in the same logical class will be spatially separate. Such a procedure is widely used in any experimental work. More uniquely, the stimuli in Piagetian tasks are often designed to lead away from the logical relationship or the correct answer, to contain a "phenomenal trap" (Morf, 1962) or "contrary cue" (Smedslund, 1963).

The presence or absence of a "contrary cue" is a major difference between Genevan and non-Genevan approaches to Piagetian tasks, and warrants some close examination. We are accustomed to varying the number of cues and the ratio of irrelevant to relevant cues, but we seldom design a task so that the answer has to survive a deliberately misleading cue. What are these "contrary cues"? They are first of all stimulus features that encourage the child to use an immature mode of thought, to make a judgment based on a cue whose untempered use is characteristic of an earlier age. In conservation of length, for example, young children tend to judge two lines as equal if they begin or end at the same point. This basis for judgment is tapped by arranging lines like this, ══ , or like this, ══ ,and asking if they are equal. Similarly, judgments of number may be tied to the space occupied, judgments of the amount of water to the water level without regard to the size of the container.

Some further indication of the role of "contrary cues" can be seen in a distinction brought to my attention by M. Sinclair. (I am indebted to her also for the example of screening on a seriation task.) A distinction is drawn between stimulus arrangements that tap an immature mode of thought and arrangements that tap an illusion (an arrangement of lines like this, ⌐ , for example, for conservation of length). Moreover, the processes involved in overcoming the two kinds of difficulty are regarded as different in kind and in the course of development. In a sense, such a distinction is to be expected from a theory that draws a sharp line between perception and thought, but it is an easy distinction to miss when one works from a background that draws a less sharp line.

Finally, the importance attached to "contrary cues" can be sharply seen in some special uses of terms. In the classic conservation task, the child may be asked to predict whether the two amounts of water will be the same if the water is poured into two unidentical glasses. But these judgments, made before exposure to the diverging water levels, are referred to as "anticipation" judgments, and not "conservation" judgments (Inhelder, 1965). Similarly, the term "transmission" has been used rather than "conservation" when the child observes a gradual rather than a swift change in a critical property like water level (Inhelder & Piaget, 1963).

Why the Genevan insistence on "contrary cues" as a critical or necessary way of distinguishing among judgments? And why the tendency to give them a smaller role in American studies? Part of the answer lies in saying that "contrary cues" are a way of making sure a preoperational level of thought is not mistaken for an operational level. In this respect, contrary cues have the same function as other safeguards in Genevan work, safeguards such as suggesting to the child that his correct answer is not correct, or demanding that a correct answer be stable over time. In American studies, the more important error is likely to be of the opposite type, namely calling a weak form of a certain kind of thought not that kind at all. This error is likely to be particularly important when one is asking how far performance can be improved by special training.

But the difference in approach goes deeper than a concern with different kinds of error. First of all, there is in Piagetian work a tie between "type of thought" and "strength or stability of thought" that does not occur in other models. I am always surprised, for example, to find what are for me measures of strength—overcoming contrary cues, resisting countersuggestion, or remaining stable over time—used as indices of type, as measures of whether a certain judgment is based on an operational structure or not. The closest I can come to feeling at ease with such an inference is to think of Piaget's underlying model of thought as like a network, scaffolding, or geodesic construction that, as the last piece locks in, acquires a sturdiness it did not have before and at the same time a form and a set of interrelationships it did not have before. From such a model, it is easier to understand an inference from strength to type and an insistence that tasks should be designed to test the strength or stability of a judgment. The same inference does not come easily if one has in mind a model more like a plant at various points of growth, always the same plant even though it increases in strength and number of branches.

Behind the differences in task design there is as well a difference in ideas as to how development takes place and what the critical sources of difficulty are. Braine, for example, has urged the development of simpler and nonverbal forms of Piagetian tasks, on the grounds that we need to see what the child is capable of when he does not have to cope with verbal terms and misleading cues. The original and the changed tasks will not be comparable in difficulty level, he argues, but we will have a sharper focus on sources of difficulty (Braine, 1962). Such variations in tasks are not to date a major feature of Genevan work. It is not that variations are lacking. Anticipation judgments on conservation tasks, for example, represent a major variation. The reason seems to lie more in the feeling that the variations that appeal to many American psychologists are often based on an unhappy assumption.

This is the assumption that development proceeds by a gradual extension of mastery from one stimulus to another, or by the gradual dropping out of stimulus support. For Piaget, development may sometimes follow this route, but it does not have to. Instead, the significant aspect of development is more the way it proceeds in response to felt gaps and contradictions between two events or two pieces of knowledge. In a task for conservation of liquids, for instance, the evidence of the water levels is at odds with the child's sense of permanence or his grasp of transformations. With such conflict built into the design, the task mirrors the significant prods to growth. And the answers that survive or resolve this conflict will be the ones that mark a real achievement in thought.

DIFFERENCES IN THE USE OF ACTION

We have considered so far two differences among judgments, and with them a number of points about task procedures. Up to this point we have been predominantly concerned with the role of stimuli on Piagetian tasks. The final difference concerns the child's response.

In work with Piagetian tasks, one often finds a concern with how the child uses physical activity or "action" as a source of information or as a way of working through a problem (Gréco, 1959). In practice, Genevan procedures seem to contain three questions:

1. Does the solution depend on using a specific action or series of actions?

2. Can the problem be solved without recourse to action at all?

3. If it is solved by thought alone, is the thought only reproductive of a past action?

(1) Reliance on a specific action or series of actions is a criterion often observed in Genevan work. We see it in practice when the child is asked to carry out a task in a different way, to put the laundry on the line, for example, in the reverse order from that in a model or starting from a different point, to build a series in an ascending and a descending order, or to cope with a scrambled order of questions from the experimenter.

(2) Using and dispensing with actions appears at two levels. At one level the individual does use physical action, trying things out and observing them before he makes a judgment. At the other level the individual can use thought alone, e.g. work out in his head a system for combining pairs of colors, or draw without seeing the changes, the way a piece of wire would look at different stages of transition from curved to flat. There is an interesting middle ground. This is a point made by Gréco: an approach may be "empirical" in the sense that it is marked by

trial and error and a recourse to haphazard action, but the
thought may still be "logical" in the sense that the individual
shows by other actions that he can extend or generalize the
information he gathered by "empirical" means (Gréco, 1959).

(3) Even when a problem is solved by thought alone, is it by
reproductive thought? Is the solution achieved by direct recall of
a previous action, by a very limited extrapolation from previous
action, or by deduction from a general principle? This kind of
question appears to underlie the Genevan tendency to ask about
extended situations. The child has seen, for example, the experimenter put six beads in one glass and six in another, carefully
dropping the beads in the glasses in a one-to-one manner. The
child may feel quite sure that the number of beads in the two
glasses is the same. Will he feel as sure if we ask him how things
would be if we went on all afternoon, or will he feel that he will
have to "see"? In a different kind of check, the child may start off
with stimuli having a known functional tie to one another, eggs
to eggcups, or flowers to vases, for example, on a correspondence
task. Will the child show an equal grasp of correspondence if the
two rows of stimuli are, say, two rows of counters?

All three techniques are ways of attempting to specify the
child's use of action past or present as a way of working through
a problem. The techniques themselves are clear enough. Less
clear is the answer to a question Piaget has raised for all the
many ways of distinguishing among answers: how equivalent are
they, within a milieu and across milieus? (Piaget, 1959).

Suppose we consider two of the demands used to specify the
use of action: "do it another way" and "do it in your head." It
seems more than feasible that cultures value these ways of working differently and give varying amounts of practice in them.
To many Americans, for example, the European tradition emphasizes "in the head" or "thought alone," often with the implication that one would resort to direct exploration and an exhaustive gathering of data only when the problem could not be
thought out. In contrast, the American interest in "doing" and
"proving by doing" often appears to Europeans as a ritual rather
than a necessity.

More specifically, there are already enough data, especially in

Vernon's (1965a) work, to make one very cautious about any demand to do something in the head when the subject comes from a milieu differently schooled fom our own. It is precisely these "imaging" skills that seem to differentiate among children from several milieus. At the very least, one would like to give subjects from other milieus the chance to work out a task by more than one means. Children might well be asked, for instance, to carry out a task both by moving the actual stimuli around and by thinking the problem through without actions. By allowing for both response forms we may be better able to tell whether a poor performance is the result of a difficulty with the logical demands of the task or with the particular method imposed.

The trouble is that there is very frequently a relationship between a degree of intellectual skill and the ability to use a particular kind of response on a task, but the relationship is by no means clear. Even for our own culture, where there is a heavy stress on verbal skills as higher skills, the relationship is at best not simple, a point made by Inhelder and Piaget in discussing formal thought in adolescence. They ask:

Whether there is a simpler way to characterize formal thought than by referring to the notion of hypothesis or possibility. Now, the most prominent feature of formal thought is that it no longer deals with objects directly, but with verbal elements; and at first, we tried to contrast formal and concrete though in terms of this . . . factor. In fact, it is often sufficient to translate a concrete operation into simple propositions and deny the subject the use of manipulable objects for working out the operation . . . for the problem to become insoluble before the formal level . . . . However, this is not the whole problem, for all verbal thought is not formal and it is possible to get correct reasoning about simple propositions as early as the 7–8 year old level, provided that these propositions correspond to sufficiently concrete representations (Inhelder and Piaget, 1958, pp. 251–252).

Inhelder and Piaget's solution to this lack of a parallel between a level of thought and the use of words is one that we might well adopt for milieu studies or for any subjects whose linguistic skills are poor. Instead of asking for verbal responses to verbal stimuli, they stressed instead the child's ability to use the original, manipulable material to make up new problems or to discover new ways of solving the old problem.

Conclusions

We have considered three ways of comparing answers on Piagetian tasks, ways regarded as critical in Genevan work and likely to be overlooked or read differently from other points of view. In what manner, however, are these analyses of answers significant for studies of milieu effects? First, we can go only so far in studying milieu effects before having to come to terms with the problem of whether judgments are truly comparable, either in the way the child states or demonstrates them, or in the way he arrives at them. In addition, there are some specific points of relevance. Dependence on a particular arrangement of stimuli or on physically present stimuli, for example, acquires a special relevance when we find that children from some milieus seem to rely more than others on perceptual guidelines. And variations in the use of action sources or action models acquire special relevance when we find that these seem to be, in some groups, highly favored ways of gathering information and keeping track. Hypotheses such as these and hypotheses about the milieu features that may contribute to the different ways of thinking, are our next concern.

Skills and their background

What are the skills common to many milieus, and the skills differentiating among them? This is the first step in the process of matching environmental conditions to different ways of thinking.

By and large, milieu studies involve so many points of difference, both among milieus and among tasks, that it is hard to fit the pieces together. The fitting becomes easier as more studies at least use common tasks, a trend helped greatly by the widespread appeal of tasks developed at Geneva. There is now, for example, a group of five studies all using two or more Piagetian tasks (at least one of them a conservation task), and all concerned with varying kinds and amounts of schooling: no school in Bovet's continuing work with Algerian children; West Indian schools, both rural and urban, in Vernon's (1965b) work with Jamaicans; remote village schools in Peluffo's (1964, 1965) studies of Italian children; little or no school in Goodnow's (1962) work with Hong Kong Chinese, and little or no school in Sigel and Mermelstein's (1965) study of American Negro children from Prince Edward County, Virginia.

First, these studies provide a common result: some tasks are more affected than others by a departure from urban, Western schooling. With this result, we may begin to shift from a concept of overall lags in development to a concept of differential vulnerability among tasks. Furthermore, there is some consistency in the tasks that are more and less affected. Conservation of amount, for example, is consistently among the less affected or unaffected, and conservation of weight is almost as sturdy. From this kind of consistency, we may begin to draw hypotheses about common and differentiating skills.

1. *The more vulnerable tasks may be those requiring words, drawings, visual imagery—in general, some kind of nonmotor representation.* This kind of hypothesis has been suggested by Sigel and Mermelstein and by Vernon. It will account for the weaker performance of children with poor schooling on the verbal class-inclusion task used by Sigel and Mermelstein, on many of the Piagetian "imaging" tasks used by Vernon, and on the combinatorial tasks used by Goodnow and by Peluffo (tasks that require working out a problem in one's head).

Very clearly, this kind of hypothesis is only at the beginning stage. It demands that we look more closely at the meaning of "representational skills." Happily, a massive attack is being made on this problem. In Geneva, there is the work on *images mentales* (Inhelder, 1963, 1965; Piaget & Inhelder, 1966a, b). In the United States, there is Bruner's (1964) work on differences among enactive, iconic, and symbolic representations, and Leeper's (1963) argument that movements are, or can be, symbols. And in England, there is the continuing work by Vernon (1965a, b) on how tasks requiring different kinds of representational skills are intercorrelated in different cultures.

2. *The less vulnerable tasks may be those for which the child*

has an action model. Suppose we start with a relatively sturdy task, conservation of amount. Now we know that not all conservation tasks are equally sturdy. Conservation of length and of volume are more vulnerable than conservation of amount in Vernon's (1965b) study, and conservation of time is highly vulnerable in Leone and Bovet's (1966). Nor does the difference among conservation tasks seem to be a simple case of the sturdiest being the ones that are usually easiest.

We might entertain instead the idea that for conservation of amount there are some directly matched or directly relevant action models, actions of halving, sharing, or dividing any single item. And some practice in these actions might be expected to occur in a wide range of milieus. In contrast, there seem to be fewer actions that provide direct models for conservation of time or length, and wider variations among milieus in the practice and the value that they give to such judgments.

A stress on action as a basis for thought has always been a strong theme in Piaget's account of general development. In milieu studies, the themes of action and action models have appeared in several places (Goodnow & Bethon, 1966; Peluffo, 1965; Price-Williams, 1962). In these studies, there is the argument that children with little or no formal schooling may depend in particular on action models drawn from past experience or on cues from manipulative action in the experimental situation. The argument is nicely illustrated by some of Greenfield's work with conservation of liquids. Greenfield compared results when the water was poured by the experimenter and when it was poured by the child himself. The children were all Senegalese, attending either French or Koranic schools. For children in French schools, the two procedures gave the same results. For children in Koranic schools (these schools occupy only a small part of the child's day), the results are much better when the water is poured by the child himself (Greenfield, 1966).

3. *The critical skill may be versatility in the use of different sources of information and different models.* Any culture that is short on verbal representational skills may lean, by default, more heavily on action as a source of information and on action models as a way of keeping track. The same loss of versatility

may also hold for individuals who rely too heavily on "the word." We might expect to find, for example, the unschooled handicapped on the verbal class-inclusion task, because they cannot move the words around, and some of the highly educated handicapped on the Vygotsky classification task, because they do not move the blocks around (Hanfmann, 1941).

For this third hypothesis, examples are difficult to find even though we know intuitively that there are one-sided milieus and competitive and interfering relationships between different ways of working. One example is the tie observed by Hanfmann between education and the use of "perceptual" and "conceptual" styles on the Vygotsky task, particularly her observations on "concordant" and "discordant" uses of the two methods of approach (Hanfmann, 1941). Closer to Piagetian tasks, we may find an example in an observation by Leone and Bovet on uneven development among unschooled Algerian children. Leone and Bovet observed that these children often showed a precocious level of apparent success, on the conservation tasks, followed by a decline and then a rise to a new level of success. Behind this unevenness there appeared to be a high degree of early skill in making judgments on a perceptual or intuitive basis, a skill that had to be unlearned if the child was to move on to a grasp of the logical features of the task. Such unevenness is undoubtedly a complex phenomenon, but it suggests an area where we may be able to demonstrate how some milieus encourage a variety of ways of working while others lead to a concentration on one approach that makes it harder to learn others.

We have in hand, then, three hypotheses about common and differentiating skills, hypotheses that allow us to cut across a variety of tasks. Now we may ask: what aspects of milieu might be responsible? Put in other terms, how do we specify the critical differences between one milieu and another?

As a start, we all agree that "schooling" and "no schooling" are variables much in need of refining. We use them, like "chronological age," as hopeful summaries of past experience but we have only a general idea of what these experiences are. Furthermore, these terms carry their own hazards. It is very easy, for example, to think of "no schooling" as a state requiring no further specification, as a neutral state, a measure of what might have been if the organism had been left to itself. This is a dangerous assumption, likely to lead to the idea that all unschooled children are alike. In reality, all environments make demands, present problems, and reward particular ways of coping. And these ways of coping limit or open up other ways of coping. In other words, "no schooling" is not a baseline of untroubled nature, but the result itself of an active, even if different, form of training.

What happens if we set aside such variables as "schooling—no schooling" or "urban schools—rural schools," and instead work backwards from the skills that unite and divide various milieus? What, for example, is the critical background for skill in the use of nonmotor representations such as words, drawings, or complex visual images?

Part of the background may lie in specific training. Suppes, for instance, remarks that New Math children and Old Math parents may differ in the facility with which they use abstract symbols, a difference stemming from the child's earlier introduction to these symbols and to deliberate practice in shifting from one kind of symbol to another, from numbers to drawings of objects to x's and y's, for example (personal communication).

Bruner proposes a very interesting set of general dimensions (Bruner, 1966). He puts together a range of learning situations, starting with those observed in baboon troops and in human tribal life and moving on to school life as we know it. These learning situations, he points out, can be compared in terms of who teaches, e.g. peer or adult, in terms of a one-to-one or a one-to-many interaction, and in terms of whether the learning is on-the-job with an immediate functional purpose or out-of-context. In the light of these dimensions, the schooling we know has some special features. One particular adult, "the teacher," becomes prominent. The context is not one of immediate action. Direct imitation becomes less easy. And the medium of instruction is most often words. All these differences call for the use of abstractions and may account for the generally better performance of schoolchildren on tasks demanding nonmotor representations.

Bruner's dimensions open up the possibility of characterizing, with some specificity, learning situations both within and outside of school. In time such dimensions may make it possible for us to dispense with such variables as "schooling—no schooling." For such a purpose, the dimensions are a major beginning in themselves, and they can be multiplied. Piaget (1954) would point out, one expects, that every demand for communication with another person is a demand for recognizing other perspectives and for constructing some representational system, a construction that is further encouraged by every goal that is not the solution of an immediate and functional problem, and by every conflict between items of knowledge that is the right size for the child to cope with and work on. Vernon (1965a) would add dimensions at least for the extent of self-initiated play, for male dominance, and for the general rationality and purposefulness of the home.

For myself, I would add a dimension for the unity of a child's experience. In many milieus, the child brings to bear on a task only a small amount of experience because his experience is in fact limited. In others, he brings to bear only a small part of the experience he has had, because his experience is fragmented. In some Hong Kong schools, for example, children were encouraged to look toward the book and the adult as the sole arbiters of what many aspects of the world were like. This kind of split left them unable to bring their own experience to bear on a task defined as a "book" task (Goodnow, 1962).

In a similar vein, Suchman (1966) asks about the effects on mental development of some Koranic schools where the language is not the child's everyday language and where "reading" consists of responding to a set of written symbols with a fixed series of prayers. Actually, we need not go abroad for examples of split experiences, especially splits between life at school and life outside it. We may need to go further afield to find milieus where the child's experiences are all of a piece, where he is encouraged to trust his own experience and to bring to bear on a task all that he knows. This may be the distinguishing feature of the unschooled Eskimo groups Vernon (1965a) describes as performing so well on many tasks. Part of their "training in resourcefulness" may lie in encouraging them to make active and full use of all their experience.

A description of milieu dimensions, however, is only part of the problem. The other, and harder, part lies in specifying what a particular background does. Fragmented experiences, for example, are easy to describe but, to be fully useful, they need to be related to theories about the effects of amounts and kinds of learning, either in terms of the role of overlearning, or in terms of dimensional preferences, or in terms of growth as the coordination of schema. Similarly, we may feel very sympathetic towards Vernon's hypothesis that independent and constructive play affects later skills in controlled visual and spatial imagery. But now we must fill in the gap between the activity and the imaging skill. Just what does the activity provide?

On this point, there is a very nice contribution from Piaget's work, namely a distinction among three kinds of familiarity: familiarity with certain objects; familiarity with certain operations; and familiarity with certain operations as applied to certain objects.

The first and second forms of familiarity are part of the distinction between physical and logico-arithmetic experience (Piaget & Inhelder, 1966). One can well imagine, for example, two groups supplied with the same objects, but with one cultural group encouraged to spend far more time counting, grouping, and making series out of the objects.

The second and third forms of familiarity underlie questions about the tie between a type of judgment and a type of material. On the class-inclusion task, for example, children find it easier to answer the question—are there more primroses or more flowers? —than a similar question about animals, or about brown and wooden beads. One reason suggested is that the child has in the past put together flowers to make a single group, and this tie may be evoked again in the experimental situation, making the task easier by providing a concrete referent in memory or perhaps even by simply making the whole task seem more feasible (Inhelder & Piaget, 1964).

The three forms of familiarity are valuable distinctions for milieu studies. One of the major differences, for example, between a more and a less technical society may well be familiarity with such basic operations as counting and measuring, and many differences on specific tasks may stem from a differential use of these basic techniques. An example is suggested by Maistriaux (1955). He observed that unschooled Africans almost always tested the placement of a piece of wood by an attempt at direct fit rather than by eye or by an available reference length. From such a first-hand approach, with its avoidance of measuring against a standard, many handicaps on tasks of construction and measurement are bound to follow.

The other aspect of familiarity crucial for milieu studies is the occurrence of ties between operations and objects. Do we test only with material where the child has already had some experience with this operation as applied to this object? This is the case in Price-Williams's (1962) approach, using for a classification task familiar plant materials, already classed in some ways in the course of use and in the course of naming. Results from this kind of task are not easy to combine with Genevan results when the latter are based on extending the task to material without such past ties. But, with less schooled subjects, it may be precisely the move away from material with known functional ties that is difficult. In reading Lovell's (1961) description of Hyde's work with children in Aden, for example, what stands out is a special response to the class-inclusion task, when the tester asks if there are more brown beads or more wooden beads. With these children the response is, apparently more often than in the controls, one of wondering what *wooden* beads has to do with the question.

It may well be that one of the first things school children learn is that it is feasible or expectable to combine all kinds of material even if, on their standards, it makes no great amount of sense. The operation of combining comes to be the rewarded activity rather than the units combined. More seriously, the response of these children illustrates the need in milieu studies to tread a fine path between two points. If we do not use material that has already some past significance in relation to this task, we may never know what the unschooled child can do. But if we stop with this material, we may never know how much of his thought is replication rather than extension of past experiences.

Concluding remarks

I have indicated some of the ways in which time devoted to Piaget is one of the best investments a student of milieu effects can make. I would like to end with still another general contribution to be gleaned from Piaget's work. With Bruner (1966) we would agree that "there is no 'standard child,' and 'natural childhood' is hard to imagine outside a cultural context." What our own culture provides is not a norm, but an example of one set of skills. Skills, however, may be endlessly listed. We must have a way of putting all the things we can do into some kind of order, and some of these must be earmarked as more significant than others.

To Piaget, the debt is tremendous first of all for pointing out significant skills, such as the achievements of invariance or conservation, that crystallize past growth and serve as the essential basis for new growth. The debt is just as large for what lies behind the selection of significant skills, namely a model of how the many things we can do may be put together, put together at one level in terms of transformations or operations and at a further level in terms of how these transformations may be ordered or grouped among themselves. Without models for interrelationships among tasks and among skills, the study of milieu effects has difficulty advancing beyond a listing of differences and similarities on an indefinite number of discrete tasks.

References

Braine, M. D. S. Piaget on reasoning: a methodological critique and some alternative proposals. In W. Kessen & C. Kuhlman (Eds.), Thought in the young child. *Monogr. Soc. Res. Child Develpm.*, 1962, 83, Pp. 41–61.

Bruner, J. S. On cognitive growth. In J. S. Bruner, Rose R. Olver, & Patricia M. Greenfield (Eds.), *Studies in cognitive growth.* New York: Wiley, 1966. Pp. 1–67.

Bruner, J. S. The course of cognitive growth. *Amer. Psychol.,* 1964, 19, 1–15.

Elkind, D. Piaget's conservation problems. *Child Develpm.,* 1967, 38, 15–27.

Goodnow, Jacqueline. A test of milieu differences with some of Piaget's tasks. *Psychol. Monogr.*, 1962, **76**, No. 36 (Whole No. 555).

Goodnow, Jacqueline, & Bethon, G. Piaget's tasks: the effects of schooling and intelligence. *Child Develpm.*, 1966, **37**, 573–582.

Gréco, P. L'apprentissage dans une situation à structure opératoire concrète: les inversions successives de l'ordre linéaire par des rotations de 180. In P. Gréco & J. Piaget (Eds.), *Études d'épistémologie génétique*. Vol. VII. *L'apprentissage et connaissance*. 1959, 77–86.

Greenfield, Patricia M. On culture and conservation. In J. S. Bruner, Rose R. Olver, & Patricia M. Greenfield (Eds.), *Studies in cognitive growth*. New York: Wiley, 1966. Pp. 225–256.

Hanfmann, Eugenia. A study of personal patterns in an intellectual performance. *Charac. & Person.*, 1941, **9**, 315–325.

Inhelder, Bärbel. Les opérations de la pensée et leur symbolisme imagé. *Cahiers de Psychol.*, 1963, **6**, 143–171.

Inhelder, Bärbel. Operational thought and symbolic imagery. In P. Mussen (Ed.), European research in cognitive development. *Monogr. Soc. Res. Child Develpm.*, 1965, **30**, No. 2, Pp. 4–18.

Inhelder, Bärbel, Bovet, Magali, Sinclair, Hermina, & Smock, C. D. Letter published in *Amer. Psychol.*, 1966, **21**, 160–164.

Inhelder, Bärbel, & Piaget, J. *The growth of logical thinking from childhood to adolescence*. New York: Basic Books, 1958. Pp. 251–252.

Inhelder, Bärbel, & Piaget, J. De l'itération des actions a la récurrence élémentaire. In P. Gréco, B. Inhelder, B. Matalon, & J. Piaget (Eds.), *Études d'épistémologie génétique*. Vol. XVII. *La formation des raisonnements recurrentiels*. Paris: Presses Univer. France, 1963. Pp. 108–110.

Inhelder, Bärbel, & Piaget, J. *The early growth of logic in the child*. New York: Harper & Row, 1964.

Kohnstamm, G. A. An evaluation of part of Piaget's theory. *Acta Psychol.*, 1963, **21**, 313–356.

Leeper, R. Cited in J. S. Bruner, On cognitive growth. In J. S. Bruner, Rose R. Olver, & Patricia M. Greenfield (Eds.), *Studies in cognitive growth*. New York: Wiley, 1966. P. 20.

Leone, J. P., & Bovet, Magali. L'apprentissage de la quantification de l'inclusion et la théorie opératoire. *Acta Psychol.*, 1966, **25**, 334–356.

Lovell, K. *The growth of basic mathematical and scientific concepts in children*. New York: Philosophical Library, 1961. Pp. 47–48.

Maistriaux, R. La sous-évolution des noirs d'Afrique. Sa nature—ses causes —ses remèdes. *Revue de Psychol. des Peuples*, 1955, **10**, 397–456.

Morf, A. Recherches sur l'origine de la connexité de la suite des premiers nombres. In P. Gréco & A. Morf, *Études d'épistémologie génétique*. Vol. XIII. *Structures numériques élémentaires*. Paris: Presses Univer. France, 1962. P. 160.

Peluffo, N. Les notions de conservation et de causalité chez les enfants provenant de differents milieux physiques et socio-culturels. *Arch. Psychol., Genève*, 1962, 38, 75–90.

Peluffo, N. La nozione di conservazione del volume e le operazioni di combinazione come indici di sviluppo del pensiero operatorio in soggetti appartenenti ad ambienti fisici e socioculturali diversi. *Rivista di Psicol. sociale,* 1964, 11, 99–132.

Peluffo, N. Problemi cognitivi, strategie, piani di soluzione. *Rivista di Psicol. sociale,* 1965, 12, 91–103.

Piaget, J. Introduction to P. Gréco & J. Piaget (Eds.), *Études d'épistémologie génétique.* Vol. VII. *Apprentissage et connaissance.* 1959, Pp. 1–20.

Piaget, J. *The construction of reality in the child.* New York: Basic Books, 1964. Pp. 353–363.

Piaget, J., & Inhelder, B. *La psychologie de l'enfant.* Paris: Presses Univer. France, 1966. (a)

Piaget, J. & Inhelder, B. *L'Image mentale chez l'enfant.* Paris: Presses Univer. France, 1966. (b)

Price-Williams, D. R. A study concerning concepts of conservation of quantities among primitive children. *Acta Psychol.,* 1961, 18, 297–305.

Price-Williams, D. R. Abstract and concrete modes of classification in a primitive society. *Brit. J. educ. Psychol.,* 1962, 32, 50–61.

Sigel, I. E., & Mermelstein, E. Effects of nonschooling on Piagetian tasks of conservation. Paper presented at APA meeting, September, 1965.

Smedslund, J. Development of concrete transitivity of length in children. *Child Develpm.,* 1963, 34, 389–405.

Suchman, Rosslyn G. Cultural differences in children's color and form preferences. *J. soc. Psychol.,* 1966, 70, 3–10.

Vernon, P. E. Ability factors and environmental influences. *Amer. Psychol.,* 1965, 20, 723–733. (a)

Vernon, P. E. Environmental handicaps and intellectual development. *Brit. J. educ. Psychol.,* 1965, 35, 1–12 (Part I), 13–22 (Part II). (b)

Wallace, J. G. *Concept growth and the education of the child.* Upton Park, England: Nat. Found. educ. Res., 1965.

APPLIED PERSPECTIVES

The Piagetian System and
the World of Education

IRVING E. SIGEL

The purpose of this paper is to discuss the relevance of Piaget's system as a conceptual framework for educators in terms of identification of the child's cognitive capability, the creation of developmentally based teaching strategies, and the construction of a sequential curriculum. Granting that Piaget's work was not developed in the service of education, but rather in the service of genetic epistemology, the Piagetian system has considerable significance and relevance for the educator.

Piaget's theory is a theory of intelligence, where intelligence is

The author wishes to thank Dr. Kenneth Lovell and Dr. Carolyn Shantz for their thoughtful reaction to this paper.

This work, reported from the Center for Developmental Studies in Cognition, the Merrill-Palmer Institute, Detroit, Michigan, represents some of the investigations carried on by Drs. Carolyn Shantz and John Watson, in addition to myself. Research assistants participating in various phases of the work include Judith Griggiths, Frank Hooper, and Fred Stevens. Schools cooperating in the research with us include the City and Country School, Bloomfield Hills, Highland Park Public Schools, Livonia Public Schools, and the Merrill-Palmer Institute Preschool.

broadly conceived as an adaptation to the social and physical environment (Piaget, 1963). Intelligence is that set of actions and processes by which man assimilates knowledge and makes the necessary accommodations to this new knowledge. The actions taken in such acquisition reveal that Piaget's system of intelligence includes the processes of thought as well as the products of thought. Thus, his is a functional, not a psychometric view. More important perhaps, for the educator, is that intelligence is developmental, and describes the acquisition of knowledge in terms of defined stage sequential behaviors.

Piaget's system, while possessing many formal elements, is replete with substantive content. The growth of the intellect is examined through the vehicle of acquisition of concepts and problems such as number (Piaget, 1952), space (Piaget & Inhelder, 1963), and geometry (Piaget, Inhelder, & Szeminska, 1960). His interest in the content as well as in the quality of intellectual growth makes his contribution uniquely relevant to education.

In addition to developmental orientation and the detailing of the sequence of concept development, Piaget is interested in the mental operations involved in knowledge acquisition. Specification of the processes involved in learning substantive concepts extends our understanding of how knowledge is acquired. In essence, Piaget's conceptualization of the psychology of intelligence is developmental in format, substantive in content, and operational in behavior. These characteristics make the theory eminently germane, if not essential, for education.

The congruence rests, of course, on a conception of the educational endeavor as guiding a developing organism through the stages of intellectual growth, providing him with appropriate organization of subject matter (curriculum), introducing information at appropriate time levels (spacing and sequencing), in an appropriate manner (teaching strategy).

Efforts have been and are currently under way to adapt various aspects of Piagetian theory to the educational enterprise. These are frequently piecemeal efforts, emphasizing one or more aspects—sometimes unrelated to the rest of the curriculum. Discussion of these among other applications can be found in

Lunzer (1960), Lovell (1961), Peel (1960), Flavell (1963), Sigel (1964), and Wallace (1965).

It may be fortuitous, but it is certainly fortunate, that the work of Piaget has become increasingly available to the English reading public during the period of great ferment and change in the American educational scene. I believe educators today are reaching out for rationales by which to guide their activities. I hope the following discussion will provide some additional bases for searching in depth into Piagetian works.

Relationship between Piagetian theory and teacher awareness of development

Educators must have a conceptual framework within which and by which to establish programs, devise teaching strategies, and embark on innovations. A conceptual framework provides the basis for a coherent and rational program. Working within a coherent system, the educator is in a position to establish criteria by which to assess the child's developmental level and to establish relevant levels of curriculum content. Innovations can be established more rationally and integrally, since bases for innovation can be derived within the system.

Karplus illustrates the condition when he says,

. . . you will probably all agree that there is a transition between children's preoperational thinking at kindergarten age and some of their thinking in terms of propositions when the pupils leave elementary school at twelve years or so. It seems to me that in general this transition in children's thinking is not recognized by present educational practice in the United States. *Teachers with whom I have been in contact have not seemed to be much aware that there is such a change taking place and I would say that most instruction above the kindergarten takes place on what one might call the formal level.* (Italics ours.) As an unfortunate consequence of this fact many students never understand the intent of instruction and become dissatisfied with school by the time they are fourteen or sixteen (Karplus, 1964, p. 113).

Knowledge of some of the principles of intellectual development from a Piagetian framework would enable the teacher to
define the level at which children are functioning and thereby
gear the content and the mode of instruction appropriately.

Piaget's theory holds that the acquisition of knowledge comes
about through different cognitive modalities, at different age
levels. For teachers this is crucial, since it indicates that knowledge is not acquired the same way at each developmental level.
For example, the young preschool child:

. . . is not satisfied with speaking, he must needs "play out" what he
thinks and symbolize his ideas by means of gestures or objects, and
represent things by imitation, drawing and construction. In short,
from the point of view of expression itself, the child at the outset is
still midway between the use of collective signs and that of the individual symbol, both still being necessary, no doubt, but the second
being much more so in the child than in the adult (Piaget, 1963, p.
159).

A second principle is that although cognitive growth appears
to be a continuous process, it proceeds in discontinuous ways
with spurts and plateaus of achievement. Thus, for the educator,
it is important to be aware of the fact that cognitive structures
are not fixed or given but develop and, in the process of adaptation, become modified and reconstituted as new structures at
subsequent points in time. The process of structures being built,
decomposed, and recombined highlights the dynamics of mental
growth. Piaget's system is one of changing gestalts or wholes that
are reorganized and redefined in the course of growth.

This proposition raises some intriguing challenges for the
curriculum builder, e.g. can a curriculum be built that fits the
pattern of changing gestalts in a dialectic way in contrast to
increasing bits of information in an additive way? In effect, can
appropriate wholes be discovered in social studies, for example,
and sequences established? We shall have occasion to discuss
this later.

A third important set of principles for the educator relates to
the role of language. Language, a key mode of communication
receives considerable attention in the classroom. The teacher can
gain new perspective by examining language from the Piagetian

point of view. For Piaget, language is the tool by which thoughts are expressed, having been preceded by actions which are internalized and eventually defined in verbal and symbolic forms. Language conveys to the individual an already prepared organization of thought, concepts, and relationships. It is not thought, since thought can occur without language:

. . . the child begins by borrowing from this collection (language) only as much as suits him, remaining disdainfully ignorant of everything that exceeds his mental level. And again, that which is borrowed is assimilated in accordance with his intellectual structure; a word intended to carry a general concept at first engenders only a half-individual, half-socialised pre-concept (the word "bird" thus evokes the familiar canary, etc.) (Piaget, 1963, p. 159).

Social interaction and stimulation is a fourth significant consideration for the development of intelligence. The school provides just such a social context. Piaget, interestingly enough, has been criticized for underplaying the role of socialization experiences as an influence in cognitive growth. Yet he *does* make explicit the significance of social interaction in the development of logical thought. He clearly states:

The human being is immersed right from birth in a social environment which affects him just as much as his physical environment. Society, even more, in a sense, than the physical environment, changes the very structure of the individual, because it not only compels him to recognize facts, but also provides him with a ready-made system of signs, which modify his thought; it presents him with new values and it imposes on him an infinite series of obligations. It is therefore quite evident that social life affects intelligence through the three media of language (signs), the content of interaction (intellectual values) and rules imposed on thought (collective logical or prelogical norms) (Piaget, 1963, p. 156).

The social context furthers children's learning the meaning of cooperation and consequently, objectivity. Initially the child is egocentric in thought and deed, but with confrontation from the social and physical world, sociocentrism evolves. The initial egocentricity, as expressed in thought and language, is explained as:

. . . nothing more than a lack of co-ordination, a failure to "group" relations with other individuals as well as with other objects. There is nothing here that is not perfectly natural; the primacy of one's own point of view, like intuitive centralisation, in accordance with the subject's own action, is merely the expression of an original failure to differentiate, of an assimilation that distorts because it is determined by the only point of view that is possible at first (Piaget, 1963, p. 161).

With confrontation from social agents (peers, teachers, parents) as well as the inanimate environment, the child acquires an objectified view of self and the world around him:

. . . without interchange of thought and co-operation with others, the individual would never come to group his operations into a coherent whole: in this sense, therefore, operational grouping presupposes social life (Piaget, 1963, p. 163).

That social interaction is essential for group logical thought, is expressed as:

. . . actual exchanges of thought obey a law of equilibrium which again could only be an operational grouping, since to co-operate is also to co-ordinate operations. The grouping is therefore a form of equilibrium of inter-individual actions as well as of individual actions, and it thus regains its autonomy at the very core of social life (Piaget, 1963, p. 164).

The significance of social life for cognitive development rests on the conceptualization of social interaction as a necessary condition for transition from one developmental level to another. The difference between a Piagetian interpretation of the value of social interaction and the more commonly held behavior theory viewpoint is that for the former socialization creates stress that induces cognitive transformation, while for the latter reinforcement systems are held to account for growth.

That development proceeds in an orderly invariant sequence is another principle relevant for the educator. Knowledge of the sequence of stages and their behavioral indices as expressed in language and thought provide the educator with the criteria upon which to gauge the "readiness" of the child to assimilate material. The *sequence* is the crucial consideration, here, not the particular age at which particular cognitive behaviors appear.

Since teaching strategy and curriculum are dependent on the educator's awareness of the child's capacity to deal with material, it is necessary for the teacher to identify the child's level of cognitive functioning. The matching of curriculum and teaching strategy to the intellectual level of the child is a tricky issue. It is easy to confuse the child's manifest level of cognitive competence with his "true" understanding. For example, just because the child uses the word "animal" correctly in everyday contexts does not mean he knows or can define the concept.

Piaget warns us not to confuse the capacity for assimilation of new material, which in a sense would be the reiteration of words, phrases, and ideas at the level of intuitive thought, with the form they take at the operational level. Intuitive thought, which is dominant up to the end of early childhood, is, according to Piaget, characterized:

. . . by a disequilibrium, still unresolved, between assimilation and accommodation. An intuitive relation always results from a "centering" of thought depending on one's own action, as opposed to a "grouping" of all the relations involved; thus the equivalence between two series of objects is recognised only in relation to the act of making them correspond, and is lost as soon as this action is replaced by another. Intuitive thought, therefore, always evinces a distorting egocentricity, since the relation that is recognised is related to the subject's action and not decentralised into an objective system (Piaget, 1963, p. 160).

Children are suggestible at this period, and thereby inclined to imitate or copy instead of correcting. This leads to a quasi-mechanistic use rather than a natural accommodation.

A further important consideration in applying these principles is the fact the child does not move on all fronts simultaneously. The child may be in one stage in one conceptual area and another in another area. In effect, the rates of growth may vary among children as well as for a particular child. The determinants of these variations are many, such as the biological and social experiences of the child (Inhelder, 1965). Empirical support for this in regard to conservation of quantity, for example, was reported by Uzgiris (1964).

In sum, then, I have selected a few Piagetian propositions that I feel are highly relevant for the educational endeavor. These are as follows: (1) intellectual development is dependent on confrontations with the social as well as physical environment; (2) intellectual development proceeds by orderly invariant sequences (stages) with transitions from stage to stage; (3) acquisition of new knowledge comes about through appropriate assimilations and accommodations resulting in equilibrated cognitive structure; (4) language is a facilitator varying in significance as a function of the developmental level of the child.

Teaching strategies derived from Piagetian conceptualizations

To this point we have discussed the relevant Piagetian concepts to orient the teacher. Now let us turn to the implications and applications to the teaching in the classroom.

Although Piaget offers a number of principles from which to derive teaching strategies for each developmental level, I can, in this paper, touch on only some. Hopefully, the discussion will stimulate the reader to follow up with additional specification.

A curriculum requires appropriate teaching strategies to be effective. A teaching strategy reflects the teacher's conception of the learning process and of the nature of the learner. If a teacher believes that maximum learning occurs through drill and repetitions, his teaching strategy will reflect this belief. If he is convinced that learning is enhanced through discovery, he will use such techniques to effect that goal.

In addition to the teacher's conception of the learner, teaching strategy can also be influenced by the nature of the subject matter. Analyses, for example, by Aschner (1960), demonstrate through classroom interaction observations that teaching strategies vary as a function of the course taught. Piaget's interest in the logic of the subject matter as well as the nature of the learner provides, by indirection at least, perspective for devising teaching strategies specific to particular subject matter areas at particular stages.

Defining the teaching situation as involving three factors, teacher's conception of the learner, the learning process, and the nature of the subject matter, the question remains how are these expressed in a teaching technique. For example, Taba, et al., discuss the significance of question-asking, just one teaching technique, and show how it reflects all three factors:

. . . the questions teachers ask set limits within which students can operate and the expectations regarding the level of cognitive operations. Questions are the carriers of whatever new cognitive system is emerging. Some questions function as invitations to heighten the performance of certain cognitive operations, while leaving the content and the directions of these operations open. Such questions invite invention, discovery, the creative use of previous knowledge. Others control and limit both the content and nature of cognitive operations (Taba, Levine, & Elzey, 1964, p. 177).

Probably any teaching strategy is the coalition of a number of factors expressed in a single act. A major thrust of a teaching strategy is to confront the child with the illogical nature of his point of view. The reason for confrontation is that it is a necessary and sufficient requirement for cognitive growth. The shift from egocentric to sociocentric thought comes about through confrontation with the animate and inanimate environment. These forces impinge on the child, inducing disequilibrium. The child strives to reconcile the discrepancies and evolves new processes by which to adapt to the new situations. Strategies employing confrontations must be consistent with the child's stage of development, because

. . . the child can receive valuable information via language or via education directed by an adult *only if he is in a state where he can understand this information. That is, to receive the information he must have a structure which enables him to assimilate this information* (Piaget, 1964a, p. 13, italics ours).

Confrontation can take a number of forms depending on the developmental level of the child. Verbal and/or nonverbal techniques ranging from questions, demonstrations and/or environmental manipulations can be employed in the service of confrontation. To be sure, the school is only one source of such experience for,

. . . when conversing with his family, the child will at every moment see his thoughts approved or contradicted, and he will discover a vast world of thought external to himself, which will instruct or impress him in various ways. From the point of view of intelligence (which is all that concerns us here), he will therefore be led to an ever more intensive exchange of intellectual values and will be forced to accept an ever-increasing number of obligatory truths (ready-made ideas and true norms of reasoning) (Piaget, 1963, p. 159).

On the basis of these considerations, the teacher is in a strategic position to influence the child's school environment. The teacher has the freedom to organize the classroom situation to express his own conceptualization of the learning situation. Creating a facilitating physical and social environment, from a Piagetian point of view, requires attention to and consideration of the setting.

Just as the physical environment is not imposed on developing intelligence all at once or as a single entity, but in such a way that acquisition can be followed step by step as a function of experience, and especially as a function of the kinds of assimilation or accommodation—varying greatly according to mental level—that govern these acquisitions, so the social environment gives rise to interactions between the developing individual and his fellow, interactions that differ greatly from one another and succeed one another according to definite laws (Piaget, 1963, p. 157).

Detailed specification of the ecology of the classroom needs to be done, with such specification dependent on the cognitive level of the children. Since activity is a significant requisite for the growth of cognitive structures, opportunities to manipulate objects and ideas in active interaction situations with others is necessary. Of particular importance is the kind of material available. Use of activity may occur, for example, with the teacher working in small groups, guiding the children's interaction with objects.

. . . good pedagogy must involve presenting the child with situations in which he himself experiments, in the broadest sense of that term—trying things out to see what happens, manipulating things, manipulating symbols, posing questions and seeking his own answers, reconciling what he finds one time with what he finds at another, comparing his findings with those of other children (Duckworth, 1964, p. 2).

Although physical arrangements in the classsroom may guide the child, the verbal interactions with peers and with teachers provide additional experiences which foster cognitive growth.

The use of language and interpretation of language in the socioeducational context deserves special attention. The teacher must be sensitive to the child's capacity for assimilating verbal language as well as be aware of the relationship between the child's language and his thought. As was alluded to earlier, the child's correct contextual use of a term is not necessarily indicative of his comprehension of that term or an accurate reflection of the child's ability to understand the logical basis of the concept. The comprehension depends on the particular stage of the child, e.g. sensorimotor, concrete, or formal. For example, a child may use such terms as "brother" and "metal" very early. The child at the concrete stage as well as the adolescent at the formal stage will use the terms correctly. But the comprehension is not equivalent. For the concrete-stage child the word brother is defined as a boy "who lives in my house." For the adolescent, brother is a relational term defined in terms of kinship and interrelationship. To comprehend the concept of brother in all its relational significance requires the child to be able to employ the mental operations of *reciprocity*. Not until the child can deal with reciprocal relations can he understand the true nature of the concept "brother" since it is a term denoting reciprocal relationships. Thus, the limited definition of brother given by young children is due to immaturity in cognitive processes not just limits of vocabulary.

Results from the analysis of a task in which children were asked to explain such words as "brother" and "animal," revealed that before the fourth and fifth grades children could not define brother in terms of a common relationship (Sigel, 1961).

Another instance demonstrating that language and thought are not isomorphic is the following: An eight-year-old girl was presented with an array of familiar three-dimensional objects and asked to sort them. The child selected a number of items that could be classified under the rubric "tools." When asked the rationale for her classification, the child said, "These are all metal." Since I had used this task with a large number of seven- and eight-year-old children, and since the term "metal" was rarely used, I was impressed with her sophistication. I asked her to tell me more about the word "metal." The girl responded, "Metal is steel." I asked if there were any other kinds of metal. She said, "No." An involved inquiry followed to determine which metals she knew, but to no avail, since for her, steel and metal were synonymous. Despite appropriate use in a particular context, her concept of metal was different from the adult's.

Quantitative terms pose similar difficulties. Such terms as "more" and "less" are used and appear to be understood by young children in their day-to-day interactions. In one study, children were tested to determine if they could identify "more," "same," and "less" in comparisons involving number, area, and length. It was found that these relational concepts were not correctly identified in every context (Griffiths, Shantz, & Sigel, 1967). Knowing "more" in terms of number does not mean the child will know "more" in terms of weight or volume. The problem is not one of vocabulary but rather of conceptual level, since the child has not acquired the mental operations necessary to comprehend the terms. The teacher should be guided by the fact that the child's knowledge may be specific to that context and not necessarily generalized to others.

Since the teacher should not take the child's verbalisms at face value as indicative of his level of thought, inquiry must be used to assess the child's level and quality of understanding. Piaget's "clinical method," which involves appropriate and cautious questioning of the child, is one such approach. As Piaget says:

. . . It is so hard not to talk too much when questioning a child, especially for the pedogogue! It is so hard not to be suggestive! And above all, it is so hard to find the middle course between systematization due to preconceived ideas and incoherence due to absence of any directing hypothesis! The good experimenter must, in fact, unite too often incompatible qualities; he must know how to observe, that is to say, to let the child talk freely, without ever checking or side-tracking his utterance and at the same time, he must constantly be alert for something definite . . . (Piaget, 1929, p. 9).

Continuing with the significance of confrontation and guidance as a means of inducing cognitive growth, let me show how some of the work at our Center relates to this issue. We began by assuming that the significant classification skills play an important role in the development of conservation. Training situations were set up in which the child was encouraged to label the various object attributes as a preliminary step to constructing, decomposing, and reconstructing of classes, i.e. decentration. The child was free to use any one or more criteria for defining the classes. The teacher in this case did not superimpose class names. Such an opportunity is quite different from the usual educational condition in which teachers and parents accept and encourage conventional taxonomies. Table 1 illustrates this open ended procedure for classification.

Our current knowledge of children's classification competence stems from studies with children whose history in classification experience is actually not known. Risking conjecture, it is likely that children employ particular classifications as a result of reinforcement of the usual and conventional. Alternatives are not accepted. If children were allowed to build classifications freely with all types acceptable, would their repertoire of responses expand, thereby extending the quality and quantity of types of classifications employed? Thus, such "normative" developmental data presented by Sigel (1953) may be interpreted as the degree to which the child has absorbed the conventional system, since he has had relatively little encouragement to employ alternatives.

In addition to the experiential history, classification behaviors are contingent upon the material involved. A group of gifted children, four-year-olds (IQs over 130), was presented with an array of pictures of animals and furniture. With such an array, few children grouped all the pictures in a single grouping, and never were animal pictures combined with any of the furniture ones. When the furniture group was later presented along with a group of human figures and no animals, many children combined the two groups. Had these children been encouraged to build classes by selecting criteria independent of the object, and combining these criteria, cross-classes might have been built. The animal and furniture items may have been combined according to similarities in structure, or function, e.g. horse and chair are similar "because you can sit on them," or by structure, "each has four legs," or "both useful for man." Abstraction of common features of highly diverse objects, while keeping the identity of the object in mind, is usually not part of teaching. Conventional taxonomies are established and are highly embedded in the cognitive system with a priori decisions of "good" or "bad" categories, thereby precluding easy establishment of other systems.

Let me digress briefly here to illustrate. I presented a group of teachers with an array of objects (pear, banana, orange) and asked them to classify any two of these three on as many bases as they could, and asked them to justify why or how they were similar. A total of seventeen different reasons were given, accepted by the group as correct and comprehensible. Yet, not one individual gave more than eight reasons. I asked the group why everyone did not give the same number of reasons since each person understood every reason. Among the explanations for this was that *not all* the reasons were good, even though correct. When asked to express the criteria for "good," the teachers engaged in an excited discussion and suggested a variety of criteria. A good response was defined on logical grounds, such as extensitivity; *but* just as often not defined, except to say that any term conventionally accepted as abstract is "better." When asked "better" for what, confusion and disagreement reigned. The teachers employed an absolute criterion in principle, not being able to explicate the rationale. It was difficult for them to take a relativistic position, i.e. a classification may be "good" in one context but not in others.

Evaluation of criteria used in classification responses of even so mundane a set of items as the pear, orange, and banana are so value laden and absolustic, a function, no doubt, of experience with a conventional taxonomy. There is difficulty in accepting alternative criteria for creating a new or alternative classes. If this is a valid generalization regarding frames of reference held by teachers, is it surprising that children are prone to classify in conventional taxonomies? In Piagetian terms, the teachers have not only minimally decentered in their evaluation criteria but have over-valued particular response types.

If, however, teachers accepted rational alternatives, they could facilitate the decentering process by providing children with opportunities to explore and to discover the variety of attributes objects possess by teaching them to value multiple class membership concepts in contrast to unitary ones, thereby contributing to appropriate relative rather than absolute bases for determining class membership. Further, objects or events can be experienced in broad terms. Might the classes children build not be so limited? Might no variations in material be less significant? In effect, a more extensive and varied world could open up to the child, which he could approach with increased flexibility. (See Table 1 for illustration of teaching strategy.)

Table 1   Portion of Verbatim Transcript of a Training Session Dealing with Multiple Attributes of Objects

Teacher:	Can you tell me what this is, Mary?
Mary:	A banana.
Teacher:	What else can you tell me about it?
Mary:	It's straight.
Teacher:	It's straight. What else?
Mary:	It has a peel.
Teacher:	It has a peel. . . . Tom, what can you tell me about it?
Tom:	Ummm . . . It has some green on it.
Teacher:	Uh-huh.
Tom:	It has some dark lines on it.
Teacher:	What can you do with it?
Tom:	You can eat it!
Teacher:	That's right! . . . Now let's see . . .
Children:	. . . I love bananas!
Teacher:	What is this?
Children:	An orange.
Teacher:	Is it really an orange?
Children:	Uh-huh . . . Yes.
Teacher:	Look at it closely.
Child:	It's an artificial one.
Teacher:	Oh, that's right, it's an artificial one . . . But, what else can you tell me about it?
Children:	You can eat it. . . . It's round.
Teacher:	Uh-huh.
Children:	. . . Orange.
Teacher:	That's right!
Child:	It has a stem.

Table 1   Portion of Verbatim Transcript of a Training Session Dealing with
           Multiple Attributes of Objects (*Continued*)

Teacher:	Now look at this one . . . What's this?
Children:	An orange. . . . Orange.
Teacher:	And what can you do with it?
Children:	You can eat it . . . and it's round.
Teacher:	It's round . . .
Child:	It has a peel . . .
Teacher:	It has a peel . . . Now, look at these two things. Are they the same?
Children:	No.
Teacher:	What's different?
Children:	This one . . . This one here is pressed in on the side a little . . . this one is lighter.
Teacher:	Do you know what this really is? This is a tangerine . . . and this is an orange. Now, tell me in what ways they are alike.
Children:	This is smaller and that's bigger.
Teacher:	I said, "In what way are they alike?"
Children:	They are both round . . . they both have a stem . . . both orange.
Teacher:	They both have a stem, both round, both orange. Anything else alike about them?
Child:	They're both fat.
Teacher:	Uh-huh. What can you do with them?
Children:	We can eat them . . .
Teacher:	We can eat them . . . Now, tell me, what's the same about all these things?
Child:	These are round, but this isn't.
Teacher:	I said, what is the same about them, not what's different about them.
Children:	They're both round . . . they're round . . . they're round . . . and they are both artificial.
Teacher:	They're all artificial, and . . . are they all round?
Child:	No.
Teacher:	What about the banana?
Child:	It's straight.
Teacher:	But . . . tell me something else that's the same about all of these things.
Child:	. . . They have . . . all have a peel.
Teacher:	That's right, too, but what can you do with all of them?
Children:	You can eat them!
Teacher:	That's right! That's the same about every one of them. Do you have a name for all of them?
Children:	Yes!

Teacher:	What?
Child:	A banana.
Teacher:	A banana? No . . . is there something that you can call all of them?
Children:	Fruit . . . fruit!
Teacher:	And what's the same about all fruit?
Children:	They are all round except bananas.
Teacher:	No . . . why do you call all of these things fruit?
Children:	Because you can eat them.
Teacher:	You can eat them.
Children:	And they are food.
Teacher:	And they are food. If I had a piece of bread here, would that be fruit too?
Children:	No.
Teacher:	Why not?
Children:	Because it is not sweet . . . not round . . .
Teacher:	Because it is not sweet. I think that's a good reason . . . and you eat bread too?
Children:	Yes.
Teacher:	But it is still not fruit . . . right?
Children:	Yes.
Teacher:	Now, can you tell me again what this is? We talked about it yesterday.
Child:	A pencil.
Teacher:	What else can you tell me about it?
Children:	It's round . . . you said you were going to put it in . . .
Teacher:	That's right . . . ah . . . Tom, what is this?
Tom:	Chalk.
Teacher:	What else can you tell me about it?
Tom:	It's white.
Teacher:	Gail, tell me what's the same about these two things?
Gail:	They are both round.
Teacher:	What else?
Gail:	. . . Ummm . . .
Teacher:	John, tell me what's the same about these two things?
John:	. . . both write.
Teacher:	That's right! There are two things that are the same about it. Tell me what they are.
John:	Well . . . I don't know.
Teacher:	What are they Mary?
Mary:	They're round and they write.
Teacher:	Very good!

The technique described in Table 1 was employed in a series of studies that started with the hypothesis that encouragement of decentration would contribute to the child's emancipation from conventional functional fixedness, thereby facilitating solution of conservation problems, since success in conservation appears to be related to decentration. The first studies utilizing this technique of multiple classification also employed seriation and reversibility exercises. The children who underwent this training were able to solve a number of conservation of quantity problems (Sigel, Roeper, & Hooper, 1966).

From the data acquired in another study of the relations of operations (multiplicative relations, multiplicative classification, reversibility) and conservation of quantity (substance, weight, and volume), the best predictor of conservation was the ability to deal with multiplicative classification problems.* Consequently Carolyn Shantz and I undertook a study examining the import of classification on conservation of substance, length and area. Preliminary results with a sample of four-year-olds indicated that 33 percent of the children in the experimental groups were conservers on posttesting, while none of the controls was able to conserve.†

In effect, we "induced the function of advanced structures at an age when the child did not utilize it voluntarily" (Szeminska, 1965, p. 51).

Is not the employment of induction techniques contraindicated by Piagetian theory? The results of Piaget's studies point to the invariant sequence of cognitive structure—and the above studies are compatible in that conservation can be induced if the training procedures embody the prerequisite operations of multiple classification, multiplicative relations, reversibility, and seriation (Sigel, Roeper, & Hooper, 1966).

Induction studies reveal that transitions can be created in children. The results from the above studies provide limited infor-

---

* The report of these data is being prepared by Hooper, Sigel, and Stevens.
† These are results of the pilot research for a study that culminated in the Shantz and Sigel report, "Logical Operations and Concepts of Conservation in Children: A Training Study," for the Office of Education Grant No. OEG-3-6-068463-1645, Project No. 6-8463.

mation since none of them examined the degree to which inductions in one area influence acquisition in other areas.

Does the employment of such teaching strategies signify efforts towards hastening the process of development, i.e. acceleration? It must be made very clear that the teaching strategies advocated in this discussion are not intended to accelerate the child's development just for the sake of getting the child to do more and more, earlier and earlier, rationalized as preparation for a complex world. There is little to justify or commend this position.

Undertaking these so-called "acceleration" or "induction" studies has value in order to assess the degree to which particular teaching strategies are compatible with the child's developmental level, and to determine the range of capability of children to handle such experiences. Susan Isaacs, for example, has pointed out that children do show signs of logical reasoning very early (Isaacs, 1930). The contention is that the signs of children's competence are there if only we *listen* to what the children *are telling* us. Thus, we do not overlook their true capability.

Such information can also prevent false starts by enabling identification of the child's limits.

. . . This is the big danger of school—false accommodation which satisfies a child because it agrees with a verbal formula he has been given. This is a false equilibrium which satisfies a child by accommodating to words—to authority and not to objects as they present themselves to him. A teacher would do better not to correct a child's schemas, but to provide situations so he will correct them himself (Piaget, quoted by Duckworth, 1964, p. 4).

The teacher has to be cognizant of Piagetian theory to evaluate the degree to which children are able to assimilate material and accommodate correctly. Further, the sophisticated teacher is not about to force new cognitive structures as such, but rather will provide the atmosphere in which optimal growth can take place.

Implications of Piagetian theory for curriculum development

Curriculum is the core of the education enterprise. It is the knowledge that the child is expected to assimilate and to accommodate. Piaget's genetic epistemological emphasis becomes immediately relevant here since his interest is in the embryogenesis of knowledge, in the development of human knowledge in general, and, in particular, in the nature of scientific knowledge (Piaget, 1964).

Piaget's theoretical model does contain principles relevant for program planning in general, as well as subject matter in particular, despite its apparent emphasis upon science and mathematics. Piaget's contribution to curriculum development resides in those writings which describe knowledge acquisition in particular fields, e.g. mathematics and physical science. We should not, however, overlook Piaget's contribution to other relevant substance areas, such as language, play, morality, and causal thought.

Curriculum must be sequentially planned within and between grades at school. Within a grade level, sequencing of material frequently involves using a simple-complex model. But, sequences also occur between grades in terms of introduction of programs at appropriate developmental levels, e.g. the introduction of reading instruction at grade one, and algebra at grade nine. Curriculum planners are concerned with establishing sequences relevant to the learner's readiness state, and appropriate to the inherent logic of the subject matter. For Piaget these two conditions interact. Whether Piaget is describing the development of number, space, or geometry, his stages describe developmental sequences in subject matter content as well as the form of children's thinking. For this reason his theory can be used as a basis for establishing curriculum planning guidelines.

Piaget's stage descriptions for each of these substantive areas provide a framework for the curriculum planner. Implicit guidelines for curriculum are present and can be viewed by the curriculum developer then from two points of view: first, the guiding principles of development as reflected in the organization of substantive knowledge, and second, in the mental organization of the learner. Having discussed the development of the individual, let us turn to an examination of content.

Let us, for the sake of illustration, discuss Piaget's description of the development of geometric operations. Piaget has indicated that topological intuitions precede projective ones, and that these in turn precede metric concepts (Piaget, 1964b). Children pay attention to the topological nature of a surface before they attend to its metric characteristics. This suggests, then, that a curriculum for Euclidean geometry might proceed as follows: topological, projective, metric. Does this mean that current practices of teaching geometry are wrong? Students begin with Euclidean geometry, and only later, if ever, proceed to topological mathematics. Such a criticism would be justified only if we ignore the developmental level of the child and the level of knowledge involved. Euclidean geometry is frequently taught in the 10th grade, when the students are fourteen to fifteen, and have attained, in most instances, formal operational thought. By this age, topological qualities are already assimilated and appropriate schemata evolved. If we were interested in teaching Euclidean geometry to children at the concrete operational stage, then it would behoove us to be concerned with the sequencing of instructions for topological and projective geometrics. The sequencing has to be carefully examined on a long term basis, since "there is complete continuity in what mathematicians term geometrical intuition between the motor element originally controlling perceptual activity and that which reappears at each successive stage of development right up to the final solution." (Piaget & Inhelder, 1963, Pp. 450–451).

The topological and projective structures to be acquired at the concrete operational level should not be confused with the operations required to deal with topology as a mathematical science. Rather topology refers to discrimination of and attention to surface qualities of objects. The distinction needs to be made between the necessary and sufficient comprehension of relevant topological information, and similarly for projective geometry. In effect, the level and quality of topological information needed as a prerequisite to comprehension of metric geometric operations must be carefully spelled out.

The above illustration with respect to geometry points out the need for a careful detailing of the sequences involved in planning the curriculum. In effect, the necessary operations required must be specified in an interdependent way so that each step is a new synthesis incorporating previous cognitions, e.g. as in number (Piaget, 1952). For physical science and mathematics, the invariant sequences are readily apparent. Is the system as applicable for other fields of knowledge, e.g. history, economics, etc.?

Application of the Piagetian model to social studies depends on how the genetic epistemological model can be used. The Piagetian system describes the general cognitive processes or operations involved in knowledge acquisition. It would therefore be reasonable to assume that information from the social environment is acquired by the same mechanisms. Thus, the social science curriculum builder may well find that the relevance of Piaget to his areas of concern lies more in the conception of mental operations than in the description of development in particular subject matter areas. How knowledge is utilized and how problems are solved are means of identifying the underlying mental operations. The teacher who observes how the child thinks and reasons in one area will be alerted to how the child thinks and reasons in other areas. For example, the teacher who knows that a child is a nonconserver should be alert to the possibility of nonconservation in social science concepts. The conservation principle is relevant to the social domain, and this was recently demonstrated by Feffer & Suchotliff (1966), who employed the concept in a study of social interaction. The concept of conservation apparently has wide applicability to many situations (Saltz & Sigel, 1967).

In effect, the curriculum builder has to determine which dimensions of the Piagetian system are relevant, e.g. the developing principles that described the child's transitions from sensorimotor to formal operations, the inherent logic of the material. In any event, the Piagetian model provides an invaluable guide. It does what all fruitful conceptual frameworks do, namely, orients the individual toward the significance of phenomena that heretofore have been overlooked or taken for granted.

Conclusions

This has been a sketchy and brief description of the relevance of Piaget for education. The foregoing should be viewed as illustrative of what can, and, in my opinion, should be done in depth.

There is no denying at the outset that the task is a formidable one and should not be viewed as a total solution to the curriculum problem. Piaget may not have envisaged the direct relationship with education proposed here (Flavell, 1963). I firmly believe that the touchstones between education and the Piagetian model are so great, however, that the educational innovator would be remiss not to examine the relationships in depth.

The mastery of any major thought system is, however, a difficult task. To comprehend Skinner, or to comprehend Piaget, means studying their writings and musing over their intentions. The question arises, *is it worth the effort?* The research literature on Piagetian concepts and ideas provides a convincing and substantial body of knowledge which lends credence to the validity and value of the system for education. To be sure, some studies point out the limitations and suggest qualifications of Piagetian hypotheses, assertions and assumptions. But, is this not only to be expected? Is it not sufficient to provide evidence showing how Piaget's work has profound contributions?

In effect, turning toward Piaget for inspiration and guidance in the educational domain will enable education to make substantial progress. Piaget forces us to reexamine our own concepts and constructs regarding children's thinking and the relationship of the development of thought to cognate areas. For him, as for many of us:

The principle goal of education is to create men who are capable of doing new things, not simply of repeating what other generations have done—men who are creative, inventive, and discoverers. The second goal of education is to form minds which can be critical, can verify, and not accept everything they are offered. The great danger today is of slogans, collective opinions, ready-made trends of thought. We have to be able to resist individually, to criticize, to distinguish between what is proven and what is not. So we need pupils who are active, who learn early to find out by themselves, partly by their own spontaneous activity and partly through material we set up for them; who learn early to tell what is verifiable and what is simply the first idea to come to them (Piaget, quoted by Duckworth, 1964, p. 5).

References

Aschner, Mary Jane. The language of teaching. *Teachers College Rec.*, 1960, **61**. Pp. 242–252.

Duckworth, Eleanor. Piaget rediscovered. In R. E. Ripple, & V. N. Rockcastle (Eds.), *Piaget rediscovered*. Ithaca, New York: Cornell Univer. Press, 1964. Pp. 1–5.

Educational Testing Service. *Let's look at first graders.* (Rev. ed.) New York: Board of Education, 1965.

Feffer, M., & Suchotliff, L. Decentering implications of social interactions. *J. Pers. soc. Psychol.*, 1966, **4**, 415–442.

Flavell, J. H. *The developmental psychology of Jean Piaget.* Princeton, N.J.: Van Nostrand, 1963.

Griffiths, Judith, Shantz, Carolyn, & Sigel, I. E. A methodological problem in conservation studies: the use of relational terms. *Child Develpm.*, 1967, **38**, 841–848.

Inhelder, Bärbel. Operational thought and symbolic imagery. In P. H. Mussen, European research in cognitive development. *Monogr. Soc. Res. Child Develpm.*, 1965, **30**, No. 2. Pp. 4–18.

Isaacs, Susan. *Intellectual growth in young children.* New York: Harcourt Brace, 1930.

Karplus, R. The science curriculum improvement study. In R. E. Ripple, & V. N. Rockcastle (Eds.), *Piaget rediscovered*. Ithaca, New York: Cornell Univer. Press, 1964. Pp. 113–118.

Lovell, K. *The growth of basic mathematical and scientific concepts in children.* London: Univer. of London Press, 1961.

Lunzer, E. A. *Recent studies in Britain based on the work of Jean Piaget.* London: Nat. Found. Educ. Res. in England and Wales, 1960.

Peel, E. A. *The pupil's thinking.* London: Oldbourne Press, 1960.

Piaget, J. *The child's conception of the world.* New York: Harcourt, Brace, 1929.

Piaget, J. *The child's conception of number.* New York: Humanities Press, 1952.

Piaget, J. *Psychology of intelligence.* New Jersey: Littlefield, Adams (rep. by arrangement with Humanities Press), 1963.

Piaget, J. Development and learning. In R. E. Ripple, & V. N. Rockcastle (Eds.), *Piaget rediscovered.* Ithaca: Cornell Univer. Press, 1964. Pp. 7–20. (a)

Piaget, J. Mother structures and the notion of number. In R. E. Ripple, & V. N. Rockcastle (Eds.), *Piaget rediscovered.* Ithaca: Cornell Univer. Press, 1964. Pp. 33–39. (b)

Piaget, J., & Inhelder, Bärbel. *The child's conception of space.* London: Routledge and Kegan Paul, 1963.

Piaget, J., Inhelder, Bärbel, & Szeminska, Alina. *The child's conception of geometry.* New York: Basic Books, 1960.

Saltz, E., & Sigel, I. E. Concept overdiscrimination in children. *J. exp. Psychol.,* 1967, **73**, 1–8.

Sigel, I. E. Developmental trends in the abstraction ability of children. *Child Develpm.,* 1953, **24**, 131–144.

Sigel, I. E. Cognitive style and personality dynamics. Interim progress report, NIMH 2983, 1961.

Sigel, I. E. The attainment of concepts. In M. L. Hoffman, & Lois V. Hoffman. *Review of child development research.* Vol. 1. New York: Russell Sage Foundation, 1964. Pp. 209–248.

Sigel, I. E., Roeper, Annemarie, & Hooper, F. H. A training procedure for acquisition of Piaget's conservation of quantity: a pilot study and its replication. *Brit. J. educ. Psychol.,* 1966, **36**, 301–311.

Szeminska, Alina. The evolution of thought: some applications of research findings to educational practice. In P. H. Mussen, European research in cognitive development. *Monogr. Soc. Res. Child Develpm.,* 1965, **30**, No. 2, Pp. 47–57.

Taba, Hilda, Levine, S., & Elzey, F. F. *Thinking in elementary school children.* Office of Educ. Cooperative Res. Project 1574, 1964.

Uzgiris, Ina C. Situational generality of conservation. *Child Develpm.,* 1964, **35**, 831–841.

Wallace, J. G. *Concept growth and the education of the child.* Slough, Eng.: Nat. Found. Educ. Res. in England and Wales, 1965.

Index

Abelson, R. P., 295n.

Abilities, involved in ontogenesis, 307–8

Abruptness of development, 78–82; aspects of problem, 79; Piaget on gradual *vs.* abrupt, 79, 81; conceptualization of, 80

Acceleration: factors responsible for, 155; limitations of, 159; value of, 483. *See also* Training.

Accommodation, x, 5, 19; defined, 8–9; related to equilibrium, 9–10; as part of theory of adaptation, 32; false, 483

Acquisitions: authenticity of, 159–63; tests for, 162

Action: difference in use of, 449–52; across milieus, 450–52, 453–54; as basis for thought, 454; in the classroom, 474–75

Action schemes: operative aspects of cognition, 339; as codes for memorizing, 343

Activity, growth of voluntary, 224

Adam, June, 372, 384

Adaptation: as function of concepts, 176–77; as discriminative response, 177; by conservation and identity, 177; to a visual stimulus, 369

Adolescence, and intellectual equilibrium, 10

Aebli, H., 101n.

Aftereffects, 366, 369, 372; decline of with age, 375; of retardates, 394

Almy, Millie, 416

Analogy, 131, 135; and horizontal *décalage*, 131

Analytic orientation, 420, 434

Animal learning, studies of, basic to S-R theory, 13

Anokhin, P. K., 265

Anticipation judgments, 447

Apparent movement, 378–86; a Type I phenomenon, 381

Applications of research, xviii-xix

Arbitrary configurations, memory of, 357–61

Area, conservation of, 412; experiments on 413–20

Aristotle, 10; on identity, 174–75; on surprise, 258

491